STUDIES IN EARLY MODERN CULTURAL,
POLITICAL AND SOCIAL HISTORY

Volume 41

AFRICANS IN EAST ANGLIA, 1467-1833

Studies in Early Modern Cultural, Political and Social History

ISSN: 1476-9107

Series editors
Tim Harris – Brown University
Stephen Taylor – Durham University
Andy Wood – Durham University

Previously published titles in the series
are listed at the back of this volume

AFRICANS
IN EAST ANGLIA
1467–1833

Richard C. Maguire

THE BOYDELL PRESS

First published 2021
The Boydell Press, Woodbridge

ISBN 978-1-78327-633-2

The Boydell Press is an imprint of Boydell & Brewer Ltd
PO Box 9, Woodbridge, Suffolk IP12 3DF, UK
and of Boydell & Brewer Inc.
668 Mt Hope Avenue, Rochester, NY 14620–2731, USA
website: www.boydellandbrewer.com

A catalogue record for this book is available
from the British Library

The publisher has no responsibility for the continued existence or accuracy of
URLs for external or third-party internet websites referred to in this book, and
does not guarantee that any content on such websites is, or will remain, accurate
or appropriate

This publication is printed on acid-free paper

Printed and bound in Great Britain by
TJ Books Ltd, Padstow, Cornwall

Contents

Illustrations

Maps

Figures

Tables

Full credit details are provided in the captions to the images in the text. The author and publisher are grateful to all the institutions and individuals for permission to reproduce the materials in which they hold copyright. Every effort has been made to trace the copyright holders; apologies are offered for any omission, and the publisher will be pleased to add any necessary acknowledgement in subsequent editions.

Acknowledgements

I am indebted to the numerous people who have assisted me over the period that this book has taken shape. Many of the staff at the Norfolk Record Office have been involved in various ways over the years, and their patience and assistance in my work since 2007 has been crucial in conducting the research upon which this book rests. I am grateful especially to John Alban, Rachel Farmer, and Nick Sellwood. My thanks also to the staff at the Suffolk Record Offices. I am grateful also to the team at the Norfolk and Norwich Racial Equality Council – Anne Matin, Julia Dyson, and Sean Whyte – who ran the original 2007 National Lottery-funded project *Norfolk's Hidden Heritage* from which this book grew. John Barney was generous in allowing me access to his notes on King's Lynn shipping, and Mary Anne Garry helped me in relation to the records of Holkham Hall. Andy Hopper pointed me toward John Secker. I am also grateful for the assistance and efficiency of Jacqui Ward and the staff at the Tasmanian Museum and Art Gallery in helping me with all matters in relation to John Dempsey's images of Cotton and Charley.

During my research I have discussed this subject at a wide range of venues in East Anglia and further afield, from village halls to universities, churches, schools, libraries, and prisons. My thanks to the many people who have invited me to speak on this subject in these locations, to those who have listened to what I have had to say, and to those who have asked me questions. These discussions have helped me think about the Africans of early modern East Anglia in new ways. The questions of the undergraduate and postgraduate students at the University of East Anglia have also helped with various issues.

My wife, Wendy, has been a pillar of strength throughout this process, especially when helping me to recover, three times, from serious illness. This book would not have happened without her. My colleagues and friends at the University of East Anglia have been a help and support in many ways. Edward Acton and John Charmley have both been great friends all the way through. Carole Rawcliffe has been of immeasurable aid in all things medieval, as has Hugh Doherty, whose encouragement at a difficult point was also welcome. Geoff Plank, Jess Sharkey, and Joel Halcomb have made me aware of areas of early modern history that might otherwise have been overlooked, and the work and collegiality of Malcolm Gaskill has been of great assistance. Sarah Spooner and Jon Gregory answered questions about country houses, and Jon also prepared the maps used in Chapter 1. Any mistakes are, of course, the fault of the writer.

Finally, thanks are due to the editors of the Studies in Early Modern Cultural, Political and Social History, especially to Andy Wood, whose support has been vital. I would like to acknowledge the work of the readers who made insightful and collegial comment upon earlier drafts. I am also grateful to the staff at Boydell and Brewer for their assistance and encouragement. Michael Middeke has shown great interest in the project from the start and, together with Elizabeth Howard, has been helpful and supportive throughout the process of developing the book.

Abbreviations

BL	British Library
BLO	Bodleian Library Oxford
CCED	Church of England Clergy Database
HA	Holkham Hall Archives
LBSO	University College of London, Legacies of British Slave-Ownership
NAS	National Archive of Scotland
NCC	Norwich Consistory Court
NRO	Norfolk Record Office
ODNB	Oxford Dictionary of National Biography
PCC	Prerogative Court of Canterbury
SRO	Suffolk Record Office
TNA	The National Archives, Kew
TAIASD	The Trans-Atlantic and Intra-American Slave Trade Database

A note on dating, currency, and references

All dates given are new style, with the year taken as beginning on 1 January, not 25 March. Currency values are given in the pre-decimal format of £ s d (pounds, shillings, and pence), with twelve pence to the shilling and twenty shillings to the pound. To provide uniformity, all volume numbers of books and periodicals have been given in Arabic numerals. For the sake of consistency, I have used the phrase 'English/British North America' throughout rather than changing description for references to North America before and after the Act of Union.

Introduction
A Social History of Africans in Early Modern Norfolk and Suffolk

This is an history of a group of working-class English people.[1] It begins in 1467 with a 'boy of the shippe' named Eylys, who sailed into the Norfolk port of Great Yarmouth as a member of a crew of 'pyrattes'.[2] The story continues, just over a century later, in 1599, when a young man named Baptist was baptised in the village of Hunstanton, in north Norfolk.[3] Moving forward nearly ninety years, to 1688, the narrative resumes in Rougham, Suffolk, with another baptism, this time of a young woman named Rosanna.[4] Nearly a century later, in 1781, a man named Jeremiah Rowland was buried in Wroxham, Norfolk.[5] In 1799, an eighteen-year-old woman named Rachel Fitshoe was 'publickly baptised' in the Norfolk market town of Diss.[6] Our story reaches a conclusion, of sorts, with the baptism of Charles Fortunatus Freeman in Norwich in 1813.[7] Births, baptisms, and burials, the basic threads from which the everyday existence of rich and poor alike was woven in early modern England. Eylys, Baptist, Rosanna, Jeremiah, Rachel, and Charles were, moreover, connected by other threads. They were all poor. They were all working people. They all lived in the English counties of Norfolk and Suffolk. And they were all linked by the way they were described in the documents that recorded them. Eylys was described as 'a More', Baptist as an 'Aethiopian', Rosanna as a 'black-amore', Jeremiah as 'a negro', Rachel as 'a black', and Charles as 'African'.

---

[1] The idea of class deployed here is largely that of Thompson, that class is a relationship and when we use the term 'working class' this does not imply an ahistorical 'it' but a suggestion that class 'happens when some men (and women), as a result of common experiences [...] feel and articulate the identity of their interests as between themselves, and as against other men (and women) whose interests are different from (and usually opposed to) theirs', E.P. Thompson, *The Making of the English Working Class* (London, 1963), pp. 10–11.

[2] See Henry Swinden, *History and Antiquities of the Ancient Burgh of Great Yarmouth* (Norwich, 1772), p. 366.

[3] NRO/PD/696/16, Baptism of Baptist, Great Ringstead, 15 April 1599.

[4] SRO/FL619/4/2, Baptism of Rosanna, Rougham, 12 February 1688.

[5] NRO/PD/390/2, Burial of Jeremiah Rowland, 15 June 1781.

[6] NRO/PD/100/364, Baptism of Rachel Fitshoe, Diss, 23 October 1799.

[7] NRO/PD26/4, Baptism of Charles Freeman, Norwich, 30 May 1813.

By these varying descriptors, the writers of the historical records indicated that Eylys, Baptist, Rosanna, Jeremiah, Rachel, and Charles were all Africans, which is the term used in this book to describe someone who was born on the continent of Africa, or someone who was descended from forebears who had been born there.[8] This African heritage provides the hub around which this book revolves, but the argument presented here is that the other descriptors already mentioned, like 'class' and 'locality', along with yet more, such as 'baptised' and 'Christian', are equally important in understanding the lives of the hundreds of Africans who lived in the region. This study seeks to come to an understanding of the lives of the Africans who lived in Norfolk and Suffolk between 1467 and 1833 that reflects the complexity of their historical experience. At its heart, the book proposes that their lives can be appreciated in a new and positive fashion if these Africans are understood to have been an integral part of the wider social group of the labouring poor. In so doing, the book suggests that the description of Eylys in 1467, that called him 'one of the same compeny' of his fellow sailors, is a crucial clue to understanding their lives.[9] This is a story, therefore, about the lives of English working people who were of African descent, rather than one about a group of outsiders to English society who were defined purely by the colour of their skin.

* * *

The roots of historic investigation into the African presence in England generally can be traced back to the publication of M. Dorothy George's 1926 book, *London Life in the Eighteenth Century*, which mentioned their presence in late-eighteenth-century London, if only briefly.[10] For most of the twentieth century this was not a subject that garnered much attention. As Norma Myers put it in the 1990s: 'Although black people have sustained a continuous presence in Britain for at least four centuries, they remain almost invisible in historical writing.'[11] The subject of an early modern African population in England was touched upon by Kenneth Little in 1948, but it was W.E. Miller's use of a Tudor subsidy return to locate four Africans in late-Tudor London

---

[8] The term 'African' is preferred here over the other commonly used term for this group of people in historic analysis, 'Black', on the grounds that it is a more 'neutral', primarily geographic, descriptor and covers all the inhabitants of the continent. I do not make a distinction between sub-Saharan Africa and North Africa as this is not apparent in the records and, in any case, this distinction is itself a contentious one, with 'North Africa' relating to a cardinal direction, but 'sub-Saharan' Africa being a culturally constructed notion with colonial-era overtones; see Herbert Ekwe-Ekwe, 'Geopolitics or Blatant Sophistry?', *Latitude: Rethinking Power Relations – for a decolonised and non-racial world* <https://www.goethe.de/prj/lat/en/dis/21909728.html> [accessed 7 October 2020].

[9] Swinden, *History*, p. 366.

[10] M. Dorothy George, *London Life in the Eighteenth Century* (London, 1930), pp. 139–43.

[11] Norma Myers, *Reconstructing the Black Past: Blacks in Britain 1780–1830* (London; Portland, OR, 1996), p. 1.

that showed this presence could be traced in the historical record as far back as the sixteenth century.[12] Other scholars have explored the records since then to expand upon the knowledge about the African population.[13]

In recent years, Imtiaz Habib, Miranda Kaufmann, and Onyeka have published important work on Africans in Tudor and Stuart England.[14] The literature on the seventeenth- and eighteenth-century African presence has tended to focus more upon the intersection between Atlantic slavery and that presence. The two-hundredth anniversary of the abolition of the slave trade in British ships in 2007 gave significant impetus to the study of African history, especially in relation to the history of the major slaving ports, and saw substantial resources poured into the subject of Britain and slavery.[15] There remains much to be learnt about

---

[12] Kenneth Little, *Negroes in Britain: A Study of Racial Relations in English Society* (London, 1948); W.E. Miller, 'Negroes in Elizabethan London', *Notes and Queries*, 8 (1961), p. 138.

[13] See for example, Rosalyn L. Knutson, 'A Caliban in St. Mildred Poultry', in Tetsuo Kishi, Roger Pringle, and Stanley Wells (eds), *Shakespeare and Cultural Traditions: the Selected Proceedings of the International Shakespeare Association World Congress, Tokyo, 1991* (Newark, NJ, 1994), pp. 110-26; Marika Sherwood, 'Blacks in Tudor England', *History Today*, 53 (October 2003), pp. 40-2; Gustav Ungerer, 'Recovering a Black African's Voice in an English Lawsuit: Jacques Francis and the Salvage Operations of the *Mary Rose* and the *Sancta Maria* and *Sanctus Edwardus*, 1545-1550', *Medieval and Renaissance Drama in England*, 17 (2005), 255-71; Gustav Ungerer, 'The presence of Africans in Elizabethan England and the performance of Titus Andronicus at Burley-on-the-Hill, 1595/96', *Medieval and Renaissance Drama in England*, 21 (2008), 19-55. A good summary of the development of the field can be found in James Walvin, *From the Fringes to the Centre: the Emergence of British Black Historical Studies* (London, 1982). The early modern period is covered in James Walvin, *Black and White: The Negro and English Society 1555-1945* (London, 1973); Peter Fryer, *Staying Power: Black People in Britain since 1504* (Atlantic Highlands, NJ, 1984); Paul Edwards and James Walvin, 'Africans in Britain, 1500-1800', in Martin L. Kilson and Robert I. Rotberg (eds), *The African Diaspora: Interpretive Essays* (Cambridge, MA, 1976), pp. 173-204; Paul Edwards, 'The Early African Presence in the British Isles,' in Jagdish S. Gundara and Ian Duffield (eds), *Essays on the History of Blacks in Britain: From Roman Times to the Mid-twentieth Century* (Aldershot, 1992), pp. 9-29; Gretchen Gerzina, *Black England: Life Before Emancipation* (London, 1995).

[14] Imtiaz Habib, *Black Lives in the English Archives, 1500-1677: Imprints of the Invisible* (Aldershot, 2008). See also Imtiaz Habib, 'Sir Peter Negro, and the blacks of early modern England: Colonial inscription and postcolonial excavation', *Literature Interpretation Theory*, 9 (1998), 15-30; Miranda Kaufmann, *Black Tudors: The Untold Story* (London, 2017); Miranda Kaufmann, 'Caspar Van Senden, Sir Thomas Sherley and the Blackamoor Project', *Historical Research*, 81 (2008), 366-71; Onyeka, *Blackamoores: Africans in Tudor England, Their Presence, Status and Origins* (London, 2013).

[15] Examples of studies published in the period around this anniversary include: Simon Schama, *Rough Crossings* (London, 2005); James Walvin, *The Trader, The Owner, The Slave: Parallel Lives in the Age of Slavery* (London, 2007); Kathleen Chater, *Untold Histories: Black People in England and Wales during the Period of the British Slave Trade, c 1660-1807* (Manchester; New York, 2009) and a number of valuable local studies, for example, Todd Gray, *Devon and the Slave Trade: Documents on African Enslavement, Abolition and Emancipation from 1562 to 1867* (Exeter, 2007); Douglas Hamilton, *Scotland, the Caribbean and the Atlantic World, 1750-1820* (Manchester, 2005).

3

the rest of the country in that context, however. In the 1800s, the Liverpool MP William Roscoe said that, 'The African trade is the trade of the nation, not of any particular place.'[16] Roscoe was referring to the contribution of the wealth generated by slavery to Britain's coffers, but his comment draws attention to the fact that slavery was a component of English life far from the great slaving ports of Bristol, London, and Liverpool and reached deep into the provinces.

There has been growing interest in the issue of the connections between provincial spaces and the history of Africans in England.[17] This book demonstrates that counties such as Norfolk and Suffolk were not insulated from the world of English/British transatlantic slavery as it developed from the early 1600s.[18] Indeed, the two counties' growing involvement with the plantation complex is proposed here as an important element in understanding the trajectory of the social history of Africans in the region between 1467 and 1833. At the same time, this study shows that Norfolk and Suffolk had an African history that predated that 'full-blooded' English/British involvement in the Atlantic slaving economy. This means that, in attempting to explore that social history, this study has found itself moving far beyond what Roscoe termed 'the African trade' and its records. For while the evidence provided by the transatlantic slaving economy is used in the story told here, it is not the only evidence that underpins that story. The fragments of evidence that allow us to think about the African presence in early modern Norfolk and Suffolk come from a far wider set of sources than one might have expected.

* * *

The evidence base for this study is diverse and fragmentary, and its very nature has made the construction of a social history of Norfolk and Suffolk's African population a slow and challenging process. As will be explained in detail

---

[16] Quoted in Gomer Williams, *History of the Liverpool Privateers: and Letters of Marque with an Account of the Liverpool Slave Trade, 1744–1812* (Liverpool, 2005, orig. 1897), p. 595.

[17] University of Nottingham's Reconnecting Diverse Rural Communities Project, for example, https://www.nottingham.ac.uk/isos/research/rural-legacies.aspx. This topic was considered at the project conference, 'Historicising and re-connecting communities: Black presences and the legacies of slavery and colonialism in rural Britain. An interdisciplinary workshop funded by the Arts and Humanities Research Council', October 2013, University of Nottingham.

[18] Such work that has drawn Norfolk and Suffolk into discussions about African history has tended to focus on the leading abolitionists, looking particularly at the Quakers, Thomas Clarkson, and the Norfolk MP, Thomas Fowell Buxton, Christopher L. Brown, *Moral Capital: Foundations of British Abolitionism* (Chapel Hill, 2006), pp. 415–44; Howard Temperley, *White Dreams, Black Africa: the Antislavery Expedition to the Niger, 1841–1842* (New Haven, CT; London, 1991). Richard G. Wilson was one of the first historians to look at the region's involvement with the slave economy, in *Greene King: A Business and Family History* (London, 1983). Recent work on Norfolk includes Richard C. Maguire, 'Presenting the History of Africans in Provincial Britain: Norfolk as a Case Study', *History*, 99 (2014), 819–38.

in Chapter One, these data have been extracted from passing references that have been judged to indicate, with varying degrees of certainty, that a person had African heritage. This information has been found in a variety of archival material, including parish registers, local government and court records, ballads, censuses, personal letters, household accounting records, tombstones, newspapers, paintings, and books. This archival research has resulted in the creation of a database that I consider to be indicative of the African presence in Norfolk and Suffolk in the early modern period, but which I suspect is not an exhaustive list of that presence. Having found this information, the difficulty was conceiving of a fashion in which it could be used to provide an understanding of that presence that went beyond listing the entries, which would have only provided a 'scattered incidence' of the Africans in the region.[19]

The key issue to be dealt with was how to glean empirically supported understandings of Norfolk and Suffolk's African history from data which for the most part consisted of a name, location, perhaps an age, and a descriptor. A good example is that of Patrick Brink, who was listed as a 'blackamor' on his 1720 burial in Bury St Edmunds, but who left no other trace in the documentary record.[20] Eventually, after many false starts, it was the nature of the evidence that provided a means of understanding how it could be used productively. This was because all the data about the Africans that I had brought together appeared within other documents which were themselves products of a specific local culture, time, and space. For example, a parish register can be understood as just a book containing names and associated information, which has been gathered for a bureaucratic purpose. In that case, looking at a King's Lynn register which recorded the baptism of 'Peter Lynn' who was also described as a 'Moore or Mulatto' in 1643, it is possible to view that African in that sense; bureaucratised, separated from the community around him, a line in a book.[21] Yet, a parish register is far more than just a book. It reflects the passage of lives in a specific geographic locale, it records the rhythm of those lives, and provides insight into the cultural ideas that bound those lives together – at that moment, and across time. In other words, that parish register is an embedded local history. From that perspective, finding any mention of an African in such a document is a reminder to an historian that *this* African lived in, and was part of, *that* local community.

Viewed in this fashion, the data I had collected changed from a simple list to a collection of microhistories, where an African appeared in a specific location, at a specific point in history. These microhistories could only be fully understood in that locality's context, and at that entry's temporal moment. Once this was done, then these local microhistories could be drawn together to provide an understanding of the wider picture, even eventually to think

---

[19] Habib, *Black*, p. 11.
[20] SRO/FL/545/4/5, Burial of Patrick Brink, Bury St Edmunds, 17 September 1720.
[21] NRO/PD/39/1, Baptism of Peter Lynn, King's Lynn, 20 May 1643.

about a story that criss-crossed the Atlantic. The methodology used here might be likened to that of an archaeologist faced with using a few fragmentary and broken tiles to reconstruct an ancient villa floor. Each tile has a specific place and meaning, which can be deduced by extracting every possible detail from its local surroundings, shape, appearance, and so on. Gradually, by focusing upon this detailed exploration of those local factors, each tile can be placed into a relationship with its fellows, providing a progressively better understanding of the overall construction of the floor. Finally, a view of the floor can be suggested, and that can then be related to what we already know about villas more widely, adding to our understanding of them. Here, I have tried to do something similar for the, apparently evanescent, glimpses into the lives of the Africans found in the records. Each mention of an African has been 'squeezed' for the maximal amount of information that it can provide by placing the entry into its local historical context first, rather than beginning with a wider theoretical framework and working inwards. These microhistories of an individual, or a collection of them, provide the building blocks for the sub-sections in each chapter, each contextualised in relation to their local Norfolk and Suffolk communities. Where there is a little more data to work with, for example with Baptist in Hunstanton in 1599, or Rosanna in Rougham in 1688, then a microhistory is more expansive; in other incidents it might be less so. These multiple microhistories are then drawn together to provide a wider, but still localised, history of the Africans involved in the regional context.

The book also looks at the local history of Norfolk and Suffolk's connections with Europe and the Atlantic world, because it is clear from the close analysis of these Africans that their presence relates to locations in those wider areas. There is a substantial chapter on the involvement of the region's population in the transatlantic economy from 1700 onwards, for example. Once again, however, the emphasis is on the way Norfolk and Suffolk's population interacted with these wider communities, rather than the other way around. Throughout, I have attempted to examine the issues here from the vantage point of the locality, even when I have been discussing events and ideas in the colonies, because it seems to me that this is a productive viewpoint from which to observe. So, when I look at planters in Virginia and Barbados in the early seventeenth century in Chapter Four, I have tried, as much as possible, to refer to planters who came from East Anglia, and think of them as people who came from Norfolk and Suffolk originally. Above all, I have tried to place the Africans we encounter in the region's archives at the centre of the story and have sought always to draw our thinking back to them, making their local social history the continuous focus for our reference.

* * *

Early modern Norfolk and Suffolk is a region that has not been examined carefully in relation to the history of Africans in early modern England. As Corfield points out, 'regional boundaries in England resist tidy mapping' and, instead, broad historical associations, reflecting shared geography, experience and culture, have created communal identities in certain locations. Norfolk and Suffolk form 'the compact East Anglian heartland' and are studied together here for that reason.[22] In recent decades there has been much research about the relationship between what Philip Curtin defines as 'the plantation complex' and other areas of England, especially the country's key slaving ports; London, Bristol, and Liverpool, and their hinterlands.[23] Norfolk and Suffolk have generally been left out of this research, since they are perceived to have been a geographical backwater for African history because the counties are in the 'wrong' place. Bounded on the north and east by the North Sea, although Norfolk and Suffolk have short sailing distances to important parts of the European continent, they have a more tricky route to the Atlantic, which tended to mean that as the Atlantic economy grew across the early modern period there was comparatively less direct trading with the Americas from their ports than there was from London and the western ports, such as Liverpool.[24] This North Sea alignment has led historians to overlook the possibility of a meaningful African presence in the two counties, on the basis that access to the Atlantic (and the slave trade and slave-plantations) was too difficult for the area's merchants. As Metters puts it in relation to King's Lynn, 'After all, Lynn faced the wrong way for all that, and provincial conservatism

[22] Penelope Corfield, 'East Anglia', in Peter Clark and David Michael Palliser (eds), *The Cambridge Urban History of Britain: Volume 2, 1540–1840* (Cambridge, 2000), pp. 31–2.

[23] Philip D. Curtin, *The Rise and Fall of the Plantation Complex: Essays in Atlantic History* (Cambridge; New York, 1990). See for example, Philip Morgan, 'British Encounters with African and African Americans, 1600–1780', in Bernard Bailyn and Philip Morgan (eds), *Strangers within the Realm: Cultural Margins of the First British Empire* (Chapel Hill, 1991), p. 159; Myers, *Reconstructing*, p. 35. For discussions of these ports' relation to the slaving economy, among many texts, see Nuala Zahedieh, *The Capital and the Colonies: London and the Atlantic Economy, 1660–1700* (Cambridge, 2010); Kenneth Morgan, *Bristol and the Atlantic Trade in the Eighteenth Century* (Cambridge, 1993), and his 'The Economic Development of Bristol, 1700–1850', in Madge Dresser and Philip Ollerenshaw (eds), *The Making of Modern Bristol* (Bristol, 1996), pp. 48–75; David Richardson, 'Slavery and Bristol's "Golden Age"', *Slavery and Abolition*, 26 (2005), 35–54; Madge Dresser, *Slavery Obscured: The Social History of the Slave Trade in an English Provincial Port* (New York, 2001); Kenneth Morgan, 'Building British Atlantic Port Cities Bristol and Liverpool in the eighteenth century', in Daniel Maudlin and Bernard L. Herman (eds), *Building the British Atlantic World: Spaces, Places, and Material Culture, 1600–1850* (Chapel Hill, 2016), pp. 212–28; Diana E. Ascott, Fiona Lewis, and Michael Power, *Liverpool, 1660–1750: People, Prosperity and Power* (Liverpool, 2006); Kenneth Morgan, 'Liverpool's Dominance in the British Slave Trade, 1740–1807', in David Richardson, Suzanne Schwarz, and Anthony Tibbles (eds), *Liverpool and Transatlantic Slavery* (Liverpool, 2007), pp. 14–42.

[24] John Barney, 'Shipping in the Port of King's Lynn, 1702–1800', *Journal of Transport History*, 20 (1999), 126–41, at p. 136.

would stifle any tendency to venture into unknown and uncertain areas.'[25] This idea has been reinforced by the presence of London to the south, which tended to act as a break on any involvement in the actual slave trade for ports further up the eastern coast of England. Furthermore, Norfolk and Suffolk's merchants have been characterised as being too insular to become involved in trade with Africa, the West Indies, and America because, as Tattersfield states, they were 'tied into a marriage of convenience' with existing trade networks involving countries such as Norway.[26]

The reality is more complex. Firstly, as will be shown in the early chapters of this book, the original appearance of an African population in Norfolk and Suffolk was not connected to the Atlantic economy, or to English/British involvement in Atlantic slavery at all, and reaches back to the fifteenth and sixteenth centuries. The early African presence in the two counties, up to around 1640, was linked to established regional trading connections with Europe and the Mediterranean. This African presence should not, consequently, be thought about in relation to Atlantic slavery and the ideas about race that grew to prominence during the period of that economic system's development. Furthermore, these trading connections were part of Norfolk and Suffolk's general mercantile activity and were not driven by any regional involvement in existing European slaving networks, so they were not the result of 'English-operated' slavery. Moreover, the evidence marshalled here leads me to propose that, while there is a possibility that some of the Africans living in the two counties in the period before the mid-1600s may have been enslaved, it seems that a proportion of the Africans living in Norfolk and Suffolk between 1467 and 1599 were not enslaved. If the evidence advanced here to support this proposal is accepted, then it points us towards a further suggestion; that the initial, and subsequent, history of the African population in the two counties – and the response of the existing populace to those Africans as they arrived, settled, lived, and worked in the region – needs to be understood in relation to a different set of ideas than those to which it might generally be connected.

The lives of the Africans we will explore here seem to point us towards an idea proposed by Roxann Wheeler, that 'skin colour and race as we know them today have not always been powerful tools to convey difference'. Wheeler's suggestion is that the focus on skin colour as a predominant marker of identity in English/British thought is best seen as a development of modernity, and as a break from previous ways of approaching difference. She proposes that this focus on skin colour can be related to the development of Enlightenment ideas in fields of inquiry such as philosophy, politics, economics, medicine, and travel, which caused 'the reification of skin colour as a discrete item of analysis'. These ideas

[25] G. A. Metters, 'The Rulers and Merchants of King's Lynn in the Early Seventeenth Century' (Unpublished Ph.D Dissertation, University of East Anglia, 1982), p. 326.
[26] Nigel Tattersfield, *The Forgotten Trade: Comprising the Log of the Daniel and Henry of 1700 and Accounts of the Slave Trade from the Minor Ports of England, 1698–1725* (London, 1991), p. 202.

then provided a means by which people could be differentiated that had not existed previously but was a response to a need to distinguish the British nation from its colonies through the identification of difference between rulers and ruled. This emphasis on skin colour was, however, a shift from previous contrasts that had been more important, such as that between Christian and heathen.[27]

The evidence about Norfolk and Suffolk presented here would appear to be supportive of this approach, and of a notion that East Anglian conceptions of difference in the early modern period should not be understood as having been fixed at its start. Rather, the data seem to suggest that these concepts were subject to alteration between 1467 and 1833. The suggestion made here, in consequence, is that the early history of Africans in Norfolk and Suffolk was not bounded and defined by the negative ideas about Africans that, as will be seen, became more evident among some in the region in later centuries. The arrival of those negative ideas was, I suggest, entwined with the region's growing connection with the newly forged economic networks of the Atlantic economy, which came to rely upon the enslavement of Africans from the mid-seventeenth century onwards. In contrast to the situation in this later period, the opening stages of African migration into the two counties are understood here in the context of a pan-European economic area, and of different social relations to those of the later world of Atlantic slavery. I suggest that this evidence allows us to consider the possibility that the responses of the existing population in Norfolk and Suffolk to Africans as they appeared in local communities from the late medieval period onwards were not dominated by pre-existing notions about 'blackness' – although these existed in certain areas of English culture – or by a set association between African heritage and enslavement.[28] Initial responses in the region were, instead, framed by ideas drawn from local memories about traditional rights, economic position, and social relations, which reflected the surrounding local religious, economic, and social order. It was only later in the early modern period, from the mid-1600s onwards, that the ideas about race that evolved in the colonies under the aegis of Enlightenment thought and colonial slavery began to affect the culture of Norfolk and Suffolk, because of a deepening involvement by Norfolk and Suffolk people in the plantation complex.

---

[27] Roxann Wheeler, *The Complexion of Race: Categories of Difference in Eighteenth-Century British Culture* (Philadelphia, 2002), Chap. 1, at p. 3.

[28] For examples of the discussion of such ideas see Kim Hall, *Things of Darkness: Economies of Race and Gender in Early Modern England* (Ithaca, NY, 1995); Ania Loomba, 'Periodization, Race, and Global Contact', *Journal of Medieval and Early Modern Studies*, 37 (2007), 595–620; Valerie Traub, 'Mapping the Global Body', in Peter Erickson and Clark Hulse (eds), *Early Modern Visual Culture: Representation, Race, and Empire in Renaissance England* (Philadelphia, 2000); Catherine Molineux, *Faces of Perfect Ebony: Encountering Atlantic Slavery in Imperial Britain* (Cambridge, MA; London, 2012); Alden T. Vaughan and Virginia Mason Vaughan, 'Before Othello: Elizabethan Representations of Sub-Saharan Africans', *William and Mary Quarterly*, 3rd ser., 54 (1997), 19–44.

The connection between Norfolk and Suffolk and 'the plantation machine' that grew to dominate the economy of the Atlantic from the early seventeenth century is, nonetheless, of crucial importance in understanding the overall history of the African population in the two counties.[29] As time progressed, ideas about Africans became entangled with the development of colonial slavery and were reconfigured as part of a dynamic process that saw racial categories and mercantile capital interact with one another increasingly after 1600, and especially after the shift towards the use of enslaved African labour that gained momentum from the 1640s onwards. This process generated 'social and economic changes in the colonies and then across the Atlantic'.[30] From the middle of the seventeenth century these social and economic changes had increasing influence on the lives of Africans living in Norfolk and Suffolk, both because regional involvement with the colonial economies created new routes for greater numbers of Africans to arrive in the two counties, and also because the new ideas about race that developed within that system began to challenge the existing ideas about Africans held in East Anglia. These new ideas, I suggest, worked in tandem with the changes to Norfolk and Suffolk's culture resulting from the advent of agrarian capitalism and the ideas of the Enlightenment about efficiency and progress, to alter gradually the social relations in Norfolk and Suffolk that had allowed Africans to enter local communities previously and had prevented them being seen purely from a perspective of ethnicity. The process would seem to be supportive of the proposal made by Kyle Grady that there was 'a flexibility in early modern notions of difference that diminishes under the more rigid racialism of the eighteenth century'.[31]

An important element in this book is the relationship between the notion of class position and the social construction of race in provincial Norfolk and Suffolk from 1467 to 1833. As Franklin Knight has suggested, 'Race can be, and has often been, employed with the most imprecise connotations and is therefore notoriously unreliable as a principal identifier.'[32] The idea of 'race' is used by groups of people to define themselves against others and also to express ideas about specific characteristics but, because it is culturally constructed, it is changeable and so difficult to use historically. Julian Pitt-Rivers suggests that 'the

[29] Trevor Burnard and John Garrigus, *The Plantation Machine: Atlantic Capitalism in French Saint-Domingue and British Jamaica* (Philadelphia, 2016).

[30] D.V. Armstrong, 'Capitalism and the Shift to Sugar and Slavery in Mid-Seventeenth-Century Barbados', *Historical Archaeology*, 53 (2019), 468–91, at p. 469; for another discussion of the emergence of capitalism in agro-industrial sugar production in the late seventeenth century see M. Meniketti, 'The Bush Hill Sugar Plantation: A West Indies Case Study in Developmental Capitalism', *Historical Archaeology*, 54 (2020), 212–39.

[31] Kyle Grady, 'Zora Neale Hurston and Humoral Theory: Comparing Racial Concepts from Early Modern England and Post-Abolition America', *Shakespeare Studies*, 46 (2018), 144-9, at p. 145.

[32] Franklin W. Knight, 'Introduction: Race and Identity in the New World', in Christopher Morris and John D. Garrigus (eds), *Assumed Identities: The Meanings of Race in the Atlantic World* (Texas, 2010), 1–17, at p. 4.

word race [...] clearly owes little to physical anthropology, but refers, however it may be defined, to the ways in which people are classified in daily life. What are called race relations are, in fact, always questions of social structure.'[33] Likewise, Barbara Fields maintains that 'many historians tend to accord race a transhistorical, almost metaphysical, status that removes it from all possibility of analysis and understanding'. Fields argues that doing so entails taking a 'position within the terrain of racialist ideology' and questions its explanatory efficacy, arguing that class is a more useful analytical tool.[34] As Andy Wood has pointed out, it is important to appreciate the difficulty in using models about social power drawn from 'frozen caste societies' such as the antebellum United States, or the slaving economies of the Caribbean, in the analysis of early modern English society, which was 'characterised by structural and cultural diversity: [...] rapid social mobility, increasing population, expanding literacy, industry and urbanisation'.[35]

With such caveats in mind, this book looks to utilise the idea of class to rethink the social history of Africans in early modern East Anglia. In recent years historians have returned to the use of class as a category of analysis in the early modern period, and suggested that, 'Instead of searching for antecedents of modern class identities, early modern historians need to rethink class as a category; as a relationship; as a structure – and thereby reconfigure the ways in which we conceptualise both the periodisation and the meaning of class.'[36] The records of the lives of the African population in early modern Norfolk and Suffolk – which are admittedly limited, partial, and fragmentary – seem to show that for much of the early modern period in Norfolk and Suffolk there was, to use the phrasing of Wheeler, an 'elasticity accorded black and white skin colour' in the region.[37] In this context of 'elasticity' the notion of class can be used to provide a different approach to understanding the situations of these Africans, alongside other notions, such as the division between Christian/heathen, and the importance of local cultures and memories.

Africans first appeared in East Anglia at an historical moment where older pre-capitalist social relations were under pressure from emergent agrarian capitalism, but those older relations had not yet succumbed to the new economic order. It is proposed in Chapters Two and Three that these earlier social relations allowed for Africans to be understood and related to in a specific fashion; one

---

[33] Julian Pitt-Rivers, 'Race, Colour and Class in Central America and the Andes', in John J. Johnson, Peter J. Bakewell, and Meredith D. Dodge (eds), *Readings in Latin American History, Volume II, The Modern Experience* (Durham, 1985), pp. 313-28, at p. 313.

[34] Barbara J. Fields, 'Ideology and Race in American History', in J. Morgan Kousser and James M. McPherson (eds), *Region, Race and Reconstruction: Essays in Honour of C. Vann Woodward* (New York, 1982), pp. 143-77, at pp. 144-5.

[35] Andy Wood, *Riot, Rebellion and Popular Politics in Early Modern England* (London, 2002), p. 18.

[36] Andy Wood, 'Fear, Hatred and the Hidden Injuries of Class in Early Modern England', *Journal of Social History*, 39 (2006), 803-26, at p. 804.

[37] Wheeler, *The Complexion*, p. 6.

where their 'class' position, along with religious affiliation, mattered more than modern concepts of 'ethnicity' or 'race'. In this environment Africans were able to enter local communities because they could be understood in terms of other social categories that more readily fitted with existing social relations. So, as we shall see when looking at the earliest example of an African in the region from 1467, a working sailor who was an African could be understood more readily in terms of his 'class' status – as a member of the mobile working poor – and his religious status, than as a 'black' person, itself a description that was not used on its own in relation to Africans in the region until nearly 200 years later.

Class is also important because the story presented here takes place within a period characterised by significant social and cultural changes that resulted from the wider social effects of the advent of agrarian capitalism in Norfolk and Suffolk. These changes led to an expansion of what Patricia Fumerton identifies as 'a large and growing number of mobile and casually employed labourers in early modern England'. Fumerton reminds us that early modern workers often moved geographically, as they sought 'various lines of gainful employment'. This was often because their work was itinerant in type (such as peddlers, carriers, entertainers, tinkers, and so on), but also because some workers shifted from one similar job to another (harvest workers, wage labourers), or people changed their jobs entirely. The result was a situation Fumerton terms 'unsettledness'.[38] As David Rollison has highlighted, this 'unsettled' condition was, in turn, a crucial building block of early modern society because 'immigrants and passers-through' were a vital element in the constitution of 'the fellowship of the town' in the period, and the constant flow of such immigrants through early modern villages and towns was constitutive of those locations' social and economic structure. Rollison's idea is that immigrants were essential for the existence of early modern towns, and that without them 'few towns in early modern England could maintain their size, let alone increase it'.[39]

The arrival of Africans in Norfolk and Suffolk can be placed into this framework. Early modern East Anglia was a mobile society, and the people of Norfolk and Suffolk were used to encountering travellers, and to travelling. Along with its substantial internal and coastal trade, which provided connections with migrants from elsewhere in the British isles, the region's foreign trade linked it with the Baltic, the Low Countries, Scotland, France, Spain, the Mediterranean, and even Iceland – reputedly reached by a fisherman from the Norfolk port of Cromer shortly after 1400.[40] Africans arriving in Norfolk and Suffolk entered, therefore, a locale that was used to newcomers arriving in villages, towns, and cities, seeking work and providing labour. The

[38] Patricia Fumerton, *Unsettled: The Culture of Mobility and the Working Poor in Early Modern England* (Chicago; London, 2006), pp. xi–xii.
[39] David Rollison, 'Exploding England: the dialectics of mobility and settlement in early modern England', *Social History*, 24 (1999), 1–16, at pp. 9–10.
[40] N.J. Williams, *The Maritime Trade of the East Anglian Ports, 1550–1590* (Oxford, 1988), pp. 69–137, at p. 85.

local population was used to engaging with 'foreigners' from many places. In consequence, it was possible for arriving Africans to join this mobile and diverse milieu. These Africans could do so because a marketplace for mobile labourers existed, and because newly arrived strangers were a staple part of the region's life. The proposal made here is that, in this environment, there was an existing social space for Africans to arrive, to move around, and to settle in as accepted members of the region's working poor. This meant that Africans who were not enslaved could find a home in a culture which utilised many religious, social, and economic understandings of social place, and did not prioritise notions of 'race' over these other longer-established ideas.

* * *

The book begins by looking at the empirical evidence of the gradual appearance of Africans in Norfolk and Suffolk from the late fifteenth century onwards. Chapter One provides the large-scale picture of this migration, using the data presented in the appendices about the Africans identified in the two counties between 1467, which saw the first documented appearance of an African in the region, and 1833, when slavery was finally ended in the British Empire. Appendix A lists people who were described in the records in ways that are taken to show that they were African, and Appendix B augments this with further data derived from the examination of surnames. These data show an extensive, numerous, and geographically dispersed African presence between 1467 and 1833. The chapter then presents these data in a series of maps that examine the appearance of the African population in Norfolk and Suffolk over time, looking for patterns in the geographic distribution of that population that might provide a general framework to understand the migration itself.

The book next moves from the general to the specific. Chapters Two and Three cover the fifteenth and sixteenth centuries, a period that saw the initial appearance of Africans in Norfolk and Suffolk, beginning in the coastal areas. They show that the appearance of these Africans was related to regional trading links with the Mediterranean economy and should not be assumed to be related to any direct local involvement with slavery. These chapters also explore the question of what was understood by 'slavery' by the population of Norfolk and Suffolk in this early period. As has been shown by the extensive discussion of the Somerset Case of 1772, the exact legal status of Africans in early modern England remains difficult to discern.[41] For the purposes of this study, the notion of 'slavery' is considered in relation to a concept of 'Classical chattel slavery', which forms a Weberian 'ideal type'. In the fullest expression of this, a 'slave' would be legally considered as property that could be sold, bequeathed, and physically damaged or destroyed with nearly complete authority by an owner. Legal enslavement in the English-speaking Atlantic world across the

---

[41] A summary can be found in James Oldham, *English Common Law in the Age of Mansfield* (Chapel Hill, 2004), 305-23.

early modern period varied in the degree to which it approached that ideal type. It came awfully close to it in the colonies in the eighteenth century, but never reached this position in England. While ideal type chattel slavery did not exist in England in the period, however, a set of legal rules developed from the sixteenth century that created a potential for Africans to exist in what has been characterised by George van Cleve as 'slavish servitude' or 'near slavery'.[42] Cleve's terms are utilised in this study to describe Africans who appear to have been held in some form of bondage in Norfolk and Suffolk.

Unfortunately, there is no evidence of any legal discussion of the status of those Africans who were living in Norfolk and Suffolk in the early modern period, nor was the matter explored in the region's books or newspapers, despite some discussion about colonial slavery in the late eighteenth and early nineteenth centuries. In the absence of such debate, I attempt to explore the reality of the status of Norfolk and Suffolk's Africans by the close examination of their interactions with their local communities. The lived relations of these Africans suggest that understandings of enslavement in the region at community level were not centred upon skin colour initially. Instead, their local situation and class position were the important determinants of their perception by contemporaries.

My proposal is that in the period up to the mid-1600s, slavery was a concept that had specific local cultural connotations, which drew on medieval roots, and were expressed clearly during the 1549 rebellions in the region.[43] This leads to a suggestion that slavery was not associated with skin colour but with social situation and, in consequence, I propose that the Africans arriving in the region were not automatically connected to enslavement by their contemporaries. Instead, their place in society was understood largely by reference to their relationship to Christianity and their class position. Once their confessional situation was dealt with, they were able to interact with society as members of the labouring poor. This interaction was made simpler because the society of Norfolk and Suffolk at this time was diverse already and its people were used to

---

[42] George Van Cleve, 'Somerset's Case and Its Antecedents in Imperial Perspective', *Law and History Review*, 24 (2006), 601–45, at pp. 603–4.

[43] This is a contrast to the suggestions of historians such as Jordan and Guasco, who see a more 'national' set of ideas in play and suggest that the English had a coherent set of ideas about slavery that were derived from Greek literature, Roman law, and the Bible, and that these theoretical understandings were then contextualised by their encounters with realities such as galley slavery in the Mediterranean, the trading and slaving activities of John Hawkins, Francis Drake, and Christopher Newport, and the experiences of English merchants who were involved in the African slave trade; see for example, Winthrop D. Jordan, *White Over Black: American Attitudes Toward the Negro, 1550–1812* (2nd edn) (Chapel Hill, 2012), pp. 55–62; Michael Guasco, *Slaves and Englishmen: Human Bondage in the Early Modern Atlantic World* (Philadelphia, PA, 2014), pp. 1–30. For similar approaches see Tamara E. Lewis, '"Like Devils out of Hell": Reassessing the African Presence in Early Modern England', *Black Theology*, 14 (2016), 107–20; Alvin O. Thompson, 'Race and Colour Prejudices and the Origin of the Trans-Atlantic Slave Trade', *Caribbean Studies*, 16 (1976–7), 29–59.

the arrival of migrants from a variety of backgrounds. These findings gradually lead to a thesis that there was an existing approach to 'difference' in Norfolk and Suffolk at the beginning of the early modern period which was not rooted in modern concepts of 'race'. While there may have been such ideas floating around in certain texts, and possibly among some members of the social elite, the proposal is made that they were not prevalent in the area's culture generally.

Chapter Four moves into the seventeenth century and explores the ways that Norfolk and Suffolk were drawn into the Atlantic world through economic links with the newly established colonies in the Americas. Jerome Handler has recently proposed that existing negative racial stereotypes about Africans, combined with other aspects of English culture, namely views of private property, enabled the enslavement of Africans in Barbados long before the subject was codified in law. Handler accepts, nonetheless, that this argument is based on 'an inference from the admittedly sparse direct evidence [that] indicates that racist assumptions about Africans and the ideological acceptability of their exploitation and enslavement were already present among the English who settled Barbados'.[44] Chapter Four explores the degree to which such an 'inference' can be made, by looking at the 'direct evidence' provided by a region of England that supplied many of the early colonists to Barbados and the rest of the English/British New World. In Chapter Five, I look for this evidence in the lived relations of Africans in labouring communities in Norfolk and Suffolk.

As will be seen in Chapters Four, Five, Six, Seven, and Eight, the evidence about the situation of Africans in early modern Norfolk and Suffolk is complex and resists easy categorisation. We can find examples of Africans who were held in conditions of slavish servitude, the majority of which come from the mid- to late seventeenth century onwards. Equally, we can find examples of Africans who were free to come and go as they pleased, to marry local people, to raise their children, and baptise them in local churches. These patterns of life seem to predate the examples of slavish servitude and reach back to the first appearance of Africans in the region. Likewise, we can find racialised conceptions of Africans in the economic choices taken by some of the region's wealthy inhabitants to invest in plantation ownership from the late seventeenth century on. At the same time, we find little evidence at the beginning of the early modern period of deeply ingrained negative cultural preconceptions about Africans across Norfolk and Suffolk that linked them automatically to enslavement.[45]

In Chapters Four, Five, and Six we will see that such ideas only became visible as some of the region's inhabitants became involved in the Atlantic economy after 1600. By following the lead of Rogers Brubaker and Frederick Cooper and looking at race as a 'category of practice' rather than one of analysis,

[44] Jerome S. Handler, 'Custom and law: The status of enslaved Africans in seventeenth-century Barbados', *Slavery & Abolition*, 37 (2016), 233–55, at p. 248.
[45] This echoes Fields' view that, 'It is easy enough to demonstrate a substantial continuity in racial "attitudes". But doing so does not demonstrate continuity of racial ideology.' Fields, 'Ideology', p. 155.

this study examines how this idea can 'crystallize at certain moments, as a powerful, compelling reality'.[46] The fulcrum on which the argument made here pivots is the appearance of a form of economic organisation that relied upon enslaved labour and drew upon an ideology about race to justify its operation. This ideology drew on ideas that had existed at some level of English culture, but which had not been dominant, or visible, in the region in the fifteenth and sixteenth centuries. My suggestion here draws on Eric Williams' proposition in *Capitalism and Slavery* that anti-African racism was a consequence of the functioning of the plantation system, not a reason for it; or, as Williams phrased it, 'A racial twist has thereby been given to what is basically an economic phenomenon. Slavery was not born of racism; rather racism was the consequence of slavery.'[47]

The local history of Africans in early modern Norfolk and Suffolk seems to show that anti-African racism was not obvious in the area's culture until after the pivot to the Atlantic economy took place in the 1600s. Negatively charged racialised ideas look to have appeared gradually in Norfolk and Suffolk in a process that lagged their appearance in the colonies and their arrival seems to have been connected to the region's growing involvement in the plantation complex. This might be seen as a process of cultural change akin to that of English/British institutional change that Acemoglu, Johnson, and Robinson have suggested was a consequence of the growth in the Atlantic trade generally.[48] Pat Hudson has added to this idea, showing, for example, how the requirements of the slaving economy helped to foster new forms of financial instruments to manage new levels of debt and credit.[49] Similarly, Nuala Zahedieh has argued

[46] Rogers Brubaker and Frederick Cooper, 'Beyond "Identity"', *Theory and Society*, 29 (2000), 1–47, at p. 5.

[47] Eric Williams, *Capitalism and Slavery* (New York, 1961, orig. 1944), p. 7. Menard usefully distils Williams' argument into three: that slavery was a means of exploiting workers and racism was its consequence, the idea that the profits of slavery helped to finance British industrialisation, and the suggestion that abolition was a consequence of the declining profitability of slavery; Russel R. Menard, 'Reckoning with Williams: "Capitalism and Slavery" and the Reconstruction of Early American History', *Callaloo*, 20, *Eric Williams and the Postcolonial Caribbean: A Special Issue* (1997), pp. 791–9 (p. 793). For a recent review of the usefulness of Williams' ideas see Trevor Burnard and Giorgio Riello, 'Slavery and the new history of capitalism', *Journal of Global History*, 15 (2020), 225–44. The literature on Williams' work is voluminous; for an excellent survey of, and response to, his work from various perspectives, see the essays in Barbara L. Solow and Stanley L. Engerman (eds), *British Capitalism and Caribbean Slavery: The Legacy of Eric Williams* (Cambridge, 1987), especially Hilary Beckles, '"The Williams Effect": Eric Williams's Capitalism and Slavery and the Growth of West Indian Political Economy', pp. 303–16.

[48] Daron Acemoglu, Simon Johnson, and James Robinson, 'The Rise of Europe: Atlantic Trade, Institutional Change, and Economic Growth', *American Economic Review*, 95 (2005), 546–79.

[49] Pat Hudson, 'Slavery, the slave trade and economic growth: a contribution to the debate', in Catherine Hall, Nicholas Draper, and Keith McClelland (eds), *Emancipation and the Remaking of the British Imperial World* (Manchester, 2014), 36–59.

that the growth of Atlantic trade was important in encouraging 'adaptive innovations', including financial innovations in British commerce, improved transport networks and manufacturing capacity, and even 'useful knowledge', since people had to acquire mathematical and mechanical skills necessary for increasingly complicated trade.[50] The historical record of Africans in Norfolk and Suffolk from 1467 to 1833 looks to be best understood in a similar fashion, seeing the development of ideas about Africans in Norfolk and Suffolk as being influenced by the notions about race that were developed in the social, economic, and political context of the decision to use enslaved African labour in the colonial plantation economies.

Menard has suggested that if a distinction is made between 'attitudes and ideology' and slavery is seen in an Atlantic context, then much scholarship, for example the discussion about 'Chesapeake gradualism', would point to the fact that 'racism, as a systematic body of thought constructed to justify existing social arrangements and defend the interests of the planters, appeared relatively late in the region, well after planters had thoroughly committed to slavery'.[51] An examination of the situation of Africans in fifteenth- and sixteenth-century Norfolk and Suffolk and the comparison of it with later periods seems to reflect this proposal. The 'attitudes' of colonial planters that eventually grew into the racist ideology of colonial capitalism drew on elements of thinking that may have existed before the creation of the slave-plantations, but these do not seem to have been dominant, or even visible, in the culture of the people from Norfolk and Suffolk who became colonists in the Americas. These attitudes, and the racism that grew from them, only became important in the context of the development of African enslavement from the mid-1600s onwards, as they formed a system of psychological justification that allowed the operation of what Marc Mvé Bekale terms the 'alienating ethics of Western capitalism'.[52]

These new economic structures, although important, were not the only element in this story. Also vital were new Enlightenment ideas. The Norfolk and Suffolk-based owners of slave-plantations who are discussed in Chapter Six conceived of their plantations as a modern and advanced form of economic organisation. As we shall see, the evidence suggests that they were, to quote Justin Roberts, 'driven by the Enlightenment commitment to progress and inspired by Newtonian universalism and Baconian empiricism' to develop new management systems for their enslaved labour force and to import new agricultural techniques onto their plantations.[53] The slaveholding systems that

---

[50] Nuala Zahedieh, 'Colonies, copper, and the market for inventive activity in England and Wales, 1680-1730', *Economic History Review*, 66 (2013), pp. 805-25; Zahedieh, *The Capital*, pp. 285 and 292.

[51] Menard, 'Reckoning', p. 794.

[52] Marc Mvé Bekale, 'Memories and mechanisms of resistance to the Atlantic slave trade: the Ekang Saga in West Central Africa's epic tale the Mvet', *Journal of African Cultural Studies*, 32 (2020), 99-113, at p. 110.

[53] Justin Roberts, *Slavery and the Enlightenment in the British Atlantic, 1750-1807* (Cambridge,

developed in the eighteenth-century Atlantic world drew on ideas of efficiency based on wider Enlightenment discussions about scientific and agricultural advance, along with those concerning moral reform. The implementation of these ideas allowed plantations to become progressively more efficient, slave ships to become swifter, and slaves to be exploited more fully. Norfolk and Suffolk's plantation owners were part of this eighteenth-century improvement movement across the British Americas, which altered the way planters and their managers conceived of their plantations, and of Africans.

Roberts' work on the influence of the Enlightenment's thought processes on the development of ideas and practice in the plantation economy, and Wheeler's suggestions about the process by which ideas of race were developed in modernity, show that Enlightenment ideas about efficiency and scientific operation were themselves constitutive of concepts of race and altered the way slaveholders thought about their slaves. Such proposals would seem to find discernible support in the history of Africans in Norfolk and Suffolk presented here. We can draw on the ideas of Patrick Deneen, who suggests that an older set of customs and rules around the understanding of other people in early modern society, which were focused on classical/Christian understandings of social relations, were changed as these new Enlightenment ideas appeared. Deneen argues that a key element in the historic construction of 'liberty' as conceived by liberalism is that it 'disassembles a world of custom and replaces it with promulgated law'.[54] This would seem to provide a useful extra level of understanding to the social history presented here. In Chapters Two and Three it is argued that Africans arriving in the fifteenth and sixteenth centuries were not viewed in relation to skin colour because the existing system of social relations was based on classical/Christian notions. The background to the changes described in later chapters is that, as time progressed, that world of custom was gradually 'disassembled' – to borrow Deneen's phrase – and reconstructed by a combination of new economic systems and changes to customary practice. The story of the changing thinking about Africans in Norfolk and Suffolk is linked, therefore, to the wider social history of the impact of agrarian capitalism and the process whereby, as Keith Wrightson puts it, 'by the end of the sixteenth century [...] a permanent proletariat had emerged, collectively designated "the poor".'[55]

Chapter Five argues, moreover, that the Africans living in the region were an integral part of the 'permanent proletariat' and that this position meant that the new colonial ideas about race were not accepted unquestioningly. The social response to Africans that had developed in Norfolk and Suffolk in the fifteenth and sixteenth centuries continued to provide the fundamental reaction to them

---

2013), p. 6; see also Marcel van der Linden, 'Reconstructing the origins of modern labour management', *Labour History*, 51 (2010), pp. 509–22.

[54] Patrick J. Deneen, *Why Liberalism Failed* (New Haven, 2019), p. xiv.

[55] Keith Wrightson, *English Society, 1580–1680* (London, 1982), p. 141.

in the seventeenth. Africans continued to live and settle in the region from 1600 to 1699. They were baptised, moved around, married local people, raised families, and worked. Some Africans were new arrivals, while others were the descendants of those who had arrived in the Tudor period. Looking at the lives of these Africans reveals that the growing anti-African racism seen in the colonies did not supplant the existing social response to Africans in Norfolk and Suffolk, but neither was it completely rejected. Africans held in forms of near slavery can be discerned in Norfolk and Suffolk during this period, far more clearly than in the Tudor, and the situation of these Africans can be linked to those social groups who were most clearly involved in profiting from the Atlantic economy, and agrarian capitalism at home, and who were embracing the new ideas of the Enlightenment, namely East Anglia's merchants and the gentry. At the same time, building on the suggestions made in earlier chapters, my examination of the social relations in the region in the 1600s involving these Africans leads me to propose that it is useful to think of these Africans in terms of class, since that notion can be used to encapsulate a variety of degrees and types of labour situation. In that case, I suggest that many of the Africans in early modern Norfolk and Suffolk can usefully be thought of as being members of the working class who also happened to be African.

Changes in thought and economy during the early modern period more generally enabled greater control of workers, of any background, in any work context, and any geographic location. In Chapters Four and Six we shall see that workers from Norfolk and Suffolk were drawn into an ever-widening economic area, that linked rural East Anglia to the sugar plantations, and which exploited workers of many backgrounds, whether from Ireland, Africa, rural Suffolk, or Norfolk. Within this changing world, there were many different forms of unfree labour. As Roberts has pointed out, the tendency in slave studies to emphasise 'the resistance paradigm' as a central theme in subaltern studies has been useful in dismantling the idea that slavery could be a 'benevolent institution'. Drawing on Sidney Mintz, however, Roberts suggests that it is also important to avoid 'fetishizing' slavery and presenting it as 'the polar opposite of freedom'. The reality faced by members of the 'permanent proletariat' was that 'From apprentices to convict slaves, the early modern Atlantic was an unfree world. Most workers were dependent, bound, or coerced in some way, denied specific bundles of rights and freedoms. The difference between slavery and other forced labour systems is more a matter of degree than kind.'[56] Understanding that there was not an absolute difference between 'free labour' and 'slave labour' in this period is an important aspect of understanding the position of Africans in Norfolk and Suffolk. Although the term 'free' is used here to suggest that an African was not held in chattel slavery or slavish servitude, it does not mean that they were free of other forms of economic coercion. Indeed, one of the useful things that the use of the concept of class in this context allows is a recognition

[56] Roberts, *Slavery*, pp. 3–4.

19

of the range of potentially unfree economic situations Africans faced, even when they were not held by overt means of control. This then leads to a recognition of the potential links that these varying situations of unfree labour created between workers in different situations across Norfolk and Suffolk.

The book moves on to explore the situation in Norfolk and Suffolk during the eighteenth and early nineteenth centuries. This was the historical moment when the ideas about race and skin colour that had been forming since the early 1600s began to become more important in local society. Chapter Six looks at the evidence of the area's involvement in the world of colonial slavery from 1700 to 1833, including slaving voyages, plantation ownership, and general trade with the slaving colonies. I argue that at this historical moment the attitudes of colonial slave societies can be seen far more clearly in the views and behaviour of some members of the merchant and landed classes in the counties, and among those members of the lower classes who were drawn into the Atlantic world. Chapters Seven and Eight examine the data concerning the African population in the two counties from 1700 onwards and explore how the lives of this population were connected, framed, and changed. Using this analysis, I propose that the ideas about race that had become so entrenched in the Americas by the eighteenth century were not simply transferred to the region. Even in this period Norfolk and Suffolk were not slave societies; they were not even societies with slaves.[57] Rather they were English counties where relatively small numbers of Africans lived and some had settled. Prevailing norms about Africans in the two counties, now centuries old, still had to be engaged with.

From 1700 onwards the region became the home of more Africans, many of whom seem to have been brought there from previous situations of chattel slavery, and some of whom seem to have remained in various degrees of 'slavish servitude' when in the region. At the same time, however, it appears that the local situation of Africans in Norfolk and Suffolk that had developed over previous centuries provided a buttress against anti-African racism. The local context continued to matter, especially among the labouring population within which most Africans lived, and many continued to see Africans as neighbours, as spouses, as colleagues, and fellow members of the labouring classes. The picture of Africans presented emphasises their embedded local context and relates that to their position as members of the local working class.[58]

The microhistories offered here suggest an historic process that ran from a beginning point where the major aspect of difference that people in Norfolk and Suffolk considered in relation to arriving Africans was that between Christian and non-Christian; this was dealt with through baptism and Africans were then allowed to enter local working communities. It seems that changes to social

---

[57] For the original conceptualisation of these ideas see Moses Finley, *Ancient Slavery and Modern Ideology* (New York, 1980). These were developed by Ira Berlin, *Many Thousands Gone: The First Two Centuries of Slavery in North America* (Cambridge, MA, 1998), esp. pp. 7–14.
[58] The one exception to this class membership is the story of Edward Steele, who is discussed in Chapter Eight.

customs caused by the onset of agrarian capitalism, the Reformation, and the Enlightenment, along with the increasing involvement of Norfolk and Suffolk in the Atlantic economy, changed the social history of Africans in Norfolk and Suffolk over time. This process exposed the inhabitants of the region to the Atlantic world's developing discourse about Africans, which was based in a significant manner on a process of their categorisation and commodification, and was used to justify their economic exploitation. This challenged the region's original ways of relating to Africans, which were simultaneously being weakened by the local social shifts caused by the growth of agrarian capitalism. The evidence then leads us to an end point where what Wheeler describes as 'our current sense of colour's intractability' can be seen clearly affecting the view of Africans being taken by many, but not all, in the region.[59] Looking at the lives of the Africans presented here, from the arrival of Eylys in the port of Yarmouth in 1467 to the involvement of three unnamed Africans in the 'Swing' riots in 1830–1, it seems that this latter notion took time to gain traction and never became completely dominant. The idea proposed to explain this situation is that the long-term African presence in those working communities, which predated the anti-African racism of the plantation era, continued to provide a connection to these original local responses about Africans that can be seen from the late 1400s and throughout the 1500s.

By working from a local and provincial perspective, over a period of 400 years, I hope that the social situation of Africans in early modern Norfolk and Suffolk can be given greater texture. There has been a tendency to present the African population in early modern England as 'overwhelmingly young, male and transient' and as 'a group of people bound together by a common history of direct or indirect English enslavement, benign or brutal, and having common ethnic or cultural characteristics'.[60] This study looks at their story from other perspectives and, in doing so, attempts to add new layers of understanding to it. The book uncovers an African population of all ages, comprising men, women, and children, that was mobile, but not necessarily transient, many of whose members were embedded in local communities, and had many means of employment. It also proposes that this population should not be thought of en masse as being held in slavery, and defined by racism, since it seems that the situation was far more nuanced than this. Finally, I suggest that these Africans might be thought of productively as members of the working class, and that doing so can provide us with a fresh understanding of their lives.

---

[59] Wheeler, The Complexion, p. 6.
[60] Dana Rabin, 'In a Country of Liberty?': Slavery, Villeinage and the Making of Whiteness in the Somerset Case (1772)', History Workshop Journal, 72 (2011), 5–29, at p. 7; Habib, Black, p. 11.

1

Identifying the African Population in Early Modern Norfolk and Suffolk

The first documented African inhabitant of Norfolk and Suffolk was a young 'boy of the shippe' called Eylys, who was described as a 'More' on his arrival in Yarmouth in 1467.[1] Over the next 400 years, Eylys was followed by a continuous stream of men and women of African heritage into the two counties. This chapter presents the core material identifying this African population and then examines that information to make some general comments about its members. Having done this, it goes on to make some broad suggestions about the drivers that lay behind this migration and an initial set of propositions about that African population in Norfolk and Suffolk. The most significant proportion of these data was drawn from the parish records of Suffolk and Norfolk.[2] The modern Diocese of Norfolk covers 573 parishes, while that of St Edmundsbury and Ipswich (Suffolk) consists of 446 parishes. With a total of 1,019 parishes in the region, it has not been possible to examine all the

---

[1] This statement excludes the suggestion made in 1980 that the characteristics of a female skull found during archaeological work on eleventh-century skeletal remains in North Elmham Park 'leave little doubt that it comes from a negress or a woman with predominantly negro genes on her chromosomes'. This view argued that 'The combined features of flattened nasals, a nasal index of 60.4 and the high Gnathic Index, gives this skull a strongly negroid character', Calvin Wells, '12. The Human Bones', in *East Anglian Archaeology Report No. 9, Norfolk, North Elmham Volume II* (Norfolk, 1980), 257–62 and 317–19, at p. 259 and p. 318. This theory assumed substantial differences in bone structure between races; however, such categorisation is no longer accepted in archaeological interpretation and, in the absence of DNA analysis, the identification is not accepted here. The remains are mentioned in Fryer, *Staying*, p. 2; Paul Edwards and James Walvin, *Black Personalities in the Era of the Slave Trade* (London, 1983), p. 4; Sue Niebrzydowski, 'The Sultana and Her Sisters: Black Women in the British Isles before 1530', *Women's History Review*, 10 (2001), 187–210, at p. 188.
[2] Prior to the formation of the modern-day Diocese of St Edmundsbury and Ipswich in 1914, the entire county of Suffolk was included in the Diocese of Norfolk. This area did not include the extreme west of Norfolk beyond the River Great Ouse, which is part of the Diocese of Ely; however, Norfolk parishes that lie in the Diocese of Ely are included in this sample. The 1914 change to the old Diocese of Norfolk means that the parish records information has been drawn from the diocesan records preserved at the Norfolk Record Office – which include those of the Deanery of Lothingland, which comprises the port of Lowestoft and its immediate hinterland and lies in the county of Suffolk – alongside material drawn from records that are held in the Suffolk Record Offices at Ipswich, Bury St Edmunds, and Lowestoft.

available parish records over the near four centuries covered by this study. This means that the evidence offered here is not a complete survey. Nonetheless, it is proposed that this material is indicative of both the geographic extent and numbers of the region's African population.

Norfolk and Suffolk form 'England's premier cereal growing province' and their shared coastline and maritime history has tended to lead to even closer affiliation.[3] Bounded on the north and east by the North Sea, the area's long coastline stretches from the Wash to Felixstowe, providing easy access to the sea from most of its inland areas. Norfolk is the fourth largest county of England and during the period covered here it was one of the richest and most important areas of the country. It was the most densely populated English county from 1000 until 1600, while its capital city, Norwich, with a population of 29,000 in 1750, was the second city of England from 1350 until the 1720s, when the wealth and commerce engendered by the slave trade allowed Bristol to displace it.[4] In Suffolk, political and economic power was traditionally divided between the towns of Ipswich, with a population of 9,000 in 1700, and Bury St Edmunds, with a population of around 5,000. The two counties' ports had strong fishing and trading fleets, together with shipbuilding industries. In 1700, the port of Yarmouth had a population near 10,000, while that of Lynn was nearing 7,000. Therefore, although not thickly urbanised, Norfolk and Suffolk had an 'interlocking mesh of pivotal towns' that provided the backdrop for a vibrant political, economic and cultural world. Norwich, for example, had one of the largest constituencies of freemen electors in the country prior to the reforms of 1832, and a correspondingly tempestuous political scene.[5]

As has already been said, Norfolk and Suffolk were not insular counties; in fact, they formed an area that was used to receiving visitors from abroad and had great experience of welcoming non-English migrants. The short sailing distances to important parts of the continent had long ensured close trading and cultural links with mainland Europe.[6] For centuries the region's food exports, along with its textiles and cloths, were exported via its many ports, notably Great Yarmouth, Lowestoft, Ipswich, and King's Lynn, which were counted among the kingdom's

---

3 Corfield, 'East', p. 32; Roger Thompson, *Mobility and Migration: East Anglian Founders of New England, 1629–1640* (Amherst, 1994), p. 14; Richard Wilson, 'Introduction', in Carole Rawcliffe, Richard Wilson, and Christine Clark (eds), *Norwich Since 1550* (London; New York, 2004), p. xxiii.

4 Wilson, 'Introduction', p. xxiv; Penelope Corfield, 'From Second City to Regional Capital', in *Norwich*, p. 157.

5 Jane Whittle, *The Development of Agrarian Capitalism: Land and Labour in Norfolk, 1440–1580* (Oxford, 2000), pp. 1–5, pp. 301–14; Naomi Riches, *The Agricultural Revolution in Norfolk* (London, 1967), pp. 18–35, pp. 76–128, pp. 147–53; Susan Mitchell Sommers, *Parliamentary Politics of a County and Its Town: General Elections in Suffolk and Ipswich in the Eighteenth Century* (Westport, CT; London, 2002), pp. 3–12.

6 Barbel Brodt, 'East Anglia', in David Michael Palliser (ed.), *The Cambridge Urban History of Britain: Volume 1, 600–1540* (Cambridge, 2000), p. 639; R. Rainbird Clarke, *East Anglia* (Wakefield, 1975), p. 13.

most significant. King's Lynn and Yarmouth were head ports for wide-ranging inland waterways, reaching to the Midlands. Yarmouth also possessed one of Europe's major herring fisheries and a half-mile-long quay 'allowed to be the finest and most extensive in England'.[7] The trading networks of Norfolk and Suffolk's merchants were concentrated on the North Sea economy, but they ranged to Moscow, the Baltic, Holland, France, Germany, Italy, Iberia, and eventually to the American colonies. Furthermore, the region's traders were 'sufficiently well-established in their own right – and sufficiently far from the City – to evade domination' by London, as happened to the economy of the more southerly Essex, for example.[8]

The appendices present the core information about the African population in early modern Norfolk and Suffolk. Appendix A provides details of the people living in the counties who have been clearly identified from the records as being of African heritage. For completeness, this includes people who were described as 'Asiatic Black', and similar terms. Appendix B extends the search for the African population through the analysis of surnames. The men, women, and children listed in Appendix A constitute the core group considered in this study. There are 159 entries in this table. Each entry provides the person's name, if it is known, the details of the description that made their identification clear, the date of that piece of information, and the archival reference. The nature of the information that provides the positive identification of a person as African varies in type and in the degree to which it is conclusive. The most common piece of identifying information is when a specific adjective describing a person appears in a book, parish record, or other document. The terms seen here as being definitive examples of African heritage include 'More', 'blackamore', 'mulatto', 'Ethiopian', 'African', 'negro', 'black', and 'man of colour' with their variants, along with references that state a person was from a location connected with transatlantic slavery, such as 'a native of Jamaica'.[9]

Additional means of identification have also been used to identify the people who are listed in Appendix A. One of these is visual representation. By looking at various pieces of art that are linked with the region in this period, several Africans have been identified from the seventeenth century and the early nineteenth century. The later examples come from pictures painted by the itinerant painter John Dempsey in Norwich in the 1820s.[10] Dempsey's

---

[7] William White, *History, Gazetteer, and Directory of Norfolk* (Sheffield, 1836 and 1845), p. 267; Richard Wilson, 'Journal of a Tour through Suffolk, Norfolk, Lincolnshire and Yorkshire in the Summer of 1741', in Christopher Harper-Bill, Carole Rawcliffe, and Richard Wilson (eds), *East Anglia's History: Studies in Honour of Norman Scarfe* (Woodbridge, 2002), 259–88, at p. 261.

[8] Corfield, 'East', p. 41.

[9] These names concur with the range of terms found by other authors; see Habib, *Black Lives*, p. 2, where he lists 'nigro', 'neger', 'neygar', 'moor', 'barbaree', 'barbaryen', 'Ethiopian', and 'Indian' in the Tudor period.

[10] For more on the collection see David Hansen, *Dempsey's People: A Folio of British Street*

work was painted from life, which means that his images of 'Charley' and 'Cotton' are unequivocally of real Africans. In the case of the identification made from two paintings from the seventeenth century, which are depictions of young African servants in paintings from Oxburgh Hall and Oxnead Hall, there is a possibility that these could be artistic motifs, rather than records of actual people. As will be discussed in Chapter Five, however, the balance of evidence suggests that these pictures are likely to have been drawn from life and so the unnamed servants are included.

Another level of evidence is provided in Appendix A by extrapolating along family lines, so when one person has been clearly identified as African in a record, any children and, in some cases, parents and siblings of that person identified elsewhere have then been included. A good example of this is provided by the Doubleday family, who lived in Norfolk during the late eighteenth and early nineteenth centuries. In 1836 James Doubleday was listed as a 'negro' in a directory.[11] Since James Doubleday's African heritage is known from this entry, his siblings, parents, and grandparents have been included, although their baptismal records do not mention their heritage. Having analysed familial relations at this level, however, there has been no attempt to trace the genealogy of families beyond that immediate level of relationship, since it requires too many extra levels of conjecture. Such family groups are gathered in the table for ease of reference, although this sometimes alters the date sequence of entries overall.

Using Surnames as an Indicator of African Heritage

Having provided the details of people who can be clearly identified as being African in Appendix A, the search is extended in Appendix B by means of the analysis of surnames. Since the derivation of English surnames is a complex area, the results obtained from this approach are, of course, less definitive than those presented in Appendix A. Nonetheless, there is a persuasive case to be made that surnames, suitably treated, can provide a strong indication of an African background. This route has been followed by other historians. Imtiaz Habib argues firmly, for example, for this method in his work on the African population of early modern London. Habib's view is that 'given the instability and informality of English naming practices' generally, it is reasonable for an historian seeking evidence of the African presence in English records to 'err on the side of aggressive inclusiveness' when looking at surnames in parish records.[12]

Portraits 1824–1844 (Canberra, 2017) and David Hansen, '"Remarkable Characters": John Dempsey and the Representation of the Urban Poor in Regency Britain', *The British Art Journal*, 11 (2010), 75–88.

[11] White, *History*, p. 770.

[12] Habib, *Black*, pp. 16 and 34.

One surname that Habib maintains is indicative of an African heritage is 'Blackamore' and its variations (for example, 'Blackmore', 'Blakemoor', and 'Blakeamoore').[13] A common explanation of this surname in early surname research was that it was not related to ethnicity and instead signified a 'dweller at a black moor', being derived from the Old English 'blaec' plus 'mór'.[14] Habib's view is that this early usage was supplanted by later use to designate an African and that the surname 'Blackamore' was 'one of the commonest, expediently derived, and ambiguous names for a black person in early modern England'.[15] This suggestion is supported by the fact that by the early modern period the term 'blackamore' was commonly used as a generic descriptor for African people. As the *Oxford English Dictionary* (OED) explains, it was a term for 'A black African; an Ethiopian (obsolete); (also) any dark-skinned person', and was formed by compounding the adjective 'black' with the noun 'Moor'.[16] The noun 'Moor' was itself 'a designator of a native or inhabitant of ancient Mauretania, a region of North Africa corresponding to parts of present-day Morocco and Algeria'.[17] The term became visible in the early sixteenth century, as shown in the 1525 example from Froissart, 'The thirde present [..] was brought in [..] by two men, fygured in the fourme of two blacke Moores richely apparelled.'[18] As a surname it may have been blended with an existing surname, derived from joining of the Middle-English 'blak' to the French 'more', from the Latin *Maurus*, and used to designate that a person had 'dark complexion'.[19] Even if the original usage may have been indicative of a person not of African descent but with a dark complexion, as Africans appeared in the English landscape the generic term 'blackamore' seems gradually to have become used as a surname that also referenced a person's African heritage. The fact that McKinley does not list Blackamoor as a surname found in Norfolk and Suffolk in the Middle Ages is also supportive of this interpretation, suggesting it was a later addition to the region's culture.[20] Evidence for this comes from the Suffolk coastal

---

[13] Ibid, pp. 95–100.

[14] See, for example, Charles Bardsley, *English Surnames: Their Sources and Significations* (London, 1815), p. 161. Matthews avoids any mention of ethnicity in discussion of this name, mentioning only 'dark men' and calling the entire subject 'hopelessly mixed together', C.M. Matthews, *English Surnames* (London, 1966), p. 271. It is suggested as 'signifying someone with a dark complexion' in Patrick Hanks, Richard Coates, and Peter McClure (eds), *The Oxford Dictionary of Family Names in Britain and Ireland* (Oxford, 2016), p. 246.

[15] Habib, *Black*, p. 47.

[16] "blackamoor, n.", *OED Online*, Oxford University Press, March 2020. Web. 12 April 2020.

[17] "Moor, n.2.", *OED Online*, Oxford University Press, March 2020. Web. 12 April 2020.

[18] Quoted in "blackamoor, n.", *OED Online*, Oxford University Press, March 2020. Web. 12 April 2020.

[19] William Browne, Percy Reaney, and Richard Wilson (eds), *A Dictionary of English Surnames* (London and New York, 2006), p. 317.

[20] McKinley discusses 'moor' only in the context of names derived from topography, but provides no examples of its use, and 'Moorman', which he describes as 'more common'; Richard Alexander McKinley, *Norfolk and Suffolk Surnames in the Middle Ages* (Volume 2 of

village of Kessingland in the 1560s, concerning a man called 'Thomas'. Thomas was identified in the parish register initially as being 'Blackamore'. Over the next decade he gained the surname 'Harrison' or variants of this surname ('Harryson', Haryson') but was also described as 'Thomas Haryson alias Blackamore' on the baptism of his children.[21] This example indicates the malleable use of the term 'blackamore' in parish records in Norfolk and Suffolk, showing its ability to morph from generalised descriptor to potential surname and back. In view of this, the surname 'Blackamore' and its alternates are accepted here as being an indicator of African ancestry.

There is some evidence that the surname 'Moore' can also be indicative of an African heritage. On 29 September 1687, a man named John Moore was given the freedom of the city of York and was listed in the freemen's roll as 'John Moore - blacke'.[22] This example provides a correlation between the surname 'Moore' and an African heritage; however, this cannot be automatically assumed. For example, in the same York roll two other men named Moore are mentioned - 'Thomas Moore' and 'Ricardi Moore, marriner' - without any mention of their ethnicity. Since John Moore was described as 'blacke' in the document it seems likely that these latter two would also have been described as such if that was the situation. In the Norwich census of 1570, there are a number of people named 'More', for example, 'John More of 45 yeris, sawer not in work & syklye, & Adry, his wife' or 'Agnes More, wedowe, of 34 yers, lame of bothe legges, & spyn white warp, have dwelt her 23 yer', but there is nothing to link them to African heritage in the document or in other sources.[23] In conse-quence, the surname 'Moore' is accepted here as being indicative of an African heritage only where other evidence suggests that identification, for example the lack of that surname in the surrounding area in that period.

Although Habib uses the surname Blackman as an identifier of African heritage in relation to the sixteenth and seventeenth centuries in London, this approach has not been adopted here. Browne *et al* and Hanks *et al* are equivocal

---

English Surnames Series) (London, 1975), p. 110 and p. 119. Because of the lack of this term in the medieval period, I have not included 'William Blakehommore' from Norwich in 1400, since this is extremely early for this term and it is not conjoined with any other term, such as 'Ethiopian' or 'Saracen', to suggest he might have been African. For mention of him see David H. Kennett, 'Caister Castle, Norfolk and the Transport of Brick and other Building Materials in the Middle Ages', in Robert Odell Bork and Andrea Kann (eds), *The Art, Science, and Technology of Medieval Travel* (London, 2008), pp. 55-67, at p. 62, and Penelope Dunn, 'Trade', in Carole Rawcliffe and Richard Wilson (eds), *Medieval Norwich* (London; New York, 2004), 213-24, at p. 228.
21 NRO/PD/105/1, Burial of Abraham, 22 April 1563; Baptism of Roger and William Haryson, 11 August 1564; Burial of Roger Haryson, 22 October 1565; Baptism of Thomas Haryson, 22 January 1566; Baptism of Michael Haryson, Kessingland, 22 January 1566.
22 'Admissions to the Freedom of York: Temp. James II (1685-88)', in *Register of the Freemen of the City of York: Vol. 2, 1559-1759*, ed. Francis Collins (Durham, 1900), pp. 161-6. *British History Online* <http://www.british-history.ac.uk/york-freemen/vol2/pp161-166> [accessed 2 February 2020].
23 John F. Pound (ed.), *The Norwich Census of the Poor 1570* (London, 1967), p. 41 and p. 53.

on the root of this name, arguing that the name was a derivation of the Old English 'Blacmann', meaning 'dark man', and stating that it was 'a personal name fairly common until the thirteenth century', but making no suggestions about whether or not it was also an ethnic marker.[24] In relation to London, Habib suggests that the surname 'Blackman', while not definitive on its own in signifying African heritage, was used commonly 'as a designator of a black man' in English parish registers in this period and was cited as such by 'Victorian colonial ethnographers'. Habib's methodology has been to look for the use of the surname Blackman in locations where African people had been located, for example in Westminster, as a means of supporting an identification of the surname with an African heritage. In such circumstances he suggests that the name should be viewed as 'an improvised ethnic descriptor of an assimilated black individual with a given Christian forename'.[25]

This approach is far more difficult to follow in Norfolk and Suffolk because there are no locations which are particularly associated with a specific African presence. A good example is the Lowestoft Lay Subsidy of 1524-5, which lists a man named Robert Blackman as receiving wages of £1.[26] There is no reference to Blackman's ethnicity. Since the compiler of the Lay Subsidy list was careful to note the background of several foreigners, who were described as Frenchmen, Dutchmen, Guernseymen and Scots, it seems unlikely that any African heritage would have been ignored. Neither is there any other evidence of an African presence in Lowestoft in this period.

The surname 'Black' is treated equally gingerly. The surname can be found across the region, but the problem with attempting to confidently correlate a surname of 'Black' with African ethnicity is that 'Black' was a traditional English surname prior to this period and is generally accepted as being derived from the appearance of a person as being 'black haired or of a dark complexion'.[27] This might, of course, mean it was used to describe someone of African descent, but it was also the name of people who were not African; for example, it was often used to describe a dyer. Examples of this surname can be found in the records, for example in sixteenth-century Yarmouth, but these records do not make mention of any African heritage. The Yarmouth records in this period were quite detailed and provided extra particulars of the place of origin of the people mentioned who came from outside the immediate locality, such as 'a man of Norwich', 'a stranger', 'a northern man', and 'a man of Rye', and numerous foreigners, such as 'a flemynge' or 'a French man', 'a duche man' or 'a scott'.[28] The lack of corroborating local evidence in relation to most mentions of the surname Black means it is rarely cited here as a marker of African heritage.

[24] Browne et al, A Dictionary, p. 316; Hanks et al, The Oxford (Oxford, 2002), p. 246.
[25] Habib, Black, p. 129.
[26] David Butcher, Medieval Lowestoft: The Origins and Growth of a Suffolk Coastal Community (Woodbridge, 2016), pp. 233-6.
[27] Browne et al, A Dictionary, p. 311.
[28] NRO/PD/28/1, Parish Records of Great Yarmouth St Nicholas with St Peter, St John, St Andrew, St James, St Paul and St Luke, April 1558-September 1653.

The Size of the African Population in Early Modern Norfolk and Suffolk

The information provided in the appendices identifies 315 African (and Asian) people in the two counties over the period 1467 to 1833. This is a statistically small number in comparison to the overall population of the two counties as estimated by historians. Table 1 uses the work of Patten and Wrigley to provide estimates for the levels of population in Norfolk and Suffolk from the early 1500s to 1801.[29]

Table 1: Estimated Population of Norfolk and Suffolk, 1520 to 1801

	1520s	1600	1700	1801
Norfolk	112,000	173,113	230,919	285,409
Suffolk	90,000	139,871	159,214	223,856
Total	202,000	312,984	390,133	509,265

Having acknowledged that the African population in Norfolk and Suffolk was small in relation to the overall population, the information does confirm, nonetheless, several important historical realities. The first is that an identifiable African population existed in both counties in this period. The second is that the data show that this population existed continuously across the early modern period, suggesting that the African population of Norfolk and Suffolk was not transient. Rather, the evidence points toward a continuous process of settlement, through practices such as baptism, marriage, and the general progress of family life. The third reality suggested is that the African population was spread widely across both counties. The data show that Africans were not confined to any specific area of the region, for example in a single parish of a port like Great Yarmouth. Instead, the evidence indicates that settled Africans could be found throughout Norfolk and Suffolk, from the city of Norwich to the port of Ipswich and to the tiny village of Hunstanton.

[29]   The figures are taken from John Patten, 'Population Distribution in Norfolk and Suffolk during the Sixteenth and Seventeenth Centuries', *Transactions of the Institute of British Geographers*, 65 (1975), 45–65; Tony Wrigley, *English county populations in the later eighteenth century* (Cambridge Group for the History of Population and Social Structure, Department of Geography, University of Cambridge. An ESRC Funded Project, Male Occupational Change and Economic Growth 1750-1851); E. A. Wrigley, 'Rickman Revisited: The Population Growth Rates of English Counties in the Early Modern Period', *The Economic History Review*, 62 (2009), 711–35.

Furthermore, in considering the proportionally small numbers presented here it is important to remember that, because it has not been possible to examine every parish record for the entire period, these examples are only an indistinct intimation of an African population that is likely to have been larger. This conclusion is not merely based upon the fact that not every parish record has been examined, but also because, even had a full examination of all parish records been possible, the resultant material would still have not identified every African living in the region. This is for two reasons. Firstly, with occasional remarkable exceptions, the lives of poor people in past centuries have tended to leave little obvious trace upon the historic record; wealth has always allowed its fortunate holders to leave a far wider range of documents, artefacts, buildings, and obvious political and social impacts behind, than those who lack wealth. Since the records show that Africans in early modern Norfolk and Suffolk were invariably poor, it is the case that they will have left little documentation to reveal their presence.

This lack of documentation makes the sampling method heavily reliant upon traces in parish records and leads on to the second reason for arguing that this sample is likely to be under-representative of the actual numbers of Africans in the regional population. This is because the presence of a specific African in any record can be hidden from an historian who is looking for them simply because that identification in the historical records is reliant upon a third party having made a note of the fact that the person being recorded was African. It can be tempting to assume that any Africans living in an area in the early modern period would have been seen primarily as such and that their ethnicity would have always been noted in documents. Therefore, it might be presumed that if the document does not describe someone as African then the person being considered was not African. This is an assumption that is dependent, however, on an understanding of skin colour as the primary determinant of ideas of difference in the early modern period, which does not appear to be correct. In this period, as the examples of the Communicant Returns of 1603, the Compton 'Census' of 1676, and the Hearth Taxes show, there was no requirement to record a person's ethnicity.[30] The same is true for parish records and for court documents.[31] In itself, this fact of bureaucratic life points towards a realisation that ideas of race were of less importance to government than they were to become in the modern era. Furthermore, this means that whenever a person was described as a 'blackamore', 'negro', 'moor', 'Ethiopian', or any of the other terms found in the parish records, then the addition of that

[30] See, for example, Anne Whiteman and Mary Clapinson (eds), *The Compton Census of 1676: A Critical Edition*, Records of Social and Economic History: New Ser., 10 (Oxford, 1986); Alan D. Dyer and David M. Palliser (eds), *The Diocesan Population Returns for 1563 and 1603* (Oxford, 2005); Peter Seaman (ed.), *Norfolk Hearth Tax Exemption Certificates 1670–1674: Norwich, Great Yarmouth, King's Lynn and Thetford* (London, 2001).
[31] W.E. Tate, *The Parish Chest: A Study of the Records of Parochial Administration in England* (Chichester, 1983).

description was a question of historical chance, a result of an individual decision made by the person making the record, not of bureaucratic design.

The records that have been examined here show categorically that it cannot be assumed that such a decision was always made by the clerk involved. Appendix A contains several instances where people were recorded in parish records but were not identified as being African in that entry, although a separate record provides that information. For example, the burial register made no mention of Samuel Turner's background when he was interred on 15 February 1819; it was only a separate coroner's inquest that mentioned he was from Martinique.[32] The African heritage of the Snoringe family in north Norfolk was identified because of a witness statement in a court case in 1636.[33] They had been recorded in parish registers for forty years previously without any mention of their ethnicity. Had there not been a trail of breadcrumbs leading to them, then they would not have been identified. Consequently, it is probable that the actual African population of the region in the early modern period was larger than the numbers detailed here. While this 'known unknown' cannot be calculated, what it does do is provide some level of reassurance that the tentative suggestions that are made here about the African population using this limited set of data relate to a wider population that cannot be identified exactly.

The Gender Composition of the African Population in Early Modern Norfolk and Suffolk

The African population can also be considered in relation to gender. Looking at the Africans identified in Appendix A, there were thirty-five females in a total group of 160. This constitutes 22 per cent of the sample. This proportion increases in the samples of the surname Blackamore and its variants. In the period 1500–99, there were nine women from a sample size of eighteen (50 per cent). In the period 1600–99, there were twenty-five women in a group of fifty-five (46 per cent), and in the period 1700–99, there were thirty-four women in a group of eighty-one (42 per cent). It is clear from this that the numbers of female Africans in the region through this period were significant. In the sixteenth and early seventeenth centuries, many of these women were the children of African men who had migrated to the region and, consequently, they do not appear to have been held in conditions of near slavery, and, for most, there is no evidence of enslavement previously. This situation altered from the late seventeenth century onwards, however. Although female descendants of previously settled Africans can be identified in that period, it also becomes possible to identify an increasing number of African women in the region who would seem to have arrived because of the interface of the region with colonial slavery.

[32] NRO/PD/106/21, Burial of Samuel Turner, Norwich, St George, Tombland, 15 February 1819; NRO/NCR/Case6a/25, Death of Samuel Turner, 12 February 1819.
[33] NRO/NQS/C/S3/30, Examination of John Cole, 19 April 1636.

Our understanding of the situation of these later female migrants, and of the male migrants, can be enhanced by consideration of their age at their baptism. Baptismal records provide a significant proportion of the information about the African population in early modern Norfolk and Suffolk, and it is important to consider the information provided by baptismal records not only in terms of the actual data provided by those records, but also through consideration of the cultural significance of the act of baptism itself, which was the primary process by which all people – regardless of social station, ethnicity, or gender – were welcomed into the local community in early modern England. This aspect of baptism will be discussed in detail later, but it is relevant to this large-scale analysis of the data. The Africans identified contain a smaller sub-group who were baptised as infants, who can, therefore, be identified as the children of Africans who had settled previously in the region; second-generation settlers, as it were. There is then another sub-group of Africans who were baptised as adults.[34]

Adult baptism provides a potential indicator that there had been a change in cultural and social situation for those African migrants. We can begin with an initial proposal that where the register notes that an African was baptised as an adult then this is a strong indicator that they had arrived in Norfolk and Suffolk as a non-Christian, since the Catholic Church and the Anglican Church eschew the concept of second baptism. In that case, such baptisms provide a clue that an African may have been previously enslaved outside England, or even held in slavish servitude in Norfolk and Suffolk. In general, the conclusion drawn from such situations would seem to change over time. In the period from 1467 to around 1640 it is suggested that adult baptism is an indicator that the African was previously Muslim, or of a non-Christian religious background relating to other African origins. It will be suggested that in this early period this is not necessarily a definitive indicator of a connection with enslavement before their arrival in the region, or after their arrival, although it may be a pointer to such a situation. The conclusion drawn from adult baptism in the period after around 1640 is different. This later period coincides with the advent of slaveholding in the colonies and the appearance of plantation owners in the region, along with increasing involvement with the Atlantic economic area. As is discussed in Chapters Four and Five, over much of this period the issue of the baptism of slaves was controversial, and many slaves were not baptised in the colonies. This means that the increasing number of incidents of adult baptism from 1640 onwards is likely to be an indicator that the African in question had been held in a position of enslavement in the English/British colonies before coming to England, and that this situation may have continued in Norfolk and Suffolk. This suggestion gains support from an analysis of the proximity of these Africans to the homes of known slaveowners in the region, who are listed in Appendix C and discussed in Chapter Six.

[34] The term 'adult baptism' is used here to indicate any baptism that did not take place when the person was an infant. It includes the baptism of older children, therefore.

The Geographical Distribution of the African Population in Early Modern Norfolk and Suffolk

Maps One, Two, and Three utilise the information in Appendix A and provide visual representations of the geographic dispersal of the African population across Norfolk and Suffolk over the early modern period. The data in these three maps suggest that the historic appearance of Africans in the region might be usefully understood as emanating initially from the coast and then gradually spreading inland over time. As Map 1 shows, considering the period from 1467 to 1599, virtually all the Africans identified were living either in ports or in villages and towns lying in the hinterland of ports. Norfolk and Suffolk were major maritime-trading counties, involved in both the coastal and Baltic trades, and trading further afield into southern Europe. Alongside the major ports of Lynn, Yarmouth, Lowestoft, and Ipswich, there were numerous smaller ports such as those at Heacham, Kessingland, and Wells. The long coastline and plethora of maritime locations provided many points through which Africans could arrive in the two counties in consequence of the area's maritime trading network. This concentration around ports would seem to indicate that the appearance of these early Africans was probably connected to the region's maritime trade.

The next issue to consider is the impetus that lay behind their journey to Norfolk and Suffolk in the period from 1467 to 1599. The general choice in explaining this is between an idea that these Africans arrived as free individuals, choosing to live and work in Norfolk and Suffolk, or that they arrived as enslaved people, with no choice about their entry into the region. Historians such as Kaufmann and Onyeka have argued that Elizabethan involvement in slaving has tended to be over-emphasised and misinterpreted and should not be understood to prove that all Africans in England in this period were enslaved. The research on the African population in Tudor England generally has found both free and enslaved Africans living elsewhere in the country and, therefore, it seems reasonable to assume a similar pattern in Norfolk and Suffolk.[35] The analysis here, therefore, builds on this work on the wider Tudor population and allows for the possibility of both enslaved and free Africans in the region in the Tudor period. In Chapter Two it is suggested that if enslavement was involved before 1599, then it should be considered in relation to the Mediterranean and connected to the internal African slaving networks of the period. As will be seen, the links between Norfolk and Suffolk's local ports and the Mediterranean make this suggestion a reasonable one. In this context, since none of the Africans in this period were openly identified as being enslaved, the fifteenth- and sixteenth-century population distribution makes it possible to argue that a proportion of the African population were free agents, who had arrived in the region through their own volition. They may have been previously enslaved,

---

[35] Kaufmann, *Black*, p. 9. Kaufmann's work provides examples of free Africans in the Tudor period, as does Onyeka, *Blackamores*; see also Miranda Kaufmann, 'Sir Pedro Negro: What Colour was His Skin?', *Notes and Queries*, 253 (2008), 142–6.

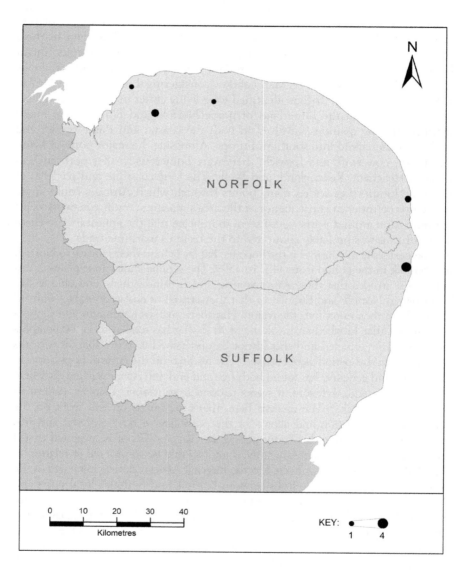

Map 1: Locations where Africans have been identified in Norfolk and Suffolk, 1467 to 1599

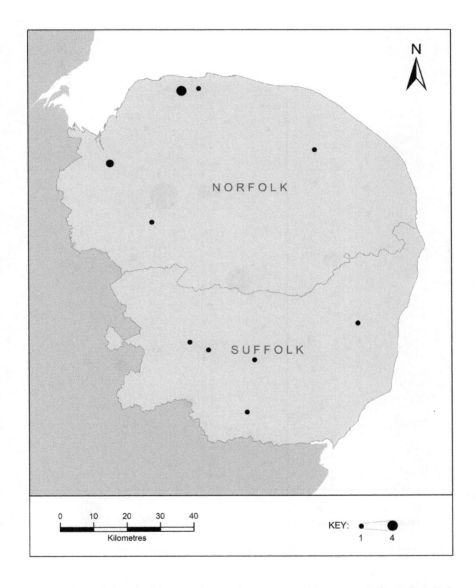

Map 2: Locations where Africans have been identified in Norfolk and Suffolk, 1600 to 1699

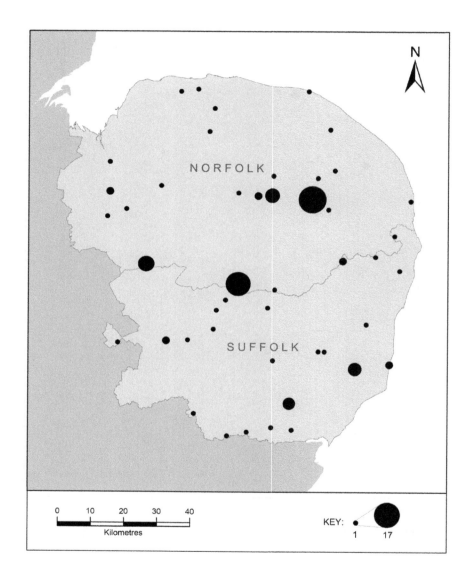

Map 3: Locations where Africans have been identified in Norfolk and Suffolk, 1700 to 1833

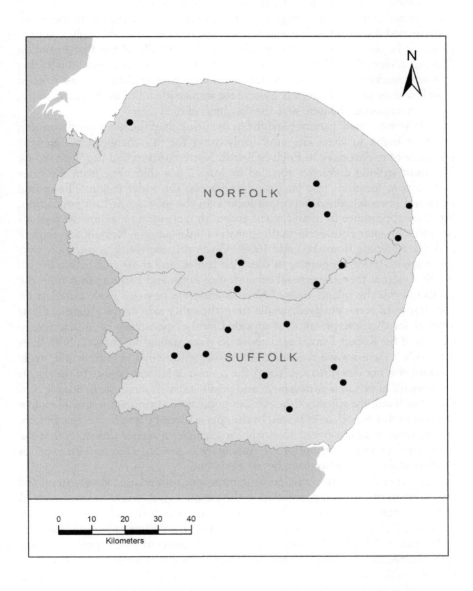

Map 4: Locations where plantation-owning families have been identified in
Norfolk and Suffolk, 1680 to 1833

but there is little clear-cut evidence to show actual enslavement in Norfolk and Suffolk, and considerable evidence to show that some of these Africans were able to move around freely and settle in local communities. This accumulation of evidence makes it possible to suggest that the appearance of an African in the region in this period should not be linked automatically to enslavement, although, of course, it cannot be discounted as a factor. The fact that virtually all the first-generation Africans in Norfolk and Suffolk identified in this period were male may indicate that they were working freely as crew members on ships passing along the East Anglian coast before settling in the region. Most of the women identified in this early sample, such as the Snoring children, were the daughters of such men.

This 'port-focused' pattern persisted in the first half of the seventeenth century, but then began to alter. The most likely driver for this change is the growing influence of enslavement in English/British North America and the West Indies. The most striking difference revealed by Map 2 is a shift away from the coast and ports to locations that lay inland and across the wider region. The coastal areas and ports remained important locales for the growing African population, but their appearance in inland towns shows an increasing range for the region's Africans. Chapter Four explores the growth of links between Norfolk and Suffolk and the Americas from the early 1600s. Given this increasing connection with the nascent slaving economies in the West Indies, and those in English/British North America, then the general expansion of range and location away from the coasts towards the inland areas of Norfolk and Suffolk seems likely to reflect an appearance of some enslaved people from the other side of the Atlantic. Clear support for this interpretation is provided by the appearance of 'a blackamore woman of Sir Robert Davers aged about 16 years' named Rosanna in Suffolk in the 1680s.[36] Davers was a Barbadian slaveowner who retired to Suffolk and, while Rosanna was not described as a 'slave', the context of her appearance in the region is suggestive of previous enslavement and possible slavish servitude in Suffolk. On the other hand, the spread of the African population continued to include a free element in this period, as indicated by the appearance of the surname Blackamore and its variants in the city of Norwich, for example. It seems, therefore, that the seventeenth-century distribution of Africans was not an issue of 'either/or' in relation to slavery and freedom, but of 'both/and'.

This general suggestion of a growing impact of transatlantic slavery upon the expansion of the African population in the region would appear to be confirmed by the information in Map 3, which looks at the eighteenth and early nineteenth centuries. The fact that most (over 70 per cent) of the Africans identified as living in Norfolk and Suffolk between 1467 and 1833 appeared in the eighteenth and early nineteenth centuries is certainly suggestive of a mounting impact from this human traffic. Furthermore, as a comparison with Map 4 reveals, the geographic spread of Africans in the region in this latter period plots rather suggestively onto the locations of families and residents who had direct connections with

---

[36] SRO/FL619/4/2, Baptism of Rosanna, Rougham, 12 February 1688.

transatlantic slavery as the owners of slave-plantations, who are listed in Appendix C. The coincidence of the residences of these plantation-owning families and the locations of Africans in the two counties suggests that their arrival in the region in the period after 1682 was associated with the region's involvement with the plantation economy.

The Terminology Used to Describe Africans, 1467 to 1833

Table 2 lists the various terms used to describe Africans in the documents over the period from 1467 to 1833, dividing this usage into three periods. Where a record provides two descriptors for an African, for example Baptist in 1599 being described as an 'Aethiopian' and as a 'Blackamore', both terms have been noted in the total under the relevant heading. Where a person has been identified from familial relations, but the record makes no reference to African heritage, this has been recorded as 'not specified', and identifications from paintings have not been included.

Table 2: Terminology used in records to describe Africans in Norfolk and Suffolk, 1467 to 1833

	1467–1599	1600–99	1700–1833
'more', 'moor'	2	2	–
'blackamore'	6	7	4
'Aethiopian'[37]	1	–	–
'niger'	1	2	–
'black'	–	4	31
'negro'	–	–	16
'mulatto'	–	1	6
'man of colour'	–	–	6
'African'	–	–	5
'Native of' (Caribbean island)	–	–	7
'Turk/Morocco'	–	–	2
India/East Indies	–	–	6
Not specified	4	7	30

---

[37] Greek: Αἰθιοπία, romanized: Aithiopia; also known as Ethiopia.

This table indicates that there was a change in the terminology used to describe Africans across the early modern period. In the period 1467 to 1599, the terms 'more', 'blackamore', 'Aethiopian', and 'niger' were used. As will be proposed in Chapters Two and Three, it is possible to suggest that these terms relate more to the notion of difference based around the distinction between Christian/heathen than they relate to an idea of difference focused on skin colour, although clearly 'blackamore' and 'niger' are indicative of an awareness of that attribute. The period 1600 to 1699 saw continued use of 'blackamore', but importantly, this period saw the appearance of the terms 'black' and 'mulatto'. These examples would appear to indicate a gradual shift in terminology that was reflective of the growth of the influence of the ideas about race being developed in the colonies. The continuation of this process of accentuation of focus upon outward skin colour can be seen clearly in the period 1700–1833 when the terminology used reflected the influence of colonial ideas ever more strongly. This is most clear in the use of the term 'negro', which appeared in a parish register in the region for the first time in 1732, although some plantation owners had used the term in their wills prior to this.[38] Handler argues that by this date this term had gained a status in the colonies whereby it 'became for the English and other northern Europeans (including the Dutch), synonymous with "slave"'.[39] The terms being used to describe Africans from 1700 onwards, therefore, were increasingly connecting that heritage to the status of slavery and would seem to indicate a strengthening cultural association between Africans and enslavement.

The terminology in use also became ever more focused on the outward appearance of the individual as opposed to any, more subtle, concepts of shared humanity, such as religious belief or class position. The term 'moor' and its related terms of 'blackamoor' and 'Aethiopian' can be seen as a description of confessional status, and their superseding in regularity of use by terms like the more racialist 'black', 'mulatto', and 'negro' as being indicative of the shift taking place. The term 'black' (as opposed to 'blackamore') appeared in the registers only from the mid-seventeenth century, when a boy at Holkham was described as 'ye black boy'.[40] The *OED* states that, originally, the word 'negro' was 'Either (i) a borrowing from Spanish. Or (ii) a borrowing from Portuguese. Etymons: Spanish negro; Portuguese negro', and that it came to be associated with Africans, although it was originally used as a synonym for 'More'.[41]

---

[38] NA/PROB/11/588/339, Will of Sir Robert Davers of Rushbrooke, Suffolk, 13 December 1722. Will of Sir Robert Davers, Second Baronet, 14 March 1714, S.H.A. Hervey (ed.), *Rushbrook Parish Registers, 1567–1850, with Jermyn and Davers Annals* (Woodbridge, 1903), pp. 174–6.

[39] Handler, 'Custom', p. 237.

[40] HA/F/JC(Y) 23, 25, 57, all 1662.

[41] 'Negro, n. and adj.'. *OED* Online (Oxford University Press) <https://www.oed.com/view/Entry/125898?redirectedFrom=negro> (accessed 8 October 2020).

This shift in terminology would seem to be significant and seems indicative of a greater awareness of skin colour. It is redolent of the alteration that can be seen with the word 'slav', which became the root of 'slave' because for centuries, especially prior to the fall of Constantinople, the Genoese and Venetians had been purchasing captive Circassians, Armenians, Tatars, Mingelians, and Bulgarians – generically termed 'slavs' – for use as enslaved labour. When African slaves began to be used in that region they were initially described as *sclavi negri*, literally 'black slavs'.[42] If we accept that 'blackamore' was itself a term that had added a greater sense of significance in respect of outward appearance – in the form of skin colour – to the earlier, and Christian/heathen-focused, term 'More', then the move to drop the older, confessional, element from the compounded word and to focus upon the colour-oriented element of the word seems to hint that traditional ideas and understandings of Africans were under pressure.

The harder-edged term 'black' focused the mind of the user, consciously or unconsciously, on that one external and physical aspect of the person to whom they were referring, removing layers of understanding about alternative ways of seeing them from view. The term 'More' provided, in contrast, a multi-faceted picture to the user, reader, or hearer, suggesting at one and the same time understandings of the person being described as someone from Africa, someone who might have been a Muslim at one time, but who might now have become a Christian, and offered ways of relating to that person that did not depend on making specific connections to ideas about skin colour. The shift to 'blackamore' might therefore be taken as evidence of a beginning of a movement to highlight outward appearances, but also a term that remained balanced, to some degree, by the older element. The truncation of the word to leave only the colour-focused element seems to be evidence of a definitive move towards the classification of Africans in one fashion, which performed a distancing role in human interaction. The use of such terms cut off alternative ways of seeing Africans, rendering them one-dimensional, as it were, and so reflected the gradual process taking place in the colonial context. The crucial point here is that all these latter terms concentrated specifically on the colour of the person's skin as the primary focus of difference. The change over time would seem to provide an indication of a cultural move towards the acceptance of such racialised terminology in the region in the later periods.

There seems also to be another shift from around 1790 onwards. This would appear to be related to the arguments over abolition and slavery that appeared in English culture at this juncture and can be seen in Norfolk and Suffolk's newspapers. At this point, there was a change toward the use of terms such as 'man of colour', 'African', or 'native of Jamaica'. These terms seem to reflect a fluctuating cultural situation, where certain elements in Norfolk and Suffolk

---

[42] David Brion Davis, 'Foreword', in David Eltis and David Richardson (eds), *Atlas of the Atlantic Slave Trade* (New Haven; London, 2010), p. xix.

society were becoming less comfortable with the slavery-related descriptors and were seeking different terms to use when denoting ethnicity and heritage, while continuing to accept such differentiation. It may be that 'man of colour' was felt by abolitionist-inclined clerks and newspaper editors to be less problematic than 'negro', for example. Yet, these terms remained critically different from those used in the period 1467 to 1599, with that earlier emphasis on a variety of ways of seeing social status. The strong relationship that had been created between skin colour and enslaveement in the period from the mid-seventeenth century, and its underlying ideas of anti-African racism, was retained. The phrase 'man of colour' may have been less overtly about slavery and 'race' than 'negro' or 'black', but it was still focused on the skin colour of the person involved. That person was being defined and socially situated by this one characteristic, which by this time had become intimately associated with ideas of inferiority. In a similar fashion, descriptions which mentioned that a person was 'a native of Jamaica' were still highlighting that they were from a slave colony and had been one of those slaves. Such terms were not used for returning planters. Nor were they used, significantly, in the one example we have of an African who moved into a middle-class situation in the period, Edward Steele.

The shifting terminology used in the records over the 370 years from 1467 to 1833 is, therefore, a useful indicator of the changing approach to Africans in Norfolk and Suffolk over the period and can be understood as being constitutive of the ideas being held about them in any given period. The data presented here about the terminology used to describe Africans from 1467 to 1833 suggest that the terms available for people to think about Africans changed in the period, and that the underpinning notions connected with those terms also altered. In the earlier period people in Norfolk and Suffolk were thinking about Africans using words that focused on the geographical location that they came from and their confessional status, as evidenced in the terms 'More' and 'Aethiopian'. In the later period, from around the 1640s, a gradual process is indicated wherein the terms used to describe Africans were increasingly anchored on underlying notions of slavery and inferiority. This meant that the very ability of people to conceive of alternate ways of looking at Africans was being subtly limited by the language in use, even as the institutions of slavery were under question from the late 1700s. By the eighteenth and nineteenth centuries, the language being used in the culture of the two counties made it increasingly difficult for people, especially those in the literate and more educated sections of society, to think about Africans without those thoughts being framed by the notions of slavery and inferiority.

The information presented in this chapter allows several basic suggestions to be made about the history of Norfolk and Suffolk's African population. First, that there was an African presence in the two counties from the mid-fifteenth century onward. Second, that this presence was continuous and did not reflect a transient population of Africans who were merely passing through the area. Rather, Africans were settling down in Norfolk and Suffolk throughout the early modern period. Third, that this population settled initially in the coastal areas, suggesting that there was a maritime link with their original arrival in the area. Fourth, that this population gradually spread from these coastal locations to towns and villages throughout Norfolk and Suffolk and was not limited to any specific area. Fifth, it appears that there was a spike in the numbers of Africans arriving in the region from 1700 onwards, which correlates with the increase in local involvement in the transatlantic slaving economy over the eighteenth century. This relates to a sixth point, that this population consisted of both male and female Africans, the ratio of which changed over time. It seems that the initial group of African migrants who arrived in Norfolk and Suffolk in the period 1467 to 1599 was largely male, once again suggesting some form of maritime link for these migrants. Female Africans in this early period were mainly the children of such migrants. More female Africans appeared from the seventeenth century onwards, and this pattern was accelerated in the eighteenth century. This would seem to correlate with the increasing involvement of the region with the Atlantic slaving economy and suggests the possibility that many of these later African women were originally household slaves, who were then brought to England by their owners. Finally, it appears that there was also a shift in the language used to describe Africans over the period, which was at once representative and constitutive of the way Africans were conceived.

2

Beginnings: The Establishment of the African Population, 1467–1599

A 'More' in Great Yarmouth

In 1524-5, a witness statement was made by a sixty-eight-year-old man called William Pigott, who came from the village of Corton, near Great Yarmouth. The statement was part of the evidence in a dispute between Yarmouth and the neighbouring town of Caister about the extent of the borough boundaries.[1] Pigott recalled the construction, fifty years earlier, of a 'peyer of gallouse' on the sands 'south of Cokle water', where, he said, 'were put to execucon dyvers pyrattys, rovers upon the sea'. Pigott then added an extra detail, 'that one Eylys a More, beyng one of the same compeny, and then within age, callyd a boy of the shippe, for that he was then within age, was not put to execucon, but levyd many yeerys after.'[2]

The date of this mass-hanging of the 'pyrattes' can be determined with some accuracy. Pigott suggested the events had happened half a century before, and comparison with the other witness statements from the case suggests that the hanging took place between 1467 and 1469.[3] This would place Eylys in England before the

[1] See Swinden, *History*, pp. 360-72. Yarmouth's leaders were attempting to use sworn depositions from locals, aged from fifty to eighty-seven, to prove the location of a stretch of water previously known as the 'Grubbys Haven, otherwise cald Coclewater', which had since silted up and had marked the boundary between Yarmouth and Caister previously. This case has been highlighted for its significance in understanding the importance of landscape and oral tradition to early modern popular memory in Andy Wood, 'Tales from the "Yarmouth Hutch": Civic Identities and Hidden Histories in an Urban Archive', *Past and Present*, 230 (2016), 213-30.

[2] Swinden, *History*, p. 366. A substantial number of Yarmouth's archival records were lost in the eighteenth century, including it appears the documents covering the case of Eylys and the 'pyrattys'. The exact provenance of the documents Swinden used is unclear. Swinden stated that the documents were in a collection he termed '16 H.8', p. 360. He used a similar annotation for related documents in 'the sessions roll', which indicates that they may have been in the Quarter Sessions Rolls, although they cannot be found at the Norfolk Record Office. They also do not appear in the Rolls for Henry VIII at the National Archives.

[3] Other witnesses also referred to the scaffold and mass-hanging but did not mention Eylys. Pigott was sixty-eight at the time of his statement, meaning he was born in 1457. Assuming he could remember events from the age of around ten, then it seems reasonable to conjecture

mention of two men from 'Indea' in the Subsidy Rolls of 1483-4, and forty years before the mention of John Blanke 'the blacke Trumpet' at the court of Henry VII in 1507.[4] The term used by Pigott to describe Eylys was 'a More'. The OED shows the breadth of meaning that was given to this word in the early modern period:

> 'Originally: a native or inhabitant of ancient Mauretania, a region of North Africa corresponding to parts of present-day Morocco and Algeria. Later usually: a member of a Muslim people of mixed Berber and Arab descent inhabiting north-western Africa (now mainly present-day Mauritania), who in the 8th cent. conquered Spain. In the Middle Ages, and as late as the 17th cent., the Moors were widely supposed to be mostly black or very dark-skinned [...].'[5]

The OED definition here is extremely useful, since it argues that the word was 'Originally without depreciatory force' and avoids any association between its use and anti-African negativity.[6] The focus is, instead, on the minimum understanding of the term that can be derived from the sources that make mention of the noun. These are that 'Moor' was used in relation to an African geographic location, the possession of dark skin, and to confessional allegiance, that is as a referral to a Muslim. In the fifteenth and sixteenth centuries all these associations can be found. In Bartholomaeus Anglicus the term is associated with geography, 'Men of Africa or Moors'.[7] Hall's Union, which discusses 'how the famous citie of Granado, which many yeres had bene possessed of the Moores or Mawritane nacion, beyng infideles & unchristened people', makes the direct connection to Muslim belief.[8] In Federici, from 1588, the religious aspect is also the focus, 'always whereas I haue spoken of Moores are of the sect of Mahomet'.[9] The OED suggests that whereas the 'semantic development from "inhabitant of North Africa" to "dark brown,

---

that the pirate incident might have occurred around 1467. The statements of Robert Wheymond, Richard Swalowe, Richard Russe, Henry Iberd, and Adam Godfrey confirm a date around 1467-9; Swinden, History, pp. 360-72. Finch-Crisp records, 'Fourteen persons hanged at one time upon a gallows erected on the beach' in 1467, William Finch-Crisp, Chronological Retrospect of the History of Yarmouth and Neighbourhood, from A.D. 46 to 1884 (Great Yarmouth; London, 1884), p. 159.

4   See Sherwood, 'Blacks', p. 40. John Blanke has been discussed by Kaufmann, Black, pp. 8-31, and in Miranda Kaufmann, 'Blanke, John (fl. 1507-1512), royal trumpeter'. ODNB <https://www.oxforddnb.com/view/10.1093/ref:odnb/9780198614128.001.0001/odnb-9780198614128-e-107145> (accessed 31 December 2019).

5   'Moor, n.2', OED Online (Oxford University Press), March 2020. Web. 12 April 2020.

6   This is cross-referenced from 'blackamoor, n.', OED Online (Oxford University Press), March 2020. Web. 12 April 2020.

7   Robert Steele (ed.), Medieval Lore from Bartholomaeus Anglicus (trans. from the Latin by John Trevisa) (London, 1893), p. 120; <https://archive.org/details/b29011152/page/120/mode/2up?q=moors>, (accessed 9 February 2019).

8   Edward Hall, The Union of the two Noble and Illustrate Famelies of Lancastre [and] Yorke, 1st edn. plus variant, 1548 (1 vol.), (London), f.xxiij.

9   Cesare Federici, Voyage and trauaile (trans. Thomas Hickock) (London, 1588). Facsimile

black" [...] occurred already in post-classical Latin and may also be seen in Hellenistic Greek', the semantic development to 'Muslim' would seem to be a late medieval and early modern occurrence.[10]

What can be made of Pigott's use of the term 'More' to describe Eylys? One response would be to augment the discussion of the word in the *OED* and to assume that this term carried within it an automatic element of anti-African racism, and, following Kim Hall's argument, to accept that 'the absence of a term for race in the Renaissance and of a distinct and coherent racial ideology does not make early modern English culture (or Shakespeare) race-neutral'.[11] In this approach, the term cannot be a simple description because it needs first to be placed in an 'unuttered context' and understood in that fashion.[12] This is the method that Anthony Barthelemy follows, suggesting that there was an already strong correlation between sinfulness and black skin, as well as between Muslims and sin because of their non-Christian status. In this case, he suggests that '*Perhaps* the physical blackness of Moors was originally meant as a metaphor for their alleged spiritual blackness', but this then became elided with skin colour and its negativity conflated in one term, 'the consolidation of sign and sinner was complete'.[13] Perhaps.

Yet, Pigott's description is different from the sources used by Hall, Barthelemy, and others. It is a legal document, the witness statement of an elderly labouring man, who was probably illiterate, and describes his memory and understanding of a real set of events, not an historian's theoretical idea, or a contemporary literary device. If Barthelemy's interpretation is accepted as the only way of reading the use of the term 'Moor', or of understanding late medieval and early modern English responses to African heritage, then what is to be made of the historical circumstances that Pigott relates? Firstly, that from a group of captive 'pyrattes' numbering fifteen, only the 'More' was spared execution.[14] Secondly, that this 'More' was then welcomed into the same port which had hung his fellow 'pyrattes' and proceeded to live there for 'many yeerys'. It seems reasonable to ask how this outcome came about if Africans were conceived of only in negative terms? The circumstances in which Eylys appeared in Yarmouth were at the extreme of human experience, and were not the norm for the port,

---

edition published online at < http://tei.it.ox.ac.uk/tcp/Texts-HTML/free/A00/A00611.html> (University of Oxford Text Archive), f.23.

[10] 'Moor, n.2', *OED Online* (Oxford University Press), March 2020. Web. 12 April 2020.

[11] Hall, *Things*, p. 261.

[12] Lynda E. Boose, '"The getting of a lawful race": racial discourse in early modern England and the unrepresentable black woman', in Margo Hendricks and Patricia A. Parker (eds), *Women, "Race", and Writing in the Early Modern Period* (London, 1994), 35–54, at pp. 35–6.

[13] Anthony G. Barthelemy, *Black Face, Maligned Race: The Representation of Blacks in English Drama from Shakespeare to Southerne* (Baton Rouge, 1987); 11–12. My italics.

[14] The number of those executed comes from other witness statements. Adam Godfrey remembered seeing 'hangyng at one time upon the same galows XIIII or XV persons', and Richard Swalowe saw 'XIII or XV persons upon the same', Swinden, *History*, p. 365–6.

where mass hangings are hardly ever recorded.[15] The ferocity of response around this event indicates that feelings were strong in the town in relation to Eylys and the 'pyrattes'. The crew had been captured and the court determined that for their criminality they should be hung on the coast outside Yarmouth's walls. Afterward, their corpses were left hanging on the gallows as a warning against such activity. Another witness, Richard Russe, remembered his father telling him as they looked at the dead sailors on the gibbet, 'Thow sest how thevys be served, therfor be thow ware by them.'[16] Why did the townsfolk who acted in a fashion that indicates a sense of outrage and anxiety about these 'pyrattes' not include the only African on the gallows, if the association between Africans and sinfulness was, in Barthelemy's words, 'complete'?

This historic reality would seem to allow for an alternative reading. Pigott's description of Eylys is a rare and revealing source with which to approach the question of attitudes to 'blackness' in the early modern period precisely because it was made by an uneducated working man and describes a real set of events in a local English context. As such, Pigott's is a voice that provides evidence of the ideas about Africans held by what Hobsbawm and Rudé call that 'anonymous and undocumented body of people' so difficult to hear in historical analysis, and especially in discussions about attitudes to Africans in the early modern period.[17] There are no texts discussing the attitudes to Africans held in Norfolk and Suffolk during the fifteenth and sixteenth centuries that can be explored to examine the degree to which the negative notions that have been identified in literature were prevalent among the literate minority in the region's population, never mind the labouring poor in 1400s Great Yarmouth. In any case, as Wood has shown, in the sixteenth century the gulf between the culture of social elites and 'the commons' in the region was so significant that 'The social chauvinism embedded within early modern elite culture sometimes limited the capacity of the gentry and nobility to construe meaning from their conversations with what they called the plebs.'[18] The labouring culture of Norfolk and Suffolk in the fifteenth and sixteenth centuries was not a direct reflection of elite culture, and this means we need to remember that, in Korhonen's words, 'satiric poetry

---

[15] An earlier large-scale hanging, of eight men and two women, was recorded in 1295, according to the Yarmouth Sessions Rolls of Edward I; see Henry Harrod, 'Notes on the Records of the Corporation of Great Yarmouth', *Norfolk Archaeology*, 4 (1851), pp. 244–5. In 1613, five men, all from outside Norfolk, were tried for 'feloniously taking and carrying away' a ship called the *Sea Horse* and its cargo, and three were executed. In 1615, four men, this time all from Norfolk, were condemned to death for 'committing piracy on the high sea' around the port, Swinden, *History*, p. 739 and A.W. Ecclestone and J.L. Ecclestone, *The Rise of Great Yarmouth* (Norwich, 1959), p. 38. The written histories of Great Yarmouth record no other executions on this scale; see C.J. Palmer (ed.), *The History of Great Yarmouth by Henry Manship Esq., Temp. Queen Elizabeth* (London, 1854); Finch-Crisp, *Chronological*.

[16] Swinden, *History*, p. 367.

[17] E.J. Hobsbawm and G. Rudé, *Captain Swing* (London, 1970), pp. 12–14.

[18] Andy Wood, *The 1549 Rebellions and the Making of Early Modern England* (Cambridge, 2007), p. 122.

cannot be read as direct evidence of everyday behaviour'.[19] This cultural gap means that any suggestion that anti-African racism was a norm across all classes in the region in 1467 must remain an 'inference', as Handler puts it.[20] If that 'inference' is put aside for a moment, it is possible to argue that Pigott's short description of Eylys the 'More' is a valuable window into the views of working people in this period. Taken as such, moreover, it can be read as an indication of a lack of correlation between skin colour, negativity, and 'difference' at the starting point of the history of Africans in Norfolk and Suffolk.

This reading begins with the fact that the word 'More' cannot be linked unequivocally to anti-African sentiment in 1467. As Barthelemy admits, and the OED definition shows, 'the only certainty a reader has when he sees the word is that the person referred to is not a European Christian.'[21] The imprecision of the term is also highlighted by Kate Lowe, in her research on the African population of Renaissance Venice. Lowe finds that its Italian form, moro, was also inexact in meaning and could be used to describe Muslims generically, without giving primacy to skin colour.[22] Taking the OED's minimum definition of the word as a starting point, we can only be sure that the term 'More' was used to signify an understanding that the person being described thus was from somewhere in Africa, possibly had a darker skin, and was not a Christian. In that case, what the views of a 'More' might have been among working people in fifteenth-century Yarmouth is a question that requires considerable thought.[23] Yarmouth was an important fishing port and was also involved in the lucrative coastal trade of the period and international trade with Europe. This meant that its merchants, sailors, and labouring people were linked into trade networks that included the Baltic, Iberia, and the Mediterranean.[24] Yarmouth's autumnal herring fair attracted ships not only from the Cinque Ports, but from

[19] Anu Korhonen, 'Washing the Ethiopian white: conceptualising black skin in Renaissance England', in T.F. Earle and K.J.P. Lowe (eds), Black Africans in Renaissance Europe (Cambridge, 2007), 94–112, at p. 101.
[20] Handler, 'Custom', p. 248.
[21] Barthelemy, Black, p. 7.
[22] Kate Lowe, 'Visible Lives: Black Gondoliers and Other Black Africans in Renaissance Venice', Renaissance Quarterly, 66 (2013), 412–52 at p. 417.
[23] The emphasis in discussion of the encounter between Muslim and Christian has been to focus on the relatively more accessible, elite culture; for example, John Tolan, Saracens: Islam in the Medieval European Imagination (New York, 2002); Kathy Cawsey, 'Disorienting Orientalism: Finding Saracens in Strange Places in Late Medieval English Manuscripts', Exemplaria, 21 (2009), 380–97.
[24] M. Kowaleski, 'The Shipmaster as Entrepreneur in Medieval England', in Ben Dodds and Christian Liddy (eds), Commercial Activity, Markets and Entrepreneurs in the Middle Ages (Woodbridge; 2011), pp. 168–70; Anthony Saul, 'English towns in the late middle ages: the case of Great Yarmouth', Journal of Medieval History, 8 (1982), 75–88; A. Saul, 'The Herring Industry at Great Yarmouth, 1280–1400', Norfolk Archaeology, 38 (1983), 38–41; A. Saul, 'Great Yarmouth in the Fourteenth Century: A Study in Trade, Politics and Society' (unpublished thesis, University of Oxford, 1975), pp. 6–43, 51–3, 123.

Scandinavia, Spain, and Italy.[25] Around the 1440s there were 440 registered 'aliens' in Norfolk, of whom seventy were living in Yarmouth – the largest regional grouping of foreigners outside the city of Norwich. Those resident in Yarmouth came from Holland, Zeeland, Brabant, Utrecht, and Germany.[26] Yarmouth's inhabitants were, therefore, accustomed to meeting people from many different backgrounds in the normal course of the port's life, both abroad and on their own docks and streets. Yarmouth was not an insular location, and Pigott's statement needs to be read in that context.

In Pigott's mind there does not seem to have been any automatic correlation between Eylys' skin colour and any specific social understanding of the boy. The word 'More' was used to describe Eylys, but there is no overt indicator in the text to suppose that this term held negative connotations. There was no connection to an idea of 'blackness' – indeed that word was not used – and, tellingly, the statement rushed past the word 'More' towards other ideas that appear to have been more important to Pigott. The first of these was that Eylys was 'of the same compeny' of a crew of 'pyrattys'. This description does not mean that Eylys and his colleagues should be viewed as some exotic 'other' in this story. They were not roving pirates from North Africa or even 'Barbary slavers'.[27] Instead, it tells us that they were, almost certainly, the (with one exception) native English crew of a merchant ship that had sailed from another east coast port and had been caught when they tried to engage in some opportunistic sea-robbery around Yarmouth.

As Rodger points out, 'generations of scholars have made difficulties for themselves and their readers by using vague, anachronistic and contradictory language' in respect of the activity of 'piracy' in this period. During the fourteenth and fifteenth centuries the sea 'was widely regarded as a "march", a lawless space separating nations'. In this space all ships armed themselves and might engage in opportunistic acts of private naval warfare. The result was that 'the peaceful trader and vicious pirate' were often the same person, with their role shifting and dependent upon timing and perspective.[28] Such attacks

[25] C.G. Rye and J.G. Hurst, 'Medieval Pottery from Great Yarmouth', *Norfolk Archaeology*, 34 (1968), 279-92, at p. 291; Saul, 'English', p. 77.

[26] Nellie J. Kerling, 'Aliens in the County of Norfolk, 1436-85', *Norfolk Archaeology*, 33 (1963), 200-15, at p. 205 and p. 213.

[27] The date of the incident is too early and too far east to be related to the so-called 'Barbary' slavers. These North African pirates abducted and enslaved European Christians between 1500 and 1780 both for ransom and to work as galley slaves, labourers, and concubines for Muslim overlords in what is today Morocco, Tunisia, Algeria, and Libya; see L. Colley, *Captives: Britain, Empire and the World, 1600-1850* (London, 2002), p. 46. See also, Robert C. Davis, *Christian Slaves, Muslim Masters: White Slavery in the Mediterranean, The Barbary Coast, and Italy, 1500-1800* (Basingstoke, 2004); Martin Murphy, 'The Barbary Pirates', *Mediterranean Quarterly*, 24 (2013), 19-42.

[28] The original Latin meaning and its classical context remain the subject of discussion, but in the medieval Latin world, the term *pirata* referred generally to a form of warfare at sea with limited moral or legal boundaries; see N.A.M. Rodger, 'The Law and Language of Private Naval Warfare', *The Mariner's Mirror*, 100 (2014), 5-16, at pp. 5-7; Alfred P. Rubin, *The Law*

were happening around Yarmouth in this period. In April 1472, the merchant William Hardyngham complained that he was sailing to Holland in a ship from Lowestoft called *la Margaret* 'laden with divers goods and merchandise' when the ship was captured and despoiled in the 'Kirkely Rode' by Robert Laverok of Hull, the master of *le Trynyte*.[29]

Furthermore, the evidence of crew size for Eylys' ship, around fifteen sailors, suggests that it was a small ship, such as a *crayer*, which were used mostly in the coastal trade.[30] In 1460, David Blabour complained about the seizure of his ship by 'evildoers' from Yarmouth using 'a balinger and crayer', confirming that crayers were being used in sea-robbery in the Yarmouth area in this period.[31] Crayers were not long-range merchant ships, so Eylys and his fellows had not sailed from Africa. As Appleby has shown, such 'piracy' was local and reliant on support in home ports, which provided the operating bases for ships and markets for stolen goods.[32] This all makes it probable that Eylys and his fellows were the crew of a small coastal trader from a port on the east coast. This element of Pigott's statement revolved, consequently, not around Eylys as an exotic 'other', but upon Eylys' role as a sailor and a member of an English crew of local working men. It was, therefore, a description of his class position.

Having established that fact, Pigott then concentrated on Eylys' age. In contrast to the fleeting reference to him as a 'More', the statement spent far more time on the fact that Eylys was 'within age' and was a 'boy of the shippe'. The description 'within age' suggests that Eylys was in the age group around the ages of 'reason' and 'discretion' – that is between about seven and fourteen.[33]

---

of Piracy (Irvington-on-Hudson, NY, 1998), pp. 1–18; Daniel Heller-Roazen, *The Enemy of All: Piracy and the Law of Nations* (New York, 2009), pp. 93–100.

[29] *Calendar of the Patent Rolls preserved in the Public Record Office. Edward IV. Henry VI. A.D. 1467–1477* (London, 1900), p. 353 <https://dcms.lds.org/delivery/DeliveryManagerServlet?dps_pid=IE100801> [accessed 1 March 2019]. Kirkley Roads was the generic name given to the inshore reaches of the sea around Yarmouth and Lowestoft, which by this date were under Yarmouth's jurisdiction. The area had been annexed from the jurisdiction of Lowestoft in the fourteenth century, see Butcher, *Medieval*, pp. 142–3.

[30] The most common type of vessel used for commerce-raiding in the period was the *ballinger*, which had a crew of around forty. The *crayer* was a small ship of 20–50 tons used on the coastal trade and had a crew of around twenty, Susan Rose, *England's Medieval Navy 1066–1509* (Havertown, 2013), pp. 71–2; Robert Southey, *Lives of the British Admirals: With an Introductory View of the Naval History of England, Volume 2* (London, 1833), p. 94.

[31] *Calendar of the Patent Rolls preserved in the Public Record Office. Henry VI. A.D. 1452–1461* (London, 1910), p. 607 <https://dcms.lds.org/delivery/DeliveryManagerServlet?dps_pid=IE47017> [accessed 20 July 2019].

[32] J.C. Appleby, 'Pirates and Communities: Scenes from Elizabethan England and Wales', in J.C. Appleby and P. Dalton (eds), *Outlaws in Medieval and Early Modern England: Crime, Government and Society, c.1066–c.1600* (Farnham, 2009), 149–72, at p. 149; see also David J. Starkey, 'Voluntaries and Sea Robbers: A review of the academic literature on privateering, corsairing, buccaneering and piracy', *The Mariner's Mirror*, 97 (2011), 127–47.

[33] M Pelling, 'Child health as a social value in early modern England', *Social History of Medicine*, 1 (1988), 135–64, at pp. 137–8.

This might be taken to be proof that Eylys was somehow enslaved, since it might be argued that it would have been difficult for a child to have made the journey from Africa to Norfolk on their own. As will be seen in subsequent chapters, in later centuries there is a potential correlation that can be made between age at baptism and a status of near slavery, just two examples being the ten-year-old 'Peter Lynn' in King's Lynn in 1643 and Stephen Tucker, 'a negro boy about nine years of age', who was baptised in Nayland in 1766.[34] These examples do not fit with that of Eylys, however, because they are drawn from a later period when Norfolk and Suffolk were becoming involved in the developing world of English colonial slavery.

In 1467, by contrast, direct English involvement in African slavery was unknown, and the enslavement of Africans was dominated by the Spanish and Portuguese empires. The first explicit English involvement in slavery would come only a century later, with the activity of men such as John Hawkins.[35] As Heywood and Thornton have recently pointed out, 'Hawkins's attacks, in fact, were an anomaly not repeated by anyone else' and the English did not entertain entry into the slave trade as a credible option. Indeed, full-blown English engagement in the trade in African slaves was not even underway when the English arrived in Virginia in the early 1600s, and even then, 'Had it not been for warfare in Europe during the period, it might have been many more years before England entered the trade.'[36] The minimal English relationship to the slaving economy in the fifteenth century consisted largely in a few English merchants living in Andalusia who owned and traded African slaves in the Portuguese sphere of influence during the 1480s.[37] While it is possible, theoreti-

---

[34] NRO/PD/39/1, Baptism of Peter Lynn, St Margaret's, King's Lynn, 20 May 1643; SRO/FB64/D1/2, Baptism of Stephen Tucker, Nayland, 26 November 1766.

[35] James Walvin, *The Black Presence: A documentary history of the Negro in England, 1555-1860* (London, 1971), pp. 48-51; K.R. Andrews, *Trade, Plunder and Settlement: Maritime Enterprise and the Genesis of the British Empire, 1480-1630* (Cambridge, 1984), pp. 116-28; Kenneth R. Andrews, *Spanish Caribbean: Trade and Plunder, 1530-1630* (New Haven, 1978), pp. 113-33. Portuguese and Spanish merchants began utilising enslaved African labour on their newly established sugar plantations off the African coast on islands such as São Thomé and Principe in the fifteenth century; see Sidney M. Greenfield, 'Madeira and the Beginnings of New World Sugar Cane Cultivation and Plantation Slavery: A Study in Institution Building', in Vera Rubin and Arthur Tuden (eds), *Comparative Perspectives on Slavery in New World Plantation Societies* (New York, 1977), pp. 536-52; Alberto Vieira, 'Sugar Islands: The Sugar Economy of Madeira and the Canaries, 1450-1650', in Stuart B. Schwartz (ed.), *Tropical Babylons: Sugar and the Making of the Atlantic World, 1450-1680* (Chapel Hill, 2004), pp. 42-84. The practice of using enslaved Africans for labour was given momentum after 1560 by the creation of a small sugar industry by the Portuguese in Brazil. It was this early experimentation that began a link between plantation work and Africans in the minds of Europeans. By 1650 perhaps 200,000 Africans had been taken to Brazil and perhaps 268,000 to the Spanish colonies; Robin Blackburn, *The Making of New World Slavery: From the Baroque to the Modern, 1492-1800* (London, 1997), pp. 142-4 and p. 168.

[36] Linda M. Heywood and John K. Thornton, 'In Search of the 1619 African Arrivals', *The Virginia Magazine of History and Biography*, 127 (2019), 200-11, at p. 202 and p. 201.

[37] Gustav Ungerer, 'Portia and the Prince of Morocco', *Shakespeare Studies*, 31 (2003), 90-3.

cally, that Eylys could have been an enslaved African purchased in Iberia, this is unlikely, not only because English involvement in such activity was so small, but also because the size of Eylys' ship was too small for a trading voyage to Portugal. Moreover, it would have been an odd purchase for the captain of such a small ship to make, since in 1467 no ready market existed in England for such a youth.

Eylys' youth was not, therefore, an indicator of enslavement. Moreover, Pigott's description was constructed in such a fashion that it emphasised the exact opposite, showing that Eylys was not being held on the ship in some form of chattel servitude. Pigott was clear that Eylys was 'one of the same compeny' and 'a boy of the shippe'. By using the word 'same' Pigott was making it plain that Eylys was part of the crew, and that as the 'boy of the shippe' he was the youngest member of that crew. The employment of children on ships in this period was common. A substantial proportion of the labour force in most towns in this period was provided via migration from rural hinterlands by young boys. Migrant boys as young as twelve can be found in the tithing rolls from Essex from 1350–1525, and research has shown substantial levels of migration among children between the ages of seven and fourteen years into cities such as Norwich.[38] Analysis of the remains of the crew from the *Mary Rose* identified eighteen crew between the ages of ten and eighteen years and found that the crew's average age was young, between eighteen and twenty-five.[39] The key point being made here by Pigott was that Eylys was an ordinary boy sailor, working on an English ship like many others, and a common sight in Yarmouth.

Faced with this understanding of Eylys, the reference to Eylys as a 'More' does not have to be read in terms of unspoken anti-African racism. As Fields has argued, 'key reference points are most immediately given by the social circumstances under which contact occurs.'[40] Returning to the idea that the term 'More' was variable in meaning, but usually referred to three things – that a person was from Africa, that they had a darker skin, and that they were generally a non-Christian – then Pigott's use of the word can be read simply as an explanation of those factors. First, that he realised that Eylys was originally from somewhere in Africa which, given the wide-ranging trading experience of Yarmouth's people, was a place that was not completely unknown to them. Second, that Eylys had skin which was darker than the norm for Yarmouth. Finally, that Eylys was not a Christian. The rest of Pigott's statement can then be understood as showing that this background was not a problem, or of any real interest. The fact that only Eylys was not executed, and that he 'levyd many yeerys after' in the port is proof of this. It is probable that his heritage was

---

[38] Pelling, 'Child', 135–64. For more on child labour see Francine Michaud, 'From apprentice to wage-earner: child labour before and after the Black Death', in J. Rosenthal (ed.), *Essays on Medieval Childhood: Responses to Recent Debates* (Donington, 2007), pp. 73–90; Mary Lewis, 'Work and the Adolescent in Medieval England (AD 900–1550): The Osteological Evidence', *Medieval Archaeology*, 60 (2016), 138–71.

[39] A. Stirland, *The Men of the Mary Rose: Raising the Dead* (Gloucestershire, 2005).

[40] Fields, 'Ideology', p. 147.

unimportant because the issue of real significance was his non-Christian status, and this could be altered. Eylys could be baptised, as would happen to Africans across the region hundreds of times in the next few centuries.

Indeed, to an evangelical religion like Christianity, the prospect of converting a 'More' was a positive thing. Non-Christian Moors were not a threatening 'other' when they arrived in England in the form of a young working boy on his own; they were an opportunity to evangelise. In any case, this 'difference' was not the focus of Pigott's attention and, by extension, it was not the focus of attention for the Yarmouth community. The most important factors in determining the response to Eylys in 1467 do not seem to have been associated with unspoken ideas about 'blackness'. The key considerations determining his fate were his age and his situation as a labouring boy engaged in the maritime industry. Pigott was focused on Eylys' profession as a sailor, in which sense this was an issue of class, and upon his youth. It was the combination of these two factors that determined the outcome of his story. Eylys was not 'exotic' or 'other'. He was a sailor, which was something that Pigott and his fellows in Yarmouth understood. Equally importantly he was a 'boy', whose age was crucial in his survival. As Pigott put it, 'for that he was then within age, was not put to execucon'. The gallows had beckoned, but because the people of Yarmouth looked at Eylys and saw a working-class boy sailor, he was spared the rope.

John in Great Yarmouth

The story of Eylys indicates that we should not assume that Africans faced automatic prejudice in fifteenth- and sixteenth-century Norfolk and Suffolk. That is not to aver that such ideas may not have been present, but it is to say that we should be alert to the possibility that alternate approaches existed. Pigott's words suggest that, at least for the working community of Yarmouth, welcoming views appear to have been possible. A further hint of this potential can be discerned a century later, when the burial records of the church of St Nicholas in Great Yarmouth record the burial on 2 August 1589 of a man described as 'John the niger'.[41]

No other details exist for John but, given the circumstances of Eylys' story in the late 1400s, it should not be a surprise that Yarmouth was home to another African. In the sixteenth century Yarmouth continued to be a busy port, full of foreigners, with a major fishing industry, that was used as a key stopover for ships travelling from London to Scotland. It was also used by ships travelling to continental Europe, as Norfolk's merchants traded with ports in Italy such as Genoa, Livorno, Naples, Messina, and Venice, along with others in Spain, Portugal, Norway, and the Baltic. In this environment Yarmouth's population increased from around 3,000 in 1524 to 5,000 in 1600.[42]

41 NRO/PD28/1, Burial of John, St Nicholas, Great Yarmouth, 2 August 1589.
42 David Harris Sacks and Michael Lynch, 'Ports 1540–1700', in David Michael Palliser, Peter

The interaction between Yarmouth's fishing industry and the Mediterranean trade is probably crucial in understanding John's appearance in the port in the late 1500s. By the late sixteenth century, Yarmouth's merchants were taking advantage of the popularity of red herring in Italy and exporting considerable amounts of the fish to Italy. This new mercantile effort underpinned the noticeable increase in traffic from Yarmouth to Livorno (Leghorn) in the 1580s and 1590s.[43] Slavery was common in Livorno, but slaves there were not exclusively African. Livorno used slaves from many backgrounds extensively in crewing its state-owned galleys. This slave population included Arabic-speaking North Africans and Turkish-speaking Anatolians, political prisoners, Jewish slaves, heretical Germans, Englishmen, Armenians, Schismatic Greeks, Christian criminals condemned to forced labour (*forzati*), and indentured servants voluntarily working off financial debts (*bonavoglie*). It also included a significant number of Africans, who had usually been previously enslaved on Maghrebi ships traveling from North African ports which had then been captured by the Italians.[44]

The increased trade of Yarmouth's merchants with Livorno provides a possible explanation for the arrival of John in Yarmouth. It may be that he was a free Moorish sailor, who had joined a Yarmouth merchant crew while they were on a trading mission to Livorno, but his description suggests a different story. The term 'niger' was derived from Latin words for the colour black – *Niger*, *Nigra*, and *Nigrum*. Indeed, on the baptism of a woman named Christiana in Sibton, Suffolk, in 1634 the Latin 'niger' was directly translated by the official as meaning 'blackamore'.[45] The descriptor was used in nearby Essex in 1586, when 'Anthonius Niger' was recorded as marrying a woman named Agnes Krynge.[46] Eylys had been described clearly as 'a More', indicating a North

Clark, and Martin J. Daunton, *The Cambridge Urban History of Britain*, Volume 2 (Cambridge, 2000), pp. 377–424; Robert Tittler, 'The English Fishing Industry in the Sixteenth Century: The Case of Great Yarmouth', *Albion*, 9 (1977), 40–60, at pp. 44–6.

[43] Williams, *Maritime*, pp. 128–9.

[44] Stephanie Nadalo, 'Negotiating Slavery in a Tolerant Frontier: Livorno's Turkish Bagno (1547–1747)', *Mediaevalia*, 32 (2011), 275–324 (p. 291). Many studies on Tuscany's early modern slaves have been published in Italian and French. Those in English include Franco Angiolini, 'Slaves and Slavery in the Early Modern Tuscany (1500–1700)', *Italian History & Culture*, 3 (1997), 67–82; Salvatore Bono, 'Slave Histories and Memories in the Mediterranean World', in Maria Fusaro, Colin Heywood, and Mohamed-Salah Omri (eds), *Trade and Cultural Exchange in the Early Modern Mediterranean: Braudel's Maritime Legacy* (London; New York, 2010), 97–116; Robert C. Davis, 'The Geography of Slaving in the Early Modern Mediterranean', *Journal of Medieval and Early Modern Studies*, 37 (2007), 57–74, at p. 62.

[45] The record reads 'Christiana niger anglice blackamore', SRO/FC61/D1/1, Baptism of Christiana, Sibton, 25 December 1634.

[46] Essex Record Office, D/P/27/1/2, Marriage of Anthonius Niger and Agneta Krynge, 29 May 1586. See also the marriage of John Niger to Jane Arnold in Clerkenwell, 15 November 1576, *England Marriages 1538–1973*.

African heritage, and emphasising his non-Christian status. The use of 'niger' in relation to John highlights that non-Christian origin and might suggest that he was not Arabic in background. Although such a distinction might have eluded some in Tudor Norfolk, it was unlikely to have escaped the cosmopolitan inhabitants of Yarmouth. The compilers of the Yarmouth register in this period were especially sensitive to the background of foreigners and were able to distinguish between them. For example, Flemings, such as James who was buried in 1563, were differentiated from Dutch people, such as 'A Duche woman' buried in March 1567. [47]

Yarmouth's connection with Livorno is suggestive of some role for enslavement in John's story, but not by the English. Lowe finds that in fifteenth- and sixteenth-century Venice 'nearly all sub-Saharan Africans probably arrived [...] as slaves with the very few known not to be slaves being envoys from African countries or pilgrims from Ethiopia'.[48] Most of the African captives in Italy came originally from the Sudanese regions of Africa closest to Chad or from territories of the Songhai Empire in West Africa. John may have been from such an area, before being enslaved by one of the Barbary regencies of the North African coast. He may then have been taken to Italy via a coastal port such as Algiers or Tripoli.[49] Once in Italy, he may have been a galley-slave, but it is also possible that he had been in domestic servitude, since this was the ultimate fate of many such people.[50] Enslavement may have been part of John's background and, theoretically, he might have been purchased by a wealthy Yarmouth merchant and brought back to Norfolk to be held in near slavery; however, the lack of any hint of a connection to a 'master' of any sort in his description tends to undermine that explanation. It seems more likely that he was free before he made his journey to Yarmouth. In Livorno, Muslim slaves could gain manumission by converting to Christianity. This may have been the case for John, but if he was not from North Africa, John may not have been a Muslim, unless he had converted in a period of Muslim enslavement.[51] Nonetheless, it was normal in Venice for slaves to be freed on the death of a master or mistress, or after having completed a specified number of years' service. John might, therefore, have been an African who had been enslaved in Livorno, before being freed on one of these grounds, who had then obtained passage to England on a Yarmouth ship. The fact of John's burial indicates that he was considered sufficiently part of Yarmouth's community from a religious

---

[47] NRO/PD/28/1, 'James a flemyge', burial 20 October 1563, 'A foreign man', 23 June 1579; 'A Duche woman', 31 March 1567, 'A Duche Childe', burial 8 June 1585; NRO/PD/28/1, 'A duche man', burial 8 July 1579.
[48] Lowe, 'Visible', p. 420.
[49] Chouki El Hamel, Black Morocco: A History of Slavery, Race, and Islam (Cambridge, 2012), pp. 145-52.
[50] Paul H.D. Kaplan, 'Italy, 1490-1700', in David Bindman and Henry Louis Gates Jr. (eds), The Image of the Black in Western Art, Volume III: From the "Age of Discovery" to the Age of Abolition, Part 1: Artists of the Renaissance and Baroque (Cambridge, MA; London, 2010), 95-9; Lowe, 'Visible', pp. 419-21.
[51] Nadalo, 'Negotiating', p. 298.

perspective to be afforded what a later register entry would call 'a Christian burial'.[52] It may be that, like Eylys, he had arrived in Yarmouth and 'levyd many yeerys after' as part of its labouring community. Once again, the evidence of John's relations with the community of Yarmouth points towards the importance of religious identity over race, and away from any assumption of enslavement.

'Blackamores' in Sixteenth-Century Norfolk and Suffolk

The Suffolk port of Ipswich seems to have been a point of arrival for other Africans in the sixteenth century. Roger Blackamore was listed as being the father of two children; Robert, who was baptised in February 1544, and his sister Anne, who was baptised there in 1546.[53] Ipswich was a large, busy, and successful port, with an expanding population that included many foreigners.[54] Because Ipswich was closely associated with the export of cloth, the port's trading links were predominantly with the North Sea economy – the Low Countries, France, and the Baltic – rather than with the Mediterranean.[55] With the lack of significant links to Italy, Roger's route to Suffolk is unclear. He may, of course, have arrived through Yarmouth or Lowestoft, which lie around thirty-six miles to the north-east, a good distance, but not an impossible one for a migrant to travel. It seems more probable, however, that he arrived in Ipswich directly, perhaps on a ship plying the coastal trade, or on one from the Low Countries. Before that, it seems most probable that he had travelled from the Mediterranean, as was suggested with John and Eylys.

The family appear to have relocated in the second half of the century to the villages of Hadleigh and Layham, which lie close to one another and only eleven miles south-west of Ipswich. The villages were the locations for the baptism of Elizabeth Blackamoore in 1575 and the baptism of Awdry Blackamore in 1578.[56] In the latter case, the father of Awdry was 'Robt. Blackamore', and he was also named as the father of Edward, Robert, Anne, Alice, Thomas, and John between 1578 and 1593.[57] The proximity of Hadleigh and Layham suggests that

---

[52] See SRO/FB74/D1/4, Burial of Ben Ali, 'a native of Morrocco (sic) aged between fifty and sixty years who being found dead in this parish and on whom the coroner having taken his inquest was admitted to Christian burial', Higham, 2 November 1789.

[53] *England Births & Baptisms 1538–1975*, Baptism of Robert Blackamoore, Ipswich, February 1544; Baptism of Anne Blackamore, Ipswich, August 1546.

[54] Nicholas Amor, *Late Medieval Ipswich: Trade and Industry* (Woodbridge, 2011), p. 29. Estimates of the town's population are that it rose from around 3,000 or 4,000 in the 1520s to 8,000 a century later; Jonathan Barry, *The Tudor and Stuart Town 1530–1688: A Reader in English Urban History* (London, 1990), p. 44.

[55] Henryk Zins, *England and the Baltic in the Elizabethan Era* (Manchester, 1972), p. 105, pp. 134–7, p. 260.

[56] *England Births & Baptisms 1538–1975*, Baptism of Elizabeth Blackamoore, Hadleigh, 26 December 1575, and baptism of Awdry Blackamore, Layham, 17 April 1578.

[57] *England Births & Baptisms 1538–1975*, Baptism of Awdry Blackamore, Layham, 17 April

Robert was the father of Elizabeth in Hadleigh as well. Margaret Blackamore, who was married in Hadleigh in 1585, was possibly another of Robert's children, presumably older than Elizabeth and born elsewhere.[58]

Twenty years after Roger was mentioned in the Ipswich register, several burials of Blackamores are recorded in the port. The first is the burial of Joan Blackmore in January of 1562.[59] The burials of Thomas Blackeamore in 1565 and Clement Blackmore in 1569 are recorded there.[60] No further information is available for these three. Joan might have been Roger Blackamore's wife; the surname is spelt differently, but the normality of variation in the spelling of names in this period means that this disparity is not particularly significant. Alternatively, all three could be other children of Roger Blackamore. Finally, they could be entirely unrelated to Roger. Since their baptisms are not recorded in the Ipswich register it is possible that they were all visitors to the port and that their presence is an indicator that Ipswich was a point at which several Africans, including Roger, came into the region in the period 1540 to 1560.

The presence of the Blackamore family around Hadleigh and Ipswich highlights a situation that points toward the acceptance of Africans into working communities in the fifteenth and sixteenth centuries, that of marriage to non-Africans.[61] This subject of such marriages has been discussed by Kaufmann, who has provided other examples of this occurrence in Tudor England. For example, both James IV's African drummer and John Blanke, Henry VIII's African trumpeter, are known to have married.[62] The Blackamore family in Suffolk and the Haryson family in Kessingland, who will be discussed below, provide examples of this crucial process of social integration in sixteenth-century Norfolk and Suffolk. The fact that the children of these unions were baptised, and the clergy were willing to marry the couples concerned, is indicative of a significant degree of acceptance of Africans into local working communities from their first arrival.

1578; Baptism of Edward Blackamore, Layham, 28 February 1579; Baptism of Robert Blackamore, Layham, 17 April 1582; Baptism of Anne Blackamore, 3 January 1584 and burial of Anne Blackamore, Layham, 6 January 1584; Baptism of Thomas Blackamore, Layham, 10 April 1586; Baptism of Alice Blackamore, Layham, 17 November 1590; Baptism of John Blackamore, Layham, 5 January 1594.

[58] *England, Boyd's Marriage Indexes, 1538–1850*, Marriage of Margaret Blackamore, Hadleigh, 1585.

[59] *National Burial Index for England & Wales*, Burial of Joan Blackmore, Ipswich St Lawrence, 7 January 1562.

[60] *National Burial Index for England & Wales*, Burial of Thomas Blackeamore, Ipswich, 10 March 1565; Burial of Clement Blackmore, Ipswich St Nicholas, 1 May 1569.

[61] Rather than use the term 'white', which would be at odds with the argument being made about such concepts in the early modern period, the term 'non-African' is used hereafter. This avoids the reification of the concept of 'white' in the text and avoids making an untested assumption that the existing population of Norfolk and Suffolk was ethnically uniform.

[62] Miranda Kaufmann, '"Making the Beast with two Backs" – Interracial Relationships in Early Modern England', *Literature Compass*, 12 (2015), 22–37, at p. 26.

African Women

These examples also highlight the presence of African women in sixteenth-century Norfolk and Suffolk.[63] Kaufmann has shown that we should assume nothing about the status of African women in Tudor and early Stuart England. There are examples of women who worked as servants, such as Mary Fillis in London, women who were prostitutes, like Anne Cobie of Westminster, and women of independent means, such as Cattelena of Almondsbury.[64] Unfortunately, the hints provided toward the presence of African women in Norfolk and Suffolk do not help us understand much more than the potential presence. Nonetheless, other Blackamore women are visible; for example, Marable Blackamore was buried in Woodbridge, near Ipswich, in 1559, and Margery Blackamore was married in Thorndon, near Eye, in 1547.[65]

There is also the mention of the baptism of someone named 'Margareta Moor' in Little Walsingham, a village very close to the north Norfolk coast, in 1566.[66] The similarity of this Norfolk record to that of 'Margareta, a Moore', who was buried in London five years later, in 1571, is suggestive of potential African heritage.[67] Unfortunately, the Little Walsingham baptismal register does not record parental names, so it is not possible to determine if Margareta was an infant, or if this was an adult baptism. There is only one example of a related surname in the village, that of a man named Edmund More, who was married there in 1564.[68] The lack of other Moor/More surnames in the Little Walsingham register in this period makes it possible that Edmund More was an African who settled in the village, married a local, and raised a family there, including Margareta. Little Walsingham lies only five miles from the port of Wells-next-the-Sea. In the fifteenth century, ships plying the coastal trade from London to the north of England were regular visitors to Wells, so this location fits with the idea that maritime links were the main route for Africans into the region. It may be, therefore, that Edmund More was an African sailor from one of these ships.

---

[63] For discussion of African women in Scotland in 1504, see Fryer, *Staying*, pp. 3-4.

[64] For these examples, see Kaufmann, *Black*, pp. 219-59. Also see Fryer, *Staying*, p. 8; Sherwood, 'Blacks', p. 41.

[65] *National Burial Index for England & Wales*, Burial of Marable Blackamore, Woodbridge, 10 July 1559; *Boyd's Marriage Indexes, 1538–1850*, Marriage of Margery Blackamore, Thorndon, 1547.

[66] NRO/PD/582/1, Baptism of Margareta Moor, Little Walsingham, 22 March 1567. The register is damaged, and the entry is indistinct, but it seems to be 'Margareta' as opposed to 'Margaret a'.

[67] Westminster Archives, St Martin-in-the-Fields, Vol. 1, p. 116, Burial, 'Septes fuit Margareta a Moore', 27 September 1571.

[68] NRO/PD/582/1, Marriage of Edmund More and Jane Mason, Little Walsingham, 3 July 1564.

The Blackamore/Haryson Family of Kessingland

Much more definitive is the appearance of another African in the Suffolk coastal village of Kessingland, which lies south of Lowestoft, a few years later. This points clearly to a free African and supports the suggestion that marriages to non-African locals and the baptism of the children of such unions are indicators of a willingness on the part of Norfolk and Suffolk's labouring population to accept Africans as members of their communities. In this case the family involved was the Blackamore/Haryson family. In 1563, the register records a man named Thomas Blackamore in relation to a burial of a person called 'Abraham'.[69] In the burial register Abraham was described as 'brother to the wife of Thomas Blackamore'. It seems probable that Abraham was a minor, travelling in company with the rest of his family. After this, Thomas Blackamore and his wife settled in Kessingland, raised a family, and remained there until their deaths in 1581 and 1599.[70]

Thomas appears to have taken the surname Haryson soon after his arrival. This is revealed by reference to the christening of twins called Roger and William Haryson in 1564, which lists their parents as being Thomas and Elizabeth Haryson.[71] No mention was made of the name Blackamore in relation to the baptism of the twins, but when Roger was buried the following year, in 1565, he was listed as being 'The sonne of Thomas Haryson alias Blackamore'.[72] This formula was used again in 1566 at the baptism of another son, Thomas, and of a daughter named Margaret in 1573.[73] These entries establish the family's African heritage clearly.

Where Thomas had come from before arriving in Kessingland is a matter of conjecture. The proximity of Kessingland to Lowestoft, some five miles north, means that the suggestions made in the case of John 'the niger' may also be relevant here. Although some twenty years after Thomas' arrival in Kessingland, it is known that the Lowestoft merchants John Archer and George Phifeld were heavily involved in the trade in red herring to Livorno in the 1580s, so Thomas may have arrived as a consequence of some earlier

---

[69] NRO/PD/105/1, Burial of Abraham, 22 April 1563.

[70] NRO/PD/105/1, Burial of Elizabeth Haryson, 25 March 1581; NRO/PD/105/1, Burial of Thomas Haryson, 20 December 1599.

[71] NRO/PD/105/1, Baptism of Roger and William Haryson, 11 August 1564. The marriage of Thomas and Elizabeth is not recorded, so presumably it took place before 1561, when the parish records begin. This would concur with the burial of Abraham, which suggests that Thomas was already married in 1563.

[72] NRO/PD/105/1, Burial of Roger Haryson, 22 October 1565.

[73] NRO/PD/105/1, Baptism of Thomas Haryson, 22 January 1566; NRO/PD/105/1, Burial of Margarett Haryson, May 1573. Unfortunately, the ink on the baptismal register is smeared and unreadable for the years 1571-79 (just over one page), so Margaret's baptism cannot be identified. The records show the burial of another two children with no mention of the term Blackamore; NRO/PD/105/1, Baptism of Michael Haryson, 22 January 1566; Baptism of Thomas Haryson, 18 March 1581.

Mediterranean trading links with Italy.[74] If this suggestion is correct, then Thomas may have been enslaved at an earlier point in Italy, but it is clear he was a free man on his arrival in Kessingland, where he was able to settle in the village, marry, have children, and live as any other member of the parish's labouring community.

David Butcher has examined the registers for Lowestoft and suggested that Lowestoft was home to a relatively mobile population in this period, with many people from outside the town being buried there in the 1550s. Most were from other parts of Norfolk and Suffolk or England, but he also identified 166 foreign visitors between 1551 and 1600. As was the case with Yarmouth, most of these foreigners were from the Low Countries, but Scots, Icelanders, and French were also recorded. Butcher connects these foreigners with the maritime trade and, while he found no Africans mentioned, this shows that Lowestoft, like Yarmouth, was a location where all manner of people could appear. Butcher also identified several foreign residents. In 1524 he found four Dutchmen, four Frenchmen, one Breton, two Channel Islanders, and four Scots, who were a mixture of merchants and wage-earners. In 1568 he found a Dutchman and a Frenchman working as servants and two 'Iceland boys' working for innkeepers. The area around Lowestoft was, therefore, willing to accept the settlement of foreigners in the period of Thomas Blackamore's arrival. Butcher contrasts this relative openness with the period after 1601, where the number of foreign visitors and residents fell markedly, with only thirty-eight visitors noted in the burial registers. He suggests that this was a consequence of foreign war, domestic political turmoil, and the decline of the fishing industry.[75] The arrival of Thomas Blackamore in the hinterland of Lowestoft coincided, therefore, with a specific period of openness to migrants in the area that was gradually curtailed in the seventeenth century.

On arrival, Thomas was given a description of 'Blackamore'. As has been proposed already, this term was subtly different to the word 'More' that was used to describe Eylys. The addition of the element 'black' to the original term suggests a growing awareness of skin colour in the culture at the time, but gives no necessary hint of any negativity towards dark skin. It seems that Thomas had been baptised as a Christian at some point before 1563, since all his children were baptised in the village, and Thomas and his wife were buried without demur.[76] Given that Thomas was probably originally not from a Christian region, his family's involvement in European Christian cultural practices

---

[74] David Butcher, *Lowestoft, 1550–1750: Development and Change in a Suffolk Coastal Town* (Woodbridge, 2016), pp. 42–4, pp. 168–9, p. 181.

[75] Ibid, pp. 43–6.

[76] There is a record of an Elizabeth Haryson being baptised in Yarmouth in 1563, but since the Yarmouth register did not record parental details, it is unclear if this was an infant baptism or possibly an adult baptism of the Kessingland Elizabeth, NRO/PD/28/1, Baptism of Elizabeth Haryson, 13 Aug 1563, Great Yarmouth, St Nicholas.

suggests that Thomas Blackamore was not being treated in any materially different fashion to his non-African contemporaries. He was being integrated into the local labouring community, through those rituals and customs that bound early modern society together – baptism and marriage – with no overt resistance to his participation in that process.

3

'Strangers', 'Foreigners', and 'Slavery'

'Strangers' and 'Foreigners'

As the discussions of Lowestoft and Yarmouth make clear, 'strangers' and 'foreigners' were not uncommon in Tudor Norfolk and Suffolk, but these social categories were not equated with any notion of race; they were associated with other factors. In the censuses of 'aliens' that were being carried out in the region during the fifteenth century, the underlying idea of threat and 'difference' was driven by government in response to the idea of a potential 'internal enemy'. For example, the 1436 census was a response to the instigation of new hostilities with Philip, Duke of Burgundy, which made people from his territories – Burgundy, Nevers, Picardy, Artois, Flanders, Brabant, Zeeland, Holland, and Limberg – all potential enemies of the crown. In this instance, the term 'alien' carried a negative undertone for those in authority and government, but it was not a racially structured issue.[1]

Another 'difference' that marked out such 'aliens' was religious difference, which in the widest sense was based around a difference between Christian and non-Christian, and more specifically after the Reformation saw distinctions between Protestant and Catholic, along with a concern that immigrants might include unknown numbers of Anabaptists. It was concerns such as these that led to various censuses being taken in locations where, as the Archbishop of Canterbury put it, 'any settlement of strangers were', but this was not an issue of skin colour.[2] In late sixteenth-century Norfolk the term 'Stranger' became attached specifically to Dutch and Walloon-speaking refugees who arrived from the Low Countries from 1567 onward, fleeing persecution at home.[3] The

---

[1] Kerling, 'Aliens', p. 200.

[2] Quoted in W.J.C. Moens, *The Walloons and their Church at Norwich: 1565–1832* (London, 1888), p. 25; see also p. 38 for discussion of measures taken to ensure Anabaptists were not living in the town. For an excellent discussion of the issues surrounding Anabaptists in this period, see Eric Ives, *The Reformation Experience: Living Through the Turbulent 16th Century* (Oxford, 2012), pp. 106-9, pp. 146-7.

[3] W.C. Ewing, 'The Norwich Conspiracy of 1570', *Norfolk Archaeology*, 5 (1859), p. 74-6. See also C.W. Chitty, 'Aliens in England in the Seventeenth Century to 1660', *Race & Class*, 11 (1969), 189-201; Charles Wilson, *England's Apprenticeship, 1603-1673* (London, 1965), pp. 77-8; P.J. Bowden, *The Wool Trade in Tudor and Stuart England* (London, 1962), p. 53.

numbers of these 'Strangers' increased rapidly; by 1583 there were 4,677 recorded in Norwich. For a city whose population was no more than 12,000, this was a significant migrant population. Nonetheless, once their religious affil-iation had been ascertained and accepted, both central and local government were keen to ensure that their community was integrated into Norwich's social and economic structures. Their cloth-making skills had sufficient positive economic impact that the authorities were favourably disposed to them; as one commentator noted in the period, 'all which company of strangers, we are to confess, do live in good quyet and order, and that they traveyle [work] diligentlye to earn their livings.'[4]

While city authorities saw the Strangers' presence as positive, for those whose livelihood was affected, and possibly threatened, by the Strangers' cloth-making skills their presence may have been less desirable. In 1570, several Norwich men were condemned to death and others imprisoned for plotting to expel the Strangers from the city.[5] Although this may have owed something to the perceived economic threat of the migrants, it appears that the impetus for this plot was provided largely by the local Catholic gentry, so it was driven by a strong religious element, rather than any structured ideas about ethnicity. It is also significant that the plot came to nothing. Most local workers were uninterested in persecuting foreigners with whom they had established relations and did not support the plot. Any hostility to the Strangers and to other foreign settlers was not drawn from racial antipathy, nor was it endemic or constant. It varied in relation to religious tension, economic need, and political situation.

Such ideas and measures did not extend to Africans. There was no equiv-alent census for Africans in Tudor Norfolk and Suffolk, and they were not included in any of the censuses of foreigners. Neither was the region affected by the much-discussed incident of the Elizabethan 'Edicts of Expulsion'. These were a series of three Privy Council orders that authorised the removal of 'negars and blackamoores' from England.[6] These documents have been cited frequently as proof of racial antipathy in studies of early modern England, and presented as evidence that 'the black presence was both perceived and constructed as a threat by the state.'[7] Hall has suggested that this was an example of scapegoating,

4 For details of numbers, see Moens, *The Walloons*, pp. 26–34, pp. 44-5, at p. 27.
5 Ewing, 'The Norwich', pp. 75–6; Moens, *The Walloons*, p. 27. For more discussion, see Laura Hunt Yungblut, '"Mayntayninge the indigente and nedie": The institutionalization of social responsibility in the case of the resident alien communities in Elizabethan Norwich and Colchester', in Randolph Vigne and Charles Littleton (eds), *From strangers to citizens: the integration of immigrant communities in Britain, Ireland, and colonial America, 1550–1750* (Brighton, 2001), pp. 99–105.
6 Paul L. Hughes and James F. Larkin (eds), *Tudor Royal Proclamations Vol. 3: The Later Tudors, 1588–1603* (New Haven, 1969), pp. 221–2.
7 Ania Loomba, *Gender, Race, Renaissance Drama* (Manchester, 1989), p. 43. See also Eldred D. Jones, *The Elizabethan Image of Africa* (Washington, DC, 1971), p. 20; Kim F. Hall, 'Guess Who's Coming to Dinner? Colonization and Miscegenation in "The Merchant of Venice"', *Renaissance Drama*, 23 (1992), 87–111.

drawing on 'a series of associations about Moors as a group that seem to persist in contemporary Anglo-American racial discourse: in times of economic stress, visible minorities often become the scapegoat for a national problem.'[8] Given that the numbers involved were tiny, ten and eighty-nine, the suggestion that these 'warrants' provided a scapegoat for a national economic crisis is questionable.

Recently, moreover, historians have reframed the analysis of this issue and pointed towards political and economic explanations of these 'Edicts', rather than ideas of 'race'.[9] Weissbord has suggested that the Edicts were an economic response to connections between the Iberian slave trade and Elizabethan England and proposed that they were not about racial antipathy. They did not expel Africans from England as 'undesirable subjects'. Instead, she proposes they 'authorize the gift of blacks – as commodities – in reward for services rendered'.[10] Kaufmann looks to greed for the reason behind this event and dismisses this 'so-called deportation of Africans' as an 'unsuccessful money-making bid by a foreign merchant and a bankrupt courtier'.[11] Emily Bartels proposes that the Elizabethan 'Edicts' were part of a prisoner exchange, and links the discussion not to skin colour, but to political position. As she puts it, 'the Negroes from the Baskerville campaign came to England as prisoners of the Anglo-Spanish war, and it was that political position, I would argue—more than, say, any presumed African identity, heritage or history—that made them especially useful to the queen.'[12]

These explanations step back from an automatic framework of interpretation that begins and ends with a suggestion that fundamental ideas about Africans already existed in the Tudor period and were driving policy. Instead, they frame the issue in a specific moment and situation and show how it was related to human greed and existing economic and political structures. The Tudor state centrally was uninterested in the Africans in the kingdom *per se*; they only became of interest when someone proposed to make money out of them, or when political gain could be perceived in relation to them. Furthermore, dominant cultural ideas about their African heritage were not the reason they were chosen in this incident. They were chosen because a market existed in which such people could be sold; their heritage was merely a factor that allowed that market to be entered. Nascent capitalist markets already accorded the status of commodity to certain Africans, but only in specific contexts. These contexts were not universal, nor were they exclusively limited to Africans. As the example of Livorno showed, people of any background could be enslaved and

---

[8] Kim Hall, 'Reading What Isn't There: "Black" Studies in Early Modern England', *Stanford Humanities Review*, 3 (1993), 22–33, at p. 28.
[9] Emily Weissbourd, '"Those in Their Possession": Race, Slavery, and Queen Elizabeth's "Edicts of Expulsion"', *Huntington Library Quarterly*, 78 (2015), 1–19; Kaufmann, 'Caspar', pp. 366–71; Onyeka, *Blackamoores*, pp. 46–99.
[10] Weissbourd, 'Those', p. 2.
[11] Kaufmann, 'Making', p. 25.
[12] Emily Bartels, *Speaking of the Moor: From Alcazar to Othello* (Philadelphia, 2008), p. 106.

sold in such markets. Similarly, the Tudor Vagrancy Laws of 1547 indicate that the Tudor polity was willing to contemplate the enslavement of anyone in the right set of circumstances, since these laws based the potential enslavement of a person on 'criminal' vagrancy, not on civil status.[13]

In the century and a half after Eylys arrived in 1467, there is no record of any discussion – political, cultural, or economic – relating to the arrival of such Africans in Norfolk and Suffolk and no apparent concern, or even interest, in the subject. The discussions about the presence of foreigners that did take place were not framed by notions about skin colour. Rather, they were delineated by specific situation, either local, as in the case of the 'Strangers' in Norwich, or national, when the central government grew concerned about the defence of the realm in respect of the subjects of foreign lords who were antipathetic to England. In the mid-sixteenth century, discussions about 'strangers' were framed in similar contexts, but to these were added concerns about their religious affiliation, in the period after the break from Rome, and discussions about their economic effects in a region focused on the cloth industry.[14] In these circumstances a tiny number of Africans, who had no specific economic or political position, and so posed no threat, and who were not heretical Christians, but pagans or Muslims who could be converted to Christianity, were of no interest.

'Slavery' and Africans in Sixteenth-Century Norfolk and Suffolk

The suggestion that the Elizabethan warrants were about economics and that the Africans involved were being perceived as commodities raises the possibility of some form of equivalence in English culture in this period between being an African and being enslaved. It is difficult to find evidence in Norfolk and Suffolk of any such equivalence in the 1500s. None of the descriptions of Africans in the local records in this period make any overt reference to enslavement. Moreover, the most important reference to enslavement in the region's popular culture in the 1500s suggests that the social environment those Africans entered was one where ideas about enslavement had a specific local, social, and economic context, which did not correlate skin colour and enslavement.

This reference occurred during the popular uprisings that took place across Norfolk and Suffolk, and elsewhere, in 1549. The main uprising in the region began with enclosure riots in Attleborough and then nearby Wymondham in late June and early July. It then saw the assumption of leadership by the local landowner, Robert Kett. The rebels marched to Norwich and made camp on

---

[13] The Vagrancy Act 1547, 1 Edw. 6 c.3. For a discussion, see C.S.L. Davies, 'Slavery and Protector Somerset: The Vagrancy Act of 1547', *The Economic History Review*, 2nd set, 20 (1966), 533–49.

[14] The statutes commanding gypsies to leave the realm were more closely related to ethnicity, and show that such potential did exist, but there was nothing like that legislation in respect of Africans.

Mousehold Heath, where they organised an alternative government. The roots of the uprising were complex and underpinned by 'the conflict between lord and tenant in the rural economy', but the ideas of the ordinary people involved in the uprising regarding the need for 'good government' were empowered by the way that religious reforms allowed other fundamentals of the political system to be questioned and reform to be demanded, and so spread far beyond the purely economic.[15] Before they were crushed by royal forces in August, the rebels sent a petition of twenty-nine demands to the king that ran from requests that 'no man shall enclose any more' to others aimed at reducing corruption. In this list of demands, however, was one stating 'We pray thatt all bonde men may be made ffre for god made all ffre with his precious blode sheddyng.'[16]

The rebels were not referring to enslaved Africans with their reference to 'bonde men' in 1549. As Andy Wood has shown, this statement about 'bonde men' needs to be understood in a dual fashion. First, it had a specific Norfolk context, where it was focused on the 'growing hostility to the maintenance of serfdom upon the estates of the attainted Duke of Norfolk'. Second, it was part of a tradition of hostility to the notion of bondage that had very deep roots.[17] This terminology was a reminder that the inhabitants of Norfolk and Suffolk in the sixteenth century possessed a set of ideas about the subject of human bondage, although slavery no longer existed in a legal sense. In eleventh-century England around ten per cent of the population had been slaves.[18] This legal enslavement had died out in the twelfth and thirteenth centuries, probably for reasons of economic efficiency, but its legacy could be discerned by the rebels in 1549 within the economic structures of Tudor society, namely in remnants of the concepts of serfdom and villeinage.[19] In 1485, Norfolk and Suffolk contained 115 manors with serfs and even in 1560 there remained thirty-five manors with such bondmen.[20] The local idea of 'bonde men' in the rebel

[15] For a discussion of the difficulty of separating politics, economics, and religion, see Wood, *The 1549*, pp. 177–84. For discussions of these uprisings generally, see Anthony Fletcher and Diarmaid MacCulloch, *Tudor Rebellions*, 6th edn (London, 2015), pp. 66–89; Diarmaid MacCulloch, 'Kett's Rebellion in Context', in Paul Slack (ed.), *Rebellion, Popular Protest and the Social Order in Early Modern England* (New York, 1984), pp. 36–59; Wood, *Riot*, esp. 54–70; Jane Whittle, 'Lords and Tenants in Kett's Rebellion 1549', *Past & Present*, 207 (2010), 3–52, at p. 3.

[16] British Library Harley MS 304, ff. 75r–78v, 'Kett's Demands Being in Rebellion'.

[17] Wood, *The 1549*, p. 181.

[18] F.W. Maitland, *Domesday Book and Beyond: Three Essays in the Early History of England* (Cambridge, 1897), pp. 26–36.

[19] David A.E. Pelteret, *Slavery in Early Medieval England: From the Reign of Alfred to the Early Twelfth Century* (Woodbridge, 1995); Ross Samson, 'The End of Medieval Slavery', in Allen J. Frantzen and Douglas Moffat (eds), *The Work of Work: Servitude, Slavery, and Labour in Medieval England* (Glasgow, 1994), pp. 95–124.

[20] Diarmaid MacCulloch, 'Bondmen under the Tudors', in Claire Cross, David Loades, and J.J. Scarisbrick (eds), *Law and Government under the Tudors* (Cambridge, 1988), p. 94 (Table 10). In his discussion of the roots of English colonial slavery, Guasco has recently argued that

demands drew, therefore, on an historical sense that slavery had existed in the region's past, that the vestiges of that practice still lingered in the region in the Tudor present, and that this remnant was an unacceptable situation because all Englishmen should be free. This context then enhanced a concern among the labouring poor about the potential for the imposition of new forms of economic bondage resulting from the changes caused by the advent of agrarian capitalism.

In the context of Norfolk and Suffolk's African history, the rebels' statement is of great importance. Much as Pigott's description offered a rare glimpse of the thinking about Africans from a working-class perspective in the fifteenth century, the rebels' demand provides an insight into thinking about slavery among the labouring classes a century later. Wood has shown that the ideas of 1549 in respect of bondage could be traced back to the medieval period, for example, the argument of a group of serfs in 1310, while pleading to a royal court that 'In the beginning everyman in the world was free and the law is so favourable to liberty that he who is once found free and of free estate in that there is record shall be held free forever.' Accepting Hilton's suggestion that these ideas were drawing upon radical Christian traditions, Wood argues for 'an important continuity' between these medieval ideas and the ideas of the rebels. He suggests that, in this sense, the Mousehold articles need to be read both locally and more widely, as 'the manifestation of a generic language of late medieval anti-seigneurialism'. There was a religious aspect to this which cannot be unbound from the economic. Bondage was a 'fundamental element in the feudal mode of production, but contemporaries were more likely to interpret it in spiritual terms – as an insult to Christ's sufferings upon the cross'.[21]

The idea of human bondage had, therefore, a specific local meaning, one that drew on ideas about the nature of social relations and which were imbued with radical Christian ideas, with notions about the 'commonwealth' and social justice. Terms like 'slave', 'hireling', and 'bondman' were considered insults in early modern England. The reasons for this association were not related to ideas of race, but class. They drew on 'the endurance of a deep social memory of the humiliations endured by labouring people under late feudalism' and notions that commoners should not be too deferential in their relations with

---

serfdom and villeinage should be seen as equivalent to chattel slavery, Guasco, *Slaves*, pp. 26-30. This is not a position that is generally accepted by historians of medieval and early modern England, who argue that the institutions were fundamentally different. For discussions of serfdom and villeinage, see R.H. Hilton, 'Freedom and Villeinage in England', *Past & Present*, 31 (1965), 3-19; Paul Hyams, 'The Proof of Villein Status in the Common Law', *English Historical Review*, 89 (1974), 721-49; John Hatcher, 'English Serfdom and Villeinage: Towards a Reassessment', *Past & Present*, 90 (1981), 3-39; Chris Given-Wilson, 'Service, Serfdom and English Labour Legislation, 1350-1500', in Anne Curry and Elizabeth Matthew (eds), *Concepts and Patterns of Service in the Later Middle Ages* (Woodbridge; 2000), pp. 21-37.
[21] Wood, *The 1549*, p. 182.

social superiors.[22] These notions were bound up with regional class identities, as highlighted by Savage, which pitted plebeian identities against emergent notions of the 'middling sort'.[23] In the Neville/Woods narrative of the 1549 rebellion in Norfolk, the voice ascribed to the labouring class was very specific about the situation of slavery as a political statement that was derived from an understanding of unequal and oppressive class relations. The rebel complaints were set against an idea that 'great men' were 'consumed with vain pleasures, thirst only after gain' and that, in contrast, the poverty of the labouring classes meant 'But that condition of possessing land seemeth miserable & slavish.'[24] Of course, the passage must not read as a verbatim account of a rebel speech, but it does provide, nonetheless, 'important insights into both the representation of the rebel voice and of plebeian political language'.[25] In relation to ideas about slavery, such speech confirms that the condition of slavery was seen in the culture of the lower orders as one that could affect any person, and was dependent not on any racial characteristics, but upon economic position and the loss of correctly-ordered social relations. It was both a potential physical situation that related to the reorganisation of traditional economic structures, 'that condition of possessing land', and a possible political and social status, the consequence of alterations to the established social relations of Tudor England.

The arrival of Africans in Norfolk and Suffolk did not occur, therefore, in a local culture where there were no views about enslavement, or one where enslavement was already equated with Africans because they were considered inferior and dangerous. Contemporary memories of historic forms of bondage and enslavement that had affected Englishmen previously were powerful. These then fed into the labouring class interpretation of, and opposition to, ongoing social and economic change. Concepts of race were not an element in the construction of such notions and, consequently, Africans were not automatically categorised as slaves. Rather, poor people conceived themselves to be a group who could be enslaved if they did not resist. Although 'rebel languages of class were multifarious and heterogeneous', and used 'interchangeable' terms such as 'the commons' and 'poverty', along with 'the estate of poverty' and 'the commonalty', the idea that the members of this class should not be enslaved was a common thread, as was a sense that their oppression already meant they were being 'enslaved' by new economic orderings.[26]

---

[22] Wood, 'Fear', p. 806.

[23] M. Savage, 'Space, networks and class formation', in N. Kirk (ed.), Social class and Marxism: Defences and Challenges (Abingdon, Oxon; New York, 1996), pp. 58–86.

[24] R. Woods, Norfolk furies and their foyle (London, 1615), B2., ProQuest, https://search-pro-quest-com.uea.idm.oclc.org/docview/2240885474?accountid=10637 [accessed 2 February 2020].

[25] Wood, The 1549, p. 97.

[26] Wood, The 1549, p. 175; M.L. Bush, The Pilgrimage of Grace: A Study of the Rebel Armies of October 1536 (Manchester, 1996), p. 285.

Since these ideas were predicated on social divisions that reflected economic position and religious views, and not on race, they not only meant that slavery was not linked to race, but they allowed for the possibility of African migrants being accepted into 'the commons', because such Africans were likely to be fellow members of the poorest sections of fifteenth- and sixteenth-century society and so share a class position with non-Africans. As Pigott's statement showed, Eylys was understood primarily as a member of a group of poor sailors, rather than being an African 'other'. An African could, therefore, be viewed as part of the 'estate of poverty' since these were the social understandings that dominated the views of the labouring classes.

These popular notions were strengthened, in fact, precisely because enslavement was possible in sixteenth-century England and it was not linked to racial heritage in its actual manifestations. Furthermore, Norfolk and Suffolk's people had encountered real slavery in places such as Livorno, and, again, in that situation enslavement was not defined by racial categorisation, but by individual circumstance. The Tudor statesman Thomas Smith appears to have acknowledged the existence of some enslaved people in England in 1565 when he compared villeinage and slavery. 'Neither of the one sort or the other do we have any number in England. And of the first I never knew any in the realm in my time; of the second so few there be, that it is almost not worth the speaking.'[27] Yet, while there were some slaves in England, the population understood that this situation was not decided upon by skin colour. The potential for Africans to be enslaved existed, but only because it existed for other groups, such as vagabonds and criminals, and by extension the poor generally, if their circumstances worsened. Enslavement was a consequence of a specific situational potential based on a confluence of circumstance. Indeed, one of the most important discussions of slavery in Tudor England involved not an African, but a Russian. Known as Cartwright's Case, this situation came to law in Star Chamber in 1567, when it was reported that 'one Cartwright brought a slave from Russia, and would scourge him, for which he was questioned; and it was resolved that England was too pure an air for slaves to breathe in'.[28]

As Jonathan Bush points out, Cartwright's Case is extremely helpful in understanding thinking about slavery in the Tudor period from a legal perspective. He shows that the legal discussion around Cartwright's Case reveals generic points about enslavement in Tudor culture. Firstly, that there were many situations of employment in Tudor England where 'nothing could have been less true than that English labour was free – even legally free', and there was, of course, the much discussed issue of the law passed in 1547 in respect of vagrancy.[29]

[27] C.H. Williams (ed.), *English Historical Documents 1485–1558* (New York, 1967), pp. 1029–30.
[28] John C. Hurd, *The Law of Freedom and Bondage in The United States* (1858), p. 179 https://archive.org/details/lawoffreedombond00hurd/page/180/mode/2up [accessed 7 September 2017].
[29] Jonathan A. Bush, 'The First Slave (And Why He Matters)', *Cardozo Law Review*, 18

Secondly, in respect of legal freedom, Tudor jurists decided that everyone under English common law was free, in that 'Freedom and slavery referred not to the circumstances of one's employment, but to one's personal legal status.'[30] Villeinage had, to all intents and purposes, disappeared, since even where it still existed it was not worth the effort for a lord to enforce his rights. This reflected the general view, which Cartwright's Case pointed to, that slavery was no longer a normal thing in England. The speed with which the Vagrancy Act of 1547 was repealed also points to this reality. Yet, the mere fact that Cartwright had considered bringing a Russian slave to England, and the continued mentions of examples of penal slavery and galley-slaves in the period, show that the idea of enslavement could be accepted in certain circumstances. The query about it shows that these circumstances were not dependent on racial characteristics; instead they were dependent on situation. As Norfolk and Suffolk sailors and merchants would have seen in Livorno, anyone could be enslaved in the right set of circumstances – Christian and non-Christian, African and non-African.

This can then be elided with the gradual appearance of some Africans in Tudor society as a direct consequence of the activities of Hawkins, Drake, and Raleigh.[31] The circumstances in which these Africans had been acquired, as already enslaved, meant their situational status had begun in some form of slavish servitude, and its continuation could be justified on these grounds in England. This approach can be discerned as far back as 1259, when 'an Ethiopian of the name of Bartholomew, sometime a Saracen slave (*servus*) of Roger de Lyntin' in Windsor, was recorded as 'having run away from his said lord'. A royal order was granted to de Lyntin instructing all subjects to arrest the runaway.[32] The term Saracen was an ancient one, used 'among the later Greeks and Romans, a name for the nomadic peoples of the Syro-Arabian desert which harassed the Syrian confines of the Empire; hence, an Arab; by extension, a Muslim, esp. with reference to the Crusades.'[33] Here it denoted Bartholomew's religious affiliation, since the geographic descriptor had already been provided by the word 'Ethiopian', which will be discussed in a moment in relation to Baptist at Hunstanton. So, Bartholomew had been a non-Christian African, although the phrase 'sometime a Saracen' indicates that he had probably

(1996), 610–15, at p. 610. The literature on the issue of vagrancy is voluminous; for work related directly to Norwich, see John F. Pound, 'An Elizabethan Census of the Poor: The Treatment of Vagrancy in Norwich, 1570–1580', *University of Birmingham Historical Journal*, 8 (1961–2), 135–51.

[30] Bush, 'The First', p. 611.

[31] For discussions of these voyages see, among many, Hugh Thomas, *The Slave Trade: The Story of the Atlantic Slave Trade, 1440–1870* (New York, 1999), pp. 154–6; David B. Quinn, 'Turks, Moors, Blacks, and Others in Drake's West Indian Voyage', *Terrae Incognitae*, 14 (1982), 97–104.

[32] The case is discussed in Michael Ray, 'A Black Slave on the run in Thirteenth-Century England', *Nottingham Medieval Studies*, 51 (2007), 111–19.

[33] 'Saracen, n. and adj.', *OED Online*, Oxford University Press, March 2020. Web. 13 April 2020.

converted to Christianity. The term *servus* does not imply chattel slavery necessarily, but since de Lyntin was treating Bartholomew as a 'runaway' there was
clearly a type of servitude involved in this instance.

Bush argues that this case provides a basic framework to understand slavery
and villeinage in medieval European law. Roger de Lyntin was an Italian, so
Bartholomew was originally a non-Christian African who had been held in
slavish servitude in Italy by a foreigner before arriving in England.[34] Bush
suggests that this shows a general acceptance of a legal principle that if a person
was enslaved in some fashion under a foreign regime, then that status could
continue in England, even if they had become a Christian.[35] Bartholomew
reveals, therefore, the sort of memories relating to ideas of enslavement and
near slavery that the Norfolk rebels were drawing upon in 1549, which provide
a means of understanding popular thinking about the subject in the period, and
which would have been reinforced by experience in places like Livorno. These
memories and experiences allowed for the validity of continuing slavery for a
person who was previously enslaved abroad. This meant people in Norfolk and
Suffolk could encounter an African, or even another non-African Christian,
like Cartwright's Russian, in a situation of enslavement and accept that such
a position could continue. This was not because of their skin colour, but
because it was also accepted that a foreigner who had been enslaved before
arriving in England could continue to be enslaved in the country. At the same
time, other memories and ideas also existed that convinced the rebels that
English people should not be enslaved. These made it possible to encounter
an African such as Thomas Blackamore in Kessingland and see him as an
English labouring man who was free.

As has been discussed by numerous historians in relation to the legal cases
concerning enslaved Africans in England in the seventeenth and eighteenth
centuries, traces of these ideas can be perceived in legal opinion of later
centuries; for example, in the first edition of his *Commentaries*, Blackstone
asserted that under the common law slaves were emancipated upon arrival
in England.[36] Those discussions took place in a different situation, however,

[34] He is described as an Italian, a knight of Apulia, in A.E.Stamp (ed.), *Calendar of Close Rolls,
Henry III, Volume 10, 1256–1259* (London, 1932), at p. 444, <https://babel.hathitrust.org/
cgi/pt?id=mdp.35112103127173&view=1up&seq=5> [accessed 17 May 2018].
[35] Bush identified five elements shown by this case; 1) that a master was free to travel with
his slave, retaining ownership rights during and after the sojourn (the sojourner rule); 2) that
foreign or non-Christian status, or both, might justify enslavement (the initial enslavement
rule); 3) that conversion to Christianity ('sometime a Saracen' implies presently not a Saracen)
need not act to manumit a slave (the conversion rule); 4) that a foreign determination of slave
status should be accepted (the comity rule); and 5) that once found to be a fugitive according
to foreign law, a slave should be returned (the fugitive rendition rule), see Bush, 'The First',
p. 618.
[36] William Blackstone, *Commentaries on the Laws of England* (Oxford, 1765; facsimile edn,
Chicago: University of Chicago Press, 1979), 1: 123. The discussion of statements such as this
has been extensive, and no agreement has been reached; examples include Seymour Drescher,

one where Africans were being ascribed a place as enslaved objects within an economic system that had been constructed in the Americas and relied upon such commodification for self-justification. This was not the situation in sixteenth-century Norfolk and Suffolk. Africans had not been attributed that specific position, because there was no economic or social need for that intellectual move to be made in the 1500s. At that time Norfolk and Suffolk were not embedded into an economic system that was founded on African slavery. The economic system of importance was emergent agrarian capitalism, in which 'East Anglia was especially precocious'.[37] Agrarian capitalism did not require enslaved labourers; it had other means of extracting the required labour from workers. It required the remodelling of patterns of land use and the destruction of traditional understandings of common rights and community. It was the class tensions that were associated with this change that dominated social relations.

The Africans that arrived in the region in the Tudor period came into a situation dominated by class struggle, and not racial demarcation. The labouring classes were struggling against 'the entrepreneurial energies of the wealthier yeoman farmers and the cash-grabbing fiscal seigneurialism of the gentry'.[38] Issues of 'race' had no role in that situation. In the memory and the culture of the labouring classes, these were the matters that were significant and threatened their freedom. The labouring classes viewed the condition of bondage in general with antipathy and did not link skin colour and enslavement. The real correlation was between an idea of bondage that drew on historical memory and social constructions such as villeinage – which were themselves related to relative economic position and to their specific historical situation – and not to African heritage, or to a small number of Africans who came to live in their villages and towns.

Baptist in Hunstanton, 1599

Africans could, therefore, be understood as fellow members of 'the commons' by the working population of sixteenth-century Norfolk and Suffolk, because they shared multiple characteristics with the non-African members of that social strata; their work roles, their economic position, and their poverty. The characteristic

---

Capitalism and Antislavery: British Mobilization in Comparative Perspective (New York, 1986), 31-2; Jerome Nadelhaft, 'The Somersett Case and Slavery: Myth, Reality, and Repercussions', *Journal of Negro History*, 51 (1966), 193-208; William R. Cotter, 'The Somerset Case and the Abolition of Slavery in England', *History*, 79 (1994), 31-56; William M. Wiecek, 'Somerset: Lord Mansfield and the Legitimacy of Slavery in the Anglo-American World', *University of Chicago Law Review*, 42 (1974), 86-146; A. Leon Higginbotham Jr., *In the Matter of Colour: Race and the American Legal Process, The Colonial Period* (New York, 1978), pp. 313-29; James Oldham, 'New Light on Mansfield and Slavery', *Journal of British Studies*, 27 (1988), 45-68; Rabin, 'In a Country of Liberty?', pp. 5-29.
[37] Wood, *The 1549*, p. 14.
[38] Ibid.

that needed to be dealt with before these Africans could be considered fully part of 'the commons' and of local communities was confessional. Belonging to the Christian community was critical to membership of these social groups and to be accepted into the 'poorality' it was necessary to be a Christian. This is not to argue that all members of the labouring classes, or indeed any classes, in this period were equally motivated by religious devotion, but it is to accept that in the late medieval and early modern sixteenth century the world was understood by everyone through what Charles Taylor describes as 'the immanent frame', which accepted the existence of other levels of reality outside the everyday, whether or not people then took account of these realities in their actions.[39] In this world to be a 'heathen' was to be separated from the basic social relations that held society together. Christian status was passed on to English people through the practice of baptism and, as the baptism of an African named Baptist in the small Norfolk village of Hunstanton in 1599 shows, it was a position that could be obtained by an African migrant, with the consequence that he or she was then able to become part of the other communities that existed in the period.

There are two separate documents that mention this baptism. The first is a remark in the flyleaf of the parish register of Ringstead, the parish lying to the east of Hunstanton, where Lawrence Hockenhull, the rector of Ringstead, wrote that, 'Baptist the Aethiopian or Blacke a more of Hunstanton Hall was baptised by me Lawrence Hockenhull at Hunstanton the 15th day of April 1599'.[40] The second record of the baptism is in the Hunstanton parish register. The entry reads, 'Baptist quidam morianus bapt. 15 Dies Aprilis prenominatus Lewys.'[41] Since the Ringstead entry confirms that Baptist was the name of the 'Black a more' being baptised, then it appears that the word 'morianus' in the Hunstanton register was an attempt by the writer to use the Latin word *Maurus*, 'a Moor', to create the term 'Moorish'. If that is so, and taking account of the Ringstead entry, then this line would seem to be best translated as 'Baptist somebody Moorish baptised on 15th day of April before named Lewys.'[42]

Hunstanton lies less than three miles north of a small but well-used port, Heacham. In the sixteenth century Heacham was accessible by larger ships and was known as one of the 'principal harbours' in the Wash, providing a 'convenient haven' for ships plying the coastal route along the east of England.[43]

[39] For these ideas see Charles Taylor, A *Secular Age* (Cambridge, MA; London, 2007), especially pp. 25–148.
[40] NRO/PD/696/16, Parish Register, Great Ringstead, 15 April 1599.
[41] NRO/PD 698/1, Parish Register, Baptism of Baptist, Old Hunstanton (St Mary's), 15 April 1599.
[42] Since the Ringstead entry confirms that Baptist is the name of the 'black a moor', this helps with the Latin translation because 'Baptist' is confirmed as the person's name. In that case *quidam* can be translated as 'somebody'.
[43] Daniel Gurney, 'Household and Privy Purse Accounts of the Lestranges of Hunstanton, from A.D. 1519 to A.D. 1578: Communicated to the Society of Antiquaries' (London, 1834),

Furthermore, the village had a small, but thriving, merchant community with international connections; ships had been departing from Heacham for the Baltic in the fourteenth century.[44] One of its merchant families was the Rolfes, whose most famous member was John Rolfe, who would become Secretary and Recorder General of the Virginia Colony, a key figure in the foundation of the Virginia tobacco trade, and Member of the Council and first Legislative Assembly in America in 1619.[45] He would bring his Native American wife, Metoaka (better known as Pocahontas), to visit Heacham in 1616. Although John Rolfe first left for America in 1609, a decade after Baptist appeared in Hunstanton, and Baptist's appearance is far too early to be connected to the Americas, the important point is that the Rolfes had lived in the village since at least 1539 and were successful merchants who were heavily involved in the King's Lynn merchant community.[46] The family's trade in the sixteenth century appears to have been international, as hinted at by the brass plaque to the elder John Rolfe (1562–94) in Heacham Church, which describes his business as 'exporting and importing such things as England abounded in or needed'. His sons all appear to have become merchants, with John emigrating to the Virginia colony and his youngest son, Henry, becoming a merchant in London, and a member of the Virginia Company.[47]

Further trading links can be found in the family that owned three of the four manors at Hunstanton, and who owned Hunstanton Hall, where Hockenhull noted the baptism had taken place; the Lestrange family. The Lestranges' wealth was drawn largely from their landholdings and agriculture, and in the first half of the century they had been heavily involved in court, and were later closely linked with the Howards.[48] As the family's fortunes waxed in the first seventy years of the sixteenth century, they also became involved in the maritime trade, owning a ship that sailed from Heacham and mainly trading with the northern border region, sailing for example to Newcastle with malt during 1547–8, returning with coals. Although too early to be directly relevant to Baptist, the

p. 4; *The History and Antiquities of the County of Norfolk: Smithdon, Taverham, Tunstead, Walsham, and Wayland* (Norwich, 1781), pp. 27–30.

[44] Henry Bolingbroke sailed from Heacham for the Baltic on crusade in 1392, Timothy Guard, *Chivalry, Kingship and Crusade: The English Experience in the Fourteenth Century,* (Cambridge, 2013), pp. 72–97.

[45] A. Neville Rolfe, 'The Ancestral Home of John Rolfe', *William and Mary Quarterly,* 13 (April 1933), p. 137.

[46] 'Historical and Genealogical Notes and Queries', *The Virginia Magazine of History and Biography,* 19 (1911), 193–205.

[47] 'The Ancestors and Descendants of John Rolfe with Notices of Some Connected Families', *The Virginia Magazine of History and Biography,* 21 (1913), pp. 105–6. <http://www.jstor.org/stable/4243251> [accessed 1 March 2018].

[48] Sir Thomas Lestrange was one of the trusted courtiers of Henry VIII: J. Rowe, 'Lestrange [Le Strange], Sir Thomas (c. 1490–1545), landowner and administrator'. ODNB https://www.oxforddnb.com/view/10.1093/ref:odnb/9780198614128.001.0001/odnb-9780198614128-e-16515. [accessed 21 September 2017].

household accounts of Sir Thomas mention sales of malted barley to Dutch and Flemish merchants.[49] Cord Oestmann suggests that the family's involvement in merchant activity may have been substantial, but largely unrecorded because it took place outside registered ports.[50] Sir Nicholas was made a freeman of the port of King's Lynn in 1566, an honour that supports the notion of his involvement in merchant trade and suggests that he may have resided in the town.[51]

Overall, Lynn's maritime trade in the period comprised three strands: overseas trade; imports from the North-East of England; and operations involving the rest of the coastal trade.[52] Lynn's coastal trade was focused upon the export of grain and the import of coal, but its ships sailed to London and to the Baltic as well.[53] Moreover, in 1578-9, Lynn merchants were sending malt, barley, and beans to the Low Countries and wheat to Spain and Portugal.[54] Indeed, there had been a regular trade between Lynn and Portugal, involving Portuguese wax, fruit, and oil, since the fifteenth century.[55]

These connections mean that there were several ways in which an African such as Baptist might have arrived at Hunstanton. The first was through a direct trading link with Portugal, which, as has been said above, was one of the leading European nations involved with slaving in the sixteenth century. The second was the connection of Lynn and Heacham merchants with Holland. Dutch-sounding names have been identified in relation to the importation of enslaved Africans into the Spanish colonies as early as 1528, but the earliest direct connections between the Dutch and enslavement are to be found around 1596, when a Rotterdam captain, called Pieter van der Haagen, brought 130 enslaved Africans into Middelburg, capital of the province of Zeeland.[56] Third, there is a possibility that Baptist had arrived in Hunstanton because of the coastal trade via London. The commercial links between Lynn and London were strong; for example, between 1607 and 1609 twice as many shipments went

---

[49] NRO/LC/P3, pp. 347, 376, 474, 492, 527; NRO/LC/P1, p. 336.
[50] Cord Oestmann, *Lordship and Community: The Lestrange Family and the Village of Hunstanton, Norfolk* (Woodbridge, 1994), p. 137. There is substantial evidence that foreign trade from ports in the area was under-recorded because of customs evasion; see G. Alan Metters, 'Corn, Coal and Commerce: Merchants and Coastal Trading in Early Jacobean King's Lynn', *International Journal of Maritime History*, 23 (2011), 149-78, at p. 151.
[51] Oestmann, *Lordship*, p. 24.
[52] Metters, 'Corn', pp. 152-3.
[53] Williams, *Maritime*, pp. 140-50 (on coal) and pp. 150-61 (on corn).
[54] Thomas Stuart Willan, *Studies in Elizabethan Foreign Trade* (Manchester, 1959), pp. 72-3. The sixteenth-century trade is also mentioned in Metters, 'The Rulers', pp. 167-8.
[55] Paul Richards, 'The Hinterland and Overseas Trade of King's Lynn 1205-1537: An Introduction', in Klaus Friedland and Paul Richards (eds), *Essays in Hanseatic History: The King's Lynn Symposium 1998* (Dereham, 2005), pp. 10-21.
[56] Johannes Postma, *The Dutch in the Atlantic Slave Trade, 1600-1815* (Cambridge, 2008), pp. 10-17. For other details of the Dutch involvement in the slave trade see P.C. Emmer, *The Dutch Slave Trade, 1500-1850* (trans. Chris Emery) (New York; Oxford, 2006).

to London from Lynn as went north.[57] Since the work that has been carried out in relation to London by Habib and others shows that the capital had a substantial African population by 1599, it is possible that an African might have come into the Lestrange household from that location. Perhaps Baptist was a sailor from London who had left his ship and moved inland, where he found a job at Hunstanton Hall.

The next issue to be addressed is the status of Baptist. It is possible that enslavement had been part of his story, and that he may have been initially taken from Africa through enslavement by North Africans, and subsequently by the Portuguese, Spanish, or Italians. The surviving Lestrange records do not make any mention of either the presence of, or purchase of, any African in the household, nor is there any mention of an African in any of the wills of the family in this period.[58] Furthermore, at the time of Baptist's baptism the Lestranges were notably less wealthy, because of a fall in their political fortunes and a series of early deaths among the heirs. In 1599 the estate was in the hands of trustees, who managed the affairs of the young Sir Hamon Lestrange.[59] By 1602 the estate rental and income were well below that needed to run the estate and 'a fraction of that enjoyed by his great-grandfather'.[60]

Since Hamon Lestrange was a minor at the date of the baptism, only fourteen years old, and in financial difficulties, it seems unlikely that he would have been able to purchase an African. Moreover, as an adult he was uninterested in trade and foreign investment, focusing his energy on his estate and having little to do with Norfolk society more widely.[61] It seems, therefore, that Sir Hamon would have been indifferent to such a move, even if he had been able to afford it. These factors combine to make the idea of the purchase of an enslaved African by the Lestrange family in this period seem improbable. In view of this, although the description of Baptist in the flyleaf of the Ringland register as being 'of Hunstanton Hall' might perhaps be taken as a hint of a form of slavish servitude, it seems unlikely.

---

[57] Metters, 'Corn', p. 155.

[58] NRO GUN 82-83, 364X3, 'Will of Sir Roger Le Strange, knt.' and a 'Letter from Sir Nicholas L'Estrange, bart. to his Son' communicated by Hamon Le Strange; NRO LEST/AE 4, Will of Sir Nicholas Le Strange, 1547; NRO LEST/AE 5, Will of Hamon Le Strange, 6 Oct 1580; NRO LEST/AE 6, Will of Thomas Le Strange 1580.

[59] The trustees were William Street, Sir Henry Hobart, Thomas Oxborough, John Peyton, and Richard Stubbe. Hamon's guardian was Henry Spelman, a trained lawyer who became an antiquarian when he found the work of a lawyer too mundane. He seems to have lived at the hall until at least 1603, so was resident in the period of Baptist's presence. There is no evidence of their involvement in trade, Oestmann, *Lordship*, p. 24. For more on the family see Elizabeth Griffiths, '"A Country Life": Sir Hamon Le Strange of Hunstanton in Norfolk (1583–1654)', in Richard W. Hoyle (ed.), *Custom, Improvement and the Landscape in Early Modern Britain* (Farnham, Surrey; Burlington, VT, 2011); R.W. Ketton-Cremer, *A Norfolk Gallery* (London, 1948), pp. 56–94.

[60] Elizabeth Griffiths (ed.), *Her Price is Above Pearls: Family and Farming Records of Alice Le Strange, 1617–1656* (Norfolk, 2015), p. 7.

[61] Griffiths, 'A Country', p. 203.

It seems more probable that the statement should be read as an exact description of the situation Hockenhull had encountered, in that Baptist was a 'Blackamore' who was working at the hall, and so 'of Hunstanton Hall'.

The baptism itself points far more strongly towards the suggestion that Baptist was not seen as different because of skin colour, however. Once again, the emphasis in the documents was on his non-Christian status. The register entry focused on him as 'somebody Moorish'. Similarly, the term 'Blacke a more' in the flyleaf note pointed towards an African heritage, but was then clarified by the term, 'Aethiopian' (Ethiopian). This word was used to describe 'A native or inhabitant of Ethiopia. Also: a black or dark-skinned person' in this period.[62] The use of this term here may have been theologically important, rather than focused on race.[63]

Some writers, such as Matthew Dimmock, have touched on references to Ethiopians in the early modern period, but largely in terms of 'the proverbial notion that "To Wash an Ethiop is Labour in Vain"'.[64] This idiom was probably derived from Jeremiah 13:23, 'Can the Ethiopian change his skin, or the leopard his spots?' Although the passage was sometimes used in discussions that touched on baptism, this was mostly among Puritans from the seventeenth century onwards.[65] Importantly for this discussion, its mention by modern scholars in relation to baptism and a negative conception of race is a consequence of a fundamental misunderstanding of scripture and the *Book of Common Prayer*.

The crucial point to understand in relation to Jeremiah 13:23 is that the passage is about sin, and not about race. The text is that of a Jewish prophet dating from about 650 BC and its use in baptism must be read through a Christian interpretation of Jewish scripture. Indeed, the original Hebrew refers to 'Cushite' (pertaining or relating to an ancient people of eastern Africa, south of Egypt). Although this was often translated in seventeenth-century Protestant sermons as 'blackamore', that was an error which was itself a reflection of the increasing influence of racialised thought in that later period. Contemporary Bibles used the correct translation, 'Ethiopian'.[66] The Ethiopian and leopard are used in Jeremiah 13:23 as examples of a living creature possessing an obvious

---

[62] 'Ethiopian, n. and adj.', *OED Online*, Oxford University Press, March 2020. Web. 12 April 2020.

[63] Habib, *Black*, p. 24.

[64] Matthew Dimmock, 'Converting and Not Converting "Strangers" in Early Modern London', *Journal of Early Modern History*, 17 (2013), 457–78, at pp. 460–2.

[65] See, for example, 'Sermon 50. Man's Destruction of himself', in John Collinges, *Several Discourses Concerning the Actual Providence of God: Divided Into Three Parts* (London, 1678), p. 647.

[66] James Strong, *New Exhaustive Concordance of the Bible* (Nashville, TN: Thomas Nelson Publishers, c. 1985), 3569 [e]. The name Cush was applied to tracts of country both in Arabia and Africa – on the very probable supposition that the descendants of the primitive Cushite tribes, who had settled in the former country, emigrated across the Red Sea to the latter region of the earth, see 'Cushite, adj. and n.', *OED Online*, Oxford University Press, March 2020. Web. 20 April 2020.

physical characteristic that cannot be changed by their own effort; there is no negativity inferred from that characteristic. Rather, it is a metaphor aimed at explaining that no-one can change their sinful nature without God's assistance. The passage does not equate a sinful nature with a different skin colour, it empha-sises the essential requirement of God's grace to overcome sin for everyone.

This is central in understanding the baptism of Africans in the period. It might be suggested in relation to the baptism of the African Mary Phyllis in London as possibly being an explanation of the phrase 'that thing which by nature she could not have' which was used in the service, that the 'thing' might be 'whiteness'. [67] As the *Book of Common Prayer* makes clear, however, this was a standard theological statement, applicable to all people of the earth, that referred specifically to the fact that, because all humans are 'conceived and borne in synne', it is their nature to be sinful, and 'no manne borne in synne, can entre into the kingdom of God (except he be regenerate, and borne a newe of water and the Holy Ghost).'[68] The nature being referred to here is the sinful nature of all humanity, not anyone's ethnicity. This sinful nature is overcome, and eternal life attained, through faith in Jesus Christ, and this is made possible by the sacrament of baptism.[69]

Hockenhull's reference to Baptist as an 'Aethiopian' should be seen in this framework and as further evidence that the fundamental sign of difference in sixteenth-century Norfolk and Suffolk was religious. His use of the term 'Ethiopian' was probably a reference to Acts 8:27–39, which recounts how the evangelist Philip was told by an angel to travel south of Jerusalem, where he met 'a man of Ethiopia, a eunuch of great authority under Candace queen of the Ethiopians who had charge of all her treasure and had come to Jerusalem for to worship'. Philip explained the Gospel to the Ethiopian and the man was converted and baptised.[70] The incident is an example of evangelisation, of the fact that Jesus had made it possible for Gentiles to become members of the

---

[67] Register of St Botolph, Aldgate: LMA P69/BOT2/A/019 item 006, f. 257r, from Dimmock, 'Converting', p. 461.

[68] 'Publique Baptysme' in the *Book of Common Prayer, 1559*, in Brian Cummings (ed.), *The Book of Common Prayer: The Texts of 1549, 1559, and 1662* (Oxford, 2011), p. 141.

[69] As Kaufmann puts it, 'a quick glance at the Book of Common Prayer (1559) shows that the minister, far from making a racial slur, in suggesting that an African could not "by nature" be baptised, was in fact merely following the order of service, in which all individuals under-going baptism were reminded that their sinful nature made them unworthy of redemption and it was only Christ's love that saved them', Kaufmann, 'Making', pp. 25–6. For discussion of the *Book of Common Prayer* in relation to the baptism of adults, see J. Neil Alexander, 'The Shape of the Classical Book of Common Prayer', in Charles Hefling and Cynthia Shattuck (eds), *The Oxford Guide to The Book of Common Prayer: A Worldwide Survey* (Oxford; New York, 2006), p. 66; Cummings, *The Book of Common Prayer*, p. 211, p. 777.

[70] Acts 8:27–39. Alongside that in Acts, Strong confirms that there are three other refer-ences to Ethiopians in the Bible. None of these are negative. Jeremiah 13:23 has already been discussed. Numbers 12:1 confirms that Moses was married to an 'Ethiopian woman'. Jeremiah 38:7 recounts how 'Ebed-melech the Ethiopian' saved Jeremiah, see Strong, *New*, p. 68.

kingdom of God.[71] The significance of this incident in relation to Baptist is that his was also a clear example of the successful evangelisation and baptism of a non-Christian. The term was being used here to clarify the situation. Baptist had been 'different' because he was 'somebody Moorish', that is a non-Christian, but his baptism had made him like the Ethiopian in Acts, a Gentile who was now Christian, and so no longer someone different. This would seem also to fit with the fact that Baptist was said to have been named Lewys previously. Technically, Lewys is a Welsh name, but it was in use as a Christian name in Norfolk in this period; for example, an infant named Lewys Lankforthe was baptised in Lynn in 1593.[72] It seems likely that Lewys was a name that he had chosen for himself, or perhaps been given, after travelling from Africa to Europe in whatever fashion, before 1599. If Baptist had been owned by the Lestrange family, then it would seem odd for them to have chosen to change his name on baptism. If, however, the baptism was a sign of genuine conversion on his part, then the choice to be newly named Baptist would signify that he had become a 'new' person in Christ.

This survey of the Africans living in Norfolk and Suffolk from 1467 to 1599 suggests that the cultural, social, and economic situation in which Africans were to be considered was not dominated by any framework predicated on negative ideas about their skin colour. There may have been ideas about 'blackness' and the exotic in English literature of the period, but these are only apparent in their absence in the region. The key idea was that a 'Moor' was unlikely to be a Christian, but since so few Africans lived in the region, their presence was not a religious threat; it was an opportunity for conversion. There were certainly ideas about 'strangers' and 'foreigners' in the region, but these were not related to African heritage, and the region was generally welcoming to foreigners in the sixteenth century. There were strong ideas about villeinage and slavery, which existed alongside notions of 'free Englishmen', and drew on long-standing notions about these matters. These ideas had informed the thinking of the 1549 rebels and popular culture more generally about bondage. This understanding of slavery was not connected to African heritage, it was a means of expressing class tensions and the self-perception of working communities that were under threat from the changes underway because of agrarian capitalism.

These ideas did not form a cultural normality that meant the Africans who were beginning to appear in the region were categorised in relation to negative ideas about skin colour. There is no written evidence that racialised ideas were being developed and considered in a systematic manner. They did not form any rigid group of concepts about those Africans, their place, or status. Indeed, the arrival of small numbers of Africans in the region over this period did not necessitate any sort of considered response from authorities, community leaders, or

---

[71] Gentile – 'Of or pertaining to any or all of the nations other than the Jewish', 'gentile, adj. and n.', *OED Online*, Oxford University Press, September 2020. <https://www.oed.com/view/Entry/77647?redirectedFrom=gentile> [accessed 22 October 2020].

[72] NRO/PD39/1, Baptism of Lewys Lankforthe, 7 October 1593, King's Lynn.

the population more widely. These Africans were few in number and spread widely across the area, so they did not form a coherent community for which people in Norfolk and Suffolk needed to articulate a social place and role, in stark contrast to the responses to the known groups of 'foreigners' arriving in the period. Neither did their arrival pose any economic threat, in contrast to the situation with the Strangers for example, or reflect any economic difficulty, as did the vagrants. Nor was there any political or religious threat that they represented, as was the case with the Catholics or Anabaptists.

It seems that in responding to Africans arriving in the region, individual circumstance mattered more than theoretical ideas. The ongoing social position of African arrivals in their new context was determined primarily by the social situation in which they were encountered, rather than by the colour of their skin. So, for example, if an individual African was encountered in a foreign port where there was slavery, such as Livorno, and that person was enslaved at that point, then it was quite possible that a Norfolk or Suffolk merchant or sailor would have accepted that status. For most Africans in the two counties, however, this was not the situation.

Eylys was encountered as a free sailor in a local English environment, that of Great Yarmouth, where enslavement was not a common cultural norm. In that circumstance, although he was 'a More', this was not the determining factor in his treatment. He was not seen primarily as an African who *should* be enslaved or treated differently because of his skin colour. Instead he was perceived in the cultural and economic situation of Yarmouth, which was a port which saw many ships, many crews, and 'foreigners' from all over Europe. In that situation his primary designators were his youth, which afforded him mercy and the avoidance of the gallows, and his class position as a young labouring 'boy of the shippe', which made him a recognisable type of person in the port's culture. Indeed, it made him a member of the working poor. His skin colour and heritage were subordinate to those factors at that moment. This class position allowed Eylys to be accepted and to take up residence in Yarmouth's working community. Thomas Blackamore was similar. Probably arriving in Kessingland as a sailor or labourer, this provided him with a class position. He was also seen initially as someone who was a 'Blackamore', but this was an issue of religious affiliation and was not filtered by any fixed ideas about race. Thomas was accepted into the village community and had children who were baptised without comment.

The lack of any over-arching framework of racialised thinking in fifteenth- and sixteenth-century Norfolk and Suffolk allowed, therefore, a variety of responses to Africans to take shape. Over the course of the seventeenth century, however, such approaches to Africans in the region would begin to face a challenge. Slavery would slowly cease to be a system encountered in another culture and only on an occasional voyage to the Mediterranean, and instead would begin to become part of the economic and social world of Norfolk and Suffolk as the colonists of the New World gradually reframed these notions concerning slavery and African heritage to suit the needs of the new slavery-based colonial economies.

4

The Seventeenth Century:
The Early Shadow of Transatlantic Slavery

The Gradual Impact of the Creation of the Slave Economy
on Norfolk and Suffolk

The fifteenth- and sixteenth-century African population in Norfolk and Suffolk was small. It seems probable that some of these Africans were free of any formal enslavement, although it is conceivable that others may have been held in some form of slavish servitude. It is imaginable, nonetheless, that some of the first-generation Africans who arrived in the ports and villages of Norfolk and Suffolk may have had some experience of enslavement in their pasts, but that this would have been in the Mediterranean or in North Africa before they had travelled to England. Their arrival in the region was not a direct consequence of the activity of people from Norfolk and Suffolk in slaving networks or economic structures that were dependent on slavery. Instead, if enslavement in some sense had been part of their personal history, it would have been tangentially connected to Norfolk and Suffolk, in that their arrival would have occurred because of the interface between the mercantile economy of the region – in the form of the trading voyages of its merchants and sailors – and the North African/Mediterranean slaving economy. The initial settlement process of the African population should probably be understood as an effect of the 'ripples' of the internal African slave trade as it then intersected with the cultures and trading patterns of the Mediterranean, which in turn interacted with the counties' trading networks. While the region was not actively involved in any slaving activities in this early period, it seems that it was possible for people in the region to be enslaved or held in a condition of slavish servitude. This was not a direct function of their skin colour, however, but related to social situation. In theory, a person who was enslaved elsewhere, and was not an English Christian, could have been purchased by someone from Norfolk and Suffolk and taken back to the region as a slave, as happened to the Russian in Cartwright's Case.

In the seventeenth century this approach to Africans in Norfolk and Suffolk would encounter a new geographic and economic situation, as the region became involved in the cultures that appeared in the newly established colonies in English/British North America and then the West Indies. The colony of Jamestown in Virginia was founded in 1607. In 1624 the island of St Christopher (St Kitts) was settled, followed by Barbados in 1627, along with Montserrat and Antigua in the 1630s. In the 1650s, Oliver Cromwell's army seized the island of Jamaica from the Spaniards.[1] By the late 1600s, these locations had developed successful economies structured around African enslavement.[2] This was especially true in the West Indies, as the colonies there shifted from economies of semi-subsistence smallholders reliant on indentured servants to ones dominated by sugar plantations operating the gang-labour system.[3] The drive to establish agricultural commodity production in the colonies in response to the appearance of a mass market in Europe for the produce of the plantations, most notably sugar, tobacco, coffee, molasses, rum, and cotton, was fundamental in the shift to the use of enslaved African labour.[4]

As David Brion Davis has argued, this development was a consequence 'of innumerable local and pragmatic choices' made in Europe, the Americas, and Africa over a long period.[5] By 1700 this process resulted in the creation of the slave plantation, which Trevor Burnard characterises as 'the most advanced form of capitalism of the eighteenth century'.[6] The development of the slave plantation over the course of the seventeenth century has increasingly been understood in relation to modern capitalistic methods of operation and organisation. Marcel van der Linden has drawn attention to the fact that on Barbadian plantations in the seventeenth century, 'The sugar planter was simultaneously a farmer and a manufacturer' running a large enterprise with hundreds of slaves to be fed, clothed, and managed in their work.[7] This was the general case across the Americas, although there were, of course, substantial differences in

[1] Richard S. Dunn, *Sugar and Slaves: The Rise of the Planter Class in the English West Indies, 1624–1713* (Chapel Hill, 1972), pp. 19–23, 149–53, 161–3.
[2] David Eltis, 'New Estimates of Exports from Barbados and Jamaica, 1665–1701', *William and Mary Quarterly*, 3rd ser., 52 (1995), 631–48, at p. 631; Dunn, *Sugar*, pp. 59–120; Larry Gragg, *Englishmen Transplanted: The English Colonization of Barbados, 1627–1660* (Oxford; New York, 2003), pp. 88–112.
[3] Richard B. Sheridan, *Sugar and Slavery: An Economic History of the British West Indies, 1623–1775* (Kingston, 1994), p. 124; Philip D. Morgan, *Slave Counterpoint: Black Culture in the Eighteenth-Century Chesapeake and Lowcountry* (Chapel Hill, London, 1998); Stuart B. Schwartz, *Sugar Plantations in the Formation of Brazilian Society: Bahia, 1550–1835* (Cambridge, 1985).
[4] Jordan Goodman, *Tobacco in History: The Cultures of Dependence* (London; New York, 1993), pp. 59–67; Sidney Mintz, *Sweetness and Power: The Place of Sugar in Modern History* (New York, 1985), pp. 37–8, 74–150.
[5] David Brion Davis, *Slavery and Human Progress* (New York, 1984), p. 61. For an excellent discussion of this, see Seymour Drescher, 'White Atlantic? The Choice for African Slave Labour in the Plantation Americas', in David Eltis, Frank D. Lewis, and Kenneth L. Sokoloff (eds), *Slavery in the Development of the Americas* (New York; Cambridge, 2004), pp. 31–69.
[6] Trevor Burnard, 'West Indian Identity in the Eighteenth Century', in Morris and Garrigus (eds), *Assumed*, 71–88, at p. 72.
[7] Marcel van der Linden, 'Reconstructing the origins of modern labour management', *Labour History*, 51 (2010), 509–22, at p. 512.

the various local economic systems that developed in English/British North America and the West Indies. These differences are not rehearsed here since the similarities between the two areas are more relevant to this discussion. The first similarity is that the planters of the Americas initially found their labour force using indentured servants, drawn from the poor, along with criminals, and prisoners from civil wars, and shifted gradually to the use of enslaved Africans to provide the requisite labourers.[8] The second is that in the same period as this shift in labour use occurred, so a set of ideas about those enslaved Africans was developed that used a newly constructed idea of race as the crucial point of social demarcation.

While an ocean separated Norfolk and Suffolk from the Americas, that ocean did not form an impenetrable barrier to the consequences of the slave-plantation economy that developed from 1600 onwards. As Malcolm Gaskill and Susan Amussen have shown, the colonies and England were not separate worlds, but a single, dynamic system.[9] Throughout the seventeenth century, the trans-atlantic connections between Old and New Worlds grew and strengthened. These links were a key element in the story of the African population that unfolded in Norfolk and Suffolk from 1600 onwards. Ships from the region were sailing to both mainland America and the West Indies from early in the seventeenth century.[10] In an age when the spectre of abject poverty and a pauper's death stood at nearly everyone's shoulder, the transatlantic world offered a high-risk opportunity for economic advancement to people willing, or forced by necessity, to take the chance. A few succeeded. Many others did not. In examining these links, the way the riches offered by the emerging world of slavery could ensnare all manner of people from Norfolk and Suffolk becomes clear, as does the fashion in which that process impacted upon the lives of the Africans who lived there after 1600. As the associations that developed between Norfolk and Suffolk and the English colonies in America and the West Indies in the seventeenth century strengthened and matured, they formed a conduit through which Africans would find themselves arriving in the two counties, and

---

[8] David Eltis, *The Rise of African Slavery in the Americas* (Cambridge, 2000), pp. 1–84; Seymour Drescher, 'Free Labour versus Slave Labour, The British and Caribbean Cases', in Stanley L. Engerman (ed.), *Terms of Labour: Slavery, Serfdom, and Free Labour* (Stanford, CA, 1999), pp. 50–86. The English use of African slaves was derivative of the practice in the Spanish and Portuguese empires. When Portuguese and Spanish merchants established sugar plantations off the African coast, on islands such as São Thomé and Principe, it was to enslaved African labour that they turned to provide a workforce; Greenfield, 'Madeira', pp. 536–52. The numbers of enslaved Africans on European plantations in the Americas grew. By 1650, some 200,000 Africans had been taken to Portuguese Brazil, and perhaps 268,000 to the Spanish colonies of South America, Blackburn, *The Making*, pp. 142–4, 168.

[9] Susan Dwyer Amussen, *Caribbean Exchanges: Slavery and the Transformation of English Society, 1640–1700* (Chapel Hill, 2007), esp. pp. 126–9, for discussion of how labour practices were affected by labour shortages; Malcolm Gaskill, *Between Two Worlds: How the English Became Americans* (Oxford, 2014).

[10] PRO/E/190/493/5: Yarmouth Port Book, Overseas 1661/2.

through which the ideas and customs surrounding emergent chattel slavery in the Americas could slowly influence the social relations affecting Africans in Norfolk and Suffolk.[11]

The Establishment of Transatlantic Connections

There were many ways in which the links between Norfolk, Suffolk, and the new colonies developed in the seventeenth century. One core area was the mercantile economy. As business opportunities opened in the New World, adventurers and merchants from the region saw the occasion for trade to be developed. At the forefront of these movements were men such as John Rolfe, whose merchant family hailed from Heacham and Lynn.[12] As we have seen, the Rolfes were an established merchant family, and while little is known of Rolfe's life in Norfolk, he was one of the early colonists of English North America, leaving for Virginia in 1609 on the *Sea Venture*, the flagship of several vessels carrying settlers, provisions, and the first group of government officials to the new colony at Jamestown. Over the next decade Rolfe would become a prominent citizen in the colony, with a major role in the creation of the tobacco industry, before his death in 1622.[13] Rolfe was followed by many other merchants, such as Richard Bartholomew, a merchant who travelled to Massachusetts in 1637 and whose brothers Henry and William were also merchants in the colony. Bartholomew returned to England in 1645 before setting off for America again in 1646. Thomas Bell came from Bury St Edmunds and set up a substantial trading operation between Massachusetts, England, and Barbados, travelling back to

---

[11] For good discussions of the economic importance of slavery and the British economy, see Williams, *Capitalism*; James A. Rawley, Stephen D. Behrendt, *The Transatlantic Slave Trade: A History* (Lincoln, NE; London, 2005), pp. 1–7; Daron Acemoglu, Simon Johnson, and James Robinson, 'The Rise of Europe: Atlantic Trade, Institutional Change, and Economic Growth', *National Bureau of Economic Research Working Paper Series* No. 9378 (2002); William Darity, Jr., 'British Industry and the West Indies Plantations', *Social Science History*, 14 (1990), 117–49; Joseph E. Inikori, 'Slavery and the Development of Industrial Capitalism in England', in *British Capitalism*, pp. 79–101; Joseph E. Inikori, *Africans and the Industrial Revolution in England* (Cambridge, 2002); David Eltis and Stanley L. Engerman, 'The Importance of Slavery and the Slave Trade to Industrializing Britain', *The Journal of Economic History*, 60 (2000), 123–44.

[12] R. Tilton, 'Rolfe, John (1585–1622), colonist and entrepreneur', *ODNB* https://www.oxforddnb.com/view/10.1093/ref:odnb/9780198614128.001.0001/odnb-9780198614128-e-24018 [accessed 6 February 2019].

[13] 'The Ancestors and Descendants of John Rolfe', (1913), pp. 105–6; 'The Ancestors and Descendants of John Rolfe with Notices of Some Connected Families (Continued)', *The Virginia Magazine of History and Biography*, 21 (1913), pp. 208–11 <http://www.jstor.org/stable/4243266>; Jane Carson, 'The Will of John Rolfe', *The Virginia Magazine of History and Biography*, 58 (1950), 58–65.

England at least three times in the period.[14] John Gedney, the forebear of the Gedney-Clarke family of Salem, Massachusetts, was born in Norwich in 1609 and sailed from Yarmouth to New England in 1637 with his wife, three children, and two servants. Described as a Norwich weaver in the passenger list, Gedney founded a dynasty that would mix trade and plantation ownership with public and military service in the colonies, first in Salem, and then across the eastern seaboard and the West Indies.[15]

Other local merchants were involved in the trade with the Americas, such as the Doughty family who owned the manor of Hanworth, a village some forty miles east of King's Lynn.[16] The family were not shipowners but were involved in foreign trade via King's Lynn. For example, between 1604 and 1614, they imported fourteen shipments of goods, including Spanish salt and wine as well as cheese, hops, figs, and onions, mainly from the Netherlands, using chartered Dutch and Scottish vessels.[17] In 1661, William Doughty noted that he was 'forthwith to pass beyond the seas towards Virginia or some other parts of America'.[18] Doughty was aiming to carry out a lengthy trading mission of a few years, taking with him 'divers goods wares merchandise and ready money to the value of one hundred pounds of lawful English money to trade and traffick with or for the same'.[19] The family's willingness to risk a substantial amount of capital in a commercial venture to the Americas suggests that they had knowledge of the area, which had presumably come from previous commercial connections with the colonies. This knowledge was augmented by familial intelligence via John Thurlow, who had journeyed to North Africa and the Americas before settling in Burnham Ulph, near the Doughtys' home, and marrying William's sister, Lydia, in the 1660s.[20]

Another local merchant was Samuel Davis of Yarmouth, who wrote to Thomas Pengelly in 1671, in respect of 'your advice as for Barbadoes'. Pengelly was a wealthy London merchant, who traded to the eastern Mediterranean

---

[14] Susan Hardman Moore, *Abandoning America: Life-stories from early New England* (Woodbridge, 2013), pp. 47-8.

[15] England Births & Baptisms 1538-1975, John Gedney, Baptism 24 January 1609, Norwich, Norfolk; Henry Fitzgilbert Waters, 'The Gedney and Clarke Families of Salem, Massachusetts', *Essex Institute Historical Collections*, 16 (1879), p. 242, <https://archive.org/details/essexinstitutehiv16esse/page/242/mode/2up?q=gedney>; for more on the Gedney-Clarkes, see S.D. Smith, 'Gedney Clarke of Salem and Barbados: Transatlantic Super-Merchant', *The New England Quarterly*, 76 (2003), 499-549, and S.D. Smith, *Slavery, Family, and Gentry Capitalism in the British Atlantic: The World of the Lascelles, 1648-1834* (Cambridge, 2006), pp. 97-9.

[16] James M. Rosenheim, 'Robert Doughty of Hanworth: A Restoration Magistrate', *Norfolk Archaeology*, 38 (1983), 296-9.

[17] Metters, *Rulers*, p. 184.

[18] Rosenheim, 'Robert', pp. 296-9; NRO/AYL/201, Will of William Doughty, c. 1661.

[19] NRO/AYL/201, Will of William Doughty, c. 1661.

[20] John Debrett, *Debrett's Peerage of England, Scotland, and Ireland* (1820), p. 538.

and the Atlantic seaboard, including Barbados.[21] Davis was one of his two main business partners in Norfolk; the other was another Yarmouth merchant, George Harper. The three men were involved in various ventures, trading to Venice, sending cloth to southern Spain, and trading shoes in return for beaver and tobacco in Virginia and for sugar in Barbados.[22] Examples such as that of Davis, Harper, and Doughty make it clear that Norfolk and Suffolk merchants were actively involved in a web of trading connections that created the opportunity for them to trade with, travel to, and profit from, areas of the globe where enslaved Africans were slowly being integrated into economic systems.[23]

Others left for the colonies to seek religious freedom. The Puritan lawyer John Winthrop, who became the first governor of the Massachusetts Bay Colony, was from Groton Manor, Suffolk, and left England as the government of Charles I began to pressurise nonconformists from 1629 onwards. Winthrop would be involved in the politics of the colony until his death in 1649.[24] He was joined by many other dissenters from the region. The Hobart family and their allies in Hingham, Massachusetts, were originally from the Norfolk parishes of Hingham and Wymondham, south of Norwich.[25] Between 1633 and 1638, at least 175 people from these parishes sailed to America, many from Ipswich on one ship, the *Diligent*, under the leadership of a dissenting minister, Robert Peck, and the Hobarts.[26] In addition to large-scale migrations such as that from Hingham, there were many individual dissenters from the region making the voyage. Nicholas Busby, a worsted weaver from Norwich, was examined for dissent at Ipswich, Suffolk, on 8 April 1637, and then sailed from Great Yarmouth for New England, along with his family.[27] Other dissenters arrived in the colonies through forcible transportation. In July 1665, Edmond Durrant, Edmond Sconce, and Nicholas Riseton appeared at the Norfolk Quarter Sessions, for a third offence of being present at a conventicle held at Wood Norton. Although Robert Longe, the Justice of the Peace, refused to pronounce judgement on the three, claiming grounds of conscience for his refusal, a warrant was issued for

---

[21] D. Lemmings, 'Pengelly, Sir Thomas (1675–1730), judge', *ODNB* <https://www.oxforddnb. com/view/10.1093/ref:odnb/9780198614128.001.0001/odnb-9780198614128-e-21837> [accessed 15 November 2019].

[22] Gaskill, *Between*, p. 241.

[23] NRO/MC/757/3/793x4, Davis to Pengelly, 21 Aug 1671; NRO/MC/484/2/747x7, Davis to Pengelly, 26 December 1673.

[24] W. Woodward, 'Winthrop, John (1606–1676), colonial governor and physician', *ODNB* <https://www.oxforddnb.com/view/10.1093/ref:odnb/9780198614128.001.0001/ odnb-9780198614128-e-29779> [accessed 19 October 2019].

[25] Francis J. Bremer, *John Winthrop: America's Forgotten Founding Father* (Oxford, 2005), pp. 360–2.

[26] Moore, *Abandoning*, pp. 232–4; Solomon Lincoln, *An Address Delivered Before the Citizens of the Town of Hingham: On the Twenty-eighth of September, 1835, Being the Two Hundredth Anniversary of the Settlement of the Town* (Hingham, MA, 1835) <https://archive.org/details/ addressdelivered1835linc> [accessed 3 February 2019].

[27] Moore, *Abandoning*, p. 72.

their transportation to Jamaica for seven years. Sconce and Riseton, it appears, were sent to King's Lynn to be shipped to the colonies, but 'finding no shipping ready were committed to gaol'. It appears that they were released later that year, but only after their families had been 'destroyed for want'. Durrant's fate is unknown, and it may be that he was sent to another port and shipped to the West Indies to labour on a plantation alongside the enslaved Africans who were beginning to dominate its labour force by this date.[28]

The region's migrants were also connected with the early stirrings of the slave plantations. William Doughty had stated his aim to be Virginia, but eventually he spent '11 years in the Island of Barbados besides other parts of the world'.[29] His letters suggest that he was able to rely on a network of Norfolk and Suffolk connections while on the island. In 1667 Doughty wrote that he had 'gained a small employment at the Silvester Plantation' and later stated that he was joined there by 'Richard Scott, a Norwich man'.[30] This would seem to have been one of two sugar plantations owned in partnership by the brothers Nathaniel and Constant Sylvester, whose mother, Mary Arnold, was originally from Suffolk.[31] The Sylvesters were major landholders on the island, with estates listed in 1679 as being 500 acres in size and staffed by '10 white servants, 220 negroes' in the parish of St George, and another of 180 acres in Christchurch worked by one non-African servant and forty Africans.[32]

The Sylvesters were not the only slaveowners on seventeenth-century Barbados with connections to Norfolk and Suffolk. Some of the most successful early settlers were members of the Frere family from Occold, Suffolk. Six Frere brothers emigrated to Barbados from 1640 to 1670 and established themselves as merchants, attorneys, and planters. Their three sisters also went to the colony and married established planters, enhancing the family's wealth. The Freres were deeply involved in the early construction of the slaving economy on the island. The 1679 census shows Tobias Frere owned land totalling 180 acres and

[28] For a good discussion of the role of indentured servants in the West Indies in this period, see Hilary McD. Beckles, 'Plantation Production and White "Proto-Slavery": White Indentured Servants and the Colonisation of the English West Indies, 1624–1645', *The Americas*, 41 (1985), 21–45. For an explanation of the differences between indentured servants and enslaved Africans, see Jerome S. Handler and Matthew C. Reilly, 'Contesting "White Slavery" in the Caribbean: Enslaved Africans and European Indentured Servants in Seventeenth-Century Barbados', *New West Indian Guide*, 91 (2017), 30–55. For the differences between English bound service and colonial unfree labour, see Amussen, *Caribbean*, pp. 107–44.
[29] NRO/AYL/535/6/2, Letter, 1667; John Chambers, *A General History of the County of Norfolk: Intended to Convey All the Information of a Norfolk Tour* (Norwich, 1829), p. 164.
[30] NRO/AYL/535/6/3, Letter, 20 December 1667, and NRO/AYL/535/6/5, Letter, 25 May 1668.
[31] Henry B. Hoff, 'The Sylvester Family of Shelter Island', *The New York Genealogical and Biographical Record*, 125 (1994).
[32] From John C. Hotten, *The Original Lists of Persons of Quality 1600–1700* (1874), pp. 461 and 475.

eighty slaves in Christchurch, while his younger brother John Frere owned 395 acres and 180 slaves in the same parish, along with another 209 acres and eighty slaves in St Philip's Parish.[33] Their brother William owned 180 acres and eighty slaves.[34] As other islands were planted in the West Indies, so migrants from Norfolk and Suffolk found themselves at the heart of the new slaving cultures being created there also. The island of Nevis, which had been settled by English colonists in the late 1620s, was home to Thomas Carter, who was 'late of ye Citie of Norwich. Planter at ye Island Neavis'. Carter arrived in London in 1656 having been captured by the Spanish and taken to Spain before escaping and catching a Dutch ship to Texel. Carter declared his intention was to 'returne to ye West Indies soe soone as he shall finde opportunitie'.[35]

Aside from the merchants, adventurers, and dissenters, the greatest number of those from Norfolk and Suffolk who crossed the Atlantic were the working poor, who could sell their labour, and risk their lives, trying to gain an economic foothold in the colonies. Between 1520 and 1630, England's population rose dramatically, from 2.3 to 4.8 million. This rise created economic pressures, such as rising prices and declining real wages which, allied with changing economic practices resulting from the advent of agrarian capitalism, created unemployment, poverty, and vagrancy. This population pressure contributed to the emigration of over 700,000 English people, over half of which would go to the Americas, in an exodus that peaked between 1630 and 1660.[36] One means by which many of these migrants sought a new life was the system of indentured servitude, by which a person would agree to service for four to five years in return for the cost of their passage, board, lodging, and various freedom dues. Such indentured servants provided an integral element of the early colonial workforce.[37] One of the most successful men who chose this route was Adam

[33] Smith, *Slavery*, pp. 213–14.

[34] Hotten, *The Original*, p. 475.

[35] Vere Langford Oliver (ed.), *Caribbeana: being miscellaneous papers relating to the history, genealogy, topography, and antiquities of the British West Indies* (London, 1914), p. 298.

[36] Eltis, *The Rise*, pp. 37–8; David Eltis, 'Coerced and Free Migrations from the Old World to the New', in David Eltis (ed.), *Coerced and Free Migration: Global Perspectives* (Stanford, CA, 2002), pp. 33–74; James Horn, *Adapting to a New World: English Society in the Seventeenth-Century Chesapeake* (Chapel Hill; London, 1994), chapters 1 and 2; Nicholas Canny, 'English Migration into and across the Atlantic during the Seventeenth and Eighteenth Centuries', in Nicholas Canny (ed.), *Europeans on the Move: Studies on European Migration, 1500–1800* (Oxford and New York, 1994), pp. 39–75; Carl Bridenbaugh, *Vexed and Troubled Englishmen, 1590–1660* (Oxford, 1968), pp. 21–5.

[37] Russell R. Menard, *Sweet Negotiations: Sugar, Slavery, and Plantation Agriculture in Early Barbados* (Charlottesville; London, 2006), p. 36; Don Jordan and Michael Walsh, *White Cargo: The Forgotten History of Britain's White Slaves in America* (New York, 2007); John Donoghue, '"Out of the Land of Bondage": The English Revolution and the Atlantic Origins of Abolition', *American Historical Review*, 115 (2010), 943–74. For discussions of how the treatment of these indentured servants related to the creation of slavery, see Carla Gardina Pestana, *The English Atlantic in an Age of Revolution, 1640–1661* (Cambridge, MA; London,

Thoroughgood, who was baptised at St Botolph's Church in Grimston, near King's Lynn, on 14 July 1604. Around 1622 he paid for his passage to the Virginia colony by becoming an indentured servant and settled in an area south of the Chesapeake Bay. Thoroughgood returned to England in 1627, to marry Sarah Offley, the daughter of a successful London merchant, before sailing back to the colonies. Eventually he was granted a large landholding and became a leading citizen of the colony.[38]

Thoroughgood was only one of many from Norfolk and Suffolk who would tread this path throughout the century, in both English/British North America and the West Indies, with varying degrees of success. In 1683, Mary Baker sailed from Yarmouth to Maryland to work for a planter named Henry Hawkins for four years. She was joined by Robert Clay from Norwich, who was 'bound to Thomas Tench for 4 years', as was Daniel Rust of Norwich a year later. In the 1680s, Robert Day, a Norwich weaver, travelled to Virginia, to work for a merchant called John Burroughs. Other migrants included Mary Foster, Martha Shrimpson, and Mary Daykins of Norwich. Still more members of the working poor from the region went to the West Indies. The labourer Richard Ellgood travelled from Norfolk to Jamaica to work for a planter named John Pye in 1684. He was joined by John Payne and Thomas Rust, who went to work as indentured servants on the same island for seven and four years respectively. In 1684, a Norfolk man called Joshua Cross travelled to Barbados to work for Samuel Hanson; he was followed a year later by another Norfolk man, John Gravell, who went to work for Francis Hanson.[39]

Hilary Beckles has argued convincingly that the input of these indentured servants was integral to the initial success of the colonies in the 1600s.[40] Along with other historians, he has shown that these indentured servants found themselves in a situation of brutal exploitation, where a seven-year term of service was the norm, and where such terms were often varied, without any means of appeal. This system was supported by a structure of enforcement that resorted to vicious physical punishment, ranging from having ears nailed to the pillory to the use of the lash.[41] The role this approach to indentured servitude had upon the creation of enslavement in the colonies will be returned to below.

2004), pp. 205-12. For discussions of Irish indentured servants, see Hilary Beckles, 'A "riotous and unruly lot": Irish Indentured Servants and Freemen in the English West Indies, 1644-1713', William and Mary Quarterly, 47 (1990), 503-22.

[38] William Henry Tappey Squires, Through Centuries Three: A Short History of the People of Virginia (Portsmouth, VA, 1929), pp. 134-6; Raymond L. Harper, A History of Chesapeake, Virginia (Charleston, 2008), p. 101.

[39] All in Michael Ghirelli, A List of Emigrants from England to America, 1682-1692 (Baltimore, 1989), pp. 28-75. The St George parish registers of 1679 state that 'Mr Samuel Hanson' owned fifty-seven acres of land, had six white servants, and owned 105 enslaved Africans, Hotten, Original, p. 461.

[40] Beckles, 'Plantation', pp. 21-45.

[41] Gragg, Barbados, pp. 127-9; Edmund S. Morgan, American Slavery, American Freedom: The Ordeal of Colonial Virginia (New York, 1975), pp. 73-90.

As the examples of Carter and Thoroughgood show, this flow of humanity was not one way. A steady stream of people also returned from the colonies to Norfolk and Suffolk throughout the century. Some were merchants, such as Doughty, who had never intended to settle abroad permanently. Others were migrants who had decided that the life in the colonies was not to their liking. Moore has identified hundreds of these returning migrants, including Thomas Parish, who left Nayland, Suffolk, in 1635 and settled in Massachusetts. He returned to England in 1638-9 to sell some property, and then returned permanently in 1640, settling back in his home village.[42] Similarly, Clement Chaplin was a chandler in Bury St Edmunds who travelled to Massachusetts in 1635, where he lived until he returned to settle in Norfolk in the mid-1650s.[43] Dissenting clergy also returned from the colonies; for example, Robert Peck, who had led the mass exodus from Hingham in the 1630s, returned in 1641 at 'the Invitation of his Friends at Hingham in England' and took up his ministry in the parish once again.[44] The continuous flow of movement of people, of all backgrounds, created a web of connections that provided the means for Africans, and ideas about them, to be transferred across the ocean.

Colonial Ideas About the Enslavement of Africans

Africans appeared early in the story of the New World colonies. In Virginia, the earliest recorded landing of Africans was in August 1619, when Governor George Yeardley and his head of trade, Abraham Piersey, purchased '20. and odd Negroes' from the English privateer ships, the *White Lion* and the *Treasurer*.[45] The Africans had been exported originally from Angola on a Portuguese slave ship called the *São João Bautista* which was then intercepted by the English privateers.[46] It was the Norfolk-born John Rolfe who wrote about this incident to Sir Edwin Sandys.[47] The arrival of these Africans was not, however, part of

---

[42] Moore, *Abandoning*, pp. 227-8.

[43] Ibid, pp. 76-7.

[44] Ibid, p. 234.

[45] As Hacker has recently pointed out, the African presence in English North America may have predated the arrival of the *White Lion*. A census of Virginia in March 1619 counted thirty-two individuals of African descent. See William Thorndale, 'The Virginia Census of 1619', *Magazine of Virginia Genealogy*, 33 (1995), 155-70; and John Thornton, 'The African Experience of the "20. and Odd Negroes" Arriving in Virginia in 1619', *William and Mary Quarterly*, 55, no. 3 (1998), 421-34; mentioned in J. David Hacker, 'From "20. and odd" to 10 million: the growth of the slave population in the United States', *Slavery & Abolition* (2020), DOI: 10.1080/0144039X.2020.1755502.

[46] Engel Sluiter, 'New Light on the "20. and Odd Negroes" Arriving in Virginia, August 1619', *William and Mary Quarterly*, 54 (1997), pp. 396-8.

[47] See Susan Myra Kingsbury (ed.), *The Records of The Virginia Company of London*, III (Washington, 1933), p. 243; <https://archive.org/details/recordsofvirgini03virg/page/242/mode/2up?q=rolfe>.

a wider plan by the English to build colonies in the Americas founded on the use of enslaved Africans. Their capture by the English privateers was a matter of chance. The colonies were planned to be built using indentured English labour.[48] The same was true of Barbados, which was first settled in 1627, with the first ten Africans arriving on the island in that same year. They had been enslaved on a Portuguese ship and then acquired by the English colonists, but African slaves were not the planned labour force for Barbados; once again this was to be indentured servants. The exact nature of the Africans' position among the Barbadian colonists remains a matter of considerable debate, and it is not clear that they were immediately enslaved.[49] The development of the island's economy took time and did not begin with sugar production; rather it began with tobacco, indigo, and cotton, and it was only after economic crises made these unprofitable that planters turned to sugar production and eventually to African slavery.[50] Gradually, however, Barbados would go on to become the first powerhouse of the English/British slaving economy. Between 1627 and 1700 some 236,725 enslaved Africans were taken there.[51]

Within the network of connections that grew between Norfolk and Suffolk and the colonies after 1600, the potential was created for ideas to be transferred as well as goods and people. The question that will be pursued next is what evidence there is of such a transfer of ideas concerning the enslavement of Africans in the colonies, and in which direction any transfer took place. Did ideas about the enslavement of Africans, and the supporting racialised framework of thinking about Africans, come from England to the colonies, or was the process the other way around? The starting point is the argument made previously that it is difficult to distinguish a set of ideas about Africans in Norfolk and Suffolk before 1600 that offers an obvious basis for the colonial ideas that were developed. The next move is to seek to understand how that can be related to the work that has been done on the construction of ideas about the enslavement of Africans in the Americas.

The problem in discussing the appearance of the enslavement of Africans in the Americas is that, as Bush states, 'we really do not know that these first blacks, or any other blacks brought to Virginia in the first half century, were "slaves" as that term was understood.'[52] The same is true for Barbados and the other colonies. Even the exact meaning of the terms such as 'indentured servant' or the, apparently obvious, term 'servant' when used in relation to Africans is

[48] Heywood and Thornton, 'In Search', p. 204.

[49] See Handler, 'Custom', pp. 233-4; Carolyn Arena, 'Indian Slaves from Guiana in Seventeenth-Century Barbados', *Ethnohistory*, 64 (2017), 65-90, at p. 75.

[50] For a clear description of this process see Menard, *Sweet*, pp. 1-47.

[51] For the history of Barbados, see Hilary Beckles, *A History of Barbados: From Amerindian Settlement to Caribbean Single Market* (Cambridge, 2006). The numbers were taken from *Voyages: The Transatlantic Slave Trade Database*, http://www.slavevoyages.org/tast/assessment/estimates.faces, accessed 2 August 2011.

[52] Bush, 'The First', p. 602.

difficult to determine. Some historians have suggested that, as Coombs puts it, 'the *default* status for people of solely African descent, whether foreign or native-born, was life-time, hereditary bondage' from the earliest period of colonial expansion, and that this was because 'encounters with Africans' in the sixteenth century meant that a 'negative perception of "Negroes"' dominated English views of Africans.[53] A related idea is suggested by Guasco, who points to existing English views of race as the foundations of his argument that the first African captives were seen as slaves rather than servants. In this approach, the lack of use of the term 'slave' in early seventeenth-century Virginia is evidence of a 'conscious strategy to remain circumspect on the matter' rather than evidence of non-enslavement.[54]

The issue is similar in looking at the West Indies. While the date of arrival of the first Africans in Barbados is known, 1627, the status of these first Africans is not understood with any certainty. Historians are not even sure of the date that the first law enslaving Africans on the island was passed. Handler has recently suggested that the status of Africans as enslaved was decided almost from the first settlement of the island and predated any written law because English customs at the time of the island's settlement had decided these issues already. He argues that the three core ideas necessary for the enslavement of Africans to happen in the colonies were that they were 'considered chattel property, but also a property that would serve in perpetuity and whose descendants would be enslaved if their mothers were slaves'. Handler feels that these ideas 'developed out of widely accepted ideologies about slavery in the Euro-Atlantic world', which he sees as the notion that 'slaves were private property', that the slave-owner had absolute authority, and an assumption of African inferiority.[55]

The evidence from sixteenth-century Norfolk and Suffolk suggests that Handler's proposals have support in relation to ideas about slavery and property, but not in relation to the existence of norms about the inferiority of Africans and their enslavement. As has been shown, the population of Norfolk and Suffolk understood the concept of slavery and accepted its existence. Indeed, the region's working people, as represented by the 1549 rebels, understood their social position partially with reference to it – as free-born Englishmen they were not 'bonde men'. These ideas continued in the seventeenth century, when, as Amussen succinctly puts it, 'slavery was a metaphor frequently used as the antithesis of freedom to condemn the illegitimate use of power'.[56] This

---

[53] John C. Coombs, 'Others Not Christians in the Service of the English', *The Virginia Magazine of History and Biography*, 127 (2019), 212–38, at pp. 216, 229–30.

[54] Guasco, *Slaves*, pp. 204–6. For an explication of the earlier development of this discussion, see Alden T. Vaughan, 'The Origins Debate: Slavery and Racism in Seventeenth-Century Virginia', in Alden T. Vaughan, *Roots of American Racism* (New York, 1995), pp. 136–74.

[55] Handler, 'Custom', pp. 234–6.

[56] Amussen, *Caribbean*, p. 19. For the use of the concept of slavery in the period of the English revolution, see Christopher Hill, 'The Norman Yoke', in Christopher Hill (ed.), *Puritanism and Revolution: Studies in Interpretation of the English Revolution of the Seventeenth*

local evidence also suggests that Norfolk and Suffolk's population understood common-law property relations and accepted that these meant that people could be owned in certain circumstances. This supports part of Handler's argument rather well. On the other hand, as we have seen, there is no evidence from Norfolk and Suffolk that Africans were considered as inferior because of their skin colour, and no evidence of such ideas about inferiority causing connections to be drawn between skin colour and enslavement.

In the absence of these latter ideas being apparent in Norfolk and Suffolk in the period when the seventeenth-century colonies were being formed, it is possible to look towards the 'gradualist' approach that has been suggested by many historians, who point to the slow shift from a beginning position in 1619 where 'no law yet enshrined African slavery in either Maryland or Virginia, and the laws that referred to Africans were scattered and miscellaneous' to a later position where 'race' became central.[57] It was only in 1656 that the General Assembly passed legislation that appears to have acknowledged that slaves existed in Virginia. There was then a further slow accumulation of laws passed between 1660 and 1705 that led finally to a situation where Africans became legally enslaved.[58] Building on this, historians such as Heywood and Thornton have argued for a trajectory of development in racial ideology. They argue that, while Africans were held in forms of bondage from an early point in colonial history, the exact meaning of this concept was in the process of being defined throughout the century. This process of definition took time and meant both that 'the word slave did not have a fixed legal meaning of life-long, inheritable servitude' until later in the seventeenth century, and that it was not connected necessarily with race until a later point.[59] The example of Norfolk and Suffolk supports this approach and suggests that enslavement did not have a set meaning in the early history of the colonies because it did not have a set meaning in the

---

Century (London, 1969); Christopher Hill, The World Turned Upside Down: Radical Ideas During the English Revolution (Harmondsworth, 1975); David Underdown, A Freeborn People: Politics and the Nation in Seventeenth-Century England (New York, 1996); Betty Wood, 'Freedom and Bondage in English Thought', in Betty Wood, The Origins of American Slavery: Freedom and Bondage in the English Colonies (New York, 1998), pp. 9–19.

[57] Berlin, Many, 32. For discussion, see T.H. Breen and Stephen Innes, "Myne Owne Ground": Race and Freedom on Virginia's Eastern Shore, 1640–1676 (New York; Oxford, 1980), and Linda M. Heywood and John K. Thornton, Central Africans, Atlantic Creoles, and the Foundation of the Americas, 1585–1660 (Cambridge; New York, 2007); Thornton, 'The African', 421–34; Sluiter, 'New', 395–8.

[58] For varying views on whether this was intentional or unintentional, see Jordan, White, pp. 71–82; Christopher Tomlins, Freedom Bound: Law, Labour, and Civic Identity in Colonizing English America, 1580–1865 (New York, 2010), pp. 453–65; Rebecca Anne Goetz, 'Rethinking the "Unthinking Decision": Old Questions and New Problems in the History of Slavery and Race in the Colonial South', Journal of Southern History, 75 (2009), 599–612; Anthony Parent, Foul Means: The Formation of a Slave Society in Virginia, 1660–1740 (Chapel Hill, 2003), pp. 105–34.

[59] Heywood and Thornton, Central, pp. 312–23.

places that colonists came from. The same is true for responses to Africans themselves. Reactions to them in the colonies were variable because that had been true in the English towns and villages from which colonists hailed.

This situation can also be seen in the way the terms 'black' and 'white' evolved in the colonies. Menard has argued that the distinction between 'black' and 'white' was a late seventeenth-century development and that early legislation in English/British North America placed far more distinction between 'Christians' and 'negroes'. He suggests that the earliest reference to 'whiteness' in this context can be found in a George Fox tract of 1672 ('To the Ministers, Teachers and Priests'). The relatively late appearance of the idea of 'whiteness' is supported by a comment made by Morgan Godwyn in 1680, when he told his readers that white 'was the general name for Europeans'.[60] Grant has also noted that the first census of South Carolina, in 1708, did not prioritise a 'racialized phenotype' but divided the population along various grounds; age (child/adult), legal status (free/servant/slave), phenotype (white/Negro/Indian), and adults divided by sex (men/women). For Grant, 'This multiplicity of divisions betrayed the inchoate and relatively unstable status of "white" identity at this point.'[61]

Once again, this seems to find support in the proposal that the discernible response to Africans in fifteenth- and sixteenth-century Norfolk and Suffolk was one where skin colour was not particularly significant, but religion was. As has been discussed in Chapter One, the term 'black' (as opposed to 'blackamore') appeared in the registers only from the mid-seventeenth century, when a boy at Holkham was described as 'ye black boy'.[62] If we accept the proposal that this alteration in terminology was significant, and reflected the appearance in Norfolk and Suffolk from the mid-seventeenth century of ideas that considered the colour of a person's skin as the primary determinant of their social position, this seems to support the notion that there was a lack of any stable sense of 'white' identity in Norfolk and Suffolk before the appearance of the colonial slave plantations and the development of ideas about Africans in those locales.

Menard's view is that existing ideas about Africans were altered by planters to cement their economic position. Planters shifted from the focus on Christian/non-Christian because the use of this dichotomy did not protect their economic position; an African could become Christian, and so potentially become free, whereas an African could not become 'white'.[63] If the condition of enslavement

---

[60] Menard, *Sweet*, p. 119. For a meticulous explanation of the developments of these ideas, see Theodore Allen, *The Invention of the White Race* (London, 1997).

[61] Daragh Grant, '"Civilizing" the Colonial Subject: The Co-Evolution of State and Slavery in South Carolina, 1670-1739', *Comparative Studies in Society and History*, 57 (2015), 606-36, at p. 618. For more on the issue of Indian slavery, see Arena, 'Indian', esp. pp. 66-7; Juliana Barr, 'From Captives to Slaves: Commodifying Indian Women in the Borderlands', *Journal of American History*, 92 (2005), 19-46; Brett Rushforth, '"A Little Flesh We Offer You": The Origins of Indian Slavery in New France', *William and Mary Quarterly*, 60 (2003), 777-808.

[62] HA/F/JC(Y) 23, 25, 57, all 1662.

[63] Menard, *Sweet*, p. 119. For other similar views, see Morgan, *American*, pp. 295-337;

became conflated with African heritage, then the planters' investment in human capital was protected. The colonial context allowed for such redefinitions to occur, and economic relations required this to happen. Goetz has shown that there was a redefinition of the distinction between Christian and non-Christian, which had the effect of closing the baptismal loophole in racialised thought. Colonial society changed, therefore, long-standing English practice in baptism, and shifted it in a racialised direction, which became bound into the creation of ideas of 'black and white'.[64]

This process of economic and ideological change is revealed by recent work that has shown how existing English social customs around indentured labour were altered by the requirements of the new economic system. As has been said, many people from Norfolk and Suffolk set out to the colonies to become indentured servants, but the conditions that they found themselves working in, and the approach taken by their masters to them as indentured servants, did not reflect the ideas about indentured service to which they were accustomed in England. Donoghue has highlighted the way colonial authorities subverted traditional ideas of indentured service, for example by doubling the period of indenture if servants ran away, although this contravened both English statute and common law.[65] Beckles contends that the notion of using enslaved Africans took root because the planters in the West Indies had already changed existing ideas about indentured service in their drive to extract labour value from non-African servants. Planters developed a set of attitudes and working practices in relation to their indentured servants that replaced 'the moral-paternalistic ideology of pre-industrial England' with a form of 'proto-slavery'. The way indentured service was conceived and implemented changed so that indentured servants became seen as capital, as units of production, and planters came to hold a 'highly developed market view of labour'.[66] This redefinition of the social relations of production in relation to indentured servitude was not driven by ideas about racial difference, but by economic relations. These then set the foundations for the expansion of the use of enslaved Africans in the 1640s. The ideas about African 'difference' followed from this.

The process by which ideas that had existed in sixteenth-century England were gradually manipulated in the colonial context to relate to 'race' has also been highlighted by Grant. Looking at South Carolina from 1670 to 1739, Grant identifies that, by the turn of the eighteenth century, it was generally acknowledged by those involved in the Atlantic world 'at least in theory, that only those captured in a "just war" could lose their freedom'. Grant proposes that the colonial societies reframed this concept, which as has been shown already can

---

Blackburn, *The Making*, pp. 323–4.
[64] Rebecca Goetz, '"The Child Should Be Made a Christian": Baptism, Race, and Identity in the Seventeenth-Century Chesapeake', in Morris, *et al*, *Assumed*, pp. 46–70, at p. 47; Rebecca Anne Goetz, *The Baptism of Early Virginia: How Christianity Created Race* (Baltimore, 2012).
[65] Donoghue, 'Out', pp. 943–74.
[66] Beckles, 'Plantation', p. 23.

be seen in Norfolk and Suffolk's approaches to enslavement, and which had medieval roots exemplified in the 1259 incident involving the 'Ethiopian of the name of Bartholomew, sometime a Saracen'. These were altered to reflect a distinction Grant calls 'savage/civilised' in which 'those "savage" peoples who supposedly lived beyond the protection of laws could be freely enslaved'. Grant feels that it was this distinction that then allowed Africans and Native Americans to be systematically enslaved in English/British North America. It is significant that he links the development of these ideas in South Carolina with the ideas of John Locke, and the development of the 'power/authority' binary in the English Civil War, rather than traditional English customs and practices.[67] It was, therefore, the new Enlightenment ideas that were providing the basis for enslaving Africans, in association with the new slaveholding economy, rather than any traditional notions derived from English custom.

The evidence from colonists hailing from Norfolk and Suffolk chimes with this general thrust of interpretation. The ideas that they revealed about Africans in the colonial setting were fluid and imprecise. For example, Henry Winthrop, the second son of John Winthrop, was one of the earliest planters in Barbados, arriving around 1627. He attempted to start a tobacco plantation there, but this was unsuccessful, and he returned to England. In August 1627, he wrote to his father that there were 'here on this Iland of the weest Indyes called the Barbathes setled for a plantatyon for tobackow one which Iland here is but 3 score of christyanes and fortye slaues of negeres and Indyenes.'[68] Winthrop's discussion of the 'slaves' fits with the sixteenth-century views that were seen in Norfolk and Suffolk. He was accepting that the Africans and 'Indyenes' were enslaved, but an automatic connection between their status and their colour is not proven in this example. He did not contrast the Africans with 'white' people, but with 'christyanes', suggesting that his view of them was framed by the earlier idea that difference was dominated by religious affiliation. It seems that his understanding was delineated by the common-law notion of property and other older customary ideas which allowed him to accept that the Africans could be enslaved because that was the condition in which they had been encountered by the English; already enslaved on a Portuguese ship. This situation of previous enslavement by a foreign power, and the fact that they were captives, explains their continuing enslavement in Barbados, rather than an automatic assumption of enslaved status that had been attached to the concept of Africans.[69]

---

[67] Grant, 'Civilizing', p. 610. Grant points out that there was substantial divergence between Locke's ideas on slavery and its practice. He suggests that the key aspect was Locke's alteration of the 'power/authority' binary with three terms – force, power, and authority.

[68] Henry Winthrop, Letter to John Winthrop, 15 October 1627. Winthrop Papers (W. 1. 27; 5 Collections, VIII. 180–1.), Massachusetts Historical Society, Boston, http://www.masshist.org/publications/winthrop/index.php/view/PWF01d254., [accessed 1 June 2019].

[69] The lack of a 'black/white' distinction is also visible in his comment to Emmanuel Downing, that the island was 'without any inhabytanse of any other people of other natyones

The letters of William Doughty support this argument, since they also lack hardened ideas about Africans, enslavement, and race generally. Doughty did not discuss slavery as such, or the status of Africans *per se*. Alongside discussions about the many aspects of daily life, such as the fact that 'thread, buttons, shoes, stockings etc. are vendable here, etc', Doughty mentioned that there were 'negroes', but these were discussed in the same sentence as 'other Christian servants'. His understanding seemed, therefore, to be around the Christian/ heathen distinction, rather than a racial one. Doughty did not explain anything about enslavement or connect Africans directly with this condition. His letters instead treat the 'negroes' as another group of people within the island's population, pointing out that they had taken shelter with the other 'servants' in the Great Storm of 1668, for example.[70] Doughty was not openly conceiving of Africans as inferior, or somehow naturally deserving of enslavement. His discussion was one that reflected, in important ways, the approach to Africans that has been suggested previously, where their social status reflected the situation in which they were encountered. In Barbados, Doughty was engaging with the 'negroes' on the Sylvester plantation, who by this time numbered several hundred, but he was viewing them in the context that he encountered them, where they were already enslaved. It is important to note, however, that he was using a word to describe them that had not previously been used in Norfolk and Suffolk and would not be used again in the region until the 1720s, something that is suggestive of a change in view on Doughty's part. The context of his discussion points towards a situation where Africans held an indeterminate status in his mind, but this was being changed by his involvement in the newly emerging world of the slaveholding colony.

This seems to suggest that the ideas about Africans and enslavement that colonists brought to the Americas were variable and subject to change over time as the situation around them changed. This is not to deny that negative ideas may have existed before colonisation, but it does suggest that such ideas should not be seen to be the only way people from Norfolk and Suffolk thought about Africans and enslavement and that, at this point, these two things were often decoupled. The examples of joint action on behalf of the working settlers, namely servants and ex-servants, against the activity of planters in Barbados and Chesapeake in this era, tend to support this idea. For example, Bacon's Rebellion of 1676 was a multi-racial revolt of servants and ex-servants against the planters' attempts to increase the number of servants and their terms of service. It was, in turn, the culmination of a series of conflicts during the 1660s and

saue Inglishe men saue a matter of 50 slaues of Indyenes and blacks', Henry Winthrop, 'Letter to Emmanuel Downing, 22 August 1627'. Winthrop Papers (W. 1. 25; 5 Collections, VIII. 179–80.), <http://www.masshist.org/publications/winthrop/index.php/view/PWF01d249> [accessed 17 June 2019].

[70] NRO/AYL/535/6/5, Letter to Robert Doughty from William, at Constant Sylvester's Plantation, St George's Parish, Barbados, 25 May 1668.

1670s, which effectively ended the use of indentured labour in Chesapeake.[71] As Allen has shown, the solidarity between Africans and non-Africans in Chesapeake prevented the effective use of the notion of 'race' in Chesapeake for most of the seventeenth century.[72]

Such events are indicative of the effect that the variability of ideas in respect of Africans held by migrants from England, like Doughty, had upon the attempts by slaveholders to create societies structured by racialised constructs. While there was no direct parallel of rebellion in Barbados, Beckles has identified many examples of servant resistance on the island, from unsuccessful conspiracies to day-to-day conflict such as flight from the plantations, slowing work, theft, and arson.[73] Donoghue has developed this argument and suggests that contemporary accounts from the colonies 'construed "Christians," "negors," and "ingones" as laboring under various forms of colonial slavery'.[74] This common sense of enslavement among African and non-African workers would appear to be most convincingly explained in some sense of solidarity that transcended skin colour, and drew on earlier ideas of rights and customs as expressed in the ideas of the rebels in 1549.

It is also possible to incorporate Handler's suggestion about the importance of English notions of property in the development of African enslavement into this argument about the evolutionary change of existing custom and law in the colonial context. Handler builds on Morris' argument that English law provided the legal categories into which Africans as property could be placed and 'there was no need to adopt statutes to cover this; the common law of property already did, and it allowed wide authority to those who possessed property to use it as they pleased.' He suggests that this explains the 'likely genealogy' of the idea that enslavement was traced through matrilineal descent.[75] However, the very nature of English property law was being changed in this period in consequence of the alteration in the social relations of production being caused by the advent of English agrarian capitalism. The 'private' ownership of property had traditionally been conditioned by customary practices, giving non-owners certain use-rights to property 'owned' by someone else. The advent of agrarian capitalism had led to a process by which the concept of property was being shorn of these encumbrances.[76] The 1549 rebels were responding to these changes and challenging their implementation in areas such as land use. Such

---

[71] Morgan, American, 220–300.

[72] Allen, The Invention.

[73] Beckles, White, pp. 98–114. The idea that these were indicative of class conflict is advanced in Charles Post, 'Agrarian Class Structure and Economic Development in Colonial British North America: The Place of the American Revolution in the Origins of US Capitalism', Journal of Agrarian Change, 9 (2009), 453–83.

[74] Donoghue, 'Out', p. 944.

[75] Thomas D. Morris, Southern Slavery and the Law, 1619–1860 (Chapel Hill, 1996), p. 42; Handler, 'Custom', p. 242 (italics in original).

[76] Ellen Meiksins Wood, 'The Agrarian Origins of Capitalism', Monthly Review, 50 (1998).

widespread notions about the traditional form of property ownership were inimical to the idea of chattel slavery as it developed in the Americas since, as Handler rightly points out, that concept accepted no restrictions on the rights of the owner in relation to their human property. The ideas about the ownership of Africans that developed in the seventeenth century in the colonial context were, consequently, developments of ideas that already existed about property in England, as Handler and others suggest, but these were not traditional ideas of property ownership. They were new ideas being developed as part of the evolution of English agrarian capitalism, which, in turn, then evolved in the context of colonial slavery.

These discussions of the process by which the preceding norms of English society were reconstructed during the seventeenth and early eighteenth centuries are important in thinking about the situation of Africans in Norfolk and Suffolk. Until the middle of the seventeenth century, the colonial societies were, at most, 'societies with slaves' as opposed to 'slave societies' in the sense that their labour force was primarily European, and they did not have the social and economic infrastructure to control and utilise large numbers of African slaves. The new economic structures of plantation slavery changed the nature of these societies. The process of gradual development in respect of the ideas around Africans and their enslavement would seem, in part, to have been a consequence of the existing attitudes held in respect of Africans in places like sixteenth-century Norfolk and Suffolk, where there had been no need to really think about enslavement and race previously. Enslavement was used to discuss political and economic rights and for the labouring classes formed part of a discourse with which they resisted the changes resulting from the shift to agrarian capitalism. The few numbers of Africans and their lack of any crucial economic role in the region made it unnecessary to consider their social status as a group. This meant that many colonists who originated from the region did not arrive in the Americas with a set of fully worked-out ideas concerning the place of Africans in English society, their suitability for enslavement, or their 'natural' attributes.

As the slaveholding economies developed and the decision to use an enslaved African workforce was taken, there became a growing need to recalibrate thinking about enslavement and about the people chosen for it, but it took time to render the rather inchoate set of ideas about these matters that existed in places such as Norfolk and Suffolk in the 1500s into something that was useful in the colonial context. Peter Kolchin's suggestion that, in considering the subject of enslavement in the seventeenth century, it 'is increasingly clear that we must come to grips not so much with slavery as with slaveries' is of help here, in that the process of profit maximisation in the colonies did not immediately produce a monolithic approach to enslavement.[77] Rather, precisely because the

---

[77] Peter Kolchin, 'Variations of Slavery in the Atlantic World', *William and Mary Quarterly*, 59 (2002), 551–4, at p. 551.

ideas that preceded the colonial experience in relation to both enslavement and Africans were incoherent, the process of creating the ideological structures that supported the enslavement of Africans was gradual and variable. As Donoghue posits, it is important to realise that the institution of 'permanent, racialized chattel bondage' that came to dominate the eighteenth century 'evolved from earlier variants in the seventeenth century that formed a complex system of bondage in which race had yet to become the defining feature of chattel status'.[78] In this context, it may have been that those ideas about 'blackness' that had existed in English culture, and have been identified by historians in works of literature, became suddenly far more useful than they had been previously, and so came to be highlighted in colonial culture. The slow, but sure, result of this process was the situation where, as Post puts it, 'For the first time in history, freedom and un-freedom corresponded to differences in physical appearance, allowing the invention of race as a means of justifying and explaining the unique class position of African slaves.'[79]

This change in the colonies had the potential to affect thinking in Norfolk and Suffolk, but there was a different economic and social situation there. These alterations to English thinking about Africans only became necessary because the economic structures surrounding them altered in the colonies. The process of doing so, as Menard, Goetz, Beckles, and others have shown so convincingly, involved a radical reconstruction of fundamental cultural norms, such as baptism, that had existed in places like Norfolk and Suffolk before the colonies came into being. These factors did not apply in Norfolk and Suffolk. The few Africans living there constituted neither a tangible labour pool nor a physical threat. There was no labour-intensive economic system being constructed that needed a new group of labourers to be brought into the region from elsewhere, turned into human capital, and exploited, and for that group to be controlled and segregated. Africans in Tudor and Stuart Norfolk and Suffolk could be absorbed easily into the region's economic system without changing fundamental social norms such as baptism, marriage, and funerals. What this appears to have meant is that, although these new anti-African ideas began to filter back across the Atlantic through the seventeenth century, they still lacked the impetus to reconfigure approaches to Africans in a fundamental fashion.

[78] Donoghue, 'Out', p. 947. Indeed, Donoghue argues that 'Taking the English Atlantic as a whole in the mid-seventeenth century, those who served fixed terms as the chattel property of plantation owners outnumbered the permanently enslaved.' The suggestion that the status of indentured servants can be equated with that of enslaved Africans has been challenged; Reilly and Handler, 'Contesting', pp. 30–55.
[79] Post, 'Agrarian', pp. 468–9.

Imported Ideas? A 'Mulatto' in King's Lynn

An indication of this situation can be found in the records of a baptism in King's Lynn on 20 May 1643. On that day, the curate of the church of St Margaret's in King's Lynn, Lionel Gatford, noted in his register that he had publicly baptised 'Peter Lynn, a stranger, being as it is supposed about 11 years'. In the margin of the register Gatford noted that Peter was 'A Moore or Mulatto'.[80] This information about Peter in the parish register is augmented by a separate document, written some eighty-three years later in 1726; Cooper's *A Catalogue of Mayors of Lynn and Annual Occurrences*. This reiterated that Peter was 'supposed about 11 or 12 years old' when baptised and added two other pieces of information. The first was that Peter Lynn was 'A Blackmore of Mr Seth Hawley's' and the second was that after the service Peter 'was likewise bound out an Apprentice ye same day'.[81] The baptism of Peter Lynn was the first recorded baptism of an African in the port of King's Lynn and the first record of any African presence in the town.

It is the use of the term 'A Moore or Mulatto' in the baptism of Peter Lynn that provides the strongest evidence of some form of cultural exchange going on between Norfolk and Suffolk and the colonies in respect of ideas about the status of Africans. As Appendix A and Table 2 show, from the description of Eylys given by Pigott in the 1520s to the burial of Rachel 'the moor's wife' in 1698, the term 'Moore' was the most common descriptor used in relation to Africans in parish registers in the region during the fifteenth and sixteenth centuries, even without considering the use of it as a surname. The use of the word 'Moore' at Peter's baptism in 1643 fits clearly within this pattern.

This is not the case with the other term used by Gatford in relation to Peter; 'mulatto'. This word was used to describe 'A person having one white and one black parent.'[82] The word came originally from the Spanish and Portuguese colonial empires and was probably derived from the Spanish for mule, *mulo*, which was in turn derived from the Latin, *mulus*.[83] It became part of a set of terms that formed an integral part of the complex system of racial hierarchy that developed in the slaving structures of the colonies of Spain and Portugal, where it was being used by the late sixteenth century. The word then travelled from the Spanish sphere of influence into the English world, where it was being used by the 1590s in literature discussing Drake's and Hawkins'

---

[80] NRO/PD/39/1, Baptism of Peter Lynn, St Margaret's, King's Lynn, 20 May 1643.

[81] NRO/BL/AQ/2/13, *A Catalogue of Mayors of Lynn and Annual Occurrences*, J. Cooper 1726, date, 1643. It is unclear where Cooper gained the extra information from; he made no mention of his original source.

[82] 'mulatto, n. and adj.', *OED Online*, Oxford University Press, March 2020. Web. 13 April 2020.

[83] The Real Academia Espanol suggests its derivation to be from the word 'Mule, in the sense of hybrid', applied first to any mestizo, 'De mulo, en el sentido de híbrido, aplicado primero a cualquier mestizo', http://dle.rae.es/?id=Q2jb9eE.

voyages.[84] This context cements its appearance in English in the interface of Englishmen with the slavery of the Iberian colonial empires. As English involvement in the enslavement of Africans grew across the seventeenth and eighteenth centuries, it became far more common. As the British traveller Robert Renny explained, by 1807 it was used to designate 'a child of a black woman and a white man'.[85]

Onyeka provides only two cases of the word's use in Tudor England, one a Portuguese man in the service of the King of Portugal, Pedro Fernando, and another being 'Frances the Mulatto' who was buried at Gravesend in 1603, both of whom had Portuguese connections that would explain this early use of the term.[86] The baptism of Peter Lynn was the only instance of the use of the word 'mulatto' in any documents from Norfolk and Suffolk in the fifteenth, sixteenth, and seventeenth centuries. The word would be seen more often in the eighteenth and early nineteenth centuries, a change that can be linked in those cases convincingly to the increasing involvement of the region in the slaving economy and the arrival of plantation owners in the area.[87]

The word 'mulatto' was, however, known and understood by England's North American colonists in the seventeenth century, and this understanding was framed in the context of their evolving ideas about race. As the correlation of skin colour to slave status became stronger, terms such as 'mulatto' helped in the development of the assumption in the colonies that having two African parents was a sign of enslavement. The early laws drafted in places such as Virginia did not automatically equate a specific skin colour with slavery or freedom, in no small part because of the questions raised by the children of mixed parents. Instead, legislation such as the Virginian law of 1662 on slave status stated that the key factor was not race, but the legal position of the mother. In practice, this meant that most children with one African parent would be enslaved, as most of their mothers were slaves. Nevertheless, because some African women were freed by owners, and other children had free, white, mothers, it ensured that any 'mulatto' could never be assumed to be a slave until their personal history was known.[88]

---

[84] K.R. Andrews, *Last Voyage of Drake & Hawkins* (Hakluyt Society, Second Series, 1972), p. 220, 'Asked what person or persons came as guides to the road for the men who came to take Panama, he said their guides were a man of small stature and a tall mulatto.'

[85] Robert Renny, *An History of Jamaica* (London, 1807), p. 188.

[86] Onyeka, *Blackamoores*, pp. 362–3.

[87] See, for example, NRO/PD/197/2, Marriage of Mary Molineux 'mulatto' and Thomas Pearl, Garboldisham, 16 February 1791. This entry coincides with the arrival in the town of the plantation owner, Crisp Molineux.

[88] For recent discussion of this, see Leon Higginbotham Jr. and Barbara Kopytoff, 'Racial Purity and Interracial Sex in the Law of Colonial and Antebellum Virginia', in Werner Sollors (ed.), *Interracialism: Black-White Intermarriage in American History, Literature, and Law* (Oxford; New York, 2000), pp. 81–140. See also Jordan, *White*, pp. 167–78.

The use of this term in King's Lynn in 1643, when it had not been used in Norfolk previously, suggests several things. At the very least, it shows that the language about Africans being developed in the Americas had started to be used in the region. Even if Gatford had only heard the word in passing and did not understand it, the term must have been used in his company in Norfolk, or he might have read about it somewhere. Since Gatford chose to use the term in addition to the, far more common, term 'Moore', it seems more likely that he understood the word's nuances. The use of a specific racialised term from the colonies in the first baptism of an African in King's Lynn suggests that discussions about the status of Africans that drew on the port's colonial relations were taking place there. Gatford's exact reason for using the word cannot be known, but the curate must have understood, somehow, that Peter's parents were not both African.

There are two options for Gatford's knowledge of Peter's background. Firstly, he may have gained it from speaking with Peter prior to the baptism. Secondly, Gatford may have known this by speaking with those people who had been involved with Peter's arrival in the port. The most likely candidate here is provided in the description of Peter as 'A Blackmore of Mr Seth Hawley's'.[89] The Hawleys were a major merchant family in King's Lynn, who traded internationally; for example, Thomas Hawley was involved in the import of coal from the Netherlands.[90] The family had a number of members named Seth, but the most likely candidate as Peter's master was a man named Seth Hawley who was baptised on 6 December 1607, which would have made him thirty-six years old in 1643, and so of an acceptable age to be taking on an apprentice.[91] Seth Hawley was an important political figure in seventeenth-century Lynn, a successful merchant and businessman with various interests in the town and in Yarmouth, who owned at least one ship, the *Joshua*.[92]

The Hawleys had three potential links with the American colonies. The first is that one of the early governors of Barbados, Henry Hawley, shared a surname with them. The familial connection is difficult to show, however, since Hawley was the son of James Hawley of Brentford and there is no apparent connection

[89] NRO/BL/AQ 2/13, *A Catalogue of Mayors of Lynn and Annual Occurrences*, J. Cooper 1726, 1642/3.

[90] For the seventeenth-century trade, see Metters, 'Corn', pp. 149–78, at p. 176.

[91] NRO/PD/39/1, Baptism of 'Seathe Hawley', King's Lynn, St Margaret, 6 December 1607. Another possible candidate is the merchant 'Sethe Hawleie' who was baptised in 1583, became a freeman of the town in 1605, and was the son of a salt merchant and former mayor, *The Calendar of the Freemen of Lynn, 1292–1836* (Norwich, 1913), p. 133. NRO/PD/39/1, Baptism of Sethe Hawley, 12 February 1583, King's Lynn.

[92] Hawley's will makes it clear that he was a shipowner at the date of his death but gives no indication of any connection to the Americas or any ownership of enslaved people, TNA/PCC: Will Registers; Class: PROB 11; Piece: 350. For more on Hawley, see Peter Sykes (ed.), 'A List of the Names of those men invited to attend the Court Leet held in King's Lynn in 1663' (Norwich, 1994, SD32); Norfolk Archaeology (1888), 389; B. Mackerell, *The History and Antiquities of the Flourishing Corporation of King's-Lynn in the County of Norfolk* (Norwich, 1738), p. 66.

to King's Lynn.[93] A more solid link is provided by the Thoroughgood family. One of the daughters of the elder Seth Hawley (d.1603) married Thomas Thoroughgood, thereby linking the family with the North American colonies. The third link is a connection between the Hawleys and the Doughty family. The second wife of William Doughty's father was the widow, Dorothy Beane, who was a Hawley by birth.[94] This patchwork of connections makes it clear that the Hawley family had sufficient trading links with the West Indies and English/British North America to have acquired an enslaved African youth, and this may be the reason for Peter Lynn's arrival in the port in 1643. In the early 1640s, the enslaved population of Barbados was rapidly increasing, from around 1,000 in 1641 to 6,000 in 1643.[95] In consequence, it is possible that Peter might have been enslaved in Barbados or in Virginia and had arrived in King's Lynn as the property of the Hawleys.

This argument for previous enslavement is enhanced by the other factors apparent from Cooper's notes and the baptismal documents. The phrase 'A Blackmore of Mr Seth Hawley's' implies a position of control on the part of Hawley that is evocative of near slavery. Of course, Cooper was writing eighty years later, in a time when plantation slavery had become far more established, and he may have been adding an understanding of the relationship between Peter Lynn and Hawley that did not exist in 1643; but had become more readily made in 1726. It seems more likely, however, that Cooper was copying phrasing that he had read in his, now-lost, source from the seventeenth century. The Hawley connection suggests that he had arrived from the Americas, as does the use of the term 'mulatto'. If this evidence is added to the name he took at baptism, Peter Lynn, which was clearly a local construct, then it seems that Peter Lynn was being treated as, in some fashion, the property of the Hawleys, who had decided to name him after their home port.

The decision to name Peter Lynn after the port of his arrival is strongly redolent of a continuing control over the boy in some shape or fashion after his arrival in Norfolk, but the exact nature of Peter's situation after his baptism is unclear, and this tends to point to the inability of colonial ideas on race to remake local ideas about social relations at a fundamental level. Cooper noted that after the service Peter 'was likewise bound out an Apprentice ye same day'.[96] This is significant because it has been argued that the status of apprentice was incompatible with that of enslavement, in both England and in

[93] Beckles, 'Plantation', p. 34; J.H. Lawrence-Archer, *Monumental Inscriptions of the British West Indies from the Earliest Date* (London, 1875), <https://archive.org/details/monumenta-linscri00lawrrich/page/364/mode/2up?q=hawley> [accessed 7 June 2019], 'Monument to John Peers Esq.', p. 365. See also Gragg, *Englishmen*, pp. 37–9; Alison Games, *Migration and the Origins of the English Atlantic World* (Harvard, 1999), p. 196.
[94] Arthur Campling, *East Anglian Pedigrees* (Norfolk, 1940), p. 104 and p. 200.
[95] Postma, *The Dutch*, p. 4; Menard, *Sweet*, pp. 1–5, 31.
[96] NRO BL AQ 2/13, *A Catalogue of Mayors of Lynn and Annual Occurrences*, J Cooper 1726, 1643.

the colonies.[97] Seventeenth-century apprenticeship was not the same as slavery and should not be confused with the 'apprenticeship' system instituted for freed slaves in the former slave colonies in the 1830s.[98] Rorabaugh argues that, even in the American colonies, slavery and apprenticeship were parallel institutions that served distinct functions. Although apprenticeship was a system of partial economic exploitation and social control for young men, it was, in theory, a system of education that transmitted knowledge across generations and allowed the next generation to acquire the skills to become masters of their own crafts, and households. Slavery was not a process of training, rather one where the enslaved person had been purchased and became a tool of the master.[99]

Of course, the theory of apprenticeship in England was not necessarily matched by reality and apprentices were exploited by their masters on a regular basis.[100] Nonetheless, apprenticeship remained a specific contractual arrangement, and not a situation of chattel status. There are no apprentice records relating to Peter Lynn, although there are records of other apprentices to Seth Hawley later in the 1640s. Peter's description as an 'apprentice' may be indicative of a moment of encounter between older notions of social relations, in the form of apprenticeship as traditionally understood in Norfolk and Suffolk, and newer, reconfigured, ideas of indentured labour as 'proto-slavery' in Barbados, which were also being related to Africans in new ways. Peter Lynn may have been held on the island in an early form of slavish servitude, or perhaps as a fully enslaved African, and the notes of his baptism may indicate an early stage in the process in which this status was being recast in King's Lynn in some fashion that used the terminology and notions of traditional apprenticeship, suggesting that by this stage his status fell short of chattel slavery.

Peter Lynn is not mentioned again in the parish registers, nor in the wills of the Doughty or Hawley families. There are two potential records that may provide a clue to his later life. The burial register for St Margaret's Church, Westminster, records the burial of 'Peter Lynn' on 17 August 1650.[101] The

---

[97] Allen, The Invention, p. 103.

[98] For details of the system of apprenticeship in the British Caribbean, see William A. Green, British Slave Emancipation: The Sugar Colonies and the Great Experiment 1830–1865 (Oxford, 1976), pp. 129–61; Swithin R. Wilmot, 'Not "Full Free": The Ex-Slaves and the Apprenticeship System in Jamaica, 1834–1838', Jamaica Journal, 17 (1984), 2–10; Colleen A. Vasconcellos, Slavery, Childhood, and Abolition in Jamaica, 1788–1838 (Athens, GA, 2015), pp. 76–97.

[99] W.J. Rorabaugh, The Craft Apprentice: From Franklin to the Machine Age in America (New York; Oxford, 1988), p. 180.

[100] P. Wallis, 'Apprenticeship and Training in Premodern England', Journal of Economic History, 68 (2008), 832–61, at pp. 834–5; K.D.M. Snell, 'The apprenticeship system in British history: the fragmentation of a cultural institution', History of Education, 25 (1996), 303–21. Failure to complete the apprenticeship contract was not unusual; see Chris Minns and Patrick Wallis, 'Rules and reality: quantifying the practice of apprenticeship in early modern England', Economic History Review, 65 (2012), 556–79.

[101] Westminster Burials, St Margaret, Westminster, Middlesex, England.

proximity of St Margaret's to the River Thames makes it possible that Peter may have been working in the maritime industry at the time of his death and have been buried in the port at which the ship was docked. This may have been in a ship belonging to Hawley, or someone else, but suggests that the young man was not in near slavery at this point. Alternatively, the baptism of a boy named John Lynn in Great Yarmouth in 1675 names his father as Peter.[102] If this was the same Peter, he was now in a different local community, married, and with children, suggesting a change of status and an end to a situation of control by the Hawleys.

The fact of Peter's baptism may also be indicative of the resistance to colonial ideas about the enslavement of Africans in Norfolk and Suffolk. As will be discussed in detail in the next chapter, in relation to the baptism of Rosanna in the village of Rougham, there was strong opposition by planters in the seventeenth century to the baptism of Africans, since baptism was understood by many to mean freedom, and this led to its reconfiguration in the colonies. Yet Peter was baptised without demur in King's Lynn. It may be, therefore, that Peter's baptism is a sign that existing cultural norms about Africans continued to have weight in Norfolk and Suffolk. Whatever Peter's exact status, and it may be that he was held in some form of slavish servitude on his arrival in the port, he had to be baptised. The consequence of this was that he became part of the local labouring community and this may, in turn, have prevented any ongoing situation of slavish servitude. Peter's baptism may indicate, therefore, the beginnings of a process of cultural tension resulting from the encounter between ideas appearing out of the region's growing connections with the colonies and existing cultural practice. Older ideas were not immediately cast aside.

The sudden appearance of a specific racialised term, 'mulatto', previously unknown in the region, is suggestive, nonetheless, of the arrival of those new ideas in the counties. Rather than being a 'blackamore' or 'Ethiopian', both of which had been used in the 1500s and were more racially neutral, in the sense that they were generic terms which were not necessarily linked intellectually, or even etymologically, to slavery, Peter Lynn was described using both an older term and a newer term, one that was derived from the heart of the system of South American slavery. The word 'mulatto' carried a racialised meaning that was connected to slavery. To be a 'mulatto' was to be a mixture of two distinct 'races'; to be defined by differing skin colour. The notion of such a mixture itself required an acceptance of categories of 'black' and 'white' and for the ideas about the distinction between the two to be considered and formalised. It also required consideration of the legal status of such a person in a context that was different to that of the children of the sixteenth-century marriages between African migrants and non-Africans that were seen in Norfolk and Suffolk, such as the Haryson family in Kessingland. As the enslavement of Africans in the

[102] NRO/PD/28/4, Baptism of John Lynn, 21 September 1675.

colonial economies gathered pace and new ideas about Africans were developed, then the appearance of the term 'mulatto' in King's Lynn points toward the appearance of new questions and ideas concerning the essential position of Africans in seventeenth-century Norfolk and Suffolk. The next chapter considers the increasing population of Africans living in the region during that period and asks to what degree these new ideas became commonplace.

5

The African Population, 1600–99

Women: Christiana Niger and Rosanna Blunt

The details of the baptism of Peter Lynn seem to indicate that the ideas about enslavement being developed in the colonies began to gain some purchase in Norfolk and Suffolk from around the middle of the seventeenth century. This timeline would seem to be relevant in considering the situations of two African women who lived in the region in this period. The first was named Christiana and was mentioned in the parish register of Sibton, Suffolk, in 1634. In this Latin record, Christiana was described as 'Christiana niger', which was then rendered in English as 'blackamore', supporting the argument already made for the close equivalence between these two terms at this point.[1] This surname was also used in relation to a woman named Mary Niger, in the Suffolk village of Stowmarket, a decade later.[2]

There are no extra details in the Sibton register to link Christiana to a specific local family or hall, so her exact status, and the route by which she arrived in Suffolk, is unclear. Nonetheless, some suggestions can be proposed. This record is similar in context to those of the sixteenth century. This was an adult baptism, which suggests that Christiana was not born in England, or anywhere in Europe – since she would have been baptised in those cases. Furthermore, as with many of the early African inhabitants of Norfolk and Suffolk, Christiana was baptised in a village that was close to the coast. Sibton is not far from the small ports of Aldeburgh and Southwold and is equidistant between Ipswich and Lowestoft. This makes some form of connection with the merchant routes possible, although as a woman Christiana could not have been a crew member on a ship. This then points us towards an explanation that might involve some form of slavish servitude. The lack of any mention of a local family or place makes it difficult to be certain of this and the date, 1634, predates the widespread enslavement of Africans on the plantations in the English colonies. This would all tend to suggest that Christiana had arrived from the

---

[1] The record reads 'Christiana niger anglice blackamore', SRO/FC61/D1/1, Baptism of Christiana Niger, Sibton, 25 December 1634.

[2] The marriage of Mary Niger to Robert Bird, Stowmarket, Suffolk, in 1645, *England, Boyd's Marriage Indexes, 1538–1850*, in *Boyd's Marriage Index, 1538–1850*.

traditional origin suggested for the early African migrants into the region, the Mediterranean, as opposed to arriving because of the English/British transatlantic slaving economy. Furthermore, the terms used in Christiana's baptism fit into the older set of descriptors; she was 'niger' and 'blackamore'. The choice of Christian name might also be indicative of a baptismal 'statement' of conversion, like the suggestion made in relation to Baptist.

Much more can be said about the baptism of another African woman, named Rosanna, in Rougham, Suffolk, in 1688. The evidence from that entry makes it possible to say unequivocally, for the first time in Norfolk and Suffolk, that it refers to an African who was held in a position of near slavery. This is because the register entry recorded Rosanna as being 'a blackamore woman of Sir Robert Davers aged about 16 years'.[3] The connection with enslavement in this case is clear and unambiguous since, in 1673, the Davers family were recorded as one of the leading planter families in Barbados; they owned 600 acres, worth around £30,000. They are also known to have owned hundreds of slaves. The elder Robert Davers (d.1688) was one of the first settlers of Barbados and, having made his fortune, decided to return to England towards the end of his life. He arrived in Rougham around 1680. The family retained their plantations in the West Indies, however. His son, also called Robert Davers (1653–1722), was an important figure in Barbados, being a member of Barbados council in 1682 and baron, later chief baron, of the Exchequer and justice of the court of pleas there. He settled permanently in Rougham around 1687.[4] Since the baptism of Rosanna took place shortly thereafter, this makes it highly likely that she had been a household slave of the family brought from Barbados with him.

Rosanna's baptism provides another point of intersection, reminiscent of Peter Lynn's, between what has been suggested as the dominant approach to Africans in Norfolk and Suffolk from the fifteenth century onwards and the new, more clearly laid out, ideas in respect of Africans that had been developing in the colonies from the early 1600s. These colonial ideas were, as we have seen, formed relatively clearly by 1688. The intersection is revealed in the fact that the rector was willing to baptise Rosanna, as was the accepted norm in Norfolk, but at the same time he seems to have been willing to recognise that an African could be owned in some fashion by an Englishman in Suffolk. This was in line with the situation that has been identified for the previous century, in that the acceptance of Rosanna's status was situational, because she had been enslaved previously abroad and then brought into the parish as the property of Davers. As

---

3 SRO/FL619/4/2, Baptism of Rosanna, Rougham, 12 February 1688.
4 The elder Davers had fought for the royalist cause and left for the West Indies after the execution of Charles I. It appears he purchased land from William Byam in 1654, https://www.ucl.ac.uk/lbs/person/view/2146660239; 'DAVERS, Sir Robert, 2nd Bt. (1653–1722), of Rougham and Rushbrooke, Suff.'; Amussen, *Caribbean*, p. 151; B.D. Henning (ed.), *The History of Parliament: the House of Commons, 1660–1690* (Woodbridge, 1983), p. 197; http://www.historyofparliamentonline.org/volume/1660-1690/member/davers-sir-robert-1653-1722, [accessed 10 August 2020].

has been suggested in the discussion of Cartwright's Case and the 1549 rebellions, the culture of the region had never prevented enslavement in such a situation, it was merely that there was no direct correlation between skin colour and slavery.

At the same time, however, Davers was being forced to accede to the demands of existing local culture in respect of Rosanna, in that she was being baptised at all. Davers was opposed to the baptism of slaves in Barbados. In 1660, the king had instructed the Council of Foreign Plantations that it should look at the manner 'slaves may be best invited to the Christian Faith, and be made capable to being baptised there unto'. Some twenty years later, little had been done in this area, largely due to the opposition of planters, including Davers, who argued that the baptism of Africans was not possible. Once again, the evidence from Barbados suggests a gradual hardening of colonial views over time, with anti-African sentiment growing in response to the changing economic and social situation on the island.

Katharine Gerbner has shown that the planters' views on the baptism of slaves in Barbados changed from a general unease over the conversion of slaves on the island before the attempted rebellion of 1675, to implacable opposition to the practice thereafter. Her argument is that once African slaves had replaced European indentured servants, who were primarily Irish, as the island's primary workforce, and the larger planters had come to dominate local politics, then those planters 'finding themselves increasingly isolated, looked for ways to control their growing number of slaves'.[5] As Beckles has argued, the 'Act for the better ordering and governing of Negroes' of 1661, which would go on to form a model for slave laws in Jamaica and elsewhere, was 'built on mutual fear and suspicion' among planters toward their growing numbers of African slaves, and marked by 'tyranny and the need for constant vigilance' against them.[6] The planters espoused a variety of arguments against conversion; their core opposition was that 'converted Negroes grow more perverse and intractable than others, therefore are of less value for both labour and sale'.[7] The wording here shows plainly the link between colonial economic requirements and the construction of the ideology of race. Like any business owners, the planters wanted to protect their financial position, both as the owners of costly slaves and as plantation proprietors who now needed such slaves to work their holdings. This economic position was related to their social and political position on the island. They gradually came to conclude that this position was protected by the extreme subordination of their African workforce, as they had done in the case of their indentured non-African workforce previously. Their fear of rebellion grew in direct proportion to the numbers of enslaved Africans they imported and morphed gradually into anti-African racialism.

[5] Katharine Gerbner, 'The Ultimate Sin: Christianising Slaves in Barbados in the Seventeenth Century', *Slavery and Abolition*, 31 (2010), 57–73, at p. 1.
[6] Hilary Beckles, *Black Rebellion in Barbados: The Struggle Against Slavery, 1627–1838* (Bridgetown, 1984), p. 31.
[7] Quoted in Winnifred Winkelman, 'Barbadian Cross-currents: Church-State Confrontation with Quaker and Negro, 1660–1689' (Unpublished Ph.D. Dissertation, Loyola University Chicago, 1978), p. 189.

One aspect of this was a growing belief in the connection between baptism and a subsequent lack of discipline in Africans. Richard Ligon's description of the response of a planter to Ligon's suggestion that a slave be baptised is telling here. The planter told Ligon that 'being once a Christian, he could no more account him a Slave, and so lose the hold they had of them as Slaves, by making them Christians; and by that means should open such a gap, as all the Planters in the Iland would curse him'.[8] As Gerbner and others have pointed out, this was a 'nascent fear throughout the British colonies' in this period.[9] Slaveowners were concerned that conversion might be a route by which they could be forced to free their slaves, or that Christianity, which, as had been shown clearly to contemporaries in England in the 1640s and 1650s, was a socially revolutionary creed, would provide perilous ideas about freedom to slaves. This fear was widespread across the English colonies. Goetz has shown that the issue of baptism was a thorny one for Virginia's colonial authorities in this period, leading to events such as that in September 1667, when they passed 'An act declaring that baptisme of slaves doth not exempt them from bondage' in an attempt to end the widely accepted idea that conversion to Christianity automatically led to freedom. Goetz's argument is that over the latter part of the seventeenth century colonists 'manipulated the meaning of baptism' by linking it to ideas of race, a process which allowed them 'to flout centuries of Christian custom to argue that some, if not all, Africans might not be capable of Christian conversion at all'.[10] This gradually perverted the meaning of Christian baptism and reformulated it as a building block of the newly racialised hierarchy of the Americas.

This was not the situation in Norfolk and Suffolk, where baptism remained a fundamental social practice that was accepted as being available for all regardless of heritage. As has been seen, Africans such as the Haryson/Blackamore family and Baptist were being baptised in the area from the sixteenth century onwards, and this practice continued without check in the seventeenth, as evidenced by baptisms such as that of Peter Lynn, Christiana, and Rosanna. The question is what this continuing baptism of Africans meant. One approach to this issue has been that typified by Habib, who characterises the baptism of Africans as a 'protocolonial' activity, where a 'racial agenda' is clearly visible in the words used in the few records of such baptisms that are available. As we have seen, an example often used in this approach is the detailed account of the baptism of Mary Phyllis a 'black more' on 3 June 1597, at St Botolph's in Aldgate, London.[11]

---

[8]   Richard Ligon, A True & Exact History of the Island of Barbadoes (1673), p. 50; <https://archive.org/details/A-true-exact-history-of-the-island-of-Barbadoes-Illustrated-with-a-map-of-the-is-PHAIDRA_o_361036/page/n65/mode/2up> [accessed 3 December 2018].
[9]   Gerbner, 'The Ultimate', p. 10.
[10]   Goetz, 'The Child', pp. 46–7. For other discussion of this issue, see Warren Billings, 'The Cases of Fernando and Elizabeth Key: A Note on the Status of Blacks in Seventeenth-Century Virginia', William and Mary Quarterly, 3rd ser., 30 (1973), 467–74.
[11]   Register of St Botolph, Aldgate: LMA P69/BOT2/A/019 item 006, f. 257r, reproduced

Dimmock has challenged Habib's argument as 'a misleading teleological narrative that is not sustained by the examples'. Using other baptismal evidence from London, Dimmock argues that 'There was no coherent program of possession and domination at work' and that Africans were baptised in 'different circumstances and for different reasons'. Dimmock maintains, furthermore, that 'Neither were these baptized individuals silenced subalterns' because, in the specific case he examines, the person baptised was positively encouraged to speak about their faith as an integral part of the baptismal process.[12] The discussion of the baptism of Baptist in Chapter Three also argued against this approach to the involvement of Africans in the sacrament of baptism. As Kaufmann puts it, the idea that baptism was part of a process of racialised domination is drawn from arguments 'rooted in a modern political perspective that would have made no sense to the Tudors' and is based on a fundamental misunderstanding of the *Book of Common Prayer*.[13]

As Goetz points out, 'For the English, baptism was both a sign and seal of a covenant with God, a Protestant belief characteristic of Continental divines, and a sacrament that eased faith and salvation, a nod to residual Catholic belief and practice.'[14] Baptism was, therefore, fundamental in the construction of English identity.[15] In the context of Norfolk and Suffolk, the baptism of Africans needs to be understood from the viewpoint not of race, but of English identity and involvement in local community. From a religious perspective Africans were baptised for crucial theological reasons, which were the same for all, regardless of appearance. This theological reality underpinned baptism's social importance. People were also baptised for reasons of social and political inclusion; baptism was part of a set of services in the Prayer Book that reflected society's life-cycle – baptism, confirmation, matrimony, visitation and communion of the sick, and burial – and provided a means to unify communities.[16] The baptism

---

in Dimmock, 'Converting', p. 461 and Habib, *Black*, pp. 324–6. For discussion, see Habib, *Black*, pp. 19–20 and pp. 241–2. For this approach, see also Lewis, 'Like Devils', p. 113.

[12] Dimmock, 'Converting', pp. 474–5.

[13] Kaufmann, *Black*, pp. 148–61.

[14] Goetz, 'The Child', p. 49.

[15] For discussion, see Anna French, '"Trembling and groaning depart": Disputing the devil in Christian baptism, *Theology*, 118 (2015), 331–7; Anna French, 'Raising Christian children in early modern England: Salvation, education and the family', *Theology*, 116 (2013), 93–102; W. Coster, '"From Fire and Water": the Responsibilities of Godparents in Early Modern England', in D. Wood (ed.), *The Church and Childhood*, Studies in Church History, 31 (Woodbridge, 1994), pp. 301–12; E. Duffy, *The Stripping of the Altars: Traditional Religion in England, 1400–1580* (New Haven, CT; London, 1992), pp. 543–55.

[16] For more discussion, see, D. Cressy, *Birth, Marriage, and Death: Ritual, Religion and the Life-Cycle in Tudor and Stuart England* (Oxford; New York, 1997), pp. 95–194; W. Coster, *Baptism and Spiritual Kinship in Early Modern England* (London; New York, 2016), pp. 49–51. For an excellent summary of the discussion about the 1662 *Book of Common Prayer*, see Christopher Haigh, 'Liturgy and Liberty: The Controversy over the Book of Common Prayer, 1660–1663', *Journal of Anglican Studies*, 11 (2013), 32–64.

of arriving Africans was an automatic response to their arrival in the region, intrinsic to the normal construction of early modern society; it was a means of bringing them into the community around them. As such, it had been a social norm from the earliest point of their arrival.

This standard was not changed by the appearance of men such as Davers. Rather, the social norm was so strong that planters had to conform themselves to it. So, less than a decade after his strident opposition to the concept of the baptism of Africans in Barbados, Davers meekly allowed Rosanna to be baptised in Rougham. In the colonies, planters could oppose baptism because of the different social environment. First, in the colonies the baptism of Africans was not a long-established social norm, and Anglicanism was weak, which made it easier to alter the practice. Second, these changes were felt necessary to support the operation of the colonies as they expanded their workforce rapidly and moved decisively to the use of an enslaved African workforce. The need to control these growing African populations provided the impetus to change the approach to baptism and to maintain this stance against edicts from the London government and the established Church. Finally, the slaveholders were the social, political, and economic elite in the colonies. As such, they were the most powerful people in their specific colonial community and could make such change happen.

None of this applied in seventeenth-century Norfolk and Suffolk. While the planters could make arguments against baptism successfully in the West Indies or Virginia, and subvert its theological understanding, they had far less ability to do so in England, where the established Church was well-organised, the theology was settled, and baptism was accepted as fundamental to social functioning by social elites. There was no parallel need for any process of theological rearrangement. Indeed, such a change had the potential to cause unrest and social discord. A local precedent already existed in relation to the baptism of Africans, that they should be baptised, and this had been practised from their first arrival. The application of this social norm to Africans had then been mandated by the edict from the king and the established Church, which had made it clear that it was preferable that Africans, even when enslaved, should be converted to the Christian faith. The younger Davers, born in Barbados and acculturated to its new ideas, arrived in Norfolk and Suffolk to encounter a situation where he was no longer one of a group of men who ruled a colony, who had pressing economic and social needs to redefine social norms that existed in the metropole, and had the power to implement such change. Instead, he was now just one member of the minor gentry and, as such, he had to conform to existing social norms.

The power of existing custom can also be seen in Rosanna's eventual fate, which seems to have been freedom. Davers' will of 1714 instructed that all his property in Barbados, including his 'negroes', was to be sold to clear his debts and to provide legacies for his children.[17] His use of this term was one

---

[17] Will of Sir Robert Davers, Second Baronet, 14 March 1714, Hervey, *Rushbrook*, pp. 174-6.

of the earliest in the region, again indicative of the ongoing process of cultural exchange going on over the period. It can be seen appearing in other wills in the same period, for example that of his son, and that of Elizabeth Buxton of Stradsett Hall in 1729, which referred to her 'negro servant'.[18] Davers' will made no mention of Rosanna specifically, or of any other Africans in Rougham.[19] It seems likely that she had been freed and had left Rougham in the interim. This is because the register of nearby Bury St Edmunds records the baptism of a child named John in 1690. His parents were named as 'John and Rosanita Blunt' and were described as 'blackamores'.[20] The similarity between the names Rosanna and Rosanita is striking. Since Bury St Edmunds is only three miles from Rougham, it seems probable that Rosanna and Rosanita were the same person. It may be that John Blunt was another of the Davers family's Barbadian slaves, perhaps the 'Jone' mentioned in the elder Robert Davers' will, who was said to belong to his daughter, Anne Hartley.[21]

If this is correct, then Rosanna's life is a fascinating example of the way in which the ideas of returning planters had to bend in the face of the established culture. On arriving in Suffolk, Davers had to allow Rosanna/Rosanita to be baptised. If John was the slave 'Jone' mentioned in his father's will, then Davers had also allowed him to be baptised. He next allowed the couple to be married, and their son to be baptised. They were then freed. This sequence of events shows that the approach being taken towards Africans in seventeenth-century Norfolk and Suffolk was not a direct replication of that being created in the colonies. Forms of slavish servitude were possible, as had always been the case, because common-law ideas of property and other cultural ideas allowed it in certain situations. Davers appears to have been able to claim ownership of Rosanna, and presumably John, without challenge. Yet Davers could not resist other social requirements of the culture surrounding him. Rosanna might have been held in slavish servitude, but in Suffolk this social position still had to be conformed to church teaching. Rosanna had to be baptised.

This requirement also applied to her child. As Berry has recently shown, enslaved Africans in the colonies were held in a cycle of economic exploitation that commodified them before birth, under the doctrine of *partus sequitur*

---

[18] Will of Sir Robert Davers, Third Baronet, 26 February 1723, Hervey, *Rushbrook*, pp. 176–7; NRO/PRCC/OW, 1729, Will of Elizabeth Buxton. The will of the elder Robert Davers also uses it, but that was drafted in Barbados, not in East Anglia.
[19] NA/PROB/11/588/339, Will of Sir Robert Davers of Rushbrooke, Suffolk, 13 December 1722.
[20] SRO/FL543/4/3, Baptism of John Blunt, Bury St Edmunds, 1690.
[21] Davers stated that his daughter Anne Hartley 'hath liberty to take away all her own negroes she brought with her to my plantation and what negroes I have given her since, by name Will, Besse, Jone, Bellameno, Lettice, Phelpes, Squire, Dick, a Mallatto boy, and /20 to be paid her presently after my decease for one negroe man of hers that dyed in my service by name Hamlen'. See NA/PROB/11/391/419, Will of Sir Robert Davers, 1688.

ventrem, and continued to do so after they died.[22] In Barbados, Davers would have been able to claim ownership of baby John, because Davers owned his mother. In Suffolk, Davers neither held on to the mother, nor did he claim the child, since these ideas did not exist in Norfolk and Suffolk. Rosanna's baptism, marriage, and the baptism of her son highlights a tension, therefore. The economic and cultural interplay that was happening as the system of plantation slavery was being constructed opened routes for ideas to be transported across the ocean, as well as for previously enslaved Africans to arrive in the region. These ideas and Africans did not arrive on a blank canvas, however. The response to them had to be mediated through existing ideas; not only ideas about Africans *per se*, but also through other ideas, such as baptism, that were generally held to be applicable across all people living in Norfolk and Suffolk, without exception. Existing ideas were not easy to displace.

Country Houses

Rosanna's appearance in Davers' household makes it clear, nevertheless, that it was possible for wealthy landowners in seventeenth-century Norfolk and Suffolk to hold Africans in near slavery in their country houses and estates. The laws of property were also norms that needed to be accepted, and there are indications of other Africans being held in forms of near slavery in the region's country houses. Their presence would appear to confirm that it was not only returning colonials who owned Africans in the region in this period and conforms with what is known about country houses elsewhere. The fashion for owning African pageboys dated back to the sixteenth century and remained a clear statement of wealth and importance.[23] The first hint of such servants in the region is to be found in the records of one of its wealthiest and most important families, the Coke family at Holkham. In 1662, the household accounts of the family's country house at Hill Hall contain a note of a payment to 'John de Carlo his bill a pair of stockings for ye black boy'.[24]

The Coke family were the descendants of Sir Edward Coke (1552-1664), a lawyer, legal writer, and politician, who had been Chief Justice and Attorney General, and had built up a substantial estate on the north Norfolk coast. There

---

[22] Daina Ramey Berry, '"Broad is de road dat leads ter death": Human Capital and Enslaved Mortality', in Sven Beckert and Seth Rockman (eds), *Slavery's Capitalism: A New History of American Economic Development* (Philadelphia, 2016), pp. 146-62, at pp. 146-7.

[23] The subject of African servants in British country houses has been explored in recent years from many perspectives; see, for example, Madge Dresser, 'Slavery and West Country Houses', in Madge Dresser and Andrew Hann (eds), *Slavery and the British Country House* (Swindon, 2013), pp. 12-29; Ellen O'Brien, 'Sites of Servant Memory in the English Country House: Frederick Gorst and the Gladstone Vase', *Life Writing*, 16 (2019), 369-84; Walvin, *Black*, pp. 53-6.

[24] HA/F/JC(Y) 23, 1662.

is no evidence of the family being involved in the slave trade or in plantation ownership directly at any point. Indeed, their most famous descendant, the agriculturalist and Whig MP, Thomas William Coke, 'Coke of Norfolk', was a reformer, and was 'regarded as a staunch friend of the abolition of the slave trade'.[25] The Holkham estate lies close to the coast, with the ports of Wells-next-the-Sea, King's Lynn, and Heacham all close by, meaning that the 'black boy' might have been brought into the household through connections that the Cokes had in the locality or in London. It is most likely, however, that 'ye black boy' entered the house after the death of John Coke (1590–1661), when he was succeeded by John Coke the younger (1635–71), who had been estranged from his father since 1657, when he travelled abroad against his father's wishes.

Between 1657 and 1661 John Coke travelled to France and then to Italy, which offered the opportunity for him to have acquired an African servant. Furthermore, Philip Skippon noted in his diary that he had met Coke in Florence in 1664 and said that Coke was on his way to Constantinople.[26] John Coke had, therefore, ample opportunity to acquire a 'black boy' in his travels. It seems, furthermore, that ostentatious shows of wealth of the type represented by the ownership of such a servant were in keeping with Coke's character; the estate records show that he was a spendthrift.[27] The 'black boy' was well looked after in the house; the records show that his clothes were delivered by the carrier. They also show that the school dame purchased a book for him, which suggests that he could read.[28] There is no record of his baptism in the local church records, but since his name is not known he could be listed in the register and remain invisible if his heritage was not mentioned.[29] This lack of a name in the records enhances the likelihood that he was in a type of slavish servitude, however, since other foreign servants in the household, such as the 'sweade' Laurence Lund, were named.

The presence of Africans held in slavish servitude in other of the region's country houses in the seventeenth century is also suggested by two paintings. Neither painting can be related to any written records concerning the Africans involved, but the depictions of the Africans in each painting are marked by artistic suggestions that are redolent of subjugation and bondage, a mode of

[25] J.V. Beckett, 'Coke, Thomas William, first earl of Leicester of Holkham (1754–1842), politician and agriculturist', ODNB, <https://www.oxforddnb.com/view/10.1093/ref:odnb/9780198614128.001.0001/odnb-9780198614128-e-5831> [accessed 6 August 2012].

[26] Eveline Cruickshanks, 'Coke, John I (1635–71), of Holkham, Norf.', in Henning, The History, <http://www.historyofparliamentonline.org/volume/1660-1690/member/coke-john-i-1635-71> [accessed 1 October 2020].

[27] Christine Hiskey, Holkham: The Social, Architectural and Landscape History of a Great English Country House (Norwich, 2016), pp. 46–7.

[28] HA/F/JC(Y) 23, 25, 57, all 1662.

[29] The Holkham parish records were poorly maintained during the Interregnum, and only began to be kept correctly after 1658. It might be, therefore, that 'ye black boy' was baptised before 1658 but that this was not recorded, see NRO/PD608/1 Holkham Parish Records, 1542–1723.

representation of Africans that has been explored by Chadwick and others.[30] The most well-known of these is known as *The Paston Treasure* or *The Yarmouth Collection*. This well-known Dutch School painting of around 1663-5 is an excellent example of what is termed a 'cabinet of curiosities' or 'treasure chamber' created by wealthy aristocrats in the sixteenth or seventeenth centuries. For many years, it was displayed at Oxnead Hall, near Aylsham, which was the home of the Paston family. The painting dates from the period of Sir Robert Paston (1631-83), a leading member of Norfolk's gentry, who became the Earl of Yarmouth in 1679. The idea of such pictures was to display an individual's or family's wealth, learning, and power by providing a representation of that person's collection of expensive, rare, and exotic items.[31] An African youth is found on the left of the painting. In artistic terms, the reasons behind this youth's appearance in the painting are said to be as a representation of the 'exotic', which has been subjugated by the Paston family's wealth and power.[32] Accordingly, the depiction of this African youth in *The Paston Treasure* is not definitive proof of his existence at Oxnead Hall in the 1660s, since there are many other elements of the painting that are known to have been stock items from the artist's studio. In that case, the youth may have been a generic figure placed in the picture by the artist, with the intention of suggesting exoticism.

The example of 'ye black boy' at Holkham makes it clear, however, that Africans in the region's country houses were not necessarily recorded in parish registers, so the youth could have been real. Finding support for this suggestion is difficult, but not impossible. The parish records for Oxnead make no mention of the youth, or of any African at the hall. Neither is there any mention of him in the surviving Paston family documents.[33] Nor is there any evidence of any Paston family involvement in the slave trade or in planation ownership in the colonies. The major clue lies in the travel history of the Paston family. Although Sir Robert Paston did not travel abroad – he was a corpulent man, who was plagued by constant ill-health – his father, Sir William Paston (c.1610-63), did. In 1636, following his wife's death, the grief-stricken baronet left Oxnead and

[30] See, for example, Esther Chadwick, *Figures of Empire: Slavery and Portraiture in Eighteenth-Century Atlantic Britain* (New Haven, 2014); Agnes Lugo-Ortiz and Angela Rosenthal (eds), *Slave Portraiture in the Atlantic World* (New York, 2013).

[31] For discussion of the painting, see Robert Wenley, 'Robert Paston and the Yarmouth Collection', *Norfolk Archaeology*, 41 (1991), 113-44.

[32] Charles Ford, 'People as Property', *Oxford Art Journal*, 25 (2002), 3-16, at pp. 15-16; David Howes, 'Introduction: Empires of the Senses', in David Howes (ed.), *Empire of the Senses: The Sensual Culture Reader* (Oxford; New York, 2005), pp. 12-14; Susan M. Pearce, *On Collecting: An Investigation into Collecting in the European Tradition* (London; New York, 1995), p. 233; Esther Chadwick, '"This deepe and perfect glosse of Blacknesse": Colour, Colonialism, and *The Paston Treasure*'s Period Eye', in Andrew Moore, Nathan Flis, and Francesca Vanke (eds), *The Paston Treasure: Microcosm of the Known World* (New Haven; Norwich, 2018), p. 103.

[33] NRO/AYL, *Miscellaneous deeds and papers of the Paston family*, 1636-eighteenth century; NRO/BL/Y, *The Yarmouth Letters*, 1660-88; Daxid Yaxley (ed.), *Oxnead 1654-56: Accounts of Oxnead Hall, Home of Sir William Paston* (Dereham, 2014).

travelled across Europe, before sailing from Livorno to Egypt in September 1638, where he spent several months. The journey to Africa clearly affected him as, years later, he instructed his portrait painter to place him against a North African landscape, complete with pyramids, palm trees and a local, wearing a turban, who was being eaten by a crocodile.[34] The links to Livorno and Egypt on this trip provide potential for an African to have arrived at Oxnead at this point.

The problem is the date. The young man in *The Yarmouth Collection* is clearly too youthful to have returned with William Paston from Africa thirty years previously. If the Pastons had maintained connections with these areas, then they might have been able to acquire an African youth later in the century from these sources, but given Robert Paston's financial problems and lack of trading experience this seems unlikely. However, Robert Paston did have business dealings with the Doughty family, who might have been the source of the African.[35] A stronger option is that the youth had been brought from Algiers, since it appears from a passing reference in a letter from Sir John Clayton that Paston's son, William, was there in 1669.[36] Alternatively, the youth in the painting might have been an artistic rendition of a family memory regarding an African that William Paston had brought back with him on his return from his travels in 1640, and who had lived in the Paston household in the 1640s. If this last theory is correct, then it may be that the African at Oxnead Hall should be dated to the 1640s rather than the 1660s.[37]

A painting from Oxburgh Hall, which lies seventeen miles south of King's Lynn, provides another indication of the African presence in Norfolk and Suffolk's country houses. This painting is also of the Anglo-Dutch School, and depicts three full-length figures, standing. A boy and a girl, clearly members of a gentry family, dominate the painting and to their left stands a much less clear figure of an African boy dressed in brownish gold clothes. The painting is inscribed '1658 aged 8'. Oxburgh Hall was the seat of the Bedingfield family. In 1660, Henry Bedingfield was rewarded with a baronetcy, as recompense for his losses in the royalist cause during the Civil War, and the children may be his.[38] If

---

[34] R Ketton-Cremer, *Norfolk Assembly* (London, 1957), pp. 24–5.

[35] NRO/BL/Y/21, Letter from William Doughty, 8 October 1666. Chadwick has noted that in 1714 Robert Paston's son, the second Earl of Yarmouth, William Paston, was attempting to promote the 'Company of Adventurers to the Gold Mines in Africa', which proposed exploiting mines said to be situated on the Gold Coast, a major slaving area. This is extra evidence of a long-standing interest in the slaving economy that dated back to the 1660s. His letter can be found in NRO/AYL/304/9, Letter to the Earl of Yarmouth, 1714, and is mentioned in Chadwick, 'This deepe', p. 106.

[36] NRO/BL/Y/1/28, Letter from Sir John Clayton, 8 June 1669.

[37] The parish records make no mention of any African in this period, NRO/PD/161/1, Oxnead Parish Register, 1574–1780.

[38] National Trust Collection NT/1210329, 'A Boy and a Girl and a Blackamoor Page'. The painting was previously described as a 'Portrait of Three Children', and was thought to be Sir Henry Arundell Bedingfeld, 3rd Bt (b.1689, d.1760) with his sister and a black boy. It was thought to be dated from around 1697, but the inscription makes this unlikely.

this is correct, then the mother of the children in the painting was Margaret Paston, whom Henry had married in 1635.[39] It may be that this African was brought to the household from the Paston household. The Bedingfields had no known links with the King's Lynn trading community and were not merchants. As loyal royalist gentry they had suffered during the Interregnum and there is no evidence of foreign travel in this period, unlike that in the cases of the Paston and Coke families.

Whatever the origin of the African boy at Oxburgh, his presence there, along with that of the other youth at Oxnead Hall, as well as 'ye black boy' at Holkham, and Rosanna at Rougham, provides evidence that some gentry families across Norfolk and Suffolk acquired African servants for their households in the second half of the seventeenth century, as was the case across England. The likelihood is that there were others for whom records do not survive. Although the evidence is not conclusive, it seems probable that such people were held in some form of slavish servitude. The fact that Rosanna was part of the household of a major Barbadian planter and slave-owner provides the most obvious pointer toward this conclusion, but the other circumstantial evidence in these cases adds weight.

The maze of connections that might have caused the African youth to arrive in the Paston household at Oxnead Hall is evidence of the growing impact of the Atlantic slaving economy on the region's gentry and aristocracy. Robert Paston's interest in the growing slaving economy is representative of this. Paston was in constant financial difficulties and saw trade with Africa and the burgeoning plantation economy as an opportunity to make money. In 1664, he was one of those Members of Parliament, acting on instructions from the king, who proposed the huge grant of £2.5 million for war against the Dutch, a war which was driven, in part, by the crown's interest in the gold, ivory, and slave trade controlled by the Dutch trading stations along the coast of Africa.[40] Paston was rewarded with a range of customs duties, but this episode may have created an awareness of the potential rewards that might be provided by the burgeoning slave trade. Certainly, his letters show a strong interest in the West Indies; for example, in 1666 he wrote to tell his wife that the French had taken St Christopher from the English.[41] For members of the gentry with the interest, the connections, and the capital, the opportunity to make money in the new economic structures existed and was clearly tempting.

[39] John Debrett, *The Baronetage of England, Volume 1* (London, 1824), pp. 274-5.
[40] Gijs Rommelse, *The Second Anglo-Dutch War (1665-1667)* (Hilversum, 2006), p. 120.
[41] NRO/BL/Y/1/20, Robert Paston, 19 June 1666.

Africans and the 'Permanent Proletariat'

While the weight of evidence suggests a life of slavish servitude for those Africans found in the country houses of the region, the eventual fate of Rosanna suggests that this should not be taken automatically as being the default situation for other Africans in Norfolk and Suffolk. The evidence surrounding a man named Bedfer in King's Lynn in 1689 points strongly to a situation of freedom and suggests that, at least among the working population of the region, ideas about Africans were not shifting rapidly away from the earlier norms. The King's Lynn Poll Tax records for Chequer Ward in 1689 described a man named 'Bedfer ye Blackamore' and assessed him for the sum of one shilling.[42] Comparison with the Aid List for Chequer Ward shows that Bedfer was living at 11 King Street, which was described as being 'Mr Wm Kendall a house in his owne use & others'.[43] Little is known about Kendall; he was not recorded as a freeman of King's Lynn. In his *History of Barbados*, Ligon mentions meeting a man named Thomas Kendall on the island at some point in the 1650s, and a man named John Kendall was a major owner of land on the island in 1673.[44] There are no apparent links between these Barbadian Kendalls and William Kendall in King's Lynn.

There are no baptismal records or burial records for Bedfer in the town, so it is not clear whether he was baptised, or if he had been baptised as an adult. This removes one means of exploring his status, but the tax assessment is revealing. Kendall paid the basic rate for the poll tax, one shilling for every

---

[42] NRO/ KL/C47, Poll Tax Records 1689; Peter Sykes, 'King's Lynn. The Poll Tax and Aid of 1689: Annotated and Indexed' (2005), p. 94. The period from 1641 to 1702 saw a series of poll taxes levied across England, of which the 1689 levy was one part: Tom Arkell, 'Poll Tax, Marriage and King', in Kevin Schurer and Tom Arkell (eds), *Surveying the People* (Oxford, 1992), pp. 140–63.

[43] Sykes, 'The Poll Tax', p. 78. There is a discrepancy here, since the poll tax lists show a 'James Kendall' at this address, along with Kendall's 'wife and child' and a servant named Ann Raven, NRO/ KL/C47, Poll Tax Records 1689; Sykes, 'The Poll Tax', p. 94. It appears, however, that William and James Kendall were the same man. A 'William Kendall' was baptised at King's Lynn St Margaret's in 1669, but there is no sign of a 'James Kendall' being baptised in the records, NRO PD/39/84, Baptism of William Kendall, 24 October 1669. William Kendall had been resident at the address since at least 1684, when he was assessed for water rent, Peter Sykes, 'Notes on Houses in the Riverside Streets of King's Lynn and their known Owners and Tenants up to 1849' (2003), p. 63. A 'James Kendall' was buried in 1696, NRO/PD/69/1, Burial of James Kendall, 16 October 1696. This would appear to be the same man since Kendall was recorded in the 1693 Land Tax assessment, but he did not appear in the Quit Rental records of 1697, although his widow did, NRO KL/C47/8 Land Tax 1693; Peter Paygrave-Moore, 'King's Lynn Land Tax Assessment 1693' (Norfolk, transcribed 2000), p. 14; Peter Sykes, 'King's Lynn Borough Records: The Quit Rental of 1697, An Annotated Transcription' (Norfolk, 2004), p. 23.

[44] Ligon, *History*, p. 23; *Omitted Chapters from Hotten's Original Lists of Persons of Quality* [database online], Provo, UT, USA: Ancestry.com Operations Inc, 2006, p. 215 [accessed 5 October 2020].

member of his family, so a total of three shillings, rather than any of the higher rates paid by knights, esquires, gentlemen, doctors, and clergymen. Bedfer was assessed for the same amount, one shilling, meaning he was the only member of his household. This shows, categorically, that Bedfer was not held in slavish servitude, both because such a person could not be the only member of a household, and because they would technically be property; and property cannot pay taxes. The assessment of one shilling also shows that Bedfer was not a servant, since the wages of servants in the documents were clearly recorded as such, and they paid a different rate of tax; 2.5 per cent on wages, if these were under three pounds, and five per cent if above that sum. Kendall's servant was Ann Raven, and her wages were recorded as twenty shillings per annum, with her tax due being one shilling and sixpence.[45] Bedfer was not listed as a servant and no record was made of his wages, so he was employed in a different fashion.

An argument might be made that the fact that Bedfer was recorded at Kendall's address meant that he was being treated as a member of Kendall's family, and this indicates that he was held in near slavery within the family unit. However, all members of families within the King's Lynn Poll Tax records were recorded together, under the name of the father of the household, with no other names given. The household's total amount was then recorded as one sum. This was also the case when apprentices were members of the household.[46] Since Bedfer was identified individually, he appears, therefore, to have been neither servant, nor household member, nor apprentice. These facts also show that Bedfer was employed and not begging on the streets. Paupers were exempt from paying the tax, so Bedfer was gainfully employed somewhere in King's Lynn, presumably somewhere in the Chequer Ward. Since Chequer Ward contained the Customs House and alongside its housing could be found warehouses, breweries, and merchants' yards, it seems most likely that Bedfer was working in one of these locations and renting a room in King Street from Kendall.[47]

Bedfer was also recorded in the 1690 tax assessments register for the Chequer Ward. This time no mention was made of his racial origin; he was recorded merely as 'Bedfer'. This shortened description may reflect the fact that, as an African, Bedfer was a relatively well-known figure in the town and personally known to the tax collectors, with the consequence that they did not think the description of 'Blackamore' was needed. Alternatively, it may be that the collectors in 1690 did not think the tax record required such detail. In 1690, Bedfer's name appeared in the records below that of 'John Bassett wife and daughters' and above an entry for '3 servants', again indicating that he was neither in a family unit, nor a servant of anyone else. Interestingly, in the records many servants were not even given a name, merely being described

---

[45] Sykes, 'The Poll Tax', p. 78.
[46] See, for example, the listing of 'John Allan wife and apprentice' in the same ward, with each assessed for one shilling, NRO/ KL/C47, Poll Tax Records 1689; Sykes, 'The Poll Tax', p. 79.
[47] NRO KL/C47/8, Land Tax 1693; Paygrave-Moore, 'King's Lynn', p. 14.

as 'servant'.[48] Therefore, although Bedfer was not given a surname, he was being afforded a degree of recognition beyond that given to many non-African household servants. Furthermore, since Bedfer was still living in the same area of King's Lynn, but with a different group of people, it seems clear that he was a free agent and able to move around as he wished. What happened to him after 1690 is unknown. He was not mentioned in 1697 and does not appear in any parish register for the town, nor was he mentioned in relation to the Kendall household again.[49] There is a mention of a man named 'John Bedfer' in the Westminster Rate Books in 1702; however, aside from the shared name there is no other evidence to connect the two men.[50]

The example of Bedfer points towards the issue of employment and, more widely, to how employed Africans in the seventeenth century should be considered. There was a fundamental difference between the status of an African such as 'ye black boy' at Holkham, unnamed, and apparently held in slavish servitude, and a man like Bedfer, who, though a poor labouring man, was not held in such servitude, and who could come and go as he pleased. In relation to the fifteenth and sixteenth centuries it was suggested that once Africans were baptised then the potential existed for them to enter into membership of 'the commons'. The example of Rosanna shows that by the end of the seventeenth century baptism seems to have paved the way for eventual freedom. Men such as Bedfer suggest that these ideas can be explored more fully and help us to consider whether Africans might be understood in a different fashion to a condition of near slavery.

This is especially the case in view of the economic changes that occurred from the latter half of the sixteenth century into the seventeenth. The late sixteenth century had seen further division in rural communities, as the poor grew more numerous and richer neighbours improved their position. The yeomanry and the minor gentry became 'increasingly distanced' from their poorer neighbours. Changes in landownership led to an increase in poor, landless, labourers. These economic effects were exacerbated by the harvest failures of the 1580s and 1590s, and the divisions in English society became more marked as income was funnelled into its upper reaches, creating the 'permanent proletariat' that Wrightson has identified.[51] If Steve Hindle is correct in his view that these changes led to a 'longer-term reconstruction of social identities' in the period,

---

[48] NRO KL/C 47, Tax assessments and accounts, 1692.

[49] Sykes, 'The Quit Rental of 1697', p. 23; Sykes, 'Notes on Houses', p. 63. A William Bedfer is recorded as being married in Tregony, Cornwall, 20 August 1699, but there is no mention of his heritage, Cornwall Marriage Registers, Vol. 22, England, Boyd's Marriage Indexes, 1538–1850.

[50] John Bedfer, Castle Street, St Martin-in-the-Fields, Poor Rates 1702 (Cont.)–1705, f. 13, Westminster Rate Books 1634–1900.

[51] Wrightson, English, p. 141. For discussions of landownership, see M. Spufford, Contrasting Communities: English Villages in the Sixteenth and Seventeenth Centuries (Cambridge, 1974), pp. 46–58.

then the issue of the relationship of Africans such as Bedfer (and before him men like Thomas Blackamore and Baptist) to this emergent 'permanent proletariat' is worth considering with care.[52]

There is no detail of the nature of the work Bedfer was doing while living in Chequer Ward, although because he lived in a port it is likely that he was working in the maritime industry. In a similar fashion, since Peter Lynn was an 'apprentice' to a merchant, he was probably also engaged in maritime work. In one case, however, the exact nature of an African's work was recorded, that of Robert Smith, who was described as 'a Blackamore and Trumpeter'.[53] The information on Smith comes from the burial register of Hadleigh, Suffolk, in 1685. As was discussed in Chapter Two, Roger Blackamore had settled around Hadleigh after arriving in Ipswich in the 1540s and his family was still living there in the seventeenth century.[54] From the description of Smith, the likelihood is that he was not local to the town, but a visitor.[55] The decision of the clerk to add the details of Smith's occupation to the burial record makes more sense in a situation where Smith had been living in the town for a relatively short period, or had been passing through and had died. In these circumstances his situation as 'a Blackamore and Trumpeter' would have been somewhat novel and so more likely to have been recorded than if Smith was a locally born resident who had died in the normal course of parish life.

The most well-known example of an African trumpeter in England during the early modern period is that of 'John Blanke the blacke trumpet', who worked at the courts of Henry VII and Henry VIII.[56] Blanke was one of a number of African musicians who formed 'a very visible presence' across European courts during the Renaissance, a fashion that has been suggested to have drawn on the stereotyping of Africans as musical.[57] African musicians can

---

[52] Steve Hindle, *The State and Social Change in Early Modern England, 1550–1640* (Basingstoke; New York, 2000), p. 49.

[53] SRO/FB81/D1/3, Burial of Robert Smith, 'a Blackamore and Trumpeter', Hadleigh, 14 April 1685.

[54] Baptism of Robert Blackamoore, Ipswich, February 1544; Baptism of Anne Blackamore, Ipswich, August 1546; Baptism of Elizabeth Blackamoore, 26 December 1575, Hadleigh; Marriage of Elz Blackamore, Hadleigh, 1604. An 'Alice Blackamore' was married in Hadleigh in 1616; 'Anna Blackmor' was baptised on 25 May 1617; 'John Blackmor' was baptised on 21 February 1618; and 'Richard Blackmer' was baptised on 23 August 1620; see England Births & Baptisms 1538–1975 and England, Boyd's Marriage Indexes, 1538–1850.

[55] Several children named Robert Smith were baptised in the town in the 1630s, but no mention of their ethnicity was made, so a connection cannot be established; SRO/FB81/ D1/3, Baptism of Robert Smith, Hadleigh, 11 December 1636; Baptism of Robert Smith, Hadleigh, 6 October 1639.

[56] Kaufmann, 'Blanke'; S. Anglo, 'The court festivals of Henry VII: a study based on the account books of John Heron, Treasurer of the Chamber', *Bulletin of the John Rylands University Library*, 43 (1960-1), 12–45.

[57] Kate Lowe, 'The stereotyping of black Africans in Renaissance Europe', in T.F. Earle and K.J.P Lowe (eds), *Black Africans in Renaissance Europe* (Cambridge, 2005), pp. 17–47, at p. 39.

be found mentioned in English records as early as the fifteenth century, as can be seen from a record in Southampton describing a 'blakman that was a taboryn (drummer)' on a ship visiting the port.[58] Another mention of this profession can be found a century later, when James Woodford, the parson of Weston Longville, near Norwich, noted how he had encountered 'a black with a French horn' one evening on his way to supper. In that encounter the horn-player told Woodford that he had previously worked for the Earl of Albemarle.[59] This provides a hint of the sort of work Smith might have been engaged in around the region.

In the Renaissance period the status of such African musicians varied. Some were enslaved, such as Abdul from Meknes, who was one of a number of galley slaves who belonged to Cosimo I de'Medici.[60] In contrast, Kaufmann has argued that the fact that John Blanke 'achieved a prominent position in the royal household, was paid wages, negotiated an increase in his pay, and was able to marry' points towards him being free.[61] The balance of evidence would also seem to suggest that Robert Smith was a free man who had died while passing through the town, since there is no mention in the burial record of any relationship to an owner or a place of residence. It may be that Smith's profession was known to the clerk because he had entertained some of the town's inhabitants before his death. If this interpretation is correct, then the examples of Robert Smith and Bedfer show how Africans could operate as ordinary working people, plying their trade across the region, earning their living, and engaging with the local population. This suggests, in turn, that the more important identity for their day-to-day dealings with the population may have been their status as members of the working population, as opposed to their African heritage.

This suggestion of integration into the local working population is supported by events that occurred in the village of Great Massingham, near King's Lynn, in 1636. In April 1636, enquiries were made about a theft of items of clothing and household items from a local gentleman named Robert Cremer. The investigation focused on a local alehouse, where the stolen goods had been located. A woman named Anne Tall, who was the sister of the alehouse-keeper, and who appears to have been suspected of receiving the stolen goods, denied any involvement. In her evidence she alleged that the person who had brought the goods into the alehouse was an African, 'about two or three of the clocke in the afternoon of the same day there came into the house of her said sister a talle blacke man who termed himselfe "Blacke Will".'[62] Tall alleged that Will

---

[58] Cited in Alwyn A. Ruddock, 'Alien Merchants in Southampton in the Later Middle Ages', *English Historical Review*, 61 (1946), 1–17, at p. 12, and Habib, *Black*, p. 58. See more in Fryer, *Staying*, pp. 2–3.

[59] Ronald Blythe, James Woodforde, John Beresford (eds), *The Diary of a Country Parson, 1758–1802* (Norwich, 1999), p. 205.

[60] Lowe, 'The stereotyping', p. 39.

[61] Kaufmann, 'Blanke'.

[62] NRO/NQS/C/S3/30, examination of Anne Tall, 19 April 1636.

had owed her money and had attempted to pay the debt by offering her various household goods and clothing.[63] Tall's story was supported by another suspect in the investigation, John Cole, who came from the nearby village of Cley. Cole confirmed that the house had been visited by 'a tall blacke man', but Cole was able to provide an extra detail about him, his full name. As Cole explained, 'he termed his name (blacke Will) but this examinant saith he thinks his name is William Snoring dwelling in Burnham Market or at Wells in the said County.'[64]

The statement of the man from whom the goods had been stolen – the local gentleman, Robert Cremer – paid little overt attention to Snoring's ethnicity. Indeed, Cremer's summary of the incident makes it clear that the ethnicity of Snoring did not cause Cremer or the constables to shift their investigatory focus from Tall and Cole. It appears that Snoring was mentioned only because Cole was attempting to defend himself after having been caught in possession of the stolen goods. Cole had then alleged that he had received them from William Snoring. The ethnicity of Snoring appeared in the conversation only after Cremer and the constables spoke to Tall.[65] These statements suggest that the mention of William Snoring's skin colour, 'a tall blacke man', was given for the purposes of physical description, rather than being a shorthand marker for 'criminal'. The proceedings do not suggest that 'blacke' skin was an attribute that carried specific undertones of antipathy or criminality in the wider culture of the region in this period. Snoring's African heritage did not have any obvious effect upon the investigation or upon the approach taken by Cremer and the constables. Indeed, Cremer was rather uninterested in Snoring, possibly because Cole and Tall had been caught in possession of the goods. There is no indication in the Quarter Sessions documents that Cremer, the constables, or the magistrates jumped to any conclusions about Snoring's guilt because of his skin colour. Furthermore, it appears that Snoring was not found to be culpable. The Quarter Sessions records contain no details of any action taken against him, and it appears that he was still living in the area two years after the incident at Massingham, since he was listed as the father of a child called Thomas who was buried in 1638.[66] It seems that the due process of the law took place, and that Snoring was exonerated.

In this incident from 1636, Snoring's African heritage did not result in an automatic assumption of guilt. There was no set of characteristics that were applied to Africans that were affecting the legal process. Instead he was viewed as simply another member of the area's working class. This would seem to have been a long-term position. The family were a settled part of the Burnham landscape. William was born in Bircham Newton in 1591, to John and Alice

---

63 NRO/NQS/C/S3/30, examination of Robert Cremer, 19 April 1636.
64 NRO/NQS/C/S3/30, examination of John Cole, 19 April 1636.
65 NRO/NQS/C/S3/30, examination of Robert Cremer, 19 April 1636.
66 NRO/PD/573/1, Burial of Thomas Snoring, Burnham Westgate, 9 April 1638. Father is listed as 'Willyam Snoring'.

'Snowringe', and had at least two siblings.[67] William had been married twice, first in 1615, and then in 1626, after the death of his first wife. He was the father of several children.[68] He was a local working man. There was no question of people seeing William Snoring as a dangerous outsider because of ideas about skin colour. These ideas did not have any purchase in local culture. William Snoring was a 'tall, blacke man', but his skin colour was a known and accepted aspect of a family that had been living in the area for nearly half a century. And this may have meant that he was not seen as a 'blacke' outsider, but primarily as a member of the community, when the investigation took place. The contrast with the situation of enslaved Africans in the colonies could not have been starker.

The Surname Blackamore and the Presence of Family Units

The case of William Snoring also highlights an aspect of African history in Norfolk and Suffolk that was first seen in the 1500s with the Haryson family in Kessingland, the creation of family units. The presence of such family units reinforces the argument that Africans were regarded as ordinary members of local working populations, marrying non-Africans, having children, and settling down. This process can be traced through the examination of the surname Blackamore, which can be understood as a visible marker of a process, indicative of the creation of a stable position in working communities, where Africans ceased to be 'a blackamore' and instead became 'Blackamore'. The surname Blackamore can be found appearing rather suddenly across the region in the seventeenth century.[69] In Norwich there were a significant number of people with the surname recorded between 1600 and 1700, and these data make it possible to suggest that Norwich developed a significant presence of free Africans, who were viewed as members of its permanent proletariat. This should be no surprise, since Norwich was the economic centre of the county, and as Norfolk's only city it offered a wide range of economic opportunity for any migrant arriving there.

[67] 419 England Births & Baptisms 1538–1975, Bircham Newton, Norfolk, Baptism of William Snowringe, 1 August 1591.
[68] NRO/PD/573/1, Marriage of Wyllam Snoring and Jane Patterall, July 1615; Burial of Jane Snoring, 2 December 1624; Baptism of Richard Snoring, 3 January 1622; Baptism of Margaret Snoring, 25 November 1627; Marriage of William Snoring and Bridget Rudd, 20 August 1626; Burial of Thomas Snoring, 9 April 1638.
[69] NRO/PD/28/1, Baptism of William Blackmore, 27 September 1610; NRO/PD/548/1, Baptism of John and Ann, 'the children of Ed. Blackemore', 2 April 1626; SRO/FB64/D1/1, Marriage of Judie Blackamore, 31 October 1602, Nayland; England, Boyd's Marriage Indexes, 1538–1850, Elz Blackamore, marriage: 1604, Hadleigh. An 'Alice Blackamore' was married in Hadleigh in 1616; 'Anna Blackmor' was baptised on 25 May 1617; 'John Blackmor' was baptised on 21 February 1618; and 'Richard Blackmer' was baptised on 23 August 1620; see England Births & Baptisms 1538–1975 and England, Boyd's Marriage Indexes, 1538–1850.

The earliest mention of a potential African in seventeenth-century Norwich is the marriage of 'William Blackmor' and Mary Farrer at the church of St John Timberhill in May 1611.[70] There is no obvious baptism for William in the area, and this makes it likely that he was a migrant who had arrived in the city in the early seventeenth century. With no other records mentioning him, it is not possible to suggest where he might have originated from. Nonetheless, it seems that William was free and able to marry a local woman. The couple settled permanently in the city, and over the next few years, as their children were baptised, they moved from St John Timberhill to the parish of St Andrew and then to St Peter Parmentergate.[71] The family then lived in this area of the city permanently; their eldest son, also called William, was married at St John Timberhill in April 1637 and went on to raise his own family in the parish.[72] As was seen in the Tudor period, such unions between an African and a non-African spouse would seem to have been accepted without demur. This is in accord with evidence from elsewhere. Marriages between Africans and locals can be seen in Staplehurst, Kent, in 1616, with the marriage of the 'blackamoor' George to Marie Smith, in Deptford in 1619 when 'Samuel Munsur a blackamoure' married Jane Johnson, and London in 1617 with the marriage of 'James Curres being a Moores Christian and Margaret Person, a maid' at Holy Trinity the Less.[73]

This pattern is visible in the other Blackamore families that appeared across Norwich in the same period. In 1636, Thomas Blakemore married a woman named Elizabeth.[74] The following year the couple's child, Susannah, was baptised.[75] In the parish of St John de Sepulchre, a child named Mary Blackamore was baptised on 12 June 1641, and then sadly buried in 1642. A boy named John Blackamore was baptised in August 1644. The father of both children was noted as William Blackamore, who had married Katherine Ward at nearby Timberhill in April 1637.[76] The family of John Blakeamor and his wife Sissly appeared in St Peter Parmentergate in the 1660s.[77] The family appears to have settled into the parish very successfully, with their five children, Mary,

[70] NRO/PD/74/1, Marriage of William Blackmor and Mary Farrer, 23 May 1611.
[71] NRO/PD/74/1, Baptism of John Blackmor, 2 February 1612; Baptism of Thomasine Blackmore, 19 January 1615; NRO/PD/162/2, Baptism of William Blackmore, 28 July 1616.
[72] NRO/PD/74/41, Marriage of William Blackmore and Katheren (sic) Wardly, 12 April 1637; NRO/PD/58/1, Baptism of Thomas Blackmore, 22 October 1637; NRO/PD/71/1, Baptism of Edward Blackmore, 28 November 1652, and Burial of William Blackmore, 27 March 1655.
[73] All mentioned, along with others, in Kaufmann, 'Making', p. 26.
[74] NRO/PD/31/1, Marriage of Thomas Blakemore, 6 May 1636.
[75] NRO/PD/31/1, Baptism of Susannah Blakemore, 21 March 1637.
[76] NRO/PD/90/2, Baptism of Mary Blackamore, 15 May 1642; Burial of Mary Blackamore, 15 May 1642; and Baptism of John Blackamore, 3 August 1644. NRO/PD/74/41, Marriage of William Blackmore, 21 April 1637.
[77] NRO/PD/162/4, Baptism of Mary Blakamor, 9 May 1660; Baptism of William Blackamoor, October 1663 (exact date unclear); Baptism of John Blackemore, 6 August 1665; Baptism of Edm. Blackemore, 2 February 1668 and Christin Blakamour, 14 November 1670.

William, John, Edward, and Christin, marrying locals and having their own children baptised in the church.[78] Another family could be found in St James with Pockthorpe, to the north of the city, when Robert Blackmore married Susan Bryant in January 1665 and raised seven children.[79] In St Stephen's parish, Thomas Blackmore married Elizabeth Walwyn in November 1677 and again their family grew up in the neighbourhood.[80]

These examples all seem to reveal a process of integration into 'the poor' taking place in Norwich whereby, as such families became embedded more clearly into the parishes, they acquired the surname Blackamore. An analogous situation can be seen in 1630, when a man described as 'Johanes Brown alias Blackmore' was buried in the church of St Martin at Palace.[81] Here, it would seem that 'John the Blackmore' had gradually become known in his daily life as 'John Brown'. The common name Brown, of course, could still have had a dual meaning for those who met John, with its allusion to a dark complexion, but it was also a marker of his inclusion in the community. A similar explanation is likely in the case of Peter Le-Blacke in the village of Barningham. While Peter was not directly identified as an African in the register when he was buried in 1698, his surname is suggestive of such heritage. This identification is supported by the description of a woman named Rachel in the same village as 'the moor's wife' on her burial in 1701.[82]

The details of the lives of the various Blackamore families that were living in Norwich and elsewhere in the seventeenth century indicate, therefore, that those Africans who were living in the region (and were not being held in some form of slavish servitude) were able to move freely about, to settle in various parishes as circumstances required, and become part of the working community

[78] NRO/PD/162/4, Marriage of William Blackamoore and Sarah Newton, 29 May 1690; Baptism of Mary Blackamoore, 29 March 1691; Burial of William Blackamore, 29 April 1701; Marriage of Mary Blackamoore and Joseph King, 27 March 1687; Marriage of Christian Blackamore, 24 April 1698.

[79] NRO/PD/11/1, Marriage of Robert Blackmore and Susan Bryant, 23 January 1665; Baptism of Robert Blackmore, 18 February 1666; Burial of Robert Blackmore, 13 August 1667; Baptism of Eliz. Blackemore, 13 September 1668; Baptism of Susan Blackamore, 12 March 1672; Baptism of Robert Blackmore, 11 December 1673; Baptism of Thomas Blackamoore, 25 June 1676; Baptism of John Blackamoore, 29 February 1680; Baptism of Mary Blackamore, 23 August 1682 (Susan was noted as his wife at this point and at his burial on 25 August 1691); Burial of Robert Blackmore, 12 September 1691; Burial of Mary Blackmore, 25 August 1691; Burial of Susan Blackmore 'widow', 16 January 1692.

[80] England Marriages 1538–1973, Marriage of Thomas Blackamore and Elizabeth Walwyn, 1 November 1677. NRO/PD/484/2, Baptism of Mary Blackmore, 12 October 1678; Baptism of John Blackmore, 15 December 1679; Baptism of Elizabeth Blackmore, 13 February 1680; Burial of Mary Blackmore, 27 October 1678; Burial of John Blackmore, 26 May 1679; Burial of Eliz. Blackmore, 8 October 1683; Baptism of Thomas Blackmore, 27 February 1688; Burial of Thomas Blackmore, 3 February 1690.

[81] NRO/PD/12/1, Burial of John Brown, 30 November 1630.

[82] SRO/FL523/4/1, Burial of Peter Le-Blacke, 1701, and Rachel 'the moor's Wife' in 1698, Barningham.

around them. The evidence suggests that their surnames were in a process of evolution from being a marker of heritage, in the form 'black a moor', to a formal surname that drew on this influence but became less clearly associated with it over time. There is no evidence that these Africans were being sequestered into any specific area of the city. They appeared in various parishes across the city and moved around the parishes apparently at will. Nor does there seem to be any evidence of a self-awareness of themselves as a 'community' that stood apart from the rest of the city. There is no indication of the families having any contact; for example, there is no record of a Blackamoor marrying another person with that surname. What is more significant is their gradual entry into the labouring communities around them. As was the case with Bedfer and Robert Smith, it seems that their African heritage was less important than their class identity. In relation to the Tudor period, Onyeka suggests that Africans seem to have been 'considered as having a status akin to the white people who lived in the same parish'.[83] This seems to have been the case in the seventeenth century as well, with the status that they acquired being that of 'the poor', like that of their non-African fellows.

Working-Class Africans in Seventeenth-Century Norfolk and Suffolk

Throughout the seventeenth century, therefore, there were examples of Africans, such as the Blackamore families, who appear to have been living and settling into local communities as members of the 'permanent proletariat'. Marriages were conducted, children were baptised. There is, in the example of William Snoring, a case of an African being accused of a crime and being treated equally with others in the application of the law. Men such as Bedfer in King's Lynn and Robert Smith in Hadleigh were able to work for themselves and travel around freely. The examples of Bedfer and Robert Smith are important because they show that there were free Africans working across the region during the seventeenth century. Of course, there is no evidence that explains exactly what stories lay behind the arrival of these men. It is possible that both men may have been enslaved previously, although there is no substantive evidence to show this.

While such issues cannot be decided upon in respect of these two men, their stories, and the stories of the other people discussed here, suggest several things. The first is the variability of status of Africans in seventeenth-century Norfolk and Suffolk. There were some Africans in the region, such as Rosanna and John Blunt, who were held in slavish servitude at some point in their lives in the area. In contrast, there were also free Africans such as Bedfer and Robert Smith. There were others whose status cannot be determined; for example, Christiana Niger. Secondly, it seems that some of these people, such as Bedfer and Robert Smith, were acting in a manner that could lead them to be categorised as free working

---

[83] Onyeka, *Blackamoores*, pp. 79-80.

people. In that situation they shared a common bond with other working people, a bond that transcended their African heritage. Like their non-African fellows, they were held by the less visible bonds of economic servitude, rather than bonds that were derived from their skin colour.

This suggestion of common experience can be related to the work on such class identities by Christopher, Linebaugh, and Rediker, who have suggested that in the circumstances of the Atlantic economy, African and non-African sailors could find common class solidarity.[84] The examples of men like Bedfer and Robert Smith in seventeenth-century Norfolk and Suffolk suggest that an analogous situation could be found in provincial England. Away from the pressures of the colonial slaving economies – whose burgeoning economic structures and racially oriented societies demanded increasingly that skin colour was a defining fissure in society – the need to emphasise ethnicity did not exist. This meant that in places such as Norfolk and Suffolk economic position was more significant than racial history. Without a need to develop ideas about racial demarcation, people with an African heritage were responded to in ways that could correlate far more to economic and social situation than to skin colour. Rosanna was accepted as being in slavish servitude, not primarily because she was African, but because that was the status she held when she was brought over by the Davers family. Eventually, nonetheless, she became a free woman and lived in a working community in Bury St Edmunds, with her husband and child. On the other hand, Bedfer and Robert Smith were, primarily, poor working people, like many non-Africans around them. The colour of their skin was not particularly important in this context. Indeed, in 1690 Bedfer was not even described in relation to his racial heritage. Instead, he was being taxed like his peers and treated in a similar fashion by the authorities. It might be useful to think of people such as Bedfer and Robert Smith, and the Blackamore family members, not simply as 'African' but as free working-class Africans to highlight these characteristics.

Rediker and Linebaugh have looked at labouring people in the early modern Atlantic world and tried to understand their actions largely through a class perspective. They accept that the men and women involved 'did not often share "class" consciousness, certainly not of the class "for itself". And if they were not class conscious, neither were they race conscious, gender conscious, or nation conscious to any advanced degree.'[85] The same is true in respect of this characterisation of Africans and their fellows in Norfolk and Suffolk. These Africans were members of labouring communities that did not have consciousness of themselves as 'working class' but whose identities were, nonetheless, conformed

---

[84] Emma Christopher, *Slave Ship Sailors and Their Captive Cargoes, 1730–1807* (New York, 2006); Marcus Rediker, *Between the Devil and the Deep Blue Sea: Merchant Seamen, Pirates, and the Anglo-American Maritime World, 1700–1750* (Cambridge, 1987); Peter Linebaugh and Marcus Rediker, *The Many-Headed Hydra: The Hidden History of the Revolutionary Atlantic*, 2nd edn (Boston, 2013).

[85] Linebaugh and Rediker, *The Many-Headed*, p. 6.

predominantly by their relation to developing structures of local agrarian capitalism and the ownership of wealth. In this context, and in view of the lack of apparent emphasis upon their African heritage, a class perspective of their social position is a useful manner of considering their situation.

This returns us to the point made by Roberts, about the degree to which even chattel slavery was not 'altogether different from other systems of forced labour', from naval impressment to indentured service.[86] The situation of some of the Africans discussed in this chapter was similar. Even if Rosanna had been enslaved originally when she arrived in Suffolk, her movement across the Atlantic had changed her labour position subtly, and she would eventually cease to be in slavish servitude. Mobility had changed her social position, by moving her into a different cultural context. Her working world had been changed, and her lived experience had altered, bringing her closer to other workers in Suffolk. The labour status of an African such as Bedfer was far from that of a chattel slave in Barbados, and far more like that of the non-African working people surrounding him in King's Lynn. Africans in Norfolk and Suffolk who were not enslaved shared an experience of the working world of Norfolk and Suffolk with other members of the working poor. They were part of an early modern world in which 'most laborers (and whole groups of people, such as women or children) experienced some degree of coercion'.[87]

At the same time, however, the economic, mercantile, and social connections between the region and the slave-plantations were growing throughout the period. These connections meant that the ideas about race that were being constructed in the colonies over the course of the century could gradually seep into the culture of England. The use of the term 'mulatto' at Peter Lynn's baptism, along with the growing presence of Africans who were held in slavish servitude in country houses across the region, such as 'ye black boy' and Rosanna, shows that colonial concepts about Africans had begun to trickle into the attitudes and ideas of some of the region's population as the seventeenth century proceeded. Among the working population it seems they were less prevalent, but the wealthier social groups, who could more readily begin to access the plantation economy and its ideas, were leading the way. The appearance of the term 'negro' in their wills is one indicator of this process. Colonial concepts were beginning to gain purchase via the economic structures linking the region and the colonies, even if they had not displaced the existing approaches to Africans that had been visible from 1467 onwards.

The arrival of the Davers family in Rougham at the end of the century was a harbinger of the ever-greater influence that system would have from 1700 onwards. Robert Davers was only the first of a substantial number of planters who would make their home in the region after 1700. Gentry families from the region would also start to invest in plantations and become absentee plantation

---

[86] Roberts, *Slavery*, p. 4.
[87] Ibid, p. 4.

owners in that same period. Merchants would enhance their trading links. Even slave-ships would set sail from King's Lynn. In the eighteenth century transatlantic slavery would reach its point of greatest impact on the economic and political affairs of Britain. As the tentacles of what a group of Norwich men described in 1792 as 'that most iniquitous traffick in human blood' spread rapidly from 1700 onwards, it became impossible for Norfolk and Suffolk to remain unaffected by the ideas about Africans that were being created, or for its people to avoid involvement in the economic traffic that the plantation system engendered.[88] The next chapters will explore the ways in which groups of people in Norfolk and Suffolk became involved in that traffic, and will investigate the degree to which the world of 'peak' Atlantic slavery came to affect the region's African population, whether enslaved or free working class.

[88] NRO/COL/7/38-42, The Friars' Society – Minutes of Proceedings of Sunday and Tuesday Meetings 1791–4, Meeting of 5 February 1792.

6

Eighteenth-Century Links to the Atlantic Economy

Slavers

In early 1701, a twenty-year-old man named Nathaniel Uring signed on as second mate of a ship called the *Martha*, which was to set sail that April from London on a slaving voyage to Guinea in Africa.[1] Uring came from a Quaker household in the Norfolk village of Walsingham.[2] His introduction to the slaving economy had been through a voyage he made as a teenager to Barbados and then Virginia in 1698-9 on a merchant ship that had also sailed from London.[3] After these voyages, Uring was willing to become involved in any aspect of the slaving economy from which he could turn a profit. He traded molasses in Barbados, tobacco in Virginia, sugar in Antigua, and smuggled enslaved Africans from Jamaica to South America. He eventually retired to his home village to run a wine import business, staffed by an African who appears to have been held in near slavery.

While the seventeenth century had seen the foundations being laid, it was in the eighteenth that the British slave-based economy reached its peak of economic, social, and political importance. At the core of this expansion was sugar, which played a vital part in the growth of consumer culture in British life. This development in consumption was made possible by the appearance and success of agrarian capitalism and, in turn, contributed to industrialisation by stimulating manufacturing.[4] In 1700, the British Isles imported 23,000 tons of sugar; one hundred years later, this had grown to 245,000 tons.[5] By 1800, the colonies were providing nearly 20 per cent of England's imports, while

---

[1]   The voyage is listed in the TAIASD, https://www.slavevoyages.org/, voyage ID: 14988, the vessel owner was the Royal African Company; Nathaniel Uring, *The Voyages and Travels of Captain Nathaniel Uring* (reprinted London, 1928; first published 1726), pp. 22-4, 37.
[2]   NRO/NCC/will register, Alexander, 31 Nathaniel Uring, tobacconist, of Walsingham Parva, 1707.
[3]   Uring, *Voyages*, p. 5.
[4]   Woodruff D. Smith, *Consumption and the Making of Respectability, 1660-1800* (New York; London, 2002); Jan de Vries, *The Industrious Revolution: Consumer Behaviour and the Household Economy, 1650 to the Present* (New York, 2008); Robert C. Allen, 'Agriculture during the Industrial Revolution, 1700-1850', in Roderick Floud and Paul Johnson (eds) *The Cambridge Economic History of Modern Britain 1700-1860* (Cambridge, 2004), pp. 96-116.
[5]   Mintz, *Sweetness*, p. 73; Dunn, *Sugar*, p. 203.

purchasing nearly ten per cent of England's exports.[6] As demand for these products grew, so did the Atlantic system, which came to incorporate the governments, business communities, inhabitants, and economies of Europe, Africa, and the Americas – along with Asia, since Asian textiles were the largest single export used for enslaved Africans – into a vast trading nexus.[7] Thousands of ships plied the sea routes across the Atlantic, carrying the essential elements of a booming international economy; millions of people, foodstuffs, raw materials, and manufactured goods of all kinds. Fortunes were made (and lost) by men willing to take the huge risks entailed in engaging in this commerce over thousands of miles, via trading journeys lasting months, or even years.[8]

The numbers of Africans taken to the Americas reached their apogee during the eighteenth century, when perhaps six million were taken across the ocean.[9] The English/British slave trade increased from an average of around 15,000 slaves per year embarked from Africa in the first decade of the eighteenth century, to around 40,000 slaves per year on average a century later.[10] Overall, the transatlantic slave trade carried an estimated 12.5 million captives from Africa, with a mortality rate among the enslaved on slaving voyages of between five and 15 per cent of those embarked, depending on time and place. Around 10.7 million Africans reached the Americas over 400 years.[11] The African states situated in the coastal regions of West Africa – Sierra Leone/the Windward

[6]   Stanley L. Engerman, 'Europe, the Lesser Antilles, and Economic Expansion, 1600–1800', in Robert L. Paquette and Stanley L. Engerman (eds), *The Lesser Antilles in the Age of European Expansion* (Gainsville, FL, 1996), 147–65, at p. 160; John J. McCusker and Russell R. Menard, *The Economy of British America, 1607–1789* (Chapel Hill, NC, 1985), p. 40; Klas Rönnbäck, 'Sweet business: quantifying the value added in the British colonial sugar trade in the 18th century', *Revista de Historia Económica/Journal of Iberian and Latin American Economic History*, 32 (2014), 223–45; David Eltis and Stanley L. Engerman, 'The Importance of Slavery and the Slave Trade to Industrializing Britain', *Journal of Economic History*, 60 (2000), table 1.

[7]   S.G. Checkland, 'Finance for the West Indies, 1780–1815', *The Economic History Review*, New Series, 10 (1958), 461–9; Hugh Thomas, *The Slave Trade* (New York, 1997), pp. 76–7, 100–1, 300–1; Ralph Davis, *The Rise of the Atlantic Economies* (London, 1973), Chapter 14; Seymour Drescher, *Econocide: British Slavery in the Era of Abolition* (Pittsburgh, 1977), pp. 21–3; Dunn, *Sugar*, pp. 97, 188, 201–12.

[8]   For example, see Christopher J. French, 'Productivity in the Atlantic Shipping Industry: A Quantitative Study', *Journal of Interdisciplinary History*, 17 (1987), 613–38; David Hancock, *Citizens of the World: London Merchants and the Integration of the British Atlantic Community, 1735–1785* (Cambridge, 1995).

[9]   David Brion Davis, *Inhuman Bondage: The Rise and Fall of Slavery in the New World* (Oxford, 2006), pp. 80, 104; Eltis, 'Coerced', 33–74; Thomas, *The Slave Trade*, Table II.

[10]   Klas Rönnbäck, 'On the economic importance of the slave plantation complex to the British economy during the eighteenth century: a value-added approach', *Journal of Global History*, 13 (2018), pp. 309–27, at p. 319.

[11]   Richard Anderson, Alex Borucki, Daniel Domingues da Silva, David Eltis, Paul Lachance, Philip Misevich, and Olatunji Ojo, 'Using African Names to Identify the Origins of Captives in the Transatlantic Slave Trade: Crowd-Sourcing and the Registers of Liberated Africans, 1808–1862', *History in Africa*, 40 (2013), 165–91 at p. 166.

Coast, Senegambia, the Bight of Benin, the Gold Coast, the Bight of Biafra, and West Central Africa – worked with the European traders to provide the bulk of the people for enslavement in the Americas. Europeans such as Uring were largely restricted to the coast by the dangers of Africa and so relied on Africans to provide them with enslaved people through a 'hugely complex and geographically diverse trade system that stretched from the African coast far into the interior'.[12] Slaving captains and traders had to engage in multifaceted negotiations with the political elites of West Africa, who were willing to 'sell large numbers of slaves to whoever would pay' for them. Europeans provided goods specifically demanded by the African slave traders, such as manufactured products from Europe, and other commodities, such as silk, which were transhipped from Asia.[13]

Although the evidence is difficult to find, merchants from Norfolk and Suffolk were involved in slaving, even in some circumstances directing and financially backing slaving voyages themselves. Uring sailed from London, which was, until the rise of Liverpool and Bristol, the unchallenged centre of the English slave trade. Nonetheless, as has already been shown, some of the region's merchants and gentry had begun to make the switch to the Atlantic in the seventeenth century. This process continued in the eighteenth. The most striking evidence of this 'Atlantic pivot' is provided by the merchant community of King's Lynn. The Treasury records list a ship leaving the port for the coast of Africa in 1738.[14] The Port Book refers to the *Elizabeth*, owned by Samuel Browne, sailing on 'Trip to Africa' shipping sixty garments, aqua vitae, gunpowder, bays and other woollen cloth, calicoes, German linen, iron, English linen, lead shot, and cotton goods along with other items.[15] Such goods were all standard for use in trading for enslaved Africans, and their presence supports the argument that this appears to have been a slaving journey. The Town Dues entry referred to the local merchant Edward Everard being involved in this trip, shipping 1,000 quarters of wheat to Lisbon. Her Admiralty pass confirmed that Lisbon was the *Elizabeth*'s initial destination, with her captain being John

---

[12] David Dabydeen, John Gilmore, and Cecily Jones (eds), *Oxford Companion to Black British History* (Oxford; New York, 2007), p. 449. The crews of slave ships contained Africans; see, for example, the ship's roll for the Royal African Company ship *Bridgewater*, from 1705, which listed four crewmen identified as 'negro' and being from 'Guiny', named Isaac, Cafe, Antone, and Quanga. The passenger list also noted 'Jacko a free negro', TNA/T70/1438, Servants of the Company: lists of passengers and crews, f. 18, 1705.

[13] John K. Thornton, *Africa and Africans in the Making of the Atlantic World, 1400–1800* (Cambridge, 1998), pp. 72–97.

[14] TNA/T/64/276A/273, Record of Ships to the Coast of Africa, 1734–1754.

[15] TNA/E/190 (Port Books).

Dickson.[16] A similar journey was repeated in 1740.[17] Samuel Browne was an influential Lynn merchant, mayor, and member of one of the town's most important merchant families.[18] Everard and Browne worked in partnership on numerous occasions, and it appears that here they were working together to conduct a slaving voyage after stopping at Lisbon.[19] Browne family ships appear as regular visitors to the West Indies in this period in the port books of King's Lynn, and one of them, the *Grafton*, was closely involved in a trading network that the Brownes attempted to set up with a planter from St Christopher named Crisp Molineux in the 1760s.[20]

These two voyages are the only clear record of any direct slaving voyage from ports in Norfolk and Suffolk to Africa, but were unlikely to have been the only ones. Given the size and nature of the region's illegal economy, not all voyages were properly recorded, so it is quite possible other voyages occurred. It appears, moreover, that ships from Norfolk and Suffolk were engaged in other slaving voyages, but that these were recorded as departing from London and other ports, disguising the link. The strongest evidence for this is provided by the case of a ship named the *Charming Sally*, which set out on a slaving voyage to the Gold Coast in 1759. The ship loaded 100 slaves at Cape Coast Castle and Anomabu before sailing to the West Indies.[21] The central government records show the ship as being registered in London, but an insurance claim made by her captain and crew reveals that she was, in fact, a King's Lynn ship.[22]

Having left the Gold Coast, the *Charming Sally* was captured by French privateers near Antigua.[23] In 1760, the ship's captain, William Ayres, and a crewman named Richard Jenson made witness statements to trustees at King's Lynn who were administering a scheme for compensating maimed seamen and the families

[16] NRO/KL/C44/59, King's Lynn Town Dues book, 18 November 1738; TNA/ADM/7/83, No. 111, Admiralty Passes. Listed in the Treasury records as being 200 tons in size, with nineteen crew and four guns, references to the *Elizabeth* elsewhere show her as 90 tons. The variation in tonnage is normal for the period; tonnages quoted in Admiralty passes frequently do not bear much relation to those quoted elsewhere. This would normally be a large crew for a ship of this size, but slaving ship crews were larger than normal.
[17] TNA/T/64/276A/273, Record of Ships to the Coast of Africa, 1734-1754. Neither of these voyages is recorded in TAIASD.
[18] The Brownes owned property in Norfolk, Huntingdonshire, and Lincolnshire, alongside a considerable number of ships; NRO/PRA/525/381x7, Copy of the will of Samuel Browne of King's Lynn, Merchant, 10 September 1784.
[19] For discussion of their partnership, see Barney, 'Shipping', p. 134.
[20] NRO/BL/X6/21, Crisp Molineux to George Irvine, 26 September 1769.
[21] TAIASD, Voyage ID 75276. Cape Coast Castle was the British slaving station rented from the ruler of Efutu (and later from the leaders of the Fante confederation who absorbed Efutu in 1720), see William St Clair, *The Grand Slave Emporium* (London, 2006), pp. 39-56.
[22] TNA/BT6/3156; T70/1263; List, 12 February 1760.
[23] NRO/KL/TS/8, *Trustees for the port of King's Lynn under an Act for the relief of maimed and disabled seamen and widows and children of those killed in the merchant service*, Statements of Richard Jenson and William Ayres, 5 June, 30 June 1760 and undated.

of deceased men from the port. Ayres and his fellows were claiming compensation for the families of their crewmates who had died in the French attack. In these statements Ayres and Jenson both stated that the ship was 'the *Charming Sally* of Lynn'.[24] The court accepted that the ship was a King's Lynn vessel when it made its decision to make a financial award for the families of the dead men.[25] The statements made by Ayres and Jenson agree with all other sources in their description of the ship's voyage and fate and would appear, therefore, to be an indicator that ships from Norfolk and Suffolk may have been engaged in transatlantic slaving voyages through the eighteenth century, but were often recorded as being from London or other ports.

Other evidence points, at least tangentially, to a wider involvement in the actual business of slave-trading. Returning to the 1738 voyage of the *Elizabeth*, this was recorded in the King's Lynn Port Books as being to Lisbon.[26] It may be, therefore, that some of the other King's Lynn ships shown as sailing to Lisbon and Oporto in the eighteenth century also went on to Africa in a similar fashion. The port's records show twenty such voyages between 1738 and 1742.[27] Clearly, many of these were likely to have been merchants trading with the Iberian markets as had been the case for many years before, but the evidence of the *Elizabeth* suggests that some others may have been speculative slaving voyages. Furthermore, the port records also reveal a vibrant trade with Bristol in the period and some voyages to Liverpool. The region's merchants were, therefore, connected commercially with main English slaving ports, and such connections could easily have engendered investment opportunities and business ventures. It is also the case that ships built in the region were involved in eighteenth-century slaving voyages but were registered at other ports. The King's Lynn-built ship *Galem*, which was constructed in 1761, was used in the slave trade, but registered in Liverpool.[28] The *Galem* was joined by Yarmouth-built ships such as *Sea Nymph*, *Young Eagle*, *Westmoreland*, *Chalmers*, *City of Bruges*, *Princess Royal*, and *Duke of Buccleugh*.[29]

---

[24] NRO/KL/TS/8, Statements of Richard Jenson and William Ayres, 5 June, 30 June 1760. They confirmed that the 'first part of the voyage to Africa was on the government's orders but the second part, that which took them to the West Indies, was on the merchant service'.
[25] NRO/KL/TS/8, Statements of Richard Jenson and William Ayres, 5 June, 30 June 1760.
[26] KL/C44/59, Town Dues Book, 18 November 1738.
[27] KL/C44/59, KL/C4460, King's Lynn Town Dues Books 1738–42.
[28] TAIASD, Voyage IDs 92310, 92309 and 91068.
[29] TAIASD, Voyage IDs 25128; 18174; 84005 and 84006; 80781 and 80782; 80843; Voyage IDs 83241; 81077 to 81083. The *Chalmers* is mentioned as a slave ship owned by Archibald Dalzel of London, James A. Rawley, *London, Metropolis of the Slave Trade* (Columbia, 2003), p. 107.

Absentee Plantation Owners

As the slave-based economies developed and reached their zenith in the eighteenth and early nineteenth centuries, the ownership of plantations, and the slaves held therein, by absentee landowners who lived in Norfolk and Suffolk became more prevalent. The plantation owners identified to date in the counties are listed in Appendix C.[30] They can be placed usefully in several categories.[31] Firstly, families that gained plantations through entrepreneurial activity (for example, Thomas Bland, the Thellusson family).[32] Secondly, there were those who entered the economy via government service (for example, the Peete, Dalling, and Daniell families).[33] Third, those families that entered plantation

[30] The numbers of owners suggested by Appendix C must be taken as indicative of the depth of involvement by Norfolk and Suffolk families in plantation ownership, rather than offering a definitive list, since the data cannot be considered exhaustive. In some cases, for example the Dalling family, the records of the family held at the Norfolk Record Office contain plantation records, making the identification of the family straightforward. Other family ownership, such as the ownership of the Greenland Estate in St Christopher by the Woodley family of Eccles in Norfolk, has been identified by various other means, such as the examination of the claims made for compensation in the period after slavery was abolished in 1833. The work of extracting these data has been made far easier thanks to the excellent *Legacies of British Slave Ownership* database at University College London.

[31] This categorisation resembles that outlined by Higman, but subdivides his categories further; see B.W. Higman, *Plantation Jamaica 1750–1850: Capital and Control in a Colonial Economy* (Kingston, Jamaica, 2005), pp. 17–18.

[32] Thomas Bland was a merchant and partner in the Norwich textile import/export company of Gurney and Bland, who received a 500-acre estate in South Carolina as a minor in 1742 as a result of the business relationship and friendship between his father, Michael Bland, 'broker in London', and the Deputy Auditor of the Province of South Carolina, James St John, NRO/MC/403/1/1-9, Deeds and letters from various to Michael Bland and to his son, Thomas Bland, re 500a estate on the Winyou River near George Town in Craven County, South Carolina. The Thellusson family purchased Rendlesham House, near Woodbridge, Suffolk, in the late eighteenth century. Peter Thellusson, later Lord Rendlesham, had been a London merchant, acting as agent for leading European commercial houses, and trading to the West Indies. He had acquired the Bacolet estate in Grenada, see Thomas Kitson Cromwell, *Excursions in the County of Suffolk* (London, 1819), p. 57; SRO/HB/416/D1/3/1, Accounting records for Bacolet Estate.

[33] The Daniell family of Snettisham came to own the 'Paradise' plantation when Thomas Daniell Esq. followed a legal career that culminated in him becoming Attorney-General of the island of Dominica. Daniell died in 1806 having retired to Norfolk, Oliver, *Caribbeana*, *Volume 1*, pp. 94 and 177. Peete was the son of Richard Peete Esq. of Norwich, an alderman of the city and mayor in 1775; Charles Parkin, *The History and Antiquities of the City of Norwich* (Lynn, 1783), pp. 156 and 167; *Norfolk Chronicle*, 12 January 1788, p. 2. The Peetes may have had a previous connection with the island; a man named 'George Peete' was listed as owning an unnamed 450-acre plantation with eighteen slaves in St Andrew's parish in 1754; Frank Cundall, *Historic Jamaica* (London, 1915) pp. 138–44; Frederick G. Spurdle, *Early West Indian Government: Showing the Progress of Government in Barbados, Jamaica and the Leeward Islands, 1660–1783* (Palmerston North, New Zealand, 1962), pp. 140–3. The Dalling family gained their plantation because of John Dalling's service in Jamaica; J.

ownership through marriage into an established colonial planter dynasty, often having never left England (for example, the Berney family).[34] Fourth, there were those that inherited plantations via business or personal connections, such as the Longe, Greene, and Burton families.[35] Fifth, there was the anomaly that was the ownership of Unity Valley Pen by the Quaker banking family, the Barclays. Around 1785, David Barclay and his brother John Barclay had taken possession of this 2,000-acre cattle pen, and thirty-two enslaved Africans, in lieu of the debts of the estate of the late William Harvie. David Barclay was determined from the outset to emancipate these enslaved people, a process that took over a decade.[36]

Finally, there were returning plantation-owning families whose forebears had migrated to the West Indies from various parts of England and Scotland in the seventeenth and early eighteenth centuries, and having made fortunes there, chose to come back to England. It has been shown that alongside a desire to flaunt their wealth to a metropolitan audience, these planters 'sought to distance themselves from the fear in which all whites lived, the very real expectation that they might be cut down by disease or murdered by the enslaved'.[37] The Davers family were an early example of such a family, but this was a

---

Spain, 'Dalling, Sir John, first baronet (c. 1731–1798), army officer and colonial governor', *ODNB*, <https://www.oxforddnb.com/view/10.1093/ref:odnb/9780198614128.001.0001/odnb-9780198614128-e-53621> [accessed 6 February 2019].

[34] The Berney family of Kirby-Bedon Hall became plantation owners in the 1720s when Sir Thomas Berney married Elizabeth Folkes, the granddaughter of Samuel Hanson. The Hansons were long-established planters on the island of Barbados; the St George parish registers of 1679 state that 'Mr Samuel Hanson' owned fifty-seven acres of land, had six white servants and owned 105 enslaved Africans, Hotten, *The Original*, p. 461. The marriage meant that on the death of Samuel Hanson, the plantation came into the ownership of the Berney family. In 1792, it was described as being some 382 acres in extent, with 200 acres of rich cane land, NRO/MC/50/46/503X9, printed sale particular of Hanson Plantation, 5 April 1792.

[35] The Greenes befriended the elderly and childless Sir Patrick Blake (see below) and inherited some of his plantations in St Christopher; R. Wilson, 'Greene family (per. 1801–1920), brewers', *ODNB*. Retrieved 24 January 2020, from https://www.oxforddnb.com/view/10.1093/ref:odnb/9780198614128.001.0001/odnb-9780198614128-e-50414 [accessed 28 August 2016]. The Burton family had acquired their plantation in 1788, when two thirds of it was left to Thomas Burton of Norwich by John Vernon of Jamaica; BL, MSS. W. Ind. s. 17, MSS. W. Ind. s. 18 and MSS. W. Ind. s. 19, *Letters, documents and reports to its English owners from the agents in Jamaica managing the Chiswick sugar plantation, 1825–1847*, three volumes; mentioned in K.E. Ingram, *Sources of Jamaican History 1655–1838* (Zug, 1976). The Longe family of Spixworth appear to have obtained their slaveholding from a blend of government service and personal connections. Catherine Longe appears to have become owner of the Camp estate in St Christopher in 1817. It seems that this estate, which was previously owned by General Charles Leigh (d.1815), came to her because her husband, Francis Longe, was a close friend of Leigh and her nephew George Howes had served as Leigh's military secretary in the Caribbean from 1794-6; see, for example, NRO/MC/150/31, Letters from and concerning George Howes, military secretary to Gen. Leigh, 1794-6.

[36] Details can be found in David Barclay, *An account of the emancipation of the slaves of Unity Valley Pen, in Jamaica* (London, 1801); *Monthly Magazine*, 38 (1814), pp. 133-7.

[37] Higman, *Plantation*, p. 7.

widespread phenomenon in England over the eighteenth century. Returning planters established communities in London, Bath, and Bristol, and bought estates across the country.[38] Resented for their wealth, they were lampooned for their alleged social pretentions in plays, novels, broadsides, newspapers, and cartoons.[39] In Norfolk and Suffolk their numbers included John Scott, the Blake family, the Arcedeckne family, William Beckford, and William Colhoun.[40] Others, such as Crisp Molineux, had no intention of leaving their islands permanently. Molineux came to fight for the rights of the colonies in Parliament as part of what has been termed the 'West India lobby', a group of colonial agents, London merchants, planters, and Members of Parliament with West Indian connections who lobbied for the interests of the plantations.[41]

[38] Srinivas Aravamudan, *Tropicopolitans: Colonialism and Agency, 1688–1804* (Durham, NC, 1999), Chap. 1.

[39] Andrew J. O'Shaughnessy, *An Empire Divided: The American Revolution and the British Caribbean* (Philadelphia, PA, 2000), Chap. 1, esp. pp. 2–18.

[40] The Scotts had lived in Jamaica for at least two generations, owned the Retreat estate and may have had an interest in the Clarendon. Other members of the family remained on the island; for example, Matthew Scott was Secretary to the Commission of Compensation under the West Indian Slavery Compensation Bill and died in Jamaica in 1836. NA/PROD/11/1551, Will of John Scott, 7 January 1814; 'Thomas Scott, The Regicide', *Notes and Queries* (1883), 229–30; B.W. Higman, *Jamaica Surveyed: Plantation Maps and Plans of the Eighteenth and Nineteenth Centuries* (Kingston, Jamaica, 2001), p. 138. Sir Patrick Blake purchased the manor of Langham, near Bury St Edmunds, in 1760, using money derived from his family's ownership of plantations in Montserrat and St Christopher, Richard G. Wilson, *Greene King: A Business and Family History* (London, 1983), pp. 33–5. William Colhoun was a plantation owner who used the wealth generated by his family's long-term presence in St Christopher, Nevis, and St Croix to buy three estates in Norfolk, in Thorpe, Wretham, and Great Hockham, Richard Pares, *A West-India Fortune* (London, 1950), esp. Chap. 11; Stuart M. Nisbet, 'Sugar and the Early Mercantile Identity of Glasgow', *Scottish Archives*, 19 (2013), 65–82. The Arcedeckne family had extensive landholdings in Jamaica, notably the Golden Grove sugar plantation. The family lived at Yoxford Hall, and then Glevering Hall in Suffolk, *Proceedings of the Suffolk Institute of Archaeology*, Suffolk Institute of Archaeology (1953), 138; HD/365/3, Diaries of William Goodwin of Street Farm, Earl Soham, November 1797. Somerley, Suffolk, was the home of William Beckford Esq. who was born in Jamaica and was a member of one of Jamaica's richest planter families. He inherited his father's estates in 1756 and lived in Somerley until 1774, when he returned to Jamaica to try to rescue the plantations which were in financial difficulties. He failed in this endeavour and was incarcerated in the Fleet prison as a debtor on his return to England in 1786; NRO/YD/87/9, Youell Diaries, 23 October 1774; Jill H. Casid, *Sowing Empire: Landscape and Colonization* (Minnesota, 2005), p. 60; R. Sheridan, 'Beckford, William (1744–1799), sugar planter and historian', *ODNB*, <https://www.oxforddnb.com/view/10.1093/ref:odnb/9780198614128.001.0001/odnb-9780198614128-e-1904> [accessed 27 January 2020]; LBSO, William Beckford of Somerley, https://www.ucl.ac.uk/lbs/person/view/2146634868. [accessed 21 October 2018].

[41] Barry Higman, 'The West India Interest in Parliament, 1807–1833', *Historical Studies*, 13 (1967), 1–19; David Beck Ryden, *West Indian Slavery and British Abolition, 1783–1807* (Cambridge; New York, 2009), Chap. 3; Andrew J. O'Shaughnessy, 'The Formation of a Commercial Lobby: The West India Interest, British Colonial Policy and the American Revolution', *The Historical Journal*, 40 (1997), 71–95.

The region's plantation owners did not come from any specific area. Some were from ports, for example the Penrice family and the Burtons were from Great Yarmouth, but most were not, which suggests that plantation ownership was not linked fundamentally to any specific trading networks. There was a degree of social linkage between some of these families, mainly by marriage. The Berney and Folkes families were joined in 1776 when William Folkes' son, Robert, and Ann, the daughter of Sir John Berney, were married.[42] These linkages were not widespread, however, and do not point towards any significant influence from kinship networks. Neither was there any specific focus on any one colonial area. The plantations owned were spread across the West Indies and English/British North America. Although the records suggest that the majority were in the West Indies, this weighting may reflect the impact of the American Revolution upon later ownership records. At least one owner, Thomas Bland, appears to have lost his plantation because of the colonial revolution. Most plantations were owned in Jamaica and Barbados; again, that reflects the size and success of the economies of those islands rather than any strategic plan; people from Norfolk and Suffolk also owned plantations in St Christopher, Grenada, St Vincent, Dominica, Nevis, St Croix, and in South Carolina. In terms of date of entry into plantation ownership, there was a small involvement in the seventeenth century, with early movers into plantation ownership such as the Frere and Davers families, and then increased investment in the eighteenth century. The ownership of plantations and their slaves continued even as the regional campaign against slavery increased in impact from the late eighteenth century onwards. The Greene family only entered ownership in the 1820s, and eventually became responsible for managing and modernizing eighteen estates.[43]

The choice to own enslaved Africans on a plantation was a level of involvement in the slaving economy that was on a par with fitting out and financing a slaving ship. Plantation ownership was an active investment decision to take part in a core economic activity that required the purchase of enslaved people. It was different in its degree of involvement in the slaving economy to activities such as trading with the colonies or selling colonial goods, in that these did not involve an active choice to buy enslaved people. The merchants of King's Lynn who traded goods with the colonies were enriching themselves because of the enslavement of Africans, but they did so at arm's length from the actual business of trading and owning those Africans. This was not the case with the ownership of a plantation. To buy a plantation, or to marry into a plantation dynasty, was an investment decision, a choice to place part of a family's wealth into a specific form of asset, in this case the land of a plantation and the enslaved people held in bondage on that land, as opposed to investing it in another form of asset, for example purchasing farmland in Suffolk.

---

[42] NRO/FEL/326/551x5, Berney Marriage Settlement, 1776.
[43] Wilson, 'Greene family'.

The evidence suggests that those families in Norfolk and Suffolk who acquired slaves and plantations held their plantations for as long as they were able to. The Berney family, as an example, ran their plantation poorly and came close to bankruptcy around 1790, but avoided it. They appear to have sold that original plantation around 1809 but owned another into the 1820s.[44] Several families retained their plantations after the abolition of slavery. The Burtons kept ownership of their plantation until the 1840s, having claimed £3,119 10s 10d as compensation for the 160 enslaved people held there.[45] The Greene family carried on running their plantations into the 1840s.[46] The Dallings still owned Donnington Castle in 1847, and the Arcedeckne family retained Golden Grove until 1891.[47]

Absentee owners operated via local agents who ran the estates and shipped their produce to Britain, where it was sold and the proceeds distributed to various members of the families through an intricate network of pensions and annuities.[48] The Molineux family worked through their local contacts and also family members who had remained on the island.[49] The Burton family, who owned Chiswick plantation in Jamaica, worked through English solicitors and local agents.[50] The Arcedeckne family used a series of agents to manage their affairs, the most notable of whom was Simon Taylor.[51] The Dallings engaged the services of the planter Henry Cox to run their estate after 1800, and he appears to have brought it back into order after a previous period of poor supervision.[52] The Burton family's oversight was also, apparently, sound. The

---

[44] Deeds in the Barbados archives suggest that the Berney family sold the Hanson plantation in 1809; see J.S. Handler, with M. Conner and K. Jacobi, *Searching for a Slave Cemetery in Barbados, West Indies: A Bioarchaeological and Ethnohistorical Investigation* (Southern Illinois, 1989), p. 38. It appears that the family still owned a plantation in 1825, but it is unclear where that plantation was on the island, see *Norwich Mercury*, 29 October 1825, p. 3.

[45] TNA/T71/867, St Thomas-in-the-East claim no. 263, 30 November 1835. The family still owned the plantation in the 1840s, PROB 11/1958/444, Will of Thomas Burton of Great Yarmouth, Norfolk, 11 March 1842.

[46] J. Orbell, 'Greene, Benjamin Buck (1808–1902), merchant', ODNB, <https://www.oxforddnb.com/view/10.1093/ref:odnb/9780198614128.001.0001/odnb-9780198614128-e-48874 [accessed 24 January 2020]; Wilson, 'Greene family'.

[47] SRO/HB/26/412/1595, Sale Particulars of Golden Grove Estate, 1891.

[48] See NRO/MEA/6/10/660x7, Annuities of Donnington Castle Plantation from March 1811 to 30 April 1825.

[49] NRO/BL/F/23, Typed extracts from letter books of Crisp Molineux (1730–1792), MP for Castle Rising, 1771–1774, and King's Lynn, 1774–1790, mainly relating to King's Lynn elections [1768–1773].

[50] NRO/MC1519/1,813X9, William Wright to Susanna Wright, Chiswick, 10 April 1825, p. 6.

[51] Taylor managed the Golden Grove estate until his death in 1813 and has been studied in exceptional depth in Higman, *Plantation*, pp. 127–51 and 166–226.

[52] For mentions of Cox, see Kathleen Mary Butler, *The Economics of Emancipation: Jamaica & Barbados, 1823–1843* (Chapel Hill, 1995), pp. 59–70 and p. 162; Benjamin McMahon, *Jamaican Plantership* (London, 1839), p. 200.

Berneys appear to have had some problems with their agents, and only learned that their plantation had been 'utterly neglected if not abandoned' and had 'required good management for 25 to 30 years back' when they reached the point of bankruptcy and their trustees tried to sell it in 1790.[53]

The families' papers contain little discussion of abolition, although in 1818 William Dalling described abolitionists as 'fanatics'.[54] The evidence indicates, nevertheless, that most Norfolk and Suffolk absentee plantation owners shared an interest in the modern improvement of economic practice and associated themselves with the amelioration movement in the colonies. Detailed letters from Henry Cox in Jamaica to the Dalling family provided them with extensive information about their plantation, including weather reports, details of the work patterns in use, and productivity levels.[55] The Burton family worked with their agents to incorporate modern agricultural techniques, such as the Norfolk Four-Course System, into their operations and were recruiting Norfolk farmers to travel to their plantation in the mid-1820s as part of this programme of improvement.[56] One letter from a bookkeeper on their plantation in 1826 mentions that there was a 'hospital for the Negroes' there, confirming the family's engagement with ideas of amelioration.[57] Cox's letters to the Dallings also mention weekly doctor's visits.[58] The agents also kept owners aware of the 'increase' and 'decrease' in what was termed the 'stock' of the plantation, which included enslaved people.[59] Plantation managers used the increase and decrease in such accounts as an indicator of whether slaves were well-treated, seeing 'natural reproduction as a true test of amelioration'.[60] The surviving correspondence seems to suggest that, although their management approaches varied, the members of most plantation-owning families from Norfolk and Suffolk viewed the ownership of Africans as a necessity required to generate the cash needed to fund their lifestyles and that they appreciated that their plantations needed to be managed in a modern and efficient fashion to provide that cashflow.[61] Their letters tended to discuss slaves from the perspective of their economic utility. In 1789, the Berney family's agent told Robert Fellowes,

[53] NRO/MC/50/43/503x8, Fellowes to Folkes, 25 August 1789; NRO/MC/50/46/503x9, Printed sale particular of Hanson Plantation, 1792; NRO/FEL/539/30, Capt. Thomas Walker, 10 July 1790.
[54] NRO/MEA/6/9, William Dalling to George Peacock, undated, c.1818.
[55] NRO/MEA/6/21/660x9, Journals of Donnington Castle Plantation, written by Henry Cox, 1829–31.
[56] NRO/MC1519/1,813x9, William Wright to Susanna Wright, Chiswick, 10 April 1825, p. 6.
[57] NRO/MC1519/1,813x9, William Wright to Susanna Wright, Chiswick, 10 April 1825, p. 1.
[58] NRO/MEA/6/21/660x9, Cox to Dalling, 7 October 1830.
[59] NRO/FEL/884/556x4, Journal and ledger of Hanson plantation, Barbados, 1792, NRO/MEA/6/21/660x9, Cox to Dalling, 7 October 1830.
[60] Roberts, *Slavery*, p. 282.
[61] For the Berney estates, see NRO/MC/50/43/9, John Bond to Folkes, 15 September

for example, that 'The negroes are most of them good people', which would appear again to have been an attempt to convince Fellowes that the plantation was managed efficiently. The agent went on to state that 'some of them are old and perfectly useless', and they were insufficient in number to carry out the work needed.[62]

This evidence points towards an understanding of plantation ownership in Norfolk and Suffolk as being an active investment decision, grounded upon Enlightenment views about efficiency, moral improvement, and scientific order. The members of the families from Norfolk and Suffolk who owned plantations across the eighteenth and early nineteenth centuries – whether they had built their plantation up from nothing, bought it, inherited it, obtained it by marriage into plantation-owning families, or just received annuities from the ownership of a plantation by relatives – had made an informed business decision. The motivation behind this was always money. Plantation ownership offered a route to income and wealth, which provided access to status, to pleasure, and to power. Plantations and slaves were asset classes and were chosen with an eye to profit maximisation and income return. Detailed reports were provided about the slaves, the condition of the plantations, and the situation on the islands themselves. In general, the owners received reports and managed the plantations with an eye to modern practice and efficiency.

Merchants

Aside from slave-trading and slave-plantation ownership, the region continued to be involved in trade with the plantations. After 1700 Norfolk and Suffolk's merchants built up the links with American colonies and the West Indies that had been laid in the seventeenth century. The region's newspapers contained continuous reports of the arrival of ships from the colonies laden with sugar and other produce and of the prospects for the future production of sugar.[63] Many reports concentrated on the fluctuating fortune of conflict with the French in the West Indies.[64] A list of local merchants and other businessmen trading with the American colonies was provided in the subscribers to *The American Negotiator* in 1761. This listed five from Lynn, thirteen from Yarmouth, one from Wisbech, and twenty-two from Norwich.[65] The papers of the Gurney/Barclay

---

1790; NRO/MC/50/42503x8; Letter from George Blackman, 19 November 1789; NRO/FEL/539/28/553x7, Letter from Mr Foster, 1789.

[62] NRO/MC/50/42503x8; Letter from George Blackman, 19 November 1789.

[63] See *Norwich Mercury*, 3 September 1757, *Arrived at the Downs*, 'one hundred and four ships and vessels under their convoy from Jamaica', and *Advice from Jamaica*, 'the crops of sugar are like to be more plentiful than has been known for some years'.

[64] For example, see *Norwich Mercury*, 4 December 1756; 16 April 1757; 23 April 1757; 30 July 1757.

[65] John Wright, *The American Negotiator: Or The Various Currencies of the British Colonies in*

family show that the region's Quaker merchants were also engaged in such trade from the early eighteenth century; for example, in 1726 the 'Respected Friend Martha Hudson' was involved in shipments of flour to Barbados.[66] Other involvement can be glimpsed elsewhere. In his extensive research on the history of the port of King's Lynn, John Barney has identified about forty transatlantic voyages from the town between 1732 and 1800. In September 1714, the *Lynn Merchant*, captained by Alexander Barclay, sailed to Jamaica from King's Lynn. The ship carried a mixed cargo to the colony and returned a year later, carrying a small amount of muscovado sugar. In 1717 and 1721, ships arrived at Lynn from Campeche, in modern Mexico, carrying cochineal for the merchant Thomas Long. The *John and Ann* sailed from Lynn for New England in 1723 with a cargo including coal, iron, saddles, and scythes. The *Samuel*, which may have been owned by Samuel Browne, arrived in the port with rice from Carolina in 1732, 1733 and 1734. Other ships sailed to Carolina and New England. After Samuel Browne's death in 1741, there was a hiatus in traffic, suggesting that he may have been the guiding hand behind these early voyages. Traffic resumed in 1746, with the voyage of the *Ann and Lucy* to Carolina; this ship was owned by two Lynn men, John Bloom and Edward Bigland.[67] Several voyages were made to North Carolina, especially by the merchant Elijah Callonder, between 1767 and 1772, while custom house returns from the 1730s show occasional wine and linen being traded to the West Indies.[68] During the 1780s and 1790s, the merchants of the town appeared to shift their focus to North America, for example New York, and Canada. Whether this related to the growth in anti-slavery sentiment is difficult to determine.[69] To this involvement was added maritime investments by local absentee plantation owners, whose involvement in sugar production appears to have caused them to expand operations further along the supply chain. For example, the Berney family had a share in a ship called the *Barbadoes Planter*.[70]

Other towns were also becoming involved. For example, William Manning, a Yarmouth merchant who traded as Manning, Walker, and Hurrys, owned several ships. In June 1781, Manning's brig, the *Anson*, entered the port of San Antonio with a cargo of 200 bars of iron, two chests of tea, and twenty-one cauldrons of coals. It appears the *Anson* had sailed initially to London as part of the normal coastal trade and had then been loaded with goods for the West

---

America (1765).

[66] NRO/RQG/532/492x9, Martha Hudson/Barker. Papers regarding trade with Philadelphia and Barbados and property in America, 1706–1726. Letter from Samuel Mickle, Barbados, 21 May 1726; Hudson to John Estaugh, New Jersey, regarding payment to George Knight in Barbados, 30 November 1716.

[67] John M. Barney, 'The merchants and maritime trade of King's Lynn in the eighteenth century' (Unpublished Ph.D. Dissertation, University of East Anglia, 1997), Appendix F.

[68] Barney, 'Shipping', pp. 126–41.

[69] Barney, 'The merchants', Appendix F.

[70] NRO/FEL/539/23, Abergavenney to Folkes, 20 November 1789.

Indies, sailing direct to Jamaica.[71] Similar voyages to the Americas can be found across the period. In November 1775, the *Effingham* sailed from Yarmouth to St Christopher and Jamaica.[72] The records also show large numbers of ships that were built in towns such as Ipswich arriving in West Indian ports on trading journeys; for example, in August 1773, the *Harriett* arrived in Bridgetown, with a cargo of sugar, rum, cotton, and ginger. The ship was recorded as being built in Ipswich in 1767. There were many other similar situations.[73]

The opportunities for the region's business community did not end in direct trade with the plantations, but also in the use of plantation-produced products when they had been imported. Sugar refining was one area of such activity. In 1739, the city of Norwich received 'a present of two gold chains of One hundred guineas each, to be worn by the Sheriffs of this city for the time being' from Mr Emerson, 'a native of this city', who had a sugar-refining business in London.[74]

Sailors and Bookkeepers

As we have seen, Nathaniel Uring had signed on as a slaver voluntarily. His memoirs indicate that he found ongoing involvement in slaving operation acceptable. This was not always the case, for the job of a slaver was an unpopular one with the average British sailor. The mortality among slaving crews was high; Uring's captain died on the outward voyage and Uring recorded that while off the coast of Africa the *Martha's* surgeon and second mate died, while significant numbers of the crew fell ill.[75] Slave ships were deeply disagreeable, and highly dangerous, working environments that 'were notorious for reeking so badly that other ships at sea could smell them before they could see them'. The unpopularity of the work meant that the captains and owners of slave ships were the only group of civilian seafarers that had to use a system known as 'crimping' to obtain their crews. In a similar manner to the notorious 'pressing' of the military, the crimps entrapped sailors into debt and created a situation where a slaving voyage was the only means by which such debt could be repaid.[76]

[71] TNA/T/64/72, Ships belonging to British Persons entering Jamaica 1775–85; NRO/MC/1503/1/813x8, Bill of sale by Jacob Preston to William Manning, 29 May 1784.
[72] Peter Coldham, *Emigrants from England to the American Colonies, 1773–1776* (Baltimore, MD, 1998), p. 144.
[73] TNA/T/64/49, Ships entering Bridgetown, 1773–1775. The entry for the *Harriett* is dated 14 August 1773 (also mentioned 22 February 1774). Also included in this record are the *Chatham*, which was built in Norwich in 1767; the *Prudent Sally*, built in Ipswich in 1765; the *Gibbons*, built in Suffolk in 1766, mentioned May, October and November 1774.
[74] *Norwich Mercury*, 22 September 1739.
[75] Uring, *Voyages*, p. 47.
[76] Christopher, *Slave*, pp. 28–32.

In his short memoir written in 1775, Samuel Ward, a sailor from Great Yarmouth, remembered how on Christmas Day 1732 he had met his brothers for the first time in seventeen years. After their meeting, 'one went to Guiney [sic], another aboard a man of war' and Ward went to Florida.[77] Ward appeared to consider his brother's slaving voyage to Africa part and parcel of the differing forms of labour that he and his fellow sailors had to endure to survive. The necessities of survival for the poor, and their lack of options, made such choices at once normal and unavoidable. This can be seen in the travel narrative of another Norfolk sailor, John Secker. Secker served on various merchant vessels between 1729 and 1755, rising to the rank of chief mate, and sailed to many European destinations, as well as Arabia, the West Indies, South America, India, and Virginia. He had no illusions about the reality of slavery and recalled his concern when in 1736 his ship, the *John Snow*, sailing to Madeira, was 'chas'd & boarded by a Barbary cruiser' and he and his fellows faced the possibility of being 'carried to Barbary & made slaves'. Two years passed, however, and Secker was working as master of a riverboat in South Carolina, carrying wood to Charlestown, with Africans on his crew. Although he was the boat's master, he found the life tiresome, 'as having nothing but new negros [sic] with me (excepting one or two) & they dull & hard to manage'. Secker continued to work in this environment for several years. In 1747, when travelling in Virginia he commented on the oppressive heat, 'sometimes [sic] it has been so exceedingly hot & sultry, that I have heard it reported the negroes have fallen down dead in the field at their work'.[78] For men like Secker the practice of African enslavement was part of the reality of the world around him. His opinion on it was immaterial, the necessity was for him to survive.

Some, however, saw the opportunities that might arise from a deeper engagement with the world of slavery. Originating from Thetford in Norfolk, James King had enlisted as a sailor around 1782.[79] It appears that King deserted his ship in 1784 and then sought work in Jamaica's plantations. He wrote several letters to his parents while on the island, which reveal that he initially found life there amenable. Like Uring, King saw involvement in the slave-based economy as a means of making money and advancing himself. As he told his parents, King intended to 'take to the planting business on a sugar works as bookkeeper where I meet with all the encouragement & civilities a young man can wish for'. He was focused on the chance for wealth. 'If a man has any merit at all', he wrote, 'after being three years in Jamaica he gets an overseers [sic] berth whose wages is according to the size of the estate. Sometime £100 pa some £200.' King's long-term aim was to advance his social position – 'I hope in time to see myself proprietor or tenant of a farm in your neighbourhood' – and he accepted that his hopes for wealth were based upon the exploitation of enslaved

---

[77] NRO/COL/7/13, Autobiography of Samuel Ward 1713–1775, 21 August 1775.
[78] NRO/Y/D/41/105, *Travel narrative of John Secker, of North Walsham*.
[79] NRO/FX/323/1, 26 February 1785.

Africans.[80] He appears to have purchased slaves on the island.[81] King would die a poor man in the late 1790s, having drifted from job to job for a decade, and was apparently robbed of his last remaining goods by his executor.[82]

The decision-making process that underpinned this choice for the less wealthy is revealed in a sequence of letters written between 1824 and 1826 by William Wright, a young man from a farming background, who travelled to Jamaica from the Norfolk village of Watton to work on the Burton family's sugar estate, Chiswick St Thomas.[83] Wright made clear in his letters that the impetus behind his decision to go to the West Indies was economic. As he put it, 'if I could have gained a living by any endeavours without being a burden to anyone, I should never have left Norfolk.'[84] It seems that Wright had answered an advert in the *Norfolk Chronicle*, which asked for a man 'who thoroughly understands the breeding and management of Horses and Horned Cattle' to travel to Jamaica.[85] He mentioned that his brother, Robert, had considered becoming a sailor and that both men were attempting to make something of themselves, without relying on hand-outs from friends and relatives; 'my only desire is to gain sufficient to support me by honest industry in my own country, and to assist my Mother when age shall render her harassing life unsuitable.'[86] He saw work in Jamaica as a means of advancing his social situation and aspiration; 'it was the expectation of being able in a few years, to return and become a Norfolk farmer' that drove his decision.[87]

Wright's letters show that he made his choice with a good understanding of the situation in Jamaica before he travelled. On several occasions in his early letters Wright made it clear that he travelled to the island fully aware that it was a dangerous place for an English migrant.[88] He noted, for example, that

[80] NRO/FX/323/1-3, King from the Hallens Estate, 31 August 1784.

[81] In 1791 he told his parents, 'I have not been so fortunate as at first I expected, having lost near two hundred pounds, in Negroes & Horses & I fancy if my effects were now turned into cash, they would not fetch more than £60 or £80 pounds', NRO/FX/323/1-3, King from Kingston, Jamaica, 31 January 1791.

[82] NRO/FX/323/3, Note of William King undated, c.1817: draft affidavit of Ruth Piper, undated, circa 1886.

[83] The original letters have been lost, but transcripts of them were received by the Norfolk Record Office in 1988 (MS 34507) and are preserved as NRO/MC/1519/1/813x9, Transcripts of Letters from William Wright, travelling abroad to his mother in Watton, 1824–26.

[84] NRO/MC/1519/1/813x9, William Wright to Susanna Wright, *Simon Taylor* at sea, 13 January 1825, p. 4.

[85] *Norfolk Chronicle*, 28 August 1824, p. 3.

[86] NRO/MC/1519/1/813x9, William Wright to Susanna Wright, 13 January 1825, pp. 2–4.

[87] NRO/MC/1519/1/813x9, William Wright to Susanna Wright, Chiswick, 10 April 1825, p. 6.

[88] For details of Jamaican mortality, see Vincent Brown, *The Reaper's Garden* (Cambridge, MA, 2008), p. 2, p. 17; Burnard and Garrigus, *The Plantation*, p. 9.

when he initially viewed Jamaica 'my heart beat at the first sight of a place which might perhaps be the means of my living comfortably in England, or on the contrary might prove my grave'.[89] He seems, furthermore, to have been aware of Jamaica's poor moral reputation. As Burnard and Garrigus explain, 'the bewildering uncertainty of life in the tropics [...] meant that Jamaica came to be seen by metropolitans as a vortex of social disorder.'[90] Wright and his family seemed to have been concerned about the effect living in this environment would have on his morals, and it appears that this had been discussed with his relatives and friends before he left Norfolk. Early in his stay, he wrote that 'You must not expect any Account of the Slave Trade while I reside here. I know some of my friends expect it, but they must rest satisfied', suggesting that the issue had been of interest before his journey. He went on to assure his mother that 'No accusing Spirit shall charge me with wantonly inflicting torture on any human being [...] if a residence in this country does not destroy every spark of feeling that does honour to the heart I will try to let my conduct be such as shall not disgrace my family.' Wright's words suggest that his relatives and friends back in Norfolk had been concerned about his involvement with the slaving economy, and had, perhaps, expressed misgivings about his course of actions. Wright was, however, somewhat equivocal in his assurances, remarking that 'severity shall only be resorted to when unavoidable', intimating a willingness on his part to accept the operations of the plantation system.[91]

Although his letters contain hints of distaste, overall Wright seems to have chosen to accept the operations of the slave-based economy because of the economic opportunity the system offered. He saw a connection between business practices he knew to be efficient and modern in Norfolk, and those he encountered in Jamaica, comparing cane planting to 'the Northumberland Mode of growing turnips' for example. The key difference he perceived was that sugar cultivation was a labour-intensive practice that required large amounts of labour; 'Some idea may be formed of the labour of this process (preparing the land) when I tell you it takes 50 negroes a day to prepare an acre.'[92] He was aware that the profitability of the system depended on the use of slaves and discussed the financial penalties that resulted from using wage labour. He accepted that this meant that the 'negroes' would be worked hard, driven with whips, 'as your barrow boys do when told his horses walk too slow', and 'flogged' where necessary.[93] His explanation of why this discipline was necessary was that 'the Evil of the System is such that it is severity alone that can get the work done'.[94]

---

[89] NRO/MC/1519/1/813x9, William Wright to Susanna Wright, 13 January 1825, p. 5.

[90] Burnard and Garrigus, *The Plantation*, p. 68.

[91] NRO/MC/1519/1/813x9, Letter from William Wright, 10 April 1825, p. 14.

[92] Ibid.

[93] NRO/MC/1519/1/813x9, Letter from William Wright, 10 April 1825, pp. 1-2, 8.

[94] NRO/MC/1519/1/813x9, Letter from William Wright, 10 April 1825, p. 14.

Wright's letters also reveal the strain in his thinking brought about by the encounter with the reality of plantations. In September 1825, Wright mentioned that 'The Abolition of the Slave trade tho' a measure which as a friend to humanity I applaud, is one which as a planter I can assure you I much regret.' Wright regretted the approaching abolition, which by 1825 was understood by all to be a matter of time, because he could have made much more money if it was not to occur, but at the same time recognised that the mode of exploitation utilised in Jamaica was undesirable. The lure of financial gain, however, meant that he was willing to become involved in the system. In 1826 Wright described the abolitionists as 'saintly hypocrites' whose main aim was to make money for themselves in some unspecified fashion. He turned to racial stereotypes and described Africans as naturally 'indolent' and unable, therefore, to work in a normal economic system.[95] Wright's letters are a useful window into thinking about slavery in Norfolk and Suffolk as the nineteenth century dawned. They suggest that by this time the population of the region had a good understanding of the nature of colonial planter society and the system of slavery. This would reflect the general discussion that had been taking place in the region since 1787 in relation to the slave trade and then, in the 1820s, to slavery itself. They also suggest that there was a degree of concern among that population about the morality of the system. At the same time, the apparent ease with which Wright was able to compartmentalise any concerns he might have had so that he could profit from slavery is also revealing. As with the plantation owners, the potential to make money created a willingness for some to choose interaction with slavery.

Economic Decisions and Engagement with Atlantic Slavery

These examples indicate that those members of Norfolk and Suffolk's population who became involved in the world of colonial slavery did so largely because of economic factors. These factors took various forms, however, from passive acquiescence to active decision-making. The desire for wealth and the need to survive financially (as well as physically) were critical elements in leading such people to become involved at all levels, and with differing degrees of agency and enthusiasm. For poor working sailors like Secker, involvement was a matter of economic necessity. Poverty rendered them generally unable to object to the vicissitudes of fate. In contrast, others chose active involvement because of the potential offered by engaging with the slaving economy. For men like Uring, King, and Wright, becoming a bookkeeper promised the chance of a swift change in fortune. For merchants like Everard, Browne, and Manning, involvement was just another avenue of trade in a booming economic area. For absentee owners such as the Dallings, involvement was a means of accessing capital markets to derive investment income. Both men and women were

---

[95] NRO/MC/1519/1/813x9, Letter from William Wright, 5 May 1826, p. 3.

involved in the ownership of plantations.[96] This economic interaction with the plantation economy then created a network of social, business, and economic dealings between the region and the Americas which established, in turn, a cultural interface between these two parts of the transatlantic world. Wright appears, for example, to have known people in Jamaica before he arrived there.[97] In this context, the ideas about Africans being developed in the colonies could interact with those that already existed in the region.

In the same period that this complex network of commercial interactions drew Norfolk, Suffolk, and the slaving colonies closer together, the region remained the home of many Africans. The descendants of those Africans who had arrived in the region in the fifteenth to seventeenth centuries continued to live across the two counties. This existing group was then augmented by an influx of Africans who arrived after 1700. Over 70 per cent of the Africans who can be clearly identified as living in Norfolk and Suffolk from 1467 to 1833 lived in the region after 1700. The correlation between the growth in the region's involvement in the slaving economy in the eighteenth century and the arrival of so many Africans in the region in the eighteenth and early nineteenth centuries appears unequivocal: the primary driver for this stage of migration was the region's intensified interaction with the colonial economies.[98] Several questions are raised by this situation. Firstly, a basic question, what proportion of that eighteenth- and early nineteenth-century African population was held in a situation of slavish servitude and what proportion was not? Secondly, what economic and social roles were members of this African population fulfilling? Finally, what were the prevailing social attitudes to those Africans living in Norfolk and Suffolk during the period?

[96] For discussion of the involvement of women in the systems, see, for example, Christine Walker, 'Pursuing Her Profits: Women in Jamaica, Atlantic Slavery and a Globalising Market, 1700–60', *Gender & History*, 26 (2014), 478–501.

[97] Wright mentioned 'Mr Bradfield' in Kingston, whom he had been advised to contact on his arrival. This was, presumably, a relative of the Bradfield family who farmed near Heacham, and so were neighbours of the Wright family, NRO/MC1519/1/813x9, William Wright to Susanna Wright, Chiswick, St Thomas in the East, 14 February 1825, p. 6.

[98] The arrival of several people who were identified as being from the East Indies and India, for example John son of Solomon in Ipswich, and the nineteen-year-old Hebe Bessom and fifteen-year-old Harriot, who were baptised on the same day in Brandeston in 1784, is a reminder of the growing impact of expansion of British influence in the East as well; SRO/FL622/4/1, Baptism of John son of Solomon, Ipswich St Mary, 26 January 1781; SRO/FC105/D1/2, Baptism of Hebe Bessom, and Harriot, Brandeston, 22 May 1784.

7

Eighteenth-Century African Lives

Africans in Near Slavery

There is one example in Norfolk and Suffolk after 1700 where Africans living in the region were described as 'slaves'. This is the record of the baptism of Thomas Cross in Ipswich in 1815, when Thomas' parents, Cuffee and Amber, were described in the section of the parish register noting 'Quality, Trade or Profession' as 'negro slaves'.[1] The address of the Cross family was given as Silent Street, Ipswich, which suggests that the presence of Cuffee and Amber was related to the Worrell family, who owned plantations in Barbados. This is because the St Nicholas register also records the baptism on 23 June 1768 of Mary Hellet, who was described as 'a negro girl servant to Jonathan Worrell Esq'.[2] Jonathan Worrell (1734–1814) was a slaveowner in Barbados who lived in England from 1764.[3] Worrell lived in Ipswich at a house in Silent Street until 1781 and owned several properties in the area. He then bought Hainford Hall in Norfolk and would later move to Surrey.[4]

The Silent Street address links Cuffee and Amber Cross firmly to the Worrell family. Their arrival was probably related to the family's ownership of plantations in Barbados and the decision by two of Worrell's sons to return to the island in 1788.[5] One of these, Jonathan Worrell (1767–1843), came to own another plantation, Highland, in his own name but sold it and returned to England permanently around 1815. It is possible, therefore, that he may have lived at Silent Street while he finalised where he would live, and that he brought Cuffee and Amber with him from Highland plantation.[6] Alternatively, they may have already been resident in the property before this date. What happened

---

[1] SRO/FB94/D1/7, Baptism of Thomas Cross, Ipswich St Nicholas, 10 December 1815.
[2] SRO/FB94/D1/7, Baptism of Mary Hellet, Ipswich St Nicholas, 23 June 1768.
[3] LBSO, Jonathan Worrell senior, <https://www.ucl.ac.uk/lbs/person/view/-131609571>. [accessed 1 December 2018].
[4] Rusty Bittermann and Margaret McCallum, 'The Pursuit of Gentility in an Age of Revolution: The Family of Jonathan Worrell', *Acadiensis*, 43 (2) (2014), https://journals.lib. unb.ca/index.php/Acadiensis/article/view/22685/26326 [accessed 21 March 2018].
[5] Ibid.
[6] LBSO, Jonathan Worrell, <https://www.ucl.ac.uk/lbs/person/view/916> [accessed 21 November 2019].

to Cuffee, Amber, and Thomas after 1815 is unclear. They do not appear in the St Nicholas register again, nor do they appear in East Grinstead, where Worrell finally settled. The 1852 census for St Matthew in Ipswich records an 'anastatic printer' named Thomas Cross, who was born in Ipswich in 1820, living in St George's Street with his wife and daughter.[7] The birth year does not correlate, but this may be the same Thomas, we cannot be sure.

Although their eventual fates are unclear, Cuffee and Amber establish that enslaved Africans were being brought to Norfolk and Suffolk by plantation owners as late as 1815. It seems likely that Mary Hellet had also been brought to England in a similar fashion by the older Worrell when he returned from Barbados in 1764, since she was baptised only four years after Worrell's arrival. In view of this, Hellet was likely to have been in a condition of near slavery while living in Ipswich, a situation that would appear to have been described circumspectly in the phrasing of the parish register entry: 'a negro girl servant to Jonathan Worrell Esq.' The record of Mary Hellet's baptism suggests that in the eighteenth and early nineteenth centuries Africans held in slavish servitude were generally not recorded as such, but their status can be inferred from reference to being 'the servant of' a plantation owner, just as it was with Rosanna in the seventeenth century. Likewise, the record of Thomas Cross' baptism shows that the mention of a local geographic location that can be linked to a plantation owner is also indicative of such near enslavement.

The examination of such geographic proximity provides evidence suggesting the presence of Africans in slavish servitude elsewhere. One such location is the village of Garboldisham in the years after the planter Crisp Molineux arrived there in 1756. A decade after the planter's arrival, in 1766, the parish records mention the baptism of 'three blacks' named John Davis, Samuel Stanton, and Richard Alexander.[8] The register gives no details of their occupations, position, or previous history, although the three were all adults, since no parents were listed for them. The surnames of the men were unknown in the village prior to this entry, a strong indication of their recent arrival into Garboldisham. The connection with the Molineux family is strengthened by a later list of the enslaved Africans on the family plantation in St Christopher belonging to Thomas Crisp Molineux Montgomerie, sent to him by his estate manager around 1800. This list documents 153 enslaved people, including a twelve-month-old infant named 'Sam Stanton'.[9] This indicates that Samuel Stanton was a name being used by the Molineux family for their enslaved workers in this period. When these factors are combined with the residence of Molineux in the village, it becomes highly likely that John Davis, Samuel Stanton, and Richard

---

[7]   TNA/HO/107/1799/f436, p. 23, St George's Street, St Matthew, Ipswich, Suffolk, England.

[8]   NRO/PD/197/2, Baptism of John Davis, Samuel Stanton, and Richard Alexander, Garboldisham, 2 August 1766.

[9]   NRO/BL/F/23, Estate of Thomas Crisp Molineux Montgomerie Esquire by Luke Barnes, Manager, undated.

Alexander were Africans previously enslaved by Molineux, who had been brought over from St Christopher. Given Molineux's attitudes regarding slavery, it seems probable that they were held in slavish servitude in Norfolk, at least initially.

The Molineux family kept close contact with their home island and members of the family travelled to and from the island many times in the period. It appears that these continuing visits allowed the family to bring other Africans to Garboldisham. In 1777 a sixteen-year-old 'black serv[an]t' named Charles Molineux was baptised in the village.[10] The combination of the location, his job, the use of the planter's surname, and his adult baptism makes it very probable that Charles had been brought to the hall as a slave from St Christopher. Having established from this that Africans in the village were using the Molineux surname, we can suggest that there were other Africans in Garboldisham in this period. On 15 March 1771, an infant named Sophia Molineux was baptised, with her parents being identified as Samuel and Mary.[11] There were no members of the Molineux family named Samuel in this period, so it would appear feasible that Sophia was the child of an African named Samuel Molineux. In 1791 a Garboldisham man named Thomas Pearl married Mary Molineux, who was described as a 'mulatto'.[12] Mary's Christian name suggests that she was probably a daughter of Samuel and Mary, who appear to have married in 1763.[13] It seems, therefore, that Samuel was an African from the hall, who had taken (or been given) the surname of his master, had married a local named Mary Carman, and had raised at least one child with her.

It seems likely that the lack of racially charged epithets in the register for Samuel and Sophia before 1774 and the change to note such factors after, in the case of Charles and Mary, was a consequence of the change in rector. The rector of Garboldisham from 1748 to 1774 was William Robinson, who owed his position to the previous owner, Sir Edward Bacon.[14] Robinson mentioned the 'three blacks' in 1766, but otherwise avoided extraneous terms in the register. He was replaced by Charles Sheard Molineux, who was the illegitimate son of Crisp Molineux and had been brought up in St Christopher.[15] The arrival of the new rector coincided with the appearance of terms such as 'mulatto' in the register and reveals the way the arrival of colonials enabled the language of the new plantation economies to be transplanted into English society.

[10] NRO/PD/197/2, Baptism of Charles Molineux, 28 March 1777.
[11] NRO/PD/197/2, Baptism of Sophia Molineux, 15 March 1771.
[12] NRO/PD/197/2, Marriage of Mary Molineux and Thomas Pearl, 16 February 1791; NRO/PD/197/5, Banns of Marriage of Mary Molineux and Thomas Pearl, 30 January 1791.
[13] NRO/PD/197/4, Marriage of Samuel Molineux and Mary Carman, 4 November 1763.
[14] J. Crouse, *The History and Antiquities of the County of Norfolk* (Norwich, 1781), p. 46.
[15] CCED, Molineux, Charles Sheard (1775–1811), ID: 114187; TNA/PROB/11/1232/158, Will of Crisp Molineux of Garboldisham, Norfolk, 1792; NRO/PD/197/2, Burial of Charles Sheard Molineux, 9 August 1811; for date of birth, 9 January 1753, see CCED, ID: 145212, <http://db.theclergydatabase.org.uk/jsp/search/index.jsp> [accessed 21 March 2018].

A similar identification of near slavery is suggested in relation to the baptism of Stephen Tucker, 'a Negro Boy, about nine years of age', at Nayland, Suffolk, in 1766. The elements here are all suggestive of near slavery. An adult baptism, a teenage African, the use of the term 'Negro', and the phrasing 'surnamed Tucker', which is redolent of a name being given by a third party, rather than one chosen by Stephen.[16] The closest plantation-connected family to Nayland were the Blakes at Langham, a few miles south-east, so this is a possible explanation for Tucker's appearance. The baptism in 1755 of an infant named Barlow in Earsham points toward a similar situation. The register entry identified the father of the child to be 'Barlow a negro servant at Earsham Hall'.[17] Earsham Hall would later become the home of the Dallings, but Barlow's presence at Earsham Hall cannot be explained by reference to Sir John Dalling, since he arrived in the West Indies over a decade after Barlow appeared in Norfolk. In the 1750s Earsham Hall was in the hands of William Windham of Earsham (1705–89) whose sister, Catherine, would marry John Dalling. There is no obvious evidence of a West Indian or colonial connection for Windham, who was a landowner, rather than a merchant or entrepreneur.[18] Nonetheless, the entry relating to Barlow is suggestive of near slavery, in that Barlow was not given a surname; he was described in relation to his position at the hall, and there is no previous mention of him in the parish register.[19] It is also suggestive that the baptisms of Tucker and Barlow used the term 'negro', a word which, as we saw in Chapter Five, had not been used in the region before the arrival of the Davers family in the 1680s. In 1729 Elizabeth Barnes was described as a 'negro servant' in her mistress' will and in 1732 the term was used in the Bardwell parish register at the burial of Thomas Rundell.[20] Thereafter it became more common, for example in the 1766 baptism of 'William, a negro' in Rushbrooke.[21] By this date, the term had become, as was discussed in Chapter One, a synonym for 'slave'.[22] Its increased use in eighteenth-century Norfolk and Suffolk would seem to be indicative of the growing influence of racialised ideas in the region.

---

[16] SRO/FB64/D1/2, Baptism of Stephen Tucker, Nayland, 26 November 1766.

[17] NRO/PD/519/3, Baptism of Barlow Spence, 27 April 1755.

[18] Mary M. Drummond, 'Windham, William (?1705–89), of Earsham, Norf.', in L. Namier and J. Brooke (eds.), *The History of Parliament: the House of Commons 1754–1790* (Woodbridge, 1964), <http://www.historyofparliamentonline.org/volume/1754-1790/member/windham-william-1705-89> [accessed 1 October 2020]. The estate had been purchased with profits from the South Sea Bubble and his uncle James Windham had travelled abroad in the 1720s, NRO/WKC7/28/1-28/404x2, Family and Estate Papers of the Ketton-Cremer Family of Felbrigg Hall, 13th–20th century.

[19] The Earsham register also contains reference to the burial in 1757 of 'An old man whose name was never known here was buried September seventh he died at the hall', see NRO/PD/519/3, 7 September 1757. Since there is evidence of one African servant at the hall, it seems possible that this man was another, since he was unknown in the village, and was known only in relation to his situation at the hall.

[20] SRO/FL522/4/3, Burial of Thomas Rundell, Bardwell, 22 February 1732.

[21] Baptism of William, 29 June 1766; Hervey, *Rushbrook*, p. 19.

[22] Handler, 'Custom', p. 237.

Another group that is of interest are three men baptised at Great Saxham Church between 1777 and 1786. Thomas German and Anthrobus Morgan were both described as 'a black and adult', while John Brown was described as 'a Black and native of Jamaica aged 35 years'.[23] The adult baptism of these men is suggestive of some connection to enslavement. The owners of Great Saxham Hall were the Mills family, who did not have any overt connection to plantation holdings, but in 1805 Susanna Mills married a man named John William Hicks. Hicks lived in Bath, but owned plantations in Jamaica.[24] Since John Brown was stated to be from Jamaica, it may be that the Mills family had connections with the Hicks family earlier and the presence of German, Morgan, and Brown may have related to this relationship.

The difficulty in uncovering the exact connections between Africans living in Norfolk and Suffolk in this period and the colonies is shown graphically in respect of an African named Caesar Hockwold in Hockwold-cum-Wilton, Norfolk. In 1780 Hockwold was left an annual allowance of two shillings and sixpence per week in a codicil to the will of Cyrill Wyche Esq., of Hockwold Hall, where he was described as 'my late servant Caesar Hockwold'.[25] In 1739 Wyche's household accounting records described him as 'Caesar Hockwold Black'.[26] There is no indication exactly what Caesar's role was in the household, but the capitalised term 'Black' was used to describe him on several occasions. Wyche's records were precise and ordered. He used a variety of shorthand terms, but he did not use any form of shorthand in which 'Black' stood for some specific position. For example, the most obvious choice, 'blacksmith', was always written in full on invoices, and in any case the blacksmith in Hockwold-cum-Wilton was Samuel Lancaster. Furthermore, Hockwold was apprenticed as a shoemaker in 1740.[27] It appears, therefore, that Caesar was an African, a conclusion that is supported by the fact that the surname Hockwold does not appear in the village's parish register before Caesar's appearance.

In this case there is a possible connection with the slaving economy that could explain Caesar's arrival. The Wyche family had resided at the hall in Hockwold since around 1690.[28] Although Cyrill Wyche appears to have spent

---

[23] SRO/FL622/4/1, Baptism of Thomas German, 16 March 1777; Baptism of Anthrobus Morgan, 1 November 1780; Baptism of John Brown, 23 April 1786, all at Great Saxham.

[24] *The Monthly Magazine*, 20 (1805), p. 86; John Burke, *A Genealogical and Heraldic History of the Landed Gentry of Great Britain and Ireland* (2 vols, London, 1863), vol. 2, p. 1013; LBSO, John William Hicks II, <https://www.ucl.ac.uk/lbs/person/view/15652> [accessed 21 March 2019].

[25] TNA/PROB/11/1067/85, Will of Cyrill Wyche of Hockwold, Norfolk, June 1780.

[26] NRO/MC/42/86/527x1, 12 January 1739.

[27] NRO/MC/42/90/527x1, Robert Jackson, shoemaker 3 February 1740; NRO/MC/42/90/527x1, Edward Spinks, Shoemaker, 19 November 1742; Britain, Country Apprentices 1710–1808, IR1 Series 50 f. 8.

[28] Cyrill Wyche Esq. was born around 1704, although there is no record of his baptism. His memorial in the church of St Peter, Hockwold, provides a date of death as 10 June 1780, 'aged 76 years', indicating a birth year of 1704. He was High Sheriff of Norfolk in

most of his life on his estates in and around Hockwold-cum-Wilton, he was a business acquaintance of the King's Lynn merchant and slaver, Samuel Browne. A deed from 1736 lists Wyche as one of a group of business partners, including Samuel Browne, who leased a building in Gaywood.[29] This places Wyche as an associate of Samuel Browne in 1736, only two years before Browne engaged in his first slaving voyage. Caesar was first mentioned in 1739, one year after that voyage. The coincidence is tempting.

The baptism of Robert Yoxford, 'a Black boy brought over by Thomas Betts Esq', at Yoxford, Suffolk, in 1713 provides a clearer link.[30] The use of the phrase 'brought over' makes it clear that Robert was bound to Betts in some fashion and this description, combined with Robert's youth, the fact that he was given the name of the village, and his adult baptism, points towards him being a previously enslaved African who had arrived from either English/British North America or the West Indies. It also seems likely that at this point he was in a condition of near slavery, although as we shall see later, this did not remain the case. There is no direct link between Betts and the colonies, but in 1681 a mortgage was signed between a William Betts of Yoxford, who was described as a 'gent.', and Thomas Frere of Rendham, Suffolk.[31] This points to a link between the Frere family, who owned plantations in Barbados, and the Betts family. This Barbados connection is strengthened by the fact that a 1638 list of the inhabitants of Barbados who owned over ten acres of land recorded a 'William Betts', who may be the William Betts mentioned in the mortgage deed.[32] Thomas Betts may have been his son and might have brought Robert with him from Barbados in the early 1700s.[33]

1729, Hamon Le Strange, *Norfolk's Official Lists* (Norwich, 1890), p. 24. His grandfather was Sir Cyril Wyche, see C.I. McGrath, 'Wyche, Sir Cyril (c. 1632–1707), government official', *ODNB*, <https://www.oxforddnb.com/view/10.1093/ref:odnb/9780198614128.001.0001/odnb-9780198614128-e-30117> [accessed 7 February 2017]. Sir Cyril's elder son, Jermyn Wyche Esq., succeeded him in 1707 and died at Hockwold-cum-Wilton on 7 January 1720, leaving two daughters, Catherine and Mary, and his son, Cyrill, who succeeded to his estates, NRO/PD/311/1, Burial of Jermyn Wyche Esq, 16 January 1719; Richard Harrison, '"Jermyn Wyche, (c.1670–1720)," of Hockwold, Norf.', in D. Hayton, E. Cruickshanks, S. Handley (eds), *The History of Parliament: The House of Commons 1690–1715* (2002), <http://www.historyof-parliamentonline.org/volume/1690-1715/member/wych-%28wyche%29-jermyn-1670-1720> [accessed 1 June 2018].

[29] NRO/PD451/98, Lease for a year of the Guildhall and two acres of land in Gaywood, 1736–1737, Robert Page to Cyrill Wyche, William Browne, Samuel Browne, Edmund Rolfe, Charles Peast and Richard Hinde, 1737.

[30] SRO/FC73/D1/1, Baptism of Robert Yoxford, 25 December 1713.

[31] SRO/HA100/A/11/1, Counterpart of a mortgage, Thomas Frere of Rendham, co. Suffolk, esq., to William Betts of Yoxford, co. Suffolk, gent., 9 November 1681.

[32] The list is reprinted in P.F. Campbell, *Some Early Barbadian History* (Letchworth, 1993), p. 232. Alternatively, there is record of a John Betts, who sailed for New England from Ipswich in 1634, James Savage, A *Genealogical Dictionary of the First Settlers of New England, Volume 1* (Boston, 1860), p. 172.

[33] Betts was permanently settled in Suffolk; for example, he was listed as living at Yoxford in

The situation of Jeremiah Rowland, who was recorded in the register for Wroxham, Norfolk, as 'a negro' on his burial in 1781, is more readily explicable.[34] A memorial to Rowland in the churchyard provides the probable reason for his appearance in the village. The monument was erected by Daniel Collyer (1752–1819), who lived at Wroxham Hall and Necton Lodge. Collyer was the eldest son of Daniel Collyer Esq. (d.1773), also of Wroxham, who was a merchant in the City of London and a director of the Royal African Company in 1749.[35] Although there is no evidence of the family owning a plantation, and the will of the elder Daniel makes no mention of Jeremiah, the connection to the Royal African Company makes it likely, nonetheless, that Jeremiah had arrived in the family's possession as a consequence of involvement in the slave trade and had remained with them at Wroxham until his death.[36]

There is an equally strong likelihood that a woman named Sigismunda Beckford, who was baptised at Somerleyton in 1784, was held in slavish servitude. Sigismunda was recorded in the parish register as a 'native of Jamaica' and said to be 'aged about 40'.[37] The adult baptism and her geographic background together suggest African heritage. Somerley Hall was owned by the Jamaican planter William Beckford (1744–99), who had originally arrived there from Jamaica in 1756, at which time Sigismunda would have been around twelve. She may, therefore, have arrived on the estate with him as a child.[38] Given that Sigismunda Beckford shared a surname with the planter, and was from his home island of Jamaica, it is likely that she was a slave that Beckford had brought with him from the West Indies. Since William Beckford returned to Jamaica from 1774 to around 1786, so was not in England at the date of the baptism, it seems probable that Sigismunda had been at Somerley for most of her life. This suggestion leads to an interesting possibility to explain her status in 1784. William Beckford was arrested for debt on his arrival in England because his sugar plantations and business dealings had failed. It may be that Sigismunda had been freed from bondage at Somerley when creditors had closed in on her master. It may be, therefore, that Sigismunda's baptism marked a point of transition for her from near slavery to freedom, a change that was made possible by Beckford's financial ruin and incarceration.

1727 and taking part in elections; A copy of the poll for the Knights of the Shire for the County of S. taken at Ipswich, Aug. 30 1727 R. Goodrich, Esq.; High Sheriff. Candidates, Sir W. Barker, Sir J. Danvers, Baronets, J. Holt, Esquire (Ipswich, 1727), p. 134.

[34] Inscription in churchyard of Wroxham Church and NRO/PD/390/2, Burial of Jeremiah Rowland, 15 June 1781.

[35] Burke, Genealogical, 'Collyer of Hackford Hall', p. 246; William A. Pettigrew, Freedom's Debt: The Royal African Company and the Politics of the Atlantic Slave Trade, 1672–1752 (Chapel Hill, 2013), p. 237.

[36] NA/PROB 11/990/285, Will of Daniel Collyer of Wroxham, Norfolk, 13 August 1773.

[37] NRO/PD/577/2, Baptism of Sigismunda Beckford, 20 October 1784, Somerleyton.

[38] R.B. Sheridan, 'Planter and historian: the career of William Beckford of Jamaica and England, 1744–1799', The Jamaican Historical Review, 4 (1964), 36–58.

A similar situation appears likely for 'William, a negro', who was mentioned in the Rushbrooke parish register in 1766.[39] The most obvious clue in the case of William is the continued presence of the Davers family in the area. The family had inherited Rushbrooke Hall, Rushbrooke, via marriage in the early eighteenth century. By 1766 the Davers' fortune was almost gone, and the last male heir would die in 1806.[40] The family still owned the plantation in 1723, but it was not mentioned in the will of Jermyn Davers (d.1743). As no age was given, William might have been an enslaved servant of the family who had arrived at some point in the early 1700s from Barbados and had remained with the family for the rest of his life.

Connections between the slaving economy and an African servant can also be found at Holkham Hall in the 1730s. The parish register of Holkham records the baptism of George Calican 'a black' in 1737.[41] Calican was recorded as being a page boy when he fell ill while at the Coke family's London residence in 1742. He was treated with a 'vomit', and 'Acton water', at the family's expense, but the treatment did not save him, and he was buried at St Giles in the Fields, London, on 5 December 1742.[42] Support for the idea that he was in a form of slavish servitude comes from the connection between Thomas Coke (1697–1759) and John, second duke of Montagu, who were neighbours in Great Russell Street. Montagu's household accounts record several Africans in the period 1721 to 1745. Furthermore, he also knew Nathaniel Uring. In 1722, when the government granted the islands of St Lucia and St Vincent to Montagu, the duke had appointed Uring deputy-governor and sent him with a large flotilla to colonise the islands.[43] Given the close relations between Montagu, Uring, and the West Indies, it seems possible that the presence of George Calican at Holkham was related to Montagu and Uring in some fashion.

As has already been mentioned, an African was part of Uring's household after he retired as a wealthy man to his hometown of Walsingham to run a wine importing business. The household accounts of Holkham Hall mention Uring as a regular provider of wine to the household and, in September 1738, the house steward paid five shillings to 'Captain Uring's Black'.[44] The phrasing of this description is indicative of near slavery, in that the unnamed African was seen only in the context of his relation to Uring, as opposed to being described with more familiarity, as was the case for 'Bedfer the Blackamoore' in seventeenth-century King's Lynn, for example. There is no trace of this unnamed African in the parish records. Furthermore, having spent most of his adult life

[39] Burial of 'William', 29 June 1766, Hervey, *Rushbrook*, p. 19.
[40] Hervey, *Rushbrook*, pp. 369 and 371.
[41] NRO/PD/608/2, Baptism of George Calican, 21 August 1737.
[42] HA/A/26 to HA/A/28.
[43] Nathaniel Uring, *A Relation of the Late Intended Settlement of the Islands of St. Lucia, and St. Vincent, in America: in Right of the Duke of Montagu, and Under His Grace's Direction and Orders, in the Year 1722* (London, 1725).
[44] HA/A/26, 23 September 1738.

deeply involved in the slaving economy, it seems implausible that Uring would have had any relationship with an African that was not one of owner/enslaved. The description of the person in the Holkham records as 'Captain Uring's Black' hints, moreover, that the staff of Holkham Hall understood this situation to be one of bondage. There is no mention of any such person in Uring's will of 1742, indicating that the African was no longer part of his household by this point.[45]

'Captain Uring's Black' shows that such Africans could be found in the households of merely well-off individuals in the region as well as in the houses and estates of the very wealthy. The appearances of William Byrom at Aldeburgh in 1744 and William Strap at Ipswich in 1771 imply the presence of such Africans was often related to their master's previous connection with the slave trade or the colonies, as it had been with Uring. Both men were again described in relation to an owner described as a 'Captain'. Byrom was described as 'a blackamoor servant to Captain Rycart', while Strap was described as 'a negro servant of Captain Pricke of Nacton'.[46] Once again, the phrasing of the descriptions of Strap and Byrom is indicative of slavish servitude. It seems likely that Rycart and Pricke were sea captains since Nacton and Aldeburgh are both coastal towns; Nacton lies a few miles south-east of Ipswich on the Orwell estuary, and Aldeburgh sits on the Suffolk coast. Neither Rycart or Pricke are recorded as slaving captains, but they might have been involved in the slave trade or the general trade with the colonies and, as happened with Uring, brought an enslaved servant back to Norfolk and Suffolk. It may be that the appearance of the ten-year-old William Luccan at Mellis in 1787 reflects a similar story, although Luccan was said to have been 'brought from the East Indies by Captain William Bullock'.[47]

There are other examples of Africans in the region in the 1700s that point towards a status that might have been slavish servitude. In December 1704, the Norwich Mayor's Court Book records that permission was given for a man named David Sherrad to 'make show of a Little Black Man & his horse & living Creatures at the Angell with six servts. for the space of 21 dayes behaveing themselves civilly (sic)'.[48] The man who applied for permission, Sherrad, was a travelling showman, but there is no more information about him.[49] Neither is there more information about the background of the anonymous 'Little Black Man', but the circumstances suggest that he was under Sherrad's control,

[45] NA/PROB/11/720, Will of Nathaniel Uring, Gentleman of Walsingham, Norfolk, 12 August 1742.
[46] SRO/FC129/D1/3, Marriage of William Byrom and Sarah Knights, Aldeburgh, 16 August 1744; SRO/FB98/D1/3, Baptism of William Strap, Ipswich St Clement, 12 December 1771.
[47] SRO/FB123/D1/4, Baptism of William Luccan, Mellis, 12 April 1787; Henry Creed, *Extracts from the Registers of Mellis* (1853), p. 296.
[48] NRO/NCR/16a/26 (MF629), f. 184, Norwich Mayor's Court Book, 16 December 1704.
[49] Sherrad was not a common name in the region; the only potential clue from the Norfolk records is in NRO/PD/39/1, Baptism of Robert Sherrad, 18 August 1678.

and the description of him reduced him to the status of property. If the entry in the Court Book is read as suggesting that the 'Little Black Man & his horse' were the major point of the show, then it may be that he was a skilled horseman, who worked with Sherrad. Some support for this latter interpretation might be found in the nineteenth-century example of the circus entertainer Pablo Fanque (William Darby). Fanque, who was born in Norwich, was an example of an African who gained wealth and economic independence through his skill as a horseman and entertainer.[50] The contrast with Fanque is revealing, however. Fanque was a man in charge of his own show, known by his stage name, and clearly in control of his situation. None of this was the case for the 'Little Black Man'. As the example of Jacques Francis (Jaques Frauncys), a 'Guinea' diver kept as a slave by the Venetian Piero Paolo Corsi in the Tudor period, has shown, the possession of a sought-after skill was no guarantee of free status.[51] The balance of probability is that the 'Little Black Man' was held in some form of servitude by Sherrad.

A similar situation is likely in relation to the 'exhibit' that took place at the Half Moon Inn in Norwich in August 1783. The centrepiece of this was 'the White Negro Woman'.[52] Once again the African involved was unnamed, but in this case the 'White Negro Woman' was exhibited purely because of her non-standard appearance, rather than any specific skill. Presumably, the woman was an albino and the fact of her 'exhibition' is suggestive of the changing understanding of Africans in the region by this late part of the eighteenth century. Money could be made from her because her appearance confounded the racial norms that were starting to become accepted. The cultural tension created by an African who confused the new ideas about racial stereotyping was enough to mean that money could be made from her mere presence, without any extra support. The contrast with the 'Little Black Man' is instructive, in that in 1704 he needed to be in a show with others.

It is also significant that the term 'negro' was used to describe the African woman. The use of this descriptor, together with her nameless state, and the fact that she was set outside even the standard boundaries of race, leave little doubt that this woman was being exploited by those involved in the show. The mention of her Jamaican origin makes it possible that she had been enslaved previously. The reference to her marriage makes it improbable that she was formally enslaved at this point, but it seems clear that both her husband, and the organiser of the 'entertainment', Curtis, were controlling her. She was, therefore, deprived of any agency and was being used as a commodity, a situation made possible both by her gender and racial categorisation.

---

[50] J.M. Turner, 'Pablo Fanque "an Artiste of Colour"', *King Pole*, 89 (1990), 5-9; NRO/ PD74/44, Parish Register, All Saints Norwich, 1796.
[51] Ungerer, 'Recovering', pp. 255-71.
[52] *Norwich Mercury*, 9 August 1783.

To these Africans can also be added the details of two 'runaways' originating in Suffolk, who were mentioned in the London newspapers. In January 1741, an 'East-India Black, who goes by the Name of Oxford' was reported as having 'went away from his Master on Christmas-Day last'. Although the incident occurred in London, 'his Master' was named as Robert Gooding of Sudbury, Suffolk.[53] The Gooding family were an established one in Sudbury, but there are no details of Robert to augment this story, and no clues to link them with the slave economy. There is a similar lack of information to expand upon a second London advertisement, in 1771, for another 'runaway' named William Suza, who was described as 'a Negro Boy about seventeen Years of Age', who 'came last from Suffolk'.[54] In this case, Suza was not linked to a specific person or location in Suffolk. Nonetheless, the advertisements are further indications that Africans were held in Suffolk in slavish servitude.

'Free' Africans

In contrast to these examples, there were many Africans in the region who appear to have been operating in a social position that was not defined by the status of slavish servitude. We can begin by looking at those Africans who were descended from those who had already settled in the region before 1700, identified as the holders of the surname Blackamore and its variants. Appendix B shows that the patterns seen in the previous centuries continued into the eighteenth. There remained something of a fluidity in the naming of these Africans in the eighteenth century; for example William Blackamore, who was mentioned in St Peter Parmentergate in 1700, would see his name spelt as Blackmore in 1704.[55] This variation does not seem to be reflective of anything other than the generally unstable situation in England in this period in relation to surnames.

As might be expected, the largest proportion of people holding the surname Blackamore and its variants continued to be found in the parishes of the city of Norwich. The same parishes that figured in the seventeenth century – Norwich St Julian, St James with Pockthorpe, St Peter Parmentergate, St Stephen – all appear in the eighteenth-century records. Some of these appearances can be linked to the seventeenth-century families. For example, the Robert Blackemore baptised in Norwich St Julian in April 1700 would appear to have been the son of the Robert Blackmore who was baptised in December 1673.[56] Jane Blackamore, who was baptised in St Peter Parmentergate on 23 April 1700, would appear to be the daughter of William Blackamoore and Sarah Newton,

[53] *Daily Advertiser*, 8 January 1741.
[54] *Public Advertiser*, 13 December 1771.
[55] NRO/PD/162/4, Baptism of Jane Blackamore, 23 April 1700; Burial of Ann Blackmore, 14 January 1704.
[56] NRO/PD/31/1, Baptism of Robert Blakemore, 21 April 1700; NRO/PD/11/1, Baptism of Robert Blackmore, 11 December 1673.

who married in the same church a decade earlier.[57] It appears, therefore, that the families that had appeared in Norwich in the seventeenth century continued to live freely in the city in the eighteenth. Any new arrivals in the city also found this to be possible. These Africans continued to live as they had done before; getting married, having children, and being buried in the community around them, even as enslavement gathered strength across the Atlantic. This also appears to be true for the Blackamores that appeared elsewhere in the region over the course of the century, in places such as Thurgarton, Lowestoft, Yarmouth, and Trowse.[58]

Aside from the Blackamore families, determining the status of other Africans mentioned in this period can be difficult. Since the term 'slave' was so infrequently used, and since many entries do not provide sufficient detail to determine the Africans' exact status, in that they lack a secure connection to a country house, plantation owner, or a person who appears to have control over them, the determination of their situation becomes a matter of the balance of probabilities. These records could be recording free Africans, or they could merely be failing to provide the details that would show near slavery. The record of Thomas Rundell, who was buried at Bardwell in 1732, falls into this indeterminate category, as does that of the nineteen-year-old Charles Cook, who was baptised in Bury St Edmunds, Suffolk, in 1771.[59] Both could be connected to plantation owners who lived near Bury St Edmunds, such as the Blakes at Langham, but there is nothing substantive to help make a connection.

Another unclear example is seen in the Ellingham parish register from 1765. The entry reads, 'A negro, servant to Mr Machett'.[60] It was unusual for an African not to be named in a register entry by this date. In 1805, an unnamed African was buried in Newmarket and described as 'a pauper, an African', but otherwise Africans who were identified as such in the region's parish registers in the eighteenth century were generally named, even when they lacked a surname, as with 'William, a negro' who was buried in Rushbrooke in 1766.[61] The lack of name for the pauper in Newmarket is likely to have been the result of their economic condition; the unfortunate person was unknown in the parish

[57] NRO/PD/162/4, Baptism of Jane Blackamore, 23 April 1700; Marriage of William Blackamoore and Sarah Newton, 29 May 1690.
[58] NRO/PD/221/2, Marriage of Mary Blackmore and Humphrey Garwood, 29 August 1702; NRO/PD/589/4, Baptism of William Blackemore, 17 July 1752; NRO/PD/575/11, Marriage of Elizabeth Blackamore and Thomas Rich, 12 February 1761; NRO/PD/704/12, Marriage of Minter Blackmore and Samuel Clemence, 18 October 1762; NRO/PD/28/67, Marriage of Jonathan Blackamore and Ann Clarke, 16 January 1783; NRO/PD/216/5, Marriage of Samuel Blackmore and Susannah Piken, 5 December 1784.
[59] SRO/FL522/4/3, Burial of Thomas Rundell, Bardwell, 22 February 1732; SRO/FL541/4/4, Baptism of Charles Cook, Bury St Edmunds St James, 22 December 1773.
[60] NRO/PD/669/2, Burial, Ellingham 26 August 1765. It seems the spelling 'Machett' here is an error; the family are otherwise always noted as 'Matchett'.
[61] SRO/FL610/4/4, 'A pauper an African', Newmarket, 1805. Burial of 'William', 29 June 1766, Hervey, *Rushbrook*, p. 19.

because they were passing through, this was not a situation limited to Africans. The unnamed African in Ellingham is more difficult. The lack of a name cannot be because they were unknown to the parish since they were listed as 'a servant to Mr Machett', indicating membership of a household. A 'Mr Matchett' is mentioned as owning a shop in the village in 1777, and the family had been living in the village for many years.[62] Robert Matchett (d.1759) was described as a 'merchant' in his will.[63] There is no indication of the family having any connection with the colonies or slaveholding.

As Wrightson has noted in his analysis of wills in seventeenth-century Newcastle, the social importance of household in early modern society often meant that 'wives, children, servants and apprentices were attributed to the heads of households to which they belonged'.[64] In the Ellingham register this practice can be seen in relation to wives and children, although their Christian names were all recorded. There is no other entry in the register relating to an unnamed servant. The entry for the unnamed African would seem to indicate that the village saw them as part of Matchett's household, but we cannot be exact in identifying their status. They may have been in some form of slavish servitude or have been a servant in the more traditional sense.

Others would seem to be more clearly free or becoming free. Joseph Diana, who was baptised at Henstead, Suffolk, on 11 June 1784, is one of these. Diana was said to be 'a native Congo in Africa, aged about 16 years'.[65] This detail of Diana's Congolese origin, when connected to the boy's age, is unusual and makes it a distinct possibility that Joseph had been enslaved at some point. Yet, the baptismal entry makes no mention of any potential owner and, as Diana then proceeded to move around the region, becoming an apprentice, and then a servant to various local gentlemen over the next eight years, it seems that, even if he had been enslaved previously, he was not in such a position by 1784.[66]

This also appears to have been the situation for Henry Norbrook. The 1761 baptism in Tunstall of Hannah Norbrook described her as the 'daughter of Henry Norbrook, a negro, and Hannah his wife'.[67] It seems likely that Henry was connected to the Arcedeckne family since one of their plantations in Jamaica was named Norbrook.[68] The Arcedeckne family purchased Glevering Hall, which is only five miles from Tunstall, in 1791, and had previously rented

---

[62] 'Will Maplestone to Beccles bridewell stealing £1 2s 6d from shop of Mr Matchett of Ellingham (many of the shillings were marked with 2 letters of Mr Matchett's name', *Norwich Mercury*, 5 July 1777.

[63] NRO/NCC/will register Gooch 31, Matchett, Robert, merchant, of Ellingham, 1759. NRO/PD/669/2, burial 23 February 1759, Ellingham.

[64] Keith Wrightson, *Ralph Tailor's Summer* (New Haven, 2011), p. 107.

[65] SRO/FL/125/D1/2, Baptism of Joseph Diana, Henstead, 11 June 1784.

[66] *Norfolk Chronicle*, 18 November 1791, p. 2.

[67] SRO/FC164/D1/4, Baptism of Hannah Norbrook, Tunstall, 29 September 1761.

[68] SRO/HB26/412 and HB26/12012, Sale particulars, papers and plans, Golden Grove and Norbrook estates, Jamaica, 1804–1898.

Cockfield Hall, in nearby Yoxford, so they had a strong connection to the area in this period.[69] Henry is likely, therefore, to have been a household slave who was brought over from Jamaica. The fact that he was able to marry suggests, however, that he was no longer enslaved in 1761. As has been shown already, such marriages to non-Africans had occurred from the sixteenth century onwards and they continued in the eighteenth century. The mention of 'Miles' black wife of Lessingham' in a local Norfolk variant of the well-known 'Ballad of Arthur of Bradley', and recorded by Walter Rye at the end of the century, highlights the presence of such unions.[70] There were also marriages between Africans, such as Cuffey and Amber Cross or John and Rosanita Blunt, but most marriages involved an African marrying a non-African. Given the significance attached to marriage in the period it seems highly unlikely that an enslaved African would have been allowed to marry a free non-African. There is no specific evidence to prove this suggestion, but the *Book of Common Prayer* was clear in its requirement for any form of 'impediment' to matrimony to be declared before the ceremony. It would seem, therefore, that the marriage of an African to a non-African is indicative of freedom on the part of the African. This is significant in several cases. William Byrom was described as 'a blackamoor servant to Captain Rycart' when he married Sarah Knights, so the wording is suggestive of near slavery, but, if the suggestion regarding marriage is correct, then it seems that he was no longer in a form of slavish servitude when the marriage took place.[71]

This suggestion is supported by the fact that such marriages often led to long-term settlement in local communities. Byrom and Norbrook both lived in their respective villages long after marriage and had children; the Byroms had two, while the Norbrooks had six. Norbrook lived the rest of his life in Tunstall, being buried, aged eighty-one, in 1794.[72] The children lived in the village for many years; for example, Norbrook's daughter, Hannah, married a local man in 1783.[73] Such examples abound in the eighteenth century. Elizabeth Barnes of Stradsett may have been in servitude before her mistress' death, but afterwards she was swiftly able to marry a man named Isaac Pickerall, move with him to Bury St Edmunds, raise a family, and remain there until her death in 1748.[74] Caesar Hockwold married in 1759 and went on to have several children over the

---

[69] Nicholas Kingsley, Landed Families of Britain and Ireland, '(162) Arcedeckne of Glevering Hall', https://landedfamilies.blogspot.com/2015/04/162-arcedeckne-of-glevering-hall.html [accessed 25 March 2019].

[70] Walter Rye, 'The Ballad of Arthur of Bradley', in Charles Harold Evelyn White, *The East Anglian* (Lowestoft, 1800), pp. 177–80, <https://archive.org/details/eastanglianorno-04whitgoog/page/n190/mode/2up> [accessed 22 October 2019].

[71] SRO/FC129/D1/3, Marriage of William Byrom and Sarah Knights, Aldeburgh, 16 August 1744.

[72] SRO/FC164/D1/4, Burial of Henry Norbrook, Tunstall, 21 May 1794.

[73] SRO/FC164/D1/4, Marriage of Hannah Norbrook and William Crow, 12 June 1783.

[74] NRO/PD/13/1, Marriage of Elizabeth Barnes and Isaac Pickerall, Stradsett, 19 August 1729; NRO/PRCC/OW, 1729, Will of Elizabeth Buxton.

next twenty years, living in Hockwold-cum-Wilton until his death.[75] The Darbys were similar; married in 1791 in Norwich, they raised six children.[76] Even the issue of illegitimacy appears to have not been a major problem. Barlow at Earsham Hall in the 1750s fathered an illegitimate child, Barlow Spence, when he was in likely servitude at the hall.[77] Ann Spence, the mother of the child, was the daughter of Earsham Hall's butler, and these events seem to have led to Barlow's freedom. He and Ann were married eight years later in 1763, and Barlow had gained a surname by this point, Fielding.[78] The couple continued to live in the village and had another child, named John, in 1764.[79] It also seems that Robert Yoxford, the 'Black boy brought over by Thomas Betts Esq' to Yoxford, Suffolk, in 1713, became free and married.[80] A man named Robert Yoxford was married in the village of Darsham, less than two miles south of Yoxford, on 5 December 1729.[81]

Of special interest in this context is the marriage of Robert Taylor, described as a 'mulatto' on his son's baptism in Garboldisham.[82] He was later referred to as 'Black Bob'.[83] Robert and his wife, Mary, lived in Garboldisham for many years, raising seven children, some of whom were described as 'a mulatto infant' by the rector, Charles Sheard Molineux, whose plantation links have already been discussed.[84] Given that Taylor would appear to have been held in near slavery by the Molineux family, this marriage and the baptism of the children are extremely interesting, as Crisp Molineux was unequivocally opposed to any such measures in the West Indies. The depth of his opposition is evinced in the diary of William Wilberforce, which records the hatred of Molineux for the vicar and surgeon James Ramsay. Ramsay's attempts to alter the situation in St Christopher, which included suggestions that enslaved Africans should be encouraged to attend church and school, led to him being hounded off the island by planters, including Molineux. This animosity grew in virulence after Ramsay returned to England and published his *Essay on the Treatment and Conversion of African Slaves in the British Sugar Colonies*, which proposed a programme of preparation for emancipation that would include education,

[75] NRO/PD 311/5, Marriage of Caesar Hockwold and Elizabeth Richardson, 9 November 1759; NRO/PD/311/1, Baptism of Ann Hockwold, 17 February 1760; Burial of Ann Hockwold, 2 April 1760; Baptism of Jane Hockwold, 22 March 1762; Baptism of Caesar Hockwold, 13 November 1763; Baptism of Mary Hockwold, 29 September 1765; Baptism of John Hockwold, 25 June 1769; Baptism of Thomas Hockwold, 18 October 1767; Baptism of Sarah Hockwold, 15 September 1771.
[76] NRO/PD74/44, Marriage of John Darby and Mary Stamp, 29 March 1791.
[77] NRO/PD/519/3, Baptism of Barlow Spence, 27 April 1755.
[78] NRO/PD/519/7, Marriage of Barlow Fielding and Ann Spence, 14 April 1763.
[79] NRO/PD/519/3, Baptism of John Fielding, 22 July 1764.
[80] SRO/FC73/D1/1, Baptism of Robert Yoxford, 25 December 1713.
[81] Suffolk Marriage Index, Marriage of Robert Yoxford and Mary Garard, 5 December 1729.
[82] NRO/PD/197/2, Baptism of Robert Taylor, 23 November 1794.
[83] NRO/PD/197/2, Baptism of William Taylor, 11 March 1807.
[84] NRO/PD/197/2, Burial of William Taylor, 7 September 1803.

Christian teaching, the inculcation of family and social values, and the passing of equitable laws.[85] In Molineux's only recorded parliamentary speech, which argued strongly against any end to the slave trade, he also mounted a savage attack on Ramsay's character and professional reputation.[86] The attack broke Ramsay's fragile health and he died within a month of it.[87] Wilberforce recorded that on hearing of Ramsay's death Molineux had stated triumphantly, 'Ramsay is dead, I have killed him.'[88]

Given Molineux's opposition to Ramsay's ideas on the inculcation of Christian ideas about the family, which are predicated on marriage, then the marriage of Robert Taylor is, once again, indicative of the different cultural milieu in Norfolk and Suffolk. As had been the case with Robert Davers in 1688, planters found themselves forced to accede to long-standing local cultural norms in East Anglia. Chaloner Arcedeckne was also strongly opposed to interracial marriages, so the marriage of Henry Norbrook is equally revealing. This suggestion can also be extended to the baptisms and marriages of the other Africans in Garboldisham after the Molineux family arrived. Ramsay recorded a case of one absentee planter who had tried to allow baptism, but whose efforts had been thwarted by the contempt with which most planters on the island treated the idea of ministering the sacraments to enslaved people. Ramsay argued that the highly racialised culture of the islands made such efforts of conversion both rare and ineffective.[89] Yet, both Arcedeckne and Molineux, along with the other planters identified in Norfolk and Suffolk, allowed such events to take place while they lived in East Anglia. This was not because they arrived in the region and changed their views. As has been shown, their racialised opinions were retained up to and beyond the date of abolition. It would seem to have been a continuation of the issue identified in relation to custom and practice of baptism in sixteenth- and seventeenth-century Norfolk and Suffolk. The new ideas about race being developed in the colonies did not

[85] James Ramsay, An Essay on the Treatment and Conversion of African Slaves in the British Sugar Colonies (J. Phillips, 1784), see especially pp. 184–96.

[86] Brian Hayes, 'Molineux, Crisp (1730–92), of Garboldisham, Norfolk', in L. Namier and J. Brooke (eds), The History of Parliament: The House of Commons 1754–1790 (Woodbridge, 1964) <http://www.historyofparliamentonline.org/volume/1754-1790/member/molineux-crisp-1730-92> [accessed 1 October 2020].

[87] J. Watt, 'Ramsay, James (1733–1789), surgeon and slavery abolitionist', ODNB <https://www.oxforddnb.com/view/10.1093/ref:odnb/9780198614128.001.0001/odnb-9780198614128-e-23086> [accessed 6 February 2019].

[88] Robert and Samuel Wilberforce (eds), Life of William Wilberforce Volume One (London, 1838), pp. 234–5. Also quoted in Eric Williams, The Economic Aspect of the Abolition of the West Indian Slave Trade and Slavery (Lanham, MD, 2014), p. 229.

[89] Ramsay recorded that in this incident baptism was carried out by a minister who was 'not even ostensibly decent' purely to obtain money, or that occasionally a 'favourite slave' was baptised. The key point he made was that there was no attempt at genuine instruction in the faith even in these cases. Ramsay, An Essay, pp. 158–60, 181–2.

manage to gain adequate purchase locally to allow the planters to ignore the established norms of local society in relation to marriage and baptism.

It also seems that baptism remained an indicator of the social movement of Africans from slavish servitude to freedom. A striking example of this would appear to be provided in the baptism of Thomas Sayers, 'a Black aged 61', at Kirby Bedon, near Norwich, in 1812. Kirby Bedon Hall was the property of the Berney family, and it seems likely that Thomas arrived in the area because of their connection to the slaving economy. The plantation records of the family from 1791 mention a young slave named 'Thomas Sears' in the second gang on their estate in Barbados who would be too young to have been this man, but who might have been a relative.[90] This potential connection to the family is strengthened by his description as a 'footman' at the birth of his first daughter in 1815.[91] The note about Thomas' baptism made no mention of the Berneys, however. Instead, the emphasis was upon his salvation through baptism and his entry into the faith.

Five years had passed since the abolition of the slave trade and the attention of some in the county was turning to the institution of slavery itself. The register entry appears to have reflected this new situation. After the short mention of his background, the register went on to say that Sayers 'was publicly baptised & received into the Church as a true member & faithful believer'.[92] Even 200 years later this entry resounds with evangelical triumph. The emphasis here was, in a manner that recalls Baptist two centuries before, on the change in Thomas' status to believing Christian. The entry made it clear that, whatever his background previously, Sayers was now seen as part of the congregation. A similar turn of phrase was used in November 1807 in St Peter Hungate, Norwich, when John Gibbs, 'a black man, a native of the Island of Barbados was publickly baptised.'[93] Such status appears to have been long-term; Thomas Sayers went on to work, marry, have several children, and live in the area until the age of ninety, dying in nearby Trowse in 1838.[94]

The record of the baptism of Rachel Fitshoe at St Mary's Church, Diss, on 23 October 1799, when Rachel was described as 'a Black woman, aged 18 years', is similar.[95] Like Sayers and Gibbs, Rachel was 'publickly baptised', indicating once again that an evangelical statement was being made. The register entry did not link Rachel with any local plantation family, but Diss is close to Garboldisham, so there could have been a connection to the Molineux family. Since Rachel was a young African woman who was being baptised as an adult, then we can surmise that she had probably arrived in Norfolk having been previously enslaved and may have been in some form of near slavery at the beginning

[90] NRO/MC/50/45/503x9, Fellowes to Abergavenney, 20 December 1791.
[91] NRO/PD/481/3, Baptism of Mary Sayers, 14 January 1815.
[92] NRO/PD/481/12, Baptism of Thomas Sayers, Kirby Bedon, 3 September 1812.
[93] NRO/PD/61/3, Baptism of John Gibbs, Norwich, 15 November 1807.
[94] NRO/PD/216/14, Burial of Thomas Sayers, Trowse, 12 November 1838.
[95] NRO/PD/100/364, Baptism of Rachel Fitshoe, Diss, 23 October 1799.

of her time in the region. The lack of any mention of such connections in the record shows that by 1799 she was no longer enslaved. Diss was a town where the abolition movement had been strongly supported in 1792, holding a public meeting to sign a petition for the abolition of the slave trade, so Rachel was being baptised in a location where the ideas underpinning enslavement were being challenged.[96] In this case, it may be that Rachel was a newly freed African servant, who was seen by the congregation at Diss as someone representing the morality of their cause.

A pattern can be discerned among other female Africans in the region from early in the eighteenth century, a movement from servitude to freedom, marriage, and inclusion. Elizabeth Barnes was described in the parish register on her marriage as the 'negro maid of M Buxton of Stradsett'.[97] She was left ten pounds in the 1729 will of Elizabeth Buxton of Stradsett Hall and described as a 'negro servant'.[98] The Buxton family had no clear connection with the colonies, but since her mistress' will left no instruction to free Barnes it seems that her condition had not been full enslavement. After her mistress' death, Elizabeth was able to move with her husband to Bury St Edmunds, where the couple lived until Elizabeth's death in 1748.[99] The documentation around Elizabeth is instructive in several areas. It shows the existence of the condition of slavish servitude in the region, as opposed to chattel slavery. Elizabeth was bound to Mrs Buxton, but was not owned as chattel, since those bonds were broken by death and she was not left as property in the will. The breaking of those bonds then allowed Elizabeth to leave and marry. This suggests that she had already been able to interact with members of the local working community and develop relationships before her mistress' death. It also confirms the suggestion that marriage to a local was indicative of free status and that it could not be prevented by owners. It seems possible that Rachel Fitshoe followed this pattern. A woman listed as 'Rachel Fitch' married a man named Henry Conway in the village of Sible Hedingham in Essex in 1808. The village lies forty-four miles south of Diss along the main route to London and the similarity of surname is suggestive. This idea is supported by the age of Rachel Conway when she was buried in October 1832; fifty-two. This means that she would have been around the same age as Rachel Fitshoe in 1799.[100]

Another African who appears to have crossed the boundary of near slavery and freedom was Samuel Samuels from Spixworth Hall. Samuels was buried at Spixworth in July 1842, when he was described as 'a man of colour, a

---

[96] *Norfolk Chronicle*, 22 February 1792, p. 2.
[97] NRO/PD/13/1, Marriage of Elizabeth Barnes and Isaac Pickerall, 1729.
[98] NRO/PRCC/OW, 1729, Will of Elizabeth Buxton.
[99] SRO/FL/545/4/5, Burial of Elizabeth Pickerall, 17 March 1748.
[100] Essex Record Office, D/P 93/1/6, Banns of Rachel Fitch and Henry Conway, 5 July 1808; D/P 93/1/11, Burial of Rachel Conway, 19 October 1832.

native of Jamaica, a servant at the Hall'.[101] The 1841 census recorded Samuels as being in the household of John Longe of Spixworth Hall.[102] The Longe family owned a plantation in St Christopher, which had been inherited from General Leigh in 1816. Since Samuels was said to be from Jamaica, it is possible that he had arrived at Spixworth Hall because of the service of George Howes, a relative of the family, with Leigh in the West Indies in the mid-1790s. The register recorded Samuels' age as fifty-four, suggesting a birth in 1788, whereas the census gave it as 1796, which was the date that Howes had returned from the colonies. It may be, therefore, that Howes had brought the young Samuels back in the late 1790s, when the boy was around eight, and that Samuels had then lived at Spixworth Hall. In the burial register he was said to be living in St Martin at Oak, so it may be that in the last year of his life he had moved to Norwich. It seems Samuels was probably enslaved in St Christopher or Jamaica, then held in slavish servitude in Norfolk, before leaving that condition at some point before 1842. Whether this was because of the abolition in 1833 or had happened before is unclear.

A similar history is suggested by the record from the diary of James Woodford, of Weston Longville, Norfolk, in July 1787. Woodford recorded that 'This evening as we were going to supper, a covered cart drove into my yard with three men with it and one of them the principal was a black with a French horn.' Woodford did not name the African musician but spoke to him and noted that 'The Black told me he formerly lived with the Earl of Albemarle.'[103] He was likely to have been referring to the fourth earl, William Charles Keppel (1772–1849), who lived at Quidenham Hall, Norfolk. There is no direct evidence linking the fourth earl with the transatlantic economy; however, during the Seven Years' War his father, the third earl, George Keppel (1724–72), had commanded the land forces sent to take Havana and then became Governor of Cuba afterwards. Cuba was a major slaving economy at this time, and he bought Quidenham Hall with prize money earned from his Cuban adventures, providing the opportunity also to acquire Africans.[104] While the musician was clearly free when he met Woodford, it seems that this had followed on from some form of servitude at Quidenham Hall.

[101] NRO/PD/536/28, Burial of Samuel Samuels, 15 July 1842.

[102] TNA/HO107/16, f. 2, piece 783, p. 27, 1841.

[103] Blythe, *The Diary*, p. 205.

[104] W. Lowe, 'Keppel, George, third earl of Albemarle (1724–1772), army officer and politician', ODNB <https://www.oxforddnb.com/view/10.1093/ref:odnb/9780198614128.001.0001/odnb-9780198614128-e-15441> [accessed 6 February 2019].

Free Working-Class Africans in the Eighteenth and Early Nineteenth Centuries

The examples of the 'black with a French horn', Joseph Diana, and Henry Norbrook, along with the other free Africans living and working in Norfolk and Suffolk in this period, lead us back to the issue of employment. They also allow further exploration of the suggestion that class is a useful analytical tool in considering Africans in the period. Such people were both working class and African, as was discussed in relation to Bedfer and Robert Smith in the seventeenth century. In Kirby Bedon, Thomas Sayers worked first as a footman, and then as a labourer and husbandman, according to the entries for his children's baptisms.[105] People like Sayers, Diana, and the horn player were acting as economic agents, working on their own behalf, and making their own way in the world. As such they were free of chattel status but, of course, they did not have economic autonomy within an unequal economic system. In this context their African heritage was of little importance, what mattered was their class position. By moving away from thinking of Africans in the region in the eighteenth and early nineteenth centuries purely in terms of race and the binary of slave/free, or even in relation to the Atlantic slaving economy itself, we can look at their local class position to obtain another perspective on their lives.

We can begin by returning to Joseph Diana who, as was discussed above, was baptised at Henstead, Suffolk, in 1784. In November 1791, the *Norfolk Chronicle* reported that 'Joseph Diana, a black, servant to Daniel Jones Esq. of Fakenham' had been placed in custody at Norwich Castle, 'on suspicion of breaking open his counting room on Monday night last and stealing thereout a large sum of money and several bills'.[106] The paper alleged that, after committing the crime, Diana had fled from Fakenham to Norwich, and had been caught 'after a diligent search' at a public house, with the stolen goods still in his possession. Diana's life prior to his arrest appears to have been that of a mobile working man. He was apprenticed to a tailor named William Holyoak in Yarmouth in 1788.[107] He had moved around the region, working at various houses, including the 'service of a manufacturer of this city (Norwich)', before arriving in Fakenham.[108] His theft and subsequent conviction ended this chapter of his life. Diana was tried, convicted, and sentenced to be transported for seven years in March 1792.[109] It appears, however, that Diana avoided this fate and ended up in the Royal Navy instead. The Admiralty records of the prisoners in the various depots and prison ships during the wars with France between 1793 and 1815 mention a prisoner named 'Joseph Dian or Diana' who was listed as a seaman

[105] NRO/PD/481/12, Baptism of Thomas Sayers, Kirby Bedon, 15 December 1817.
[106] *Norfolk Chronicle*, 25 February 1792, p. 2.
[107] TNA/IR1/64/f143, 5 February 1788.
[108] *Norfolk Chronicle*, 18 November 1791, p. 2.
[109] *Norfolk Chronicle*, 16 March 1792, p. 2 and 24 March 1792, p. 2.

and died on 30 January 1805, in Valenciennes.[110] From this it appears that Diana may have joined the Royal Navy in lieu of transportation and had then died in the service of his adopted country. Looked at in this fashion, Diana's story is like that of many of his non-African contemporaries in the working class during the eighteenth century. He lived an insecure, unsettled life, which saw him seeking and finding work in various guises, falling upon hard times and into crime, before being conscripted into the Royal Navy, where he met his end in the war against Napoleonic France.

The region's newspapers contain traces of other African members of the permanent proletariat who had fallen into criminality. John Bumpstead, 'a tall black man' from Styleham, Suffolk, was described as a 'miller' in an advertisement that asserted that he had defrauded a local woman of 'ten pecks of wheat, under pretention of grinding, and afterwards absconded'.[111] There was the report of an unnamed 'thin black man' who was wanted in respect of horse theft, along with a non-African, in Pakenham, around November 1741.[112] Suspected theft was also the reason for the mention of James Pamps, 'a little black Man, aged about 35 years', in the newspapers in 1743.[113] John Ong, described as 'a stout well-made black Man, with short curl'd hair, about 25 years of age', was reported as being suspected of theft in Narford in the same year.[114] Similarly, the papers reported that John Yeldon, 'a tall black man, round-shouldered, & about fifty years of age', was suspected of housebreaking in Kettleburgh in 1773.[115]

The appearance of these men in the newspapers was a consequence of the nature of the source rather than any ingrained racial stereotyping. The same columns were full of reports of crime allegedly committed by poor non-Africans. Newspapers tend to focus on crime, so the Africans appeared in their pages when they were suspected of it, rather than being suspected of it because they were African. Indeed, as happened with William Snoring in the seventeenth century, the normal process of law appears to have run whatever the background of the suspect. In 1803, 'a man of colour' named Benjamin Grey was arrested in Bury along with a non-African sailor named Thomas Mulloy on suspicion of the theft of a barrel of porter. Both men were acquitted as 'the charge could not be substantiated'. The 'man of colour', Grey, was freed, but the non-African, Mulloy, was sent to a warship because he had been 'impertinent' to the magistrate.[116]

What these reports seem to be pointing toward is some degree of commonality of experience among the working poor, whatever their background. These men were not professional criminals, nor were they the victims of racially motivated

[110] TNA/ADM/103/631/f.42, Register of Deaths for British POWs 1794–1814.
[111] The Ipswich Journal, 4 September 1773, p. 3.
[112] The Ipswich Journal, 14 November 1741, p. 3.
[113] The Ipswich Journal, 15 January 1743, p. 3.
[114] The Ipswich Journal, 29 October 1743, p. 3.
[115] The Ipswich Journal, 19 June 1773, p. 3.
[116] The Ipswich Journal, 30 July 1803, p. 2.

accusations. Rather they were poor working men of African background who were driven to crime by the grinding poverty and treacherous economic position of the working class generally. Before turning to crime, they all were in work. Bumpstead was a miller, Ong was a servant, while Yeldon was a labourer. Their suspected crimes were all crimes of opportunity and would seem to be indicative of economic desperation. Such desperation is also clear in the mention of John Nicholls, '5 feet 9 inches high, a black man, lankey hair, with fear on his face', Martin Leverington, 'a stout black man', and Robert Tidd, who were said to have left their families 'chargeable to the parish' at Watlington in early 1776.[117] For any member of the working poor in the period, regardless of their background, eighteenth-century life was insecure and unpredictable. Illness, bad luck, or bad choices could leave anyone in the position of the unnamed 'black man begging about the streets' in Ipswich in 1789.[118]

These examples should not overshadow the stories of the Africans in the region's population who avoided slipping into criminal behaviour, or penury. For every Bumpstead, there were Africans such as the Doubledays of Colton, who managed to live and prosper without turning to crime. James Doubleday was described as a 'gardener' at the baptism of his children in the early 1800s. One of his sons, also called James, was described as a 'victualler' and a 'negro' in 1836.[119] The family had appeared in the area in 1782, when another James Doubleday had married a local woman named Ann, and appear to have been accepted into the local working class community, living and working alongside their peers for many years, with other members of the family being described as labourers in the records.[120]

Although Joseph Diana fell into crime after having become an apprentice, there were others for whom an apprenticeship appears to have been the passage to a settled life as a member of the local working poor. Robert Yoxford, the 'black boy' who had been baptised in Yoxford in 1713, was apprenticed to a carpenter named William Woolaston in the village in 1719.[121] As we have seen, Robert then married and raised a family. It seems that Yoxford had been able to move from slavish servitude to membership of the working class, and settlement with a wife and family, by means of baptism and apprenticeship. Caesar Hockwold was apprenticed as a shoemaker to Robert Jackson, from Bury St Edmunds, and then to Edward Spinks of the village of Hillborough.[122] The apprenticeship agreement

[117] *The Ipswich Journal*, 3 February 1776, p. 1. Tidd does not appear to have been an African; he was described as 'about 5 feet 7 inches high, and brown complexion'.
[118] *The Ipswich Journal*, 6 June 1789, p. 2.
[119] NRO/PD/345/3, Baptism of James Doubleday, Colton, 11 December 1814; White, *History*, p. 770 and p. 434.
[120] NRO/PD/388/1, Marriage of James Doubleday, 24 February 1782; NRO/PD/345/36, Banns of marriage, Henry Doubleday and Eliza Wilson, 28 July 1864.
[121] TNA/IR1/145/f155, 17 February 1719. The connection to Robert Yoxford from 1713 seems clear since in 1719 Robert was not listed as being 'the son of' as was the case for the other entries. He was merely stated to be 'of Yoxford'.
[122] NRO/MC/42/90/527x1, Robert Jackson, shoemaker 3 February 1740; TNA/IR1/50/

with Edward Spinks would have been an unusual statement if Hockwold was held in near slavery, since it stated that on the release from his apprenticeship Hockwold would have 'his liberty to go where and when he pleases, and to dispose of himself as he shall think proper'.[123] If Wyche was claiming ownership of Hockwold then this document would have no sense. The likelihood is, therefore, that Hockwold was free by the date of this agreement and that his apprenticeship confirmed his status. This working-class position was then passed on to his children. For example, his eldest son, also called Caesar, was apprenticed to a brickmaker called Edward Tricker in the village of Barrow in Suffolk in 1775.[124] Whatever Caesar's origins had been, the family had become firmly embedded in the local working community of Hockwold and would continue to live there for generations.

Mobility – Geography and Status

These examples return us to the issue of mobility in these Africans' lives. The parish register entries point us toward an awareness of the long journeys that had ended in Norfolk and Suffolk. The coroner's report of 1819 noted that Samuel Turner was 'a native of Martinique in the West Indies', while John Gibbs had been a 'native of Barbados'.[125] The social situation in which these men arrived in Norfolk is unclear, but the example of Samuel Samuels points us towards a suggestion of geographic and social mobility. The stories of Turner and Gibbs were, probably, like that of Samuels. They would have travelled from the West Indies to East Anglia in some form of servitude. It is likely that they settled in Norfolk, perhaps still in slavish servitude, but were freed at some later date. This changeability in status and geographical mobility was also true for women. Elizabeth Barnes appeared in Stradsett, Norfolk, and moved to Bury in Suffolk once her status had changed from 'servant' to free. We do not know Rachel Fitshoe's status exactly before she appeared in Diss, but she appears to have moved to Suffolk later.

Barlow Fielding was born in 1755 in Earsham, the illegitimate son of the 'negro servant' Barlow from Earsham Hall.[126] Although it seems probable that his father had been held in some sort of slavish servitude, no claim had been made on the young Barlow, suggesting his father had shifted situation. The younger Barlow was not mentioned again in Earsham and seems to have moved away to follow a common trade for many of the working class in the period, as a seaman. A twenty-five-year-old 'Black man' named Barlow Fielding was recorded as being a member of the crew of HMS *Montreal* in the late 1770s and then

---

f8, 14 May 1741; NRO/MC/42/90/527x1, Hillborough, Edward Spinks, Shoemakers, 19 November 1742.

[123] NRO/MC/42/90/527x1, Agreement of Edward Spinks, 12 May 1741.

[124] TNA/IR1/59, 28 August 1775.

[125] NRO/NCR/Case6a/25, Death of Samuel Turner, 12 February 1819; NRO/PD/61/3, Burial of John Gibbs, Wroxham, 1807.

[126] NRO/PD/519/3, Baptism of Barlow Spence, 27 April 1755.

HMS *Orpheus* around 1780, when the captain considered him for the position of boatswain. The ship's records note that Fielding then entered Hasler Hospital in Portsmouth.[127] Fielding appears to have remained in that region and died in 1803 in Devon.[128] There is also a possibility that William Strap, who was described as 'a negro servant of Captain Pricke of Nacton' in 1771, may have become an able seaman in the Royal Navy, since a man of that name was listed as serving on HMS *Menelaus* in 1805.[129]

Joseph Diana provides an especially fruitful example of this mobility. As we have seen, he came from the Congo where, presumably, he had originally been free. He had been enslaved in Africa and this change of status had led to his subsequent geographical movement. It seems likely that he had been taken to the West Indies in chattel slavery before he eventually travelled to Suffolk. He was possibly originally held there in near slavery, but the geographic shift caused a further change in social category and, at some point, he had moved to a free status, a shift highlighted by his baptism. That change in social status had facilitated further geographic mobility in Suffolk and then Norfolk. It also allowed Diana to change his social situation, as he became an apprentice, and then a servant. He then altered social situation again, losing his freedom, not because of his African background, but because he turned to crime. He then became a prisoner and a convicted felon. This resulted in a plan to change his geographic location with transportation to Australia. This planned movement was interrupted by another change, to conscripted Royal Navy sailor, which in turn resulted in new geographic movement, which ended in France.

The details of Diana's life provide a window into the potential mobility that it seems reasonable to suggest characterised the lives of many of the Africans who lived in Norfolk and Suffolk in the early modern period. Many were mobile within the region, and the evidence shows that a good many of them had arrived in the region from the colonies. The degree to which their class position overdetermined their African heritage is difficult to determine, but our examples show that Africans across the region were working in a variety of occupations, as servants, sailors, musicians, cobblers, millers, and labourers, throughout the eighteenth and early nineteenth centuries. As such, they were living and working as part of the region's working class.

Vivid examples of these working-class African lives can be seen in two paintings from Norwich which were painted by the itinerant miniaturist John Dempsey and are dated to the 1820s. Although there is no other information about the

---

[127] Discussed in Philip D. Morgan, 'Black Experiences in Britain's Maritime World', in David Cannadine (ed.), *Empire, the Sea and Global History* (Basingstoke, 2007), pp. 105–33. For an excellent discussion of African sailors generally, see Ray Costello, *Black Salt: Seafarers of African Descent on British Ships* (Liverpool, 2012).

[128] Plymouth and West Devon Record Office, 166/82, Burial of Barlow Fielding, 17 June 1803.

[129] NA/ADM/27/15, British Royal Navy Allotment Declarations 1795–1852, HMS *Menelaus*, Pay Book 51, 1805–10.

Figure 1: 'Cotton', Norwich c.1823 watercolour 32 x 23, The Docker collection of portraits by John Dempsey in the collection of the Tasmanian Museum and Art Gallery, Hobart

Africans in the city records, the lack of surnames and locations being particularly frustrating here, the pictures themselves can be mined for hints about the lived relations of Africans in this later period. The first is entitled a 'Black at Norwich commonly called Cotton' and depicts a haberdashery street vendor.[130] The picture of Cotton the street vendor brings to life the stories of some of the free working-class Africans we have explored in this chapter. Like Bumpstead, or Ong, he is clearly one of many of the working class whose life was being lived on the margins. He is surviving, but at any moment a turn of bad luck could tip him into penury. The generally precarious nature of the lives of the urban and rural poor is seen here, however, rather than a specifically African situation.

Dempsey's portrait of Charley, used as the cover illustration to this volume, provides a different insight, into the life of a working-class African who had managed to move from the precarious margins to the more secure realm of the tradesman. Charley stands confidently in the doorway of his shop, well-dressed, clearly the successful master of a lucrative business, exuding confidence in his place as a craftsman.[131] He has an air of agency. As David Hansen puts it, 'the proprietorial stance, the garland of shoes around him and the quality of his dress – embroidered waistcoat, carefully tied shirt collar, frock coat – all testify to professional success.'[132] This picture of Charley is a powerful piece of evidence, which presents us with a picture of success that is important for our understanding of the situation of Africans in Norfolk and Suffolk during the later early modern period. Charley's affluence reminds us that, even as the slave-holding economy waxed, it was possible for Africans in Norfolk and Suffolk to succeed and to transgress the putative boundaries that historians might accidentally create around them by making general assumptions concerning the status of Africans in the period of Atlantic slavery.

Charley was an African, but he was also a successful businessman, a skilled tradesman, a man who aspired to greater things, and was not necessarily prevented from achieving them by his African heritage. Charley's picture reminds us that the provincial world in which he and his fellow working-class Africans lived was not one that can be understood by swift recourse to rigid historical categorisations, such as fundamental racism. As we have seen throughout this chapter, the social situation in which Charley and his contemporaries lived and worked was complex and nuanced. In the final chapter we will explore three more examples of African lives in the region in the late eighteenth and early nineteenth centuries that are quite different, but all of which help us toward greater insight into this historical complexity.

---

[130] AG567 'Cotton', Norwich, c.1823 watercolour 32x23, The Docker collection of portraits by John Dempsey in the collection of the Tasmanian Museum and Art Gallery, Hobart.

[131] See cover, AG574 'Black Charley, bootmaker, Norwich' 1823, watercolour 31.5x22.7, The Docker collection of portraits by John Dempsey in the collection of the Tasmanian Museum and Art Gallery, Hobart.

[132] Hansen, '"Remarkable", p. 84.

8

The 'Three African Youths', a Gentleman, and Some Rioters

'Three African Youths'

The tapestry of stories we assembled in Chapter Seven points us toward an understanding of the history of Africans in East Anglia that underscores geographic mobility, social complexity, and unexpected turns of fortune. These stories also remind us that we should be wary of making any sort of generalisation or assumption about the experience of these Africans. Furthermore, we can see that their lives bore significant similarities to the lives of poor non-African workers in the region. Of course, for many Africans there was another layer to their experience, one where the mobility that affected the lives of many of the poor in the early modern period took a specific form because of their connection to the world of Atlantic slavery. This chapter explores three more stories that provide deeper insights into the intricacy of the situation of such Africans and into their mobility, both social and geographic, at the end of the early modern period.

The register of St Peter Mancroft Church in Norwich for 30 May 1813 records the baptism of three young men after the main Sunday service. The three were named as Paolo Loando, Edward Makenzie, and Charles Fortunatus Freeman. In each register entry the minister wrote a sentence across the two columns usually set aside to record the names of the parents of a baptised child. The phrase written was 'Born of African parents (names unknown).'[1] Clearly feeling that some further explanation was required for this unusual situation, the minister also tucked a note into the pages of the register, explaining the circumstances of the baptism. The note reads, 'These children Paolo Loando, Edward Makenzie, and Charles Fortunatus Freeman were thro. the humanity of the Hon. Captain Frederick Paul Irby of Boyland Hall Norfolk brought from Africa in His Majesty's ship Amelia March 22 1813.'[2] A week after the baptism, the *Norfolk Chronicle* added extra detail. The 'three African youths' had been 'taken out of a Portuguese slave ship' by Irby, in his position as captain of the *Amelia*, and had

---

[1] NRO/PD26/4, Baptisms, 30 May 1813, entries 23, 24, 25. The baptism is also mentioned in Charles Mackie, *Norfolk Annals, Volume I, 1801–1850* (Norwich, 1901), p. 95.
[2] Undated note inserted between f.2 and f.3 of parish register of St Peter Mancroft, NRO/PD26/4.

been 'sent by him to this City for education'. They had been baptised after the Sunday service, 'in the presence of a very numerous congregation'.[3]

Irby and the *Amelia* had recently returned from West Africa, where the ship had been engaged in anti-slave trade operations and the triple baptism has been mentioned in Mary Wills' recent work on the Royal Navy's anti-slavery patrols.[4] As Wills explains, after the passage of the Act to Abolish the Slave Trade in British Ships in 1807, 'the dominant narrative which emerged with regard to Britain's place in the changing Atlantic world was that of the world's leading abolitionist state and the principal emancipator of enslaved Africans, providing a morally just example for the rest of the world to follow.'[5]

This shift can be seen in Norfolk and Suffolk. Like the rest of England, Norfolk and Suffolk had been rocked by the debates over the slave trade that had become prominent from the 1780s. Although, as we saw in Chapter Six, the planters, some merchants, and others had engaged with the slaving economies, there were many in the region who had campaigned to end such activity. The establishment of the Society for Effecting the Abolition of the African Slave Trade in London in May 1787 had seen a rapid response in the region. A list compiled only months later details some thirty early supporters of the campaign in Norfolk, and the county delivered a petition against the trade to Parliament in February 1788.[6] In 1792 the support for the campaign reached a high point, with the Norwich Corporation drawing up a petition for the abolition of the slave trade which was stated to be 'disgraceful to a Christian country and incompatible with the sentiments or feelings of humanity'.[7] Similar petitions were drawn up in towns across the county, including Great Yarmouth, Harleston, Diss, East Dereham, Swaffham, and Wymondham.[8]

---

[3] *Norfolk Chronicle*, 5 June 1813, p. 2. A similar baptism took place in Lowestoft in 1846 when 'Thomas Alert a black boy recaptured from a Brazilian brigantine by Captain Bosanquet near the river Gabon' was baptised. In this case the register recorded his African name as 'Macarb Entcheur' and noted he was 'supposed to have been 7 or 8 years old', NRO/PD/589/7, Lowestoft, 4 October 1846.

[4] Mary Wills, *Envoys of Abolition: British Naval Officers and the Campaign Against the Slave Trade in West Africa* (Oxford, 2019), p. 128; Mary Wills, 'At War with the "Detestable Traffic": The Royal Navy's Anti-Slavery Cause in the Atlantic Ocean', in Christer Petley and John McAleer (eds), *The Royal Navy and the British Atlantic World, c. 1750–1820* (London, 2016), pp. 123–46, at p. 132.

[5] Wills, 'At War', p. 124.

[6] NRO/COL/9/59-60, Thomas Ransome, 'A list of local subscribers to anti-slavery cause, 1787'. For earlier advocates see William Richards, the pastor of King's Lynn Baptist Church in the 1770s, and some in the Quaker community who expressed opposition to the trade at their meetings in the mid-1780s; C.B. Jewson, *The Baptists in Norfolk* (London, 1957), p. 55; NRO/SF/6, Minutes of the Norfolk and Norwich Quaker Quarterly Meeting, for example, 29 December 1784 and 30 March 1785. The petition is mentioned in *Norfolk Chronicle*, 16 February 1788, p. 2.

[7] C.B. Jewson, *Jacobin City* (Glasgow, 1975), p. 28; *Norfolk Chronicle*, 11 February 1792.

[8] *Norfolk Chronicle*, 18 February 1792, p. 2; 3 March 1792, p. 2.

The debates leading to the final 1807 abolition were followed closely in the region's papers. In 1804 the Norwich Corporation toasted the prospective abolition of the slave trade at its quarterly meeting.[9] Adverts were run in the papers in 1806 advising people to vote for abolitionist candidates and the result of 1807 was welcomed by many.[10] Involvement in the new national narrative after 1807 can be seen in the gradual appearance of a new wave of support for more general anti-slavery activity across the counties, especially from the mid-1820s, with an increasing number of meetings being held and petitions being signed.[11] One of the earliest meetings in this vein was held one year after the baptism of the three Africans, on 1 July 1814 at St Andrew's Hall, Norwich, 'when resolutions were passed in favour of the abolition of the African slave trade, and it was decided to petition the House of Commons to the same effect.'[12]

In this context, the returning Captain Irby appears to have been something of a celebrity, a physical representative of this new mission.[13] It seems that Irby was genuinely engaged with this task. After being posted to the Navy's anti-slave trade operations, Irby became a subscriber and director of the anti-slave trade organisation The African Institution, paying significant subscriptions to it from 1813 into the 1820s.[14] Irby had been seriously wounded in a battle with a French frigate, the *Arethuse*, on 6 February 1813, an engagement that saw 145 of his crew killed or wounded and his ship crippled. His own wounds would prevent him from returning to service. The *Amelia* limped back to England and arrived in early 1813.[15] The African boys must have been with him on this final voyage. Irby's martial record against the French was celebrated in Norfolk and Suffolk, but his role in anti-slavery operations was given equal weight. When he was toasted at an event in Tharston, Norfolk, in July 1813, it was as 'the brave and humane Captain Irby' and then the additional phrase 'and may British valour and British humanity rescue the children of Africa from slavery' was

[9] *Norfolk Chronicle*, 23 June 1804, p. 2.
[10] *Norfolk Chronicle*, Advert 'The Friends of the Abolition of the Slave Trade', 25 October 1806, p. 3.
[11] For details of meetings in the 1820s see Mackie, *Norfolk*, pp. 220, 229, 250, 251, 276, 333. See also various papers in the collection of Edward Harbord, 3rd Baron Suffield (1781–1835), for example, NRO/GTN 5/9/43, Letters to and circulars to Lord Suffield (including draft replies) on slavery and prison discipline, 1829–34.
[12] Mackie, *Norfolk*, p. 118.
[13] For details of Irby, see J. Laughton and A. Lambert, 'Irby, Frederick Paul (1779–1844), naval officer', *ODNB* <https://www.oxforddnb.com/view/10.1093/ref:odnb/9780198614128.001.0001/odnb-9780198614128-e-14444> [accessed 12 August 2020].
[14] See *Report of the Directors of the African Institution* (London, 1813), pp. vii and 94. Irby's uncle, William Henry Irby, had married a plantation owner named Mary Blackman in 1781, so was co-owner of Blackmans in Antigua, which held 130 slaves at the date compensation was paid, see NA/T71/877, claim from W.H.R. Irby, of (24) South St., Grosvenor Sq., as owner-in-fee.
[15] See Irby's own account in the *Norfolk Chronicle*, 27 March 1813, p. 2.

added.[16] In this environment, the baptism of the three African youths was an important event that symbolised the triumph of the abolition movement and valorised regional support for it.

Little has been written about the three Africans Irby brought to Norwich in 1813, however. There is no further mention of them in the register at St Peter Mancroft, and they disappear from Norfolk's records after the baptism. The general assumption has been that Freeman, Loando, and Makenzie were rescued from enslavement and then disappeared into Norfolk society. The reality is that, although presented to Norfolk as freed Africans, the boys' situation in 1813 was rather complex. The clue that unlocks the lives of Edward Makenzie, Paulo Loando, and Charles Freeman lies in the parliamentary papers of 1827, which contain reports from the colonies listing 'captured negroes'. An 1823 return sent from the island of St Christopher notes that Freeman and Loando were both on the island on 10 September 1823.

In the return Freeman was listed as having been originally from 'Muckipara' and was stated to have been five feet tall and thirty years old. The return stated that he had been 'apprenticed to Captain Irby R.N. as a servant at Sierra Leone'. Loando was stated to have come from 'Loando', to have been five feet five inches tall and around twenty-five years old. The record stated that he had been 'apprenticed to Capt. Irby by Gov. Maxwell'.[17] Charles William Maxwell was Governor of Sierra Leone from 1811 to 1815, before he went to Dominica, and then became Governor of St Christopher from 1819 to 1832.[18] Freeman and Loando were stated to be 'of good character' and to have been 'baptised in England' – a detail which confirms, along with the mention of Irby, that these were the 'youths' from Norwich. Both were said to be churchgoers. Freeman was said to be able to read and to have originally been a servant of Governor Maxwell. In 1823 he was working 'on his own account' as a baker, while Loando remained a servant to the governor.[19]

The explanation of how Loando and Freeman came to be in St Christopher a decade after they arrived in Norwich from West Africa provides a rare insight into the backgrounds of the Africans that we encounter in the parish records. This is one of the very few examples we have where a full history of their movement, both before they arrived in Norfolk and Suffolk and after, can be pieced together. Loando and Freeman were in St Christopher in 1823 because their status in 1813 had not resulted in immediate unconditional freedom. Section VII of the British Slave Trade Abolition Act required that slaves

[16] *Norfolk Chronicle*, 30 July 1814, p. 2.
[17] 'Report concerning the Military Labourers stationed at Brimstone Hill and other liberated Negroes residing in that Island, 24 October 1823', pp. 20–1, in *Slave Trade (Three Volumes) (2), Papers relating to Slaves in the Colonies &c: Volume 22* (1827), p. 464. There is, unfortunately, no mention of Edward Makenzie.
[18] Tara Helfman, 'The Court of Vice Admiralty at Sierra Leone and the Abolition of the West African Slave Trade', *Yale Law Journal*, 115 (2006), 1122–56, at p. 1143.
[19] 'Report', pp. 20–1.

liberated from foreign ships by the Royal Navy – such as Makenzie, Loando, and Freeman – had to enlist in the armed forces or be bound 'whether of full Age or not, as Apprentices, for any Term not exceeding Fourteen Years'.[20] Analysis by Richard Anderson, Suzanne Schwarz, and others has established that, in the sixty years after British abolition of the slave trade, some 164,333 Africans were liberated from slave ships in the Atlantic and over 99,000 of these African 'recaptives' – the term used for Africans rescued from slaving ships – were then forcibly relocated to Sierra Leone.[21] The appearance of Loando, Makenzie, and Freeman in Norwich in 1813 was not a consequence of a random act of altruism by Irby, but part of a bureaucratic process, created by statute and practice, that sought to deal with these 'recaptives'. It meant that many of those individuals landed at Freetown were pressed into the service of the Royal African Corps and the Royal Navy, and others were apprenticed. Since Loando and Freeman were described in the 1823 return as having been apprenticed to Irby, this must have been their condition on arrival in Norwich in 1813.

Anderson has estimated that of the 99,466 Africans liberated at Freetown, some 24,322 were assigned roles that took them outside the colony. He has identified ninety-three of these as being assigned to the Royal Navy as apprentices between 1811 and 1815.[22] Finding Freeman, Loando, and Makenzie in the records of the 'recaptives' from Sierra Leone in the period is problematic, however, because their baptismal names are not listed in the government registers, and we do not know their African names, which were the ones normally used in those registers. Neither the baptismal register in Norwich, nor the 1823 return from St Christopher, mentioned their African names to allow a cross-reference. The 1823 return does record their heights and ages, however. Cross-referencing the dates that the *Amelia* was on station in West Africa (from December 1811 to February 1813), along with the youths' gender, heights, and ages, with the African names database for 'recaptives' arriving in Sierra Leone in 1812–13 reveals eighty-four possible Africans.[23]

[20] Suzanne Schwarz, 'Extending the African Names Database: New Evidence from Sierra Leone', *African Economic History*, 38 (2010), pp. 137–63, at p. 139.
[21] For a discussion of these numbers, see Richard Anderson, 'The Diaspora of Sierra Leone's Liberated Africans: Enlistment, Forced Migration, and "Liberation" at Freetown, 1808–1863', *African Economic History*, 41 (2013), 101–38, at p. 101; Suzanne Schwarz, 'Reconstructing the Life Histories of Liberated Africans: Sierra Leone in the Early Nineteenth Century', *History in Africa*, 39 (2012), 175–207, at pp. 175–6; Anderson, *et al*, 'Using', 165–91.
[22] Anderson, 'The Diaspora', p. 125.
[23] The height range used for this search was 40–70 inches, since we do not know how much the boys had grown since 1813. In 1823 Loando was recorded as five feet five inches and Freeman as five feet. The age range was run from twelve to eighteen, given that Freeman was said to be fourteen in Norwich, but thirty on the 1823 return, and Loando was said to be twenty-five in 1823, so would have been around fifteen in 1813; https://www.slavevoyages. org/resources/names-database [accessed 12 August 2020]. The 1814 report of the African Institution detailed all slave ships taken into Freetown in this period and records only five

The final clue in this puzzle comes from the baptism of a fourth boy that Irby brought back from Africa, Irby Amelia Frederick Heathe, who was baptised in Hampshire, a week after the three youths were baptised in Norwich. The register of All Saints, Fawley, states that Frederick was nine years old and 'a native of Popo near Whidah on the coast of Africa'.[24] Popo was a slave-trading port in the Bight of Benin (modern eastern Ghana to western Nigeria), Ouida was a port on the same coast.[25] This location is helpful. Among the eighty-four possible recaptives arriving in Freetown in 1812–13, there are five boys listed as having been embarked at Popo; all of them were taken from the Portuguese ship, San Miguel Triunfante, which began its voyage from Bahia, Brazil, in June 1811. The crew purchased most of their slaves from Popo in April 1812. The ship was intercepted and taken to Freetown soon after.[26] The boys were named Neibong, Causee, Ajassee, Toing, and Cossee; all were in the correct age range.[27] It seems probable that four of these boys were renamed Edward, Charles, Paolo, and Irby.

As we saw with Joseph Diana, the boys had moved through a variety of social and economic situations. The alterations to these situations were related in significant ways to their geographic mobility. The first change in their status had occurred within Africa and in the context of its internal slaving networks. In Africa they had been, probably, originally free.[28] They had then been enslaved by other Africans and taken to the Bight of Benin. Their African captors had subsequently sold the boys to the Portuguese at Popo. This African to European sale had altered the boys' status again, morphing it from an African form of enslavement into the form of chattel slavery that dominated the Atlantic world. They had moved into the European-dominated Atlantic area as chattel slaves. Their time in this situation was truncated by the actions of Irby and his crew, however. The boys' move from Portuguese control to British changed them to the condition of 'recaptive'. This was accompanied by another geographic shift, from the Portuguese Atlantic to British Africa. The boys were landed in Sierra Leone, and moved into a different category, as a 'Liberated African'.[29] They were then assigned the status of 'apprentice'

---

ships with slaves but does not link any with the Amelia specifically: Report of the Committee of the African Institution, 8 (London, 1814), p. 69.

[24] Hampshire Archives, Exbury Parish Register, Baptism of Irby Amelia Frederick Heathe, 6 June 1813, Exbury. Fawley lies just across the Solent from Portsmouth, where the Amelia docked in March 1813. Irby appears to have had relatives there; the minister was Adolphus Irby.

[25] David Eltis and David Richardson, Atlas of the Atlantic Slave Trade (New Haven; London, 2010), p. 112.

[26] TAIASD https://www.slavevoyages.org/voyage/database Voyage ID 7627.

[27] TAIASD https://www.slavevoyages.org/resources/names-database ID 103264, 103274, 103280, 103281, 103283.

[28] The statement that Paolo was from Loando suggests that he had come originally from what is now modern Angola.

[29] Anderson, 'African', p. 167.

and bound to the Royal Navy. This role meant that Makenzie, Loando, and Freeman could be compelled to travel to Norwich with Irby.

Their sojourn in Norwich led to them gaining another status, as baptised Christians. In Norwich, the locals perceived them to be 'free', but to the Admiralty in London, and in Sierra Leone, they remained in the social situation of 'apprentice' in the Navy. This continuing condition eventually overrode their situation in Norwich and meant that they returned, at some point, to Sierra Leone, where they became 'servants' to Governor Maxwell. This new position was one of limited freedom since they could not leave his service. It appears that Maxwell probably took them to Dominica and then to St Christopher in this state. What happened to Makenzie after 1813 is uncertain, but he may have died, since he is not recorded in the 1823 document.[30] By 1823, Freeman and Loando had changed status again. The report confirmed that they were members of a small group of 'apprentices who are free now from any obligation by indenture'. Although no longer indentured, it does not seem that they were able to do as they wished, and both were stated to be 'under the protection of His Excellency Governor Maxwell'. What this 'protection' meant for them is unclear. Freeman was now a baker and 'able to support himself at St Christopher being young and in good health', while Loando was still 'a servant', but it seems that they remained bound to the governor in some fashion. After 1823, unfortunately, the trail goes cold. All we know is that the 1823 report stated that the young men had expressed their desire to take up the British Government's offer 'to go to Trinidad as a free settler'.[31] So, it may be that Freeman and Loando eventually settled there.[32]

As Schwarz reminds us, 'In the historiography of the Atlantic slave trade, such opportunities to trace the movements of named individuals born in Africa after their embarkation on slave ships are extremely limited and usually restricted to the small number of individuals who were in position to write narratives after they had attained their freedom.'[33] Here, we have an example involving some ordinary working-class youths reconstructed by working from their local English history outwards. This example emphasises the degree to which rural provincial locations such as Norfolk and Suffolk were connected to

[30] The same is true of Irby Amelia Frederick Heathe.

[31] 'Report concerning', pp. 3-4.

[32] This account discounts the assertion in an 1813 print, entitled 'African Slavery', which shows a slave in the Portuguese settlement of Benguela with an iron collar fastened around his neck. Its caption reports, '[t]his miserable being was purchased & made free, by a British Naval Officer, for Sixty Dollars, who brought him to England in 1813, and had him Christened at Norwich when he was 14 years old, where he is now at School by the name of Charles Fortunatus Freeman', see 'African Slavery', steel engraving with colouring, 1813, National Maritime Museum, Accession No. ZBA2440; published by Edward Orme, Bond Street, London, 20 July 1813. There is no record of Irby going to Benguela, which was a significant distance from Sierra Leone and well outside the patrol area of the *Amelia*.

[33] Schwarz, 'Reconstructing', p. 178. See also her comments, Schwarz, 'Extending', p. 137.

the movement of Africans on a global scale. The boys' stories show, moreover, that we cannot afford to make any assumption when we encounter an African in the historical record. The realities of these lives are likely to confound any rapid categorisation of them, whether it is an assumption that any African encountered in early modern England must have been held in chattel slavery, or conversely, one that finding Africans mentioned in parish registers and newspapers in a situation that emphasises their apparent freedom means that they were free in our modern sense of the term. By unpacking the travels and changing social condition of Freeman, Loando, and Makenzie over time and space, we can begin to appreciate the potential for 'unsettledness' that the Atlantic world contained.

The Gentleman

In the same period that Loando, Freeman, and Makenzie arrived in Norwich for their baptism and education, another young man named Edward Steele, who was aged twenty-eight in 1813, was living in the city. We know from later correspondence that Steele read the *Norfolk Chronicle*, but what he thought about the baptism of the three Africans at St Peter Mancroft is not recorded.[34] Steele might have had reason to think about them, however, as he too was an African. Palmer's *Perlustration of Great Yarmouth* of 1875 contained the following entry:

'At No. 13 resided for many years Edward Steele, Esq., long known and highly esteemed in Yarmouth society. He was born at Barbadoes in 1785, and was for many years an officer in the East Norfolk Regiment of Militia. He died here in 1873, in his 89th year, unmarried, and having retained his faculties almost to the last.'[35]

Steele's birth in Barbados is confirmed in various censuses of the later nineteenth century, which also describe him as a 'British subject'.[36] His biography is also one of geographic movement and change in social position, but one quite different to that of Loando, Freeman, and Makenzie. The 'highly esteemed' Edward Steele Esq. of Yarmouth was born on the island of Barbados as a slave, along with his sister Katherine. The siblings were the children of a plantation owner named Joshua Steele and an enslaved 'mulatto' woman from the Byde Mill plantation called Anna Slatia.[37]

---

[34] See Edward Steele's letter 'To Timothy Steward, Esq', *Norfolk Chronicle*, 18 November 1837, p. 3.
[35] Charles John Palmer, *The Perlustration of Great Yarmouth, with Gorleston and Southtown: Volume III* (Great Yarmouth, 1875), p. 85.
[36] For example, TNA/RG10/1789/f153/8, Yarmouth, 1871.
[37] For discussion of their background, see Richard Maguire, 'The Black Middle Class in nineteenth- and early twentieth-century Norfolk', *Norfolk Archaeology*, 47 (2017), 511–22; Daniel Livesay, *Children of Uncertain Fortune: Mixed-Race Jamaicans in Britain and the Atlantic Family, 1733–1833* (Williamsburg, VA; Chapel Hill, 2018), pp. 261–3.

Joshua Steele was of Irish descent and had no connection with Norfolk or Suffolk. He had married a wealthy widow, Sarah Hopkins Osborn, who owned three Barbadian plantations – Halletts, Byde Mill House and Kendalls – that together held over 400 Africans in 1774.[38] On Sarah's death in 1757, Steele inherited the plantations and their slaves and proceeded to live off their revenues as an absentee until 1780, when falling income streams caused him to travel, aged eighty, to Barbados. Steele remained on the island until his death in 1796, running the plantations and involving himself in the amelioration movement. In this period Steele fathered Edward, who was born in 1785, and then Katherine.[39] The children remained enslaved, as did their mother, Anna Slatia. Shortly before he died, however, Steele changed his will, leaving his plantations equally to his sister, Mary Ann Steele, and to Edward and Katherine.[40]

Because Steele did not free the children a complex sequence of legal disputes followed. It was claimed that since the children were enslaved, they could not inherit. Eventually, Mary Ann Steele – who lived in Camberwell, Middlesex, England – was established as sole heir. She then emancipated Edward and Katherine and proceeded to make provision for them with sums of money that were roughly equivalent to the shares of the estate that their father wished to leave them originally. Katherine and Edward, now wealthy and no longer enslaved, were then brought to England. It appears that they landed in Lancaster and travelled to London via Liverpool, Birmingham, and Bristol.[41] Katherine went then to a finishing school in Camberwell, later married in Clerkenwell, and had at least one child. Edward was sent to school in Norwich, 'residing at the Reverend Doctor Foster's Academy'.[42] Foster was the headmaster of 'Norwich grammar school' in the 1790s and early 1800s,

[38] For Steele, see L. Gragg, 'Steele, Joshua (c. 1700–1796), plantation owner and writer on prosody', *ODNB* https://www.oxforddnb.com/view/10.1093/ref:odnb/9780198614128.001.0001/odnb-9780198614128-e-26345 [accessed 30 January 2017]. See also, 'Steele, Family of', *Notes and Queries* (1861), p. 137; David Lambert, *White Creole Culture, Politics and Identity During the Age of Abolition* (Cambridge, 2005), pp. 41–72. For Osborn, see Philip James and M.H. Combe Martin, 'General Notes', *Journal of the Royal Society of Arts*, 117 (1968), 34–45, http://www.jstor.org/stable/41371992. For the plantations, see LBSO, Joshua Steele, http://wwwdepts-live.ucl.ac.uk/lbs/person/view/2146643119/ [accessed 30 January 2017]; LBSO, 'Byde Mill [Barbados | St John]', LBSO, http://wwwdepts-live.ucl.ac.uk/lbs/estate/view/670 [accessed 30 January 2017]; 'Kendals [Barbados | St John]', http://wwwdepts-live.ucl.ac.uk/lbs/estate/view/664 [accessed 30 January 2017].
[39] Livesay spells her name 'Catherine', but the spelling Katherine is preferred here, since this is how she signed her marriage certificate and as she was also called 'Katherine' in her brother's will.
[40] James, etc., 'General', p. 229.
[41] NA/PROB/11/1319/184, Will of Mary Ann Steele, Spinster of Bloomsbury, Middlesex, Feb. 20, 1799; Livesay, *Children*, pp. 262–3.
[42] NA/PROB/11/1319/184, Will of Mary Ann Steele, Spinster of Bloomsbury, Middlesex, Feb. 20, 1799. Katherine's marriage is recorded on 17 July 1807, at St James' Church, Clerkenwell, Church of England Parish Registers, London Metropolitan Archives, London; Reference Number: p76/js1/036. The couple had at least one child, Mary Ann White, who

but records of pupils only exist from 1858.[43] After leaving school we know that Steele served with the East Norfolk Regiment of Militia for many years, being listed as a lieutenant in 1824.[44] His 1873 obituary in the *Ipswich Journal* listed him as having reached the rank of captain.[45] It appears that he was able to live as a gentleman, courtesy of the inheritance he had received through his aunt. Traces of his full social and civic life can be found in the newspapers, which show him to have been at various times a member of the Norfolk and Norwich Horticultural Society, on the committee for both the Norfolk and Norwich and Yarmouth Hospitals, and one of Yarmouth's Haven and Pier Commissioners.[46] In 1840, Steele was one of a group of local gentlemen who established a committee to raise the funds required to restore the organ for St Nicholas' Church in Yarmouth, and in 1844 he also supervised the restoration of the organ at the Chapel of St George, King Street.[47]

Three letters written by Steele in 1833 provide the only surviving correspondence from any African living in Norfolk and Suffolk between 1467 and 1833. They were all written to the Yarmouth antiquary and historian Charles John Palmer (1805–82), who would mention Steele in his *Perlustration*. The first two letters, from June and September 1833, were written in respect of Palmer's 'manuscript' entitled 'Love and Money', which Steele promised to examine and 'endeavour to form a proper opinion of it'. Having done so, he was able to inform Palmer that the manuscript was missing certain pages. The other letter relates to Palmer's invitation, in December 1833, for Steele to spend Christmas at his house. Steele declined, stating that he had already agreed to spend it with 'my old neighbour Mr Buckle at Hethersett', south of Norwich.[48]

Steele died in Yarmouth in 1873, aged eighty-eight, having lived as a member of Norfolk's middle class for seven decades. Unlike so many of the entries for other people of African descent in the records, the Great Yarmouth burial register made no mention of his heritage.[49] Indeed, in the entire period of seventy years that he lived in Norfolk, no mention was made of his African lineage. Palmer and the census mentioned that he was from Barbados, but they said nothing else. In newspaper reports, Steele was never referred to as a

---

was described in Edward's will as his 'dear niece' and the daughter of his late sister 'Katherine Anne White'; NRO, Will No. 412, Will of Edward Steele, 1873.

[43] *The Gentleman's Magazine* (1810), p. 661; James Ayres, *Art, Artisans and Apprentices: Apprentice Painters & Sculptors in the Early Modern British Tradition* (Oxford; Philadelphia, 2014), p. 442. This is now King Edward VI's Grammar School (Norwich School).

[44] Royal Norfolk Regimental Museum, (M23) West and East Norfolk Militia Scrapbook 1804–1900.

[45] *Ipswich Journal*, 2 August 1873, p. 6.

[46] See *Norfolk Chronicle*, 17 October 1829, p. 1; *Norwich Mercury*, 28 April 1838, pp. 2–3; *Norwich Mercury*, 8 July 1848, p. 2; *Norfolk Chronicle*, 27 October 1849, p. 3.

[47] Palmer (ed.), *History*, p. 261. Stephen Heywood, 'The Chapel of St George King Street, Great Yarmouth', Norfolk Historic Environment Record No. 4336 (2009).

[48] NRO/Y/L/20/1/178-180, Edward Steele, Royal Barracks, Yarmouth, 1833.

[49] NRO/PD/28/149, Burial of Edward Steele, Yarmouth, 4 August 1873, p. 154.

'man of colour' like Benjamin Grey had been in 1803, or a 'negro' like James Doubleday was in 1836. No mention was made of his personal history, unlike that of Freeman and his companions.

The most obvious reason one might suggest for this is one of class. Unlike these others, Steele was wealthy. This wealth meant that when he travelled from Barbados and arrived in Norwich in 1799, the change in social status that had occurred was from 'slave' to wealthy middle class. This social shift appears to have precluded him from being categorised a 'negro' or 'man of colour' and to have wiped away any social acknowledgement of his previous enslavement. His newly acquired status as middle class would seem to have negated his African heritage, although, of course, we cannot be sure whether he encountered anti-African racism. There is no evidence of this, however. Such terms and ideas might have been relevant in the description of working-class Africans, but they were not suitable for use in respect of a wealthy gentleman. Instead, his fortune meant that Steele became a member of the county's middle class, one who could afford to be educated at the city's best school, and then live the life of a gentleman. The nature of his journey from Barbados to Norfolk was altered by the social reality of class, therefore. Steele's wealth recalibrated his experience of the geographic and social space in which he moved. The wealth that enabled him to transcend class and racial boundaries in nineteenth-century Norfolk came, of course, from slavery itself. The money he was given by Mary Steele was the result of the sale of his father's plantations and slaves, possibly including Edward's own mother. What Edward Steele thought about this, and what he thought about as he read newspaper reports about the baptism of Africans at St Peter Mancroft, or the abolition movement in the 1820s and 1830s, cannot be known. His life demonstrates, once again, that the situation for people of African heritage in Norfolk and Suffolk in this period was complex and variegated.

The Unnamed 'Swing' Rioters

In late 1830 to early 1831, Norfolk and Suffolk were affected by a sequence of agrarian 'Swing' protests, which were part of a wider set of disturbances that took place in the south-east and central south-west of England, as well as the Midlands and the North, in the period between February 1830 and October 1831.[50] During the post-Napoleonic agrarian depression, rural workers across England were driven to action by mass unemployment and underemployment. Rural enclosures had created a landless proletariat, whose members were not being cared for by the system of poor relief, which had itself been undermined by

---

[50] These protests have been covered extensively, beginning with the masterful work by Hobsbawm and Rudé, *Captain Swing*. Hobsbawm and Rudé identified 1,475 disturbances, Holland has increased this number to 2,818; Michael Holland, *Swing Unmasked: The Agricultural Riots of 1830 to 1832 and Their Wider Implications* (Milton Keynes, 2005).

the continuing development of agrarian capitalism. In desperation, the response of rural labourers was to disturb the peace, most notoriously by smashing threshing machines, and to call for higher wages and more generous relief. The 'Swing' protests were named after the mythical avenger 'Captain Swing', whose signature could be found on many of the threatening letters received by farmers and landowners. East Anglia was a major centre of these disturbances, and one such letter was sent to the dean of Norwich Cathedral in October 1831.[51]

Amongst the records of the disturbances in Norfolk and Suffolk are two passing reports of African rioters. The first is the report of the arrest of 'a man of colour' at Little Walsingham on 26 November 1830. This unnamed 'man of colour' was 'apprehended' in possession of incendiary materials along with a man 'who says his name is Thomas Browne and Charlotte his wife'.[52] A full description was given of Browne, but not of his African accomplice, and all the party were committed to Walsingham Bridewell. Their eventual fate is unclear, since they are not mentioned in the Quarter Sessions reports for the riots. This group were different to another group of protestors mentioned in a letter written by William Howe Windham of Felbrigg Hall to Edward Harbord, third Baron Suffield, in December 1830.[53] Windham was bringing to Harbord's attention the centrality of a location in Cromer, Norfolk, called 'Allans' in the organisation of the riots. Windham went on to explain that 'Allans' had been a location where the leaders of the rioters had been seen. As he phrased it, 'The principal man's name is John Brown', and he then stated that Brown was accompanied by 'two mulattoes, or blacks'.[54] Since this group was mentioned after the incarceration of the group at Little Walsingham, and was completely different in membership, it appears that at least three Africans were involved in the 'Swing' Riots in Norfolk in late 1830.

Both reports also seem to indicate that these Africans were significant members of the rioters. Windham's letter suggests that the 'two mulattoes, or blacks' were working closely with a leading figure in the 'Swing' disturbances, 'John Brown', and went on to claim that these two Africans were deeply involved in the activity of the rioters, 'all having various combustibles and

[51] NRO/DCN/120/2D/1, Letter, postmarked 15 October 1831. Contemporary newspaper reports in Norfolk and Suffolk include 'Fire by Incendiaries', *Norwich Mercury*, 13 November 1830, p. 3; 20 November 1830, p. 2; 27 November 1830, p. 2, among many others. Activities of the protestors in the region included all those that have been generally identified – the destruction of threshing machines, incendiarism, 'mobbing', political demonstrations, food riots – see Peter Jones, 'Swing, Speenhamland and Rural Social Relations: the "Moral Economy" of the English Crowd in the Nineteenth Century', *Social History*, 32 (2007), 271–90.

[52] *Norwich Mercury*, 4 December 1830, p. 2.

[53] For Harbord, see H. Matthew, 'Harbord, Edward, third Baron Suffield (1781–1835), politician', *ODNB*, https://www.oxforddnb.com/view/10.1093/ref:odnb/9780198614128.001.0001/odnb-9780198614128-e-12232 [accessed 20 March 2020].

[54] NRO/GTN/5/9/40, William Howe Windham to Edward Harbord, 21 December 1830.

chemical preparations'.[55] This was also the case for the African in Walsingham. These Africans would appear, therefore, to have been at the heart of this local movement in 1830 and, if Windham's information was correct, then they may have had some sort of leadership role. Griffin has identified the role of local mobile groups and provocateurs in the 'Swing' disturbances, locals from one area who spread the news of protests to nearby areas, and so stirred other workers to action. The descriptions of the Africans would seem to fit into this section of the protestors. They were active in their protests, involved in acts of destruction, and moving around the locality. This is important for several reasons. First, it shows that within Norfolk's rural working communities Africans could be accepted in leadership roles. Second, if the Africans were inciting other workers to action, this meant that their fellows saw them as part of the local labouring proletariat, fellow workers, as opposed to African outsiders. Finally, it suggests that these Africans were, perhaps, politically active and involved.

The presence of these radical Africans may have particularly irked Windham since he was connected to plantation-owning families. His father, Vice-Admiral William Lukin, was married to Anne Thellusson, the daughter of the plantation owner Peter Thellusson and the sister of the first Lord Rendlesham. In 1835, Windham himself would marry Lady Sophie Elizabeth Caroline Hervey, whose family were related by marriage to the planter Charles Ellis and to other Jamaican planters, William Hervey and James Hervey.[56] In 1832, Charles Ellis would be writing letters about the hanging of rebellious Africans after the 1832 rebellion in Jamaica.[57] As we have seen with its appearance in Garboldisham after the arrival of the planter Crisp Molineux, the term 'mulatto' tended to be used by those in the region who were closely acquainted with the slave plantations. Windham's use of the term in describing the African rioters may, therefore, have reflected his personal acquaintance with, and acceptance of, the ideas of plantation society. If this is the case, then Windham's letter might indicate the malleability that the social position of Africans had in his mind. The mixing of the terms may signify that he was approaching the two Africans by blending two perspectives, a class one – that they were 'incendiaries' – and a racialised one, as indicated by his use of the colonial descriptor 'mulattoes'.

---

[55] Ibid.

[56] *The Gentleman's Magazine and Historical Review* (1855), p. 195. For details of James Hervey, see LBSO https://www.ucl.ac.uk/lbs/person/view/2146005419 [accessed 21 November 2019] and for William Hervey see LBSO https://www.ucl.ac.uk/lbs/person/view/24524 [accessed 2 March 2018]. See the marriage of the Hon. Elizabeth Catherine Caroline Hervey, daughter of John Hervey, Lord Hervey, eldest son of Frederick Hervey, 4th Earl of Bristol, to Charles Ellis (later Lord Seaford) in 1798. Ellis was the second son of John Ellis, who was a substantial planter on the island. Charles Ellis lived in England and on inheriting the Montpelier Estate in 1815 ran it as an absentee owner, although he did visit the island on occasion, Barry Higman, *Montpelier, Jamaica: A Plantation Community in Slavery and Freedom, 1739–1912* (Barbados, 1998), pp. 22–53.

[57] SRO/HA/507/4/26, Lord Seaford from Falmouth, Jamaica, 16 August 1832.

This may be an indication that class and race were held in a form of tension in Windham's mind, which made him fearful and hostile towards the men for a variety of reasons.[58]

Equally interesting is what the presence of these Africans in the riots tells us about the views their fellow 'Swing' rioters had of such Africans. In their studies of rural protest, historians such as Poole have argued that it is important to pay attention to local variation to understand social politics in this period.[59] This seems to be a viable route to follow in thinking about these Africans. Rather than taking ideas about race from the colonial context and transplanting them into provincial England without local modification, it is possible to examine the specific local context of such social relations. Griffin has shown that the protest groups were organised at a local level, based around 'pre-existing social alignments' or by using local recruitment.[60] The evidence from Norfolk in 1830 supports this view. Although one newspaper report suggested that the 'man of colour' was possibly from Kent, and at least one court official blamed the early trouble on 'strangers', this appears to have been an example of what Hobsbawm and Rudé memorably described as 'that familiar figure in the mythology of the well-fed and the contented, the subversive agitator'.[61] An examination of the backgrounds of the protestors who were convicted shows that they were all local men.[62]

This evidence points to the rioters being locals who were acting at a parish level. As Keith Snell has argued, 'parish boundaries mattered' to the labouring poor.[63] This all seems to make it possible that the African protestors were not radicals who had arrived in Norfolk from elsewhere to organise protest but were instead already living locally. There was no mention of Africans in the court cases but, since we do not know the names of the Africans, it may be that they were among the names given in the Quarter Sessions reports, but they were not described as Africans in those reports. If this is correct, then we can suggest that the Africans became involved because they were accepted members of their

---

[58] NRO/GTN/5/9/40, William Howe Windham to Edward Harbord, 21 December 1830.
[59] S. Poole, '"A Lasting and Salutary Warning": Incendiarism, Rural Order and England's Last Scene of Crime Execution', *Rural History*, 19 (2008), 163–77. See also C. Griffin, '"There Was No Law to Punish That Offence": Re-Assessing "Captain Swing": Rural Luddism and Rebellion in East Kent, 1830–31', *Southern History*, 22 (2000), 131–63; R. Wells, 'Crime and Protest in a Country Parish: Burwash 1790–1850', in J. Rule and R. Wells (eds), *Crime, Protest and Popular Politics in Southern England 1740–1850* (London, 1997), pp. 169–236.
[60] Carl Griffin, 'Swing, Swing Redivivus, or Something After Swing? On the Death Throes of a Protest Movement, December 1830–December 1833', *International Review of Social History*, 54 (2009), 459–97, and Griffin, 'There', 131–63.
[61] Hobsbawm and Rudé, *Captain*, p. 81.
[62] For the comment on 'strangers', see 'County Sessions', *Norwich Mercury*, 22 January 1831, p. 1, where the Serjeant described these strangers as wearing 'caps of sheepskin' and 'slops on their bodies' but made no mention of African heritage. For lists of the local men involved, see the reports of the 'Trials of the Rioters' at the County Sessions, *Norwich Mercury*, 8 January 1831, pp. 2–3, and 15 January 1831, pp. 2–3.
[63] K. Snell, 'The Culture of Local Xenophobia', *Social History*, 28 (2003), 1–30.

local labouring community. This raises the potential that when such Africans had settled in an area then, to their fellow members of the labouring poor, their African heritage mattered less than their membership of that local community.

This idea can be expanded upon by considering the organisation and composition of the 'Swing' protestors. Hobsbawm and Rudé placed their understanding of the rioters firmly in terms of Marxist class analysis. 'The typical English agriculturalist', they wrote, 'was a hired man, a rural proletarian.'[64] This notion of 'proletarian' rioters has been problematised by the work of historians such as Neeson and Reed, who have discussed a continuing presence of smallholding 'peasants' in the protests, but the idea remains powerful.[65] It is tempting to suggest, therefore, that the Africans were thought of as fellow labourers by the other rioters, but this suggestion needs further articulation, especially since the issue of class in relation to the 'Swing' disturbances remains a subject of contention.[66] The rioters did not share any acknowledged political or class consciousness, so the search for an understanding of the Africans' place in this community of rioters needs to be further contextualised.[67]

This can be done by drawing upon the suggestion that labouring people in the region still retained memories of the ideas relating to Africans that reached back to the 1549 rebellions. E.P. Thompson's idea of the 'moral economy of the poor' provides a starting point to connect with the suggestion of Hobsbawm and Rudé that the rioters drew on 'ancient symbols of ancient ideals'.[68] All three historians argued that eighteenth-century food rioters and the 'Swing' rioters shared a common sense of justice. The work of Roger Wells and others has shown the existence of a moral economic model running from the eighteenth century up to 1830.[69] The ideas of the working poor in such economic matters in this period were long-standing and resistant to the new ideas being pushed upon them by the development of capitalism in England and abroad. These can then be linked, however gently, through this to the ideas articulated by the Norfolk rebels in Tudor England. Harvey has written about the 'psychological

[64] Hobsbawm and Rudé, *Captain*, p. 24.
[65] J.M. Neeson, *Commoners: Common Right, Enclosure and Social Change in England, 1700–1820* (Cambridge, 1993); M. Reed, 'The Peasantry of Nineteenth-Century England: A Neglected Class?', *History Workshop*, 18 (1984), 53–76; and M. Reed, 'Nineteenth-Century Rural England: A Case for "Peasant Studies"', *Journal of Peasant Studies*, 14 (1986), 78–99.
[66] For a good summary of the ebbs and flows of this issue, see Iain Taylor, 'One For the (Farm) Workers? Perpetrator Risk and Victim Risk Transfer During the "Sevenoaks Fires" of 1830', *Rural History*, 28 (2017), 137–59.
[67] Hobsbawm and Rudé, *Captain*, pp. 217–19.
[68] E.P. Thompson, 'The Moral Economy of the English Crowd in the Eighteenth Century', *Past and Present*, 50 (1971), 76–136; see also J. Bohstedt, *The Politics of Provisions: Food Riots, Moral Economy, and Market Transition in England, c. 1550–1850* (Burlington, VT, 2010); Hobsbawm and Rudé, *Captain*, p. 18.
[69] R. Wells, 'The Moral Economy of the English Countryside', in A.J. Randall and A. Charlesworth (eds), *Moral Economy and Popular Protest: Crowds, Conflict and Authority* (Basingstoke, 1999), pp. 209–71; Jones, 'Swing', 272–91.

benefit of oral tradition' in creating long-term, popular, 'inherited' memories that linked the organisation and motivation of rebels in 1381, 1450, 1536–7 and 1549.[70] The presence of the African protestors in the 'Swing' Riots might point toward the longevity of popular 'inherited memory' across the early modern period in respect of Africans. The presence of the three unnamed African rioters may suggest that the older ideas about the nature and place of Africans that were identified in the fifteenth and sixteenth centuries still had resonance in 1830.

Conclusions

These three examples enable us to consider the relationship between geographic mobility and class mobility in the lives of Africans who lived in early modern Norfolk and Suffolk. The story of Paolo Loando, Charles Freeman, and Edward Makenzie points towards an intrinsic connection between geographical movement and social position. It also highlights the limitations engendered by their situation as poor, working, Africans. As with so many of the working poor, regardless of heritage, the three youths were buffeted and moved by the winds of circumstances that were beyond their control. As they moved within Africa, around its coast, to Norwich, back to Africa, and finally to the West Indies, the three were taken through a bewildering variety of subtly differentiated social conditions. In Africa they had been enslaved, but this was a different type of slavery to that which awaited them on the *San Miguel Triunfante*. Once 'recaptured' by Irby and his crew, they did not become 'free' in the 'ideal type' of the word, but they were not enslaved. Like so many people, African and non-African, in the Atlantic world they had transitioned into a form of unfree labour whose nature was obscure. As they travelled on the *Amelia* from Freetown to Portsmouth, there were others on the ship, conscripted sailors, whose situation was little different to theirs. In Norwich, they might have encountered poor labourers, or servants, whose economic dependency resembled their dependency on Irby, and with whom they may have felt some degree of similarity. Back in Africa with Maxwell, their condition was once more subtly changed to a form of indentured service. Finally, in the West Indies, they became members of the working poor in the final days of the slave plantations.

A similar interplay of geographic and social mobility can be seen, but in a quite different fashion, for Edward Steele. Steele was born enslaved in the West Indies, and his shift in social position took place during a voyage across the Atlantic in which he morphed from slave to wealthy middle-class youth. Edward and his sister travelled to England as paying passengers on a ship, but their ages meant that they were not completely autonomous, and decisions were still made

[70] I.M.W. Harvey, 'Was there popular politics in fifteenth-century England?', in R.H. Britnell and A.J. Pollard (eds), *The McFarlane Legacy: Studies in Late Medieval Politics and Society* (New York, 1995), pp. 155–74.

for them by their guardians, which was the reason that they were separated, and Edward came to Norwich. Freedom was an elusive status, not only because of background, but because of age. Nonetheless, the issue of age was overcome naturally, and Edward Steele's money gave him access to education, and an entrance into society.

We know little about the exact circumstances of the 'Swing' rioters, but the evidence we have garnered from the lives of the many other Africans we have explored means that we can conjecture that the three African 'Swing' rioters may have been enslaved in the West Indies before arriving in England. They may have then gradually transitioned away from positions of overt servitude into work among the rural labouring class, as did Thomas Sayers in the early 1800s. As rural labourers, it seems that they moved into active fellowship of some kind with other members of the labouring class in the region. This class affiliation meant that they shared the hardships of the post-Napoleonic economic downturn and, eventually, joined their fellows in the riots of the 1830s. Their movement across the Atlantic had resulted in a social mobility in East Anglia. As has been suggested elsewhere in this book, their African heritage placed the rioters in these specific circumstances, yet it did not separate them completely from the experience of the wider working poor around them. The Atlantic world, from Sierra Leone to the West Indies to East Anglia, was a harsh place in which to be poor and, perhaps, this shared experience allowed some sense of communal identity to exist among those in its poorest echelons, whatever their background.

Epilogue
Reconsidering the Social History of Africans in Norfolk and Suffolk

Apart from the documents that are preserved in the region's archives, there is extraordinarily little physical evidence to remind us of the presence of the Africans who lived in Norfolk and Suffolk between 1467 and 1833. Even the coastline that Eylys saw when he arrived in Yarmouth in the late fifteenth century has been altered irrevocably over the centuries; the 'Cokle water' where his fellow 'pyrattes' died has been eradicated by time and tide. Baptist resided in a village he knew as Hunstanton, but most people now associate the name with the adjacent holiday resort town of New Hunstanton that was created in the nineteenth century. The hall that 'ye black boy' lived in at Holkham was demolished in the eighteenth century to make way for Coke's magnificent Palladian mansion. Rougham Hall, where Rosanna lived after arriving from Barbados in 1688, burnt down in the 1820s and its successor is a ruin, destroyed by a Luftwaffe bomb in 1940. Garboldisham Old Hall, where Barlow Fielding lived and worked, along with Sam Stanton and his colleagues, was gutted by fire in 1955 and destroyed. The halls that do survive, such as Hockwold Hall – Caesar Hockwold's home for some portion in the 1700s – do not contain any trace of their previous African inhabitants.

The paintings of Charley and Cotton remain, but the doorway to Charley's shop stays stubbornly hidden, despite long hours spent searching Norwich's historic streets. The churches – where so many Africans were baptised, married, or buried – still stand, reminding us of the importance of the parish to our story, but, outside the parish registers which are preserved in the central county archive, those churches contain barely any obvious mention of the Africans who lived in their communities. One churchyard monumental inscription survives, erected at Wroxham in 1781 in memory of Jeremiah Rowland. It reads, 'a grateful tribute to the memory of Jer.[H] Rowland, a negro born on the island [...]'. Even there, the physical record disappears, because the bottom of the monument has fallen away, meaning that the next piece of evidence that might have led us to a greater understanding of Jeremiah Rowland's life is, tantalisingly, missing.

I would like to suggest that Jeremiah Rowland's marker might be understood as a memorial not only to him, but also to the other Africans whose lives we have touched upon here – from Eylys to Samuel Samuels – whose graves are now lost. The stone seems also to be illustrative of our memory of those lives; incomplete, gradually vanishing with the passage of time, becoming less clear

Figure 2: Memorial to Jeremiah Rowland, Wroxham Church, Norfolk
(© R.C. Maguire, 2010)

with every extra year that separates us from the moment in which it was created. The marker can, nonetheless, help us to reflect upon how we understand the social history of Africans in East Anglia. The temptation when looking at the stone is to focus on the single word 'negro' that is inscribed toward the bottom and seek to understand all that we see through that single word. This word, which has survived for over 200 years, is a reminder of the ideas held by some local people during the time in which Jeremiah lived. If the suggestion made in this book is accepted, then the use of this specific word, at that historical moment, in that place specifically, is an important indicator that Jeremiah Rowland lived in Norfolk and Suffolk at a moment in the region's history when ideas about racial categorisation that had gestated in the colonial world were becoming more important in local culture. It was a moment when the process of historical change that has been proposed here was well underway, and when local responses to Africans were changing from those which had existed in previous centuries. As such, it is an important piece of historical evidence, but I would argue that this one word should not be allowed to control the way in which we gaze upon Jeremiah's marker, and see his life.

Nor should that one word dominate our understanding of the wider social history of Jeremiah and the other Africans for whom his marker is also a memento. It is an ugly word and reminds us of an ugly aspect of the past, but to let it become the only window through which we view Jeremiah's life and the world in which he lived would be, I think, a mistake. For it is only one word in a larger context and, as I have suggested in this book, there are other words that can be used to describe Jeremiah and his fellows. It seems likely that Jeremiah may have been held in some form of slavish servitude, possibly until his death, but that condition should not be allowed to define him in our historical memory. If that word were not on the marker, we would look at it and see Jeremiah simply as another member of Norfolk's working community. Approached in that fashion, although Jeremiah's marker is crumbling, it is precious because it is a rare physical reminder of the life of someone who could also be thought of as a poor working-class man who lived in a small Norfolk village in the eighteenth century.

This study has tried to widen our view of that marker, and the other fragments that we can use to attempt to reconstruct the lives of Jeremiah Rowland, of Eylys, of Rosanna, of Barlow Fielding, of Rachel Fitshoe, of Charles Freeman, and the other characters in this story. Each one of these fragments has provided us with the opportunity to fashion a microhistory of a life; incomplete, yes, but still valuable and, for me at least, unfailingly fascinating. On their own, each of these microhistories is like Jeremiah Rowland's marker; fragmentary and partial, and in danger of being dominated by one word or idea. In the case of the history of Africans in England, the dismay that is engendered by the iniquities of the slave trade, and colonial slavery more generally, can make us want to sit in judgement and generalise about English culture and society, but I have tried to avoid doing so. In relation to a quite different historical issue, the plague that scoured

Newcastle in 1636, Keith Wrightson has written of the need for historians to think about 'the variety of human experience of the past'. This is an important thing for us to do in relation to these Africans, because the danger is that we can start to forget about the variety of their experience and instead think of them in one fashion and only in relation to a single issue. As Wrightson goes on to say:

> 'It is all too easy to homogenize past societies and people, sometimes to the point of caricature, for the purpose of constructing neat paradigms to compare and contrast with, and flatter, our own "modernity". But that is a project of narcissism rather than of history. Their lives were as complex as our own, their emotional palettes as rich, and their range of responses as varied.'[1]

Wrightson's insight here is particularly useful when we consider the lives of working-class Africans in early modern Norfolk and Suffolk, because they were individuals whose lives were as interesting, different, and unique as our own. By thinking of them in their local context, and comparing their stories to one another, we can compensate for our lack of information about them and resist the tendency to standardise their experiences. Each individual story becomes a means of reflecting upon its compatriots, and so these working people illuminate each other's lives.

My suggestion has been that this illumination can be enhanced by thinking of Rachel, Barlow, and the other Africans we have met as members of a wider social grouping, which I have tended to term the working class, but which can be termed as the permanent proletariat, or working poor. I have tried to make the case for this by pointing towards the similarities that existed between the lives of the Africans in Norfolk and Suffolk and the other members of the region's working poor. Considering the plantation system itself, Justin Roberts has argued that, for all its singular aspects, 'Slavery was, foremost, a labour system, and work was central to slaves' lives.'[2] The idea that their shared experience as labourers – subject to varying degrees of coercion, of economic instability, and geographic mobility – may have provided Norfolk and Suffolk's labouring poor, of whatever background, with a collective sense of connection has been presented here as a means of approaching their experience. Indeed, the Africans' mobility and status as migrants meant that they shared a social space with other working people, which is an element in the construction of class, since 'class is more accurately measured by movements in space'.[3] The Africans identified here seem to have been able to share in that potential for community, however inchoate. Some of them had been enslaved previously in the colonies, some were held in slavish servitude in the region, but others were free. Some of them married and many had children. They worked in a wide variety of jobs. Some moved around. Some settled down. They were baptised and buried. The fragments of their lives that we have pieced together have been offered here as pointers towards an

1 Wrightson, *Ralph*, p. 159.
2 Roberts, *Slavery*, p. 291.
3 Rollison, 'Exploding', p. 14.

understanding of their historic situations which sees them as precious and unique individuals. Simultaneously, their stories also remind us that their lives contained the opportunity, even for the ones who had been previously enslaved, for them to be remembered as part of the region's working population.

If this approach is accepted, then it would seem to open interesting and valuable ways to think about the history of Africans in early modern Norfolk and Suffolk, and England more widely. By thinking of such Africans as members of the working poor in a specific English locale we can, if we choose to do so, see them as an integral and important part of England's history because of how they lived and how they were part of a wider social setting. This means we look at them for who they were, rather than because of what was done to them. This would seem to me to be a positive thing. We might rethink how we visualise the scenes in our regional past. Perhaps the rebels on Mousehold Heath in 1549 contained free Africans among their numbers, men like Eylys or Thomas Blackamore, who wanted non-African 'bonde men' to be made free, for example. We can push that notion a little further and return to Rollison's ideas about the importance of immigrant labour in early modern communities. Rollison suggests that most towns in early modern England needed 'the tide of immigrants that flowed across the landscape in search of livelihoods' to survive as social and economic communities. As he puts it, *'movement* was literally the necessary condition of the abiding, settled, "structure".'[4]

In this reading the unsettled lives of the working poor were the bedrock upon which the, apparently settled, nature of England's provinces lay. The city of Norwich and the towns of Yarmouth, Lynn, Ipswich, Thetford, and Diss, along with the villages that lay around them, all needed this mobile working proletariat to exist. This study has suggested that an integral element of this unsettled, mobile, but essential, class of workers were the African migrants that we have found living in that community of the working poor. Their mobility, as we have seen from Eylys to Joseph Diana, Charles Freeman, and Paolo Loando, could potentially have been at the extremes of the scale, ranging from the Congo to the West Indies, and then to Norfolk or Suffolk. Nonetheless, once they arrived in that final locale of provincial England, the lived social relations of these Africans seem to have enabled them to blend into the pace and structure of the lives of the working poor surrounding them. Even those Africans who were held initially in slavish servitude in the region were gradually drawn by the customs and norms of local culture into baptism and then freedom of some sort. We might, therefore, like to consider those Africans as being part of the condition of 'movement' that Rollison suggests was indispensable in constructing the provincial world of early modern England.

Throughout this book, my aim has been to try to develop a social history of the Africans who lived in Norfolk and Suffolk in the early modern period by generating an understanding of their situation without recourse to generalised

---

[4] Rollison, 'Exploding', p. 10 (italics in original).

assumption. We have attempted to begin by looking at each appearance of an African in their localised setting, rather than seeing them in the vast, impersonal context of the Atlantic economy. Having done this, we have taken what we have learnt about the African in that local setting and tried to place this information into a relationship with wider historical issues and movements. The movement of our investigation has been to go from thinking about the African on their own, in the form of the information that can be extracted about them in the documentary entry in which they first appear, to thinking about them as a person living in their local community, and trying to understand that community, exemplified by their parish. Having done this, we have expanded our gaze to consideration of their relationship to the wider locality, moving outwards from village, town, or city to county and region. We have then bound these small individual stories together to help us fill the gaps in each and provide us with a wider and more nuanced understanding of how their social world was constituted. Finally, we have linked them to even wider social networks, such as the Atlantic world.

In this fashion, I have tried to propose that we might expand our view of Africans like Jeremiah Rowland to reach a wider, more comprehensive, understanding of their place in the counties in which they lived, and in English history more generally. Approaching them from that local perspective, it seems that we catch a glimpse of people who were from Africa originally, but who, having arrived in Norfolk and Suffolk, became a part of the area's working class and, as such, played a crucial role in producing the history of the region. They had this role not because of the negative ideas about their heritage that were created in the belly of colonial slavery, but because they were part of a group of local East Anglian people, the labouring poor, whose activity and lives were essential to the formation of the region's history. Returning one last time to Jeremiah Rowland's memorial stone from that perspective, it may be that we have then changed how we see it. Rather than focusing on one word, and one aspect of his life, we can now see the full story of his life more clearly. The marker becomes a monument to many other aspects of his existence, to those of his fellow Africans and, more widely, a testament to the significance of their lives, and the lives of their fellow workers, whatever their original background.

Appendix A: The African and Asian Population Identified in Norfolk and Suffolk, 1467–1833

Name	Description/Event	Date	Location	Reference
1. Eylys	'a more'	1467	Yarmouth	Swinden, *History* (Norwich, 1772)
2. Roger and William Haryson	Baptism: Parents: Thomas and Elizabeth Blackamore[1]	1564	Kessingland	NRO/PD/105/1
3. Thomas Haryson	Baptism: 'The sonne of Thomas Haryson alias Blackamore'	1566	Kessingland	NRO/PD/105/1
4. Edmund More	Marriage of Edmund More and Jane Mason (Parents of Margareta? Entry 5)	1564	Little Walsingham	NRO/PD/582/1
5. Margareta	Baptism: 'Moor'	1567	Little Walsingham	NRO/PD/582/1
6. Margarett Haryson	Burial: 'alias Blackamore'	1573	Kessingland	NRO/PD/105/1
7. Thomas Haryson	Baptism: 'alias Blackamore'	1581	Kessingland	NRO/PD/105/1

[1] No mention of ethnicity in 1564, but when Roger was buried in 1565, he was listed as being 'The sonne of Thomas Haryson alias Blackamore'.

8. John	Burial: 'the niger'	1589	Great Yarmouth	NRO/PD28/1
9. Baptist	Baptism: 'Aethiopian or Blacke a more'	1599	Hunstanton	NRO/PD/696/16
10. John Snowringe	Baptism: Child of John and Alice Snowringe	1587	Bircham Newton	England Births & Baptisms 1538–1975
11. John and Alice Snowringe	Baptism: Parents of William Snowringe	1587	Bircham Newton	England Births & Baptisms 1538–1975
12. Alice Snowringe	Baptism: Child of John and Alice Snowringe	1595	Bircham Newton	England Births & Baptisms 1538–1975
13. Robert Snoreng	Baptism: 'the sonn of Willyam and Joann Snoreng'	1622	Burnham Market/Westgate	NRO/PD/573/1
14. Margaret Snoreng	Baptism: 'the daughter of Willyam Snoreng and Bridget'	1627	Burnham Market/Westgate	NRO/PD/573/1
15. William Snoring	Court Papers: 'Black Will' and 'a tall blacke man'	1636	Burnham Market/Westgate	NRO/NQS/C/S3/30
16. Thomas Snoring	Burial: 'the sonn of Willyam'	1638	Burnham Market/Westgate	NRO/PD/573/1
17. Christiana Niger	Baptism: 'blackamore'	1634	Sibton	SRO/FC61/D1/1

18. Peter Lynn	Baptism: 'Moore or Mulatto'	1643	King's Lynn	NRO/BL/IIb/17
19. Mary Niger	Marriage	1645	Stowmarket	*England Marriages 1538–1973*
20. Name unknown	National Trust Collection NT/1210329, 'A Boy and a Girl and a Blackamoor Page', Anglo-Dutch School, part of the Bedingfeld collection; presented to the National Trust by Sybil Lyne-Stephens, Lady Paston-Bedingfeld (1883–1985), 1961	1658	Oxburgh Hall	National Trust, Oxburgh Hall
21. Name unknown	'Ye Black boy'	1662	Holkham Hall	Holkham Hall, F/JC(Y) 23, 25, 57, all 1662
22. Name unknown	Youth in painting 'The Yarmouth Collection'	1665	Oxnead Hall	Norfolk Museums Service
23. Jeremiah/Andrew	Baptism: 'Blackamore'	1673	King's Lynn	NRO/BL/IIb/17
24. Robert Smith	Burial: 'a Blackamore and Trumpeter'	1685	Hadleigh	SRO/FB8I/D1/3
25. Rosanna	Baptism: 'a blackamoor woman of Sir Robert Davers aged about 16 years'	1688	Rougham	SRO/FL619/4/2
26. Bedfer	Poll Tax: 'Blackamore'	1689	King's Lynn	NRO/QR1
27. John Blunt Rosanita Blunt	Baptism of John Blunt – parents were listed as 'John and Rosanita Blunt, blackamores' (Rosanita thought to be the same person as Rosanna, entry 25)	1690	Bury St Edmunds	SRO/FL543/4/3

28. John Blunt	Baptism: 'son of John and Rosanita Blunt, blackamores'	1690	Bury St Edmunds	SRO/FL543/4/3
29. Peter le-Black	Burial: His surname, plus the details of the burial of a woman named Rachel in 1698 who was described as 'the Moor's wife'[2]	1701	Barningham	SRO/FL523/4/1
30. Name unknown	'Little Black man'	1704	Norwich	NRO/NCR/16a/26 (MF629), fo.184
31. Robert Yoxford	Baptism: 'a Black boy brought over by Thomas Betts Esq.'	1713	Yoxford	SRO/FC73/D1/1
32. Patrick Brink	Buried: 'blackamor'	1720	Bury St Edmunds	SRO/FL545/4/5
33. Thomas Wright	'ESCAPE: Thomas Wright a tall black man wearing his own black hair of a sanguine complexion broke out of Beccles Gaol 13 July at night, being committed on suspicion of housebreaking. Whoever apprehends the said TW & brings him to Mr Tobias Chandler, Keeper of Gaol of Beccles aforesaid shall have 2 guineas reward paid by said Tobias Chandler'	1727	Beccles	*Norwich Gazette*
34. Thomas Rundell	Burial: 'a negro'	1732	Bardwell	SRO/FL522/4/3
35. Name unknown	'Captain Uring's Black'	1727	Holkham Hall	Holkham Hall, HA/A/26
36. Elizabeth Barnes (later married as Pickerell)	Will: 'negro servant' Burial: 'Blackamor'	1729 and 1748	Stradsett and Bury St Edmunds	NRO/PRCC/OW

[2] It seems probable that Rachel was not African herself, otherwise she would have been described as a 'moor' in her own right, rather than by reference to her husband.

Name	Description	Year	Location	Reference
37. George Calican	Servant: 'a Black'	1737	Holkham Hall	NRO/PD/608/2
38. Caesar Hockwold	'Black'	1739/49/50	Hockwold	NRO/MC/42/86/527x1
39. Ann Hockwold	Child of Caesar Hockwold	1760	Hockwold	NRO/PD/311/5
40. Jane Hockwold	Child of Caesar Hockwold	1762	Hockwold	NRO/PD/311/5
41. Caesar Hockwold	Child of Caesar Hockwold	1764	Hockwold	NRO/PD/311/5
42. Mary Hockwold	Child of Caesar Hockwold	1765	Hockwold	NRO/PD/311/5
43. Thomas Hockwold	Child of Caesar Hockwold	1767–72	Hockwold	NRO/PD/311/5
44. John Hockwold	Child of Caesar Hockwold	1769	Hockwold	NRO/PD/311/5
45. F. Hockwold	Child of Caesar Hockwold	1770	Hockwold	NRO/PD/311/5
46. Sarah Hockwold	Child of Caesar Hockwold	1771	Hockwold	NRO/PD/311/5
47. Thomas Hockwold	Child of Caesar Hockwold	1774–5	Hockwold	NRO/PD/311/5
48. Thomas Hockwold	Child of Caesar Hockwold	1775	Hockwold	NRO/PD/311/5

49. Thomas Hockwold	Child of Caesar Hockwold (entry 41)	1785	Hockwold	NRO/PD/311/5
50. Rebecca Hockwold	Daughter of Mary (entry 42)	1793	Hockwold	NRO/PD/311/5
51. Mary Hockwold	Daughter of Rebecca (entry 50)	1813	Hockwold	NRO/PD/311/5
52. Oxford	WHEREAS an East-India Black, who goes by the Name of Oxford, somewhat thin, about six Foot six Inches high, with short black curled Hair, has had the Small-Pox, and his Ears have been bored, went away from his Master on Christmas-Day last, with an old Silver laced Hat on, a black Velvet Stock round his Neck, an Olive-Colour Coat, a double-breasted red Waistcoat with Brass Buttons, and a Pair of Leather Breeches: Whoever brings him to his Master, Mr. Robert Gooding, at Sudbury in Suffolk, or to Mr. Voyce, at the Spread-Eagle Inn in Gracechurch-Street, London, shall have a Guinea Reward, and reasonable Charges. If he will return to his Master by the 31st instant, he shall be kindly receiv'd	1741	Sudbury	*Daily Advertiser*, 8 January 1741
53. Unknown	In respect of the theft of two horses - - 'the other is a black thin man, wears an old light Wigg. A little hat with a Crape Hatband, a straight Great Coat drab Colour, with a brown Cambrick Waistcoat'	1741	Pakenham	*The Ipswich Journal*, 14 November 1741
54. James Pamps	'a little black Man, aged about 35 years wearing a cap or Wigg, with a surtoit coat'	1743	Norwich	*The Ipswich Journal*, 15 January 1743
55. John Ong	Servant suspected of theft – 'a stout well-made black Man, with short curl'd hair, about 25 years of age'	1743	Narford	*The Ipswich Journal*, 29 October 1743
56. William Byrom	Marriage to Sarah Knights: William described as 'a blackamoor servant to Captain Rycart'	1744	Aldeburgh	SRO/FC129/D1/3

	Description	Year	Place	Reference
57. Sarah Byrom	'daughter of William and Sarah Byrom'	1744	Aldeburgh	SRO/FC129/D1/3
58. William Byrom	'son of William and Sarah Byrom'	1744	Aldeburgh	SRO/FC129/D1/3
59. Joseph Moulton	Baptism: 'An Asiatick Black of Madras, aged about seventeen years of age, servant to John Thompson Esq. late of Little Gadsden in Hertfordshire'	1745	Beccles	SRO/109/D2/2
60. Barlow	Baptism of child: 'a negro servant at Earsham Hall'	1755	Earsham	NRO/PD/519
61. Barlow Fielding	Baptism: 'ye base son of Ann Spence (by Barlow a negro servant at Earsham Hall)'	1755	Earsham	NRO/PD/519
62. John Fielding	Baptism: 'son of Barlow Fielding (a negro)'	1765	Earsham	NRO/PD/519
63. Unnamed	Burial: 'A negro, servant to Mr Machett'	1765	Ellingham	NRO/PD/669/2
64. Henry Norbrook	Baptism of daughter: Henry described as 'a negro'	1761	Tunstall	SRO/FC164/D1/4
65. Hannah Norbrook	Baptism: 'daughter of Henry Norbrook and Hannah his wife'	1761	Tunstall	SRO/FC164/D1/4
66. Henry Norbrook	Baptism: 'son of Henry Norbrook and Hannah his wife'	1764	Tunstall	SRO/FC164/D1/4
67. Charles Norbrook	Baptism: 'son of Henry and Hannah Norbrook'	1767	Tunstall	SRO/FC164/D1/4
68. Lettie Norbrook	Baptism: 'daughter of Henry and Hannah Norbrook'	1770	Tunstall	SRO/FC164/D1/4

69. William Norbrook	Baptism: 'son of Henry and Hannah Norbrook'	1774	Tunstall	SRO/FC164/D1/4
70. Elizabeth Norbrook	Baptism: 'daughter of Henry and Hannah Norbrook'	1777	Tunstall	SRO/FC164/D1/4
71. Stephen Tucker	Baptism: 'a negro boy about nine years of age'	1766	Nayland	SRO/FB64/D1/2
72. John Davis		1766	Garboldisham	NRO/PD/519
73. Samuel Stanton	Baptism: 'Three Blacks'			
74. Richard Alexander				
75. William	Baptism: 'a negro'	1766	Rushbrooke	Hervey (ed.), *Parish*, p. 19.
76. Mary Hellet	Baptism: 'a negro girl servant to Jonathan Worrel Esq.'	1768	Ipswich	SRO/FB94/D1/3
77. William Strap	Baptism: 'a negro servant of Captain Pricke of Nacton'	1771	Ipswich	SRO/FB98/D1/3
78. Sophia Molineux	Baptism[3]	1771	Garboldisham	NRO/PD/197/2
79. Samuel Molineux	Father of Sophia Molineux	1771	Garboldisham	NRO/PD/197/2

[3] This identification is explained in Chapter Seven.

	Description	Year	Place	Source
80. William Suza	'RUN away a Negro Boy about seventeen Years of Age, short and stout made, marked on one or both of his Temples with Scars, also on the Forehead; wears a white Coat, reddish Waistcoat, black Breeches and Stockings, the coat rather too large, blows the French Horn, and plays a little on the German Flute; came last from Suffolk. His name is William Suza. Whoever secures him and gives Notice to the Master of George's Coffee house, Coventry-street, shall receive One Guinea Reward. He is supposed to be lurking about Curzon-street, May Fair'	1771	Suffolk	*Public Advertiser*, 13 December 1771
81. John Yeldon	'Whereas John Yelden, late of Easton, Labourer, got away from the constable of Kertleburgh some time since. He was in custody for attempting to break into the Backhouse of Mr Tho. Langleys of Kertleburgh Hall. J. Yelden is a tall black man, round-shouldered, & about fifty years of age'	1773	Easton/ Kertleburgh	*The Ipswich Journal*, 19 June 1773
82. John Bumpstead	'Whereas John Bumpstead, late of Styleham, Suffolk, aforesaid, Miller, has defrauded Rachel Pulham of Hoxne of ten pecks of wheat, under pretention of grinding, and afterwards absconded [...] Bumpstead is a tall black Man, and generally speaks with a very loud Voice, and makes uncommon Motions with his Eyes when in common conversation'	1773	Easton/ Kertleburgh	*The Ipswich Journal*, 4 September 1773
83. Charles Cook	Baptism: 'a black, aged 19 years'	1773	Bury St Edmunds	SRO/FL541/4/4
84. Unknown	In respect of the theft of a horse near Bentley-Mill, Ipswich – 'a tall black man, with his own hair, Great-coat and boots'	1774	Bentley-Mill	*The Ipswich Journal*, 8 October 1774
85. John Nicholls	Advert – having left family chargeable to the parish '5 feet 9 inches high, a black man, lankey hair, with fear on his face'	1776	Watlingham	*The Ipswich Journal*, 3 February 1776
86. Martin Leverington	Advert – having left family chargeable to the parish 'a stout black man, with black hair, about 6 feet high'	1776	Watlingham	*The Ipswich Journal*, 3 February 1776

209

Name	Description	Year	Place	Reference
87. Thomas German	Baptism: 'a black and adult'	1777	Great Saxham	SRO/FL622/4/1
88. Charles Molineux	Baptism: 'Black sevt. 16 years old'	1777	Garboldisham	NRO/PD/519
89. Anthrobus Morgan	Baptism: 'a black and adult'	1780	Great Saxham	SRO/FL622/4/1
90. John son of Solomon	Baptism: 'a child brought from the East Indies and baptised at the age of 11 or 12 years'	1781	Ipswich	SRO/FB100/D1/3
91. Jeremiah Rowland	Burial: 'a negro'	1781	Wroxham	NRO/PD/390/2
92. The 'White Negro Woman'	'Mr Curtis will exhibit at the Half Moon, on the Castle Ditches, the following *lusus nature*, the White Negro Woman, who was born in Jamaica to black parents and formerly presented to George II. By her husband (a Nottinghamshire man) she has had 5 children, all of the Mulatto complexion	1783	Norwich	*Norwich Mercury*
93. Hebe Bessom	Baptism: 'a native of India aged 19'	1784	Brandeston	SRO/FC105/D1/2
94. Harriot	Baptism: 'a native of India aged 15'	1784	Brandeston	SRO/FC105/D1/2
95. Sigismunda Beckford	Baptism: 'a native of Jamaica aged 40'	1784	Somerleyton	NRO/PD/577/2
96. John Brown	Baptism and burial: 'A Black and native of Jamaica aged 35 years'	1786	Great Saxham	SRO/FL622/4/1
97. Mahomet Benaley	Charity: 'a poor Turk'	1786	King's Lynn	NRO/ BL/KL/1/13

	Description	Date	Place	Source
98. William Luccan	Baptism: 'a child brought from the East Indies by Captain William Bullock aged about 10 years'	1787	Mellis	SRO/FB123/D1/4
99. Ben Ali	Burial: 'a native of Morrocco (sic) aged between fifty and sixty years who being found dead in this parish and on whom the coroner having taken his inquest was admitted to Christian burial'	1789	Higham	SRO/FB74/D1/4
100. Unknown	'a Black with a French horn'	1789	Weston Longville	Blythe, et al, *The Diary*, p. 205
101. Unknown	'a black man begging about the streets'	1789	Ipswich	*The Ipswich Journal*, 6 June 1789
102. Joseph Dian(a)	'a native of the Congo in Africa' and later 'a Black'	1784 and 1791	Henstead, Fakenham, Norwich	SRO/FL/125/d1/2 and *Norfolk Chronicle*
103. Mary Molineux	Banns: 'a mulatto'	1791	Garboldisham	NRO/PD197/2
104. Edward Steele	Various: 'He was born at Barbadoes in 1785'	1795	Norwich and Great Yarmouth	Palmer, *Perlustration*, p. 85
105. Rachel Fitshoe	Baptism: 'a Black woman'	1799	Diss	NRO/PD/100/364
106. John Darby	Marriage: 'single man of this parish' – The father of William Darby (Pablo Fanque)	1791	Norwich	NRO/PD/484/14
107. John Richard Darby	Child of 'John Darby and Mary Stamp'	1792	Norwich	NRO/PD/26/2
108. Robert Darby	'Robert son of John Darby and Mary his wife late Mary Stamp'	1794	Norwich	NRO/PD/74/44

109. William Darby	Baptism: 'William son of John Darby and Mary his wife late Mary Stamps spinster' Burial 1797	1796	Norwich	NRO/PD/74/44
110. Elizabeth Darby	Burial: 'Daughter of William [sic] Darby and Mary his wife late Mary Stamps'	1800	Norwich	NRO/PD/74/44
111. Mary Elizabeth Darby	Burial: 'Mary Elizabeth daughter of John Darby and Mary his wife late Mary Stamps spinster, aged 2 years'	1801	Norwich	NRO/PD/74/44
112. William Darby (Pablo Fanque)	Child of 'John Darby and Mary Stamp'	1810	Norwich	St Andrew's Workhouse, Norwich, 30 March 1810
113. Robert Taylor	Banns: 'Robert Taylor, a mulatto, and Mary Driver'	1793	Garboldisham	NRO/PD/197/2
114. Robert Taylor	Baptism: 'Robert Taylor/mulatto/son of Robert Taylor'	1794	Garboldisham	NRO/PD/197/2
115. John Taylor	Baptism: 'son of Robert/mulatto man/and Mary'	1796	Garboldisham	NRO/PD/197/2
116. James Taylor	Baptism: 'son of Robert and Mary'	1798	Garboldisham	NRO/PD/197/2
117. William Taylor	Burial: 'son of Robt. and Mary mulatto infant' (Baptised 1802)	1803	Garboldisham	NRO/PD/197/2
118. Mary Taylor	Baptism: 'daughter of Robert and Mary'	1804	Garboldisham	NRO/PD/197/2

119. William Taylor	Baptism: 'son of Robert/Black Bob/and Mary'	1807	Garboldisham	NRO/PD/197/2
120. Daniel Taylor	Baptism: 'son of Robert/mulatto/and Mary'	1810	Garboldisham	NRO/PD/197/2
121. Cotton	Painting: 'Cotton', Norwich	1823	Norwich	The Docker collection of portraits by John Dempsey in the collection of the Tasmanian Museum and Art Gallery, Hobart
122. Charley	Painting: 'Black Charley, bootmaker, Norwich'	1823	Norwich	The Docker collection of portraits by John Dempsey in the collection of the Tasmanian Museum and Art Gallery, Hobart
123. Benj. Grey	'a man of colour'	1803	Bury	*The Ipswich Journal*, 30 July 1803
124. Name unknown	Burial: 'A pauper an African'	1805	Newmarket	SRO/FL610/4/4
125. John Gibbs	Baptism: 'a black man, a native of the Island of Barbados'	1807	Norwich	NRO/PD/61/3
126. John Friday	Burial: 'a black' 'supposed to be about 66 years of age'	1811	Creeting All Saints	SRO/FB12/G3/1/3

127. Thomas Sayers	Baptism: 'a Black aged 61'	1812	Kirby Bedon	NRO/PD/481/12
128. Mary Sayers	Baptism: daughter of Thomas Sayers (entry 127)	1815	Kirby Bedon	NRO/PD/481/12
129. Thomas Sayers	Baptism: son of Thomas Sayers (entry 127)	1817	Kirby Bedon	NRO/PD/481/12
130. James Sayers	Baptism: son of Thomas Sayers (entry 127)	1822	Kirby Bedon	NRO/PD/481/12
131. John Sayers	Baptism: son of Thomas Sayers (entry 127)	1833	Kirby Bedon	NRO/PD/481/12
132. Samuel Sayers	Baptism: son of Thomas Sayers (entry 127)	1825	Kirby Bedon	NRO/PD/481/12
133. Paulo Loando		1813	Norwich	NRO/PD26/4
134. Charles Fortunatus Freeman	Baptism: 'Born of African parents (sic) names unknown'			
135. Edward Makenzie				
136. Buxoo	'a Bengalese, a native of Calcutta publicly baptised at Burnham Market Church by Rev John Glasse, by the names of John Henry Martin. He was brought over to this country in a ship commanded by Capt. Glasse'	1816	Burnham Market	Mackie, *Norfolk*, p. 126
137. Cuffee Cross	Baptism of son: 'negro slaves'	1815	Ipswich	SRO/FB94/D1/7

138. Amber Cross	Baptism of son: 'negro slaves'	1815	Ipswich	SRO/FB94/D1/7
139. Thomas Cross	Baptism: 'son of Cuffee and Amber Cross'	1815	Ipswich	SRO/FB94/D1/7
140. Samuel Turner	Burial: 'Aged 69 years, or thereabouts, a native of Martinique in the West Indies'	1819	Norwich	NRO/NCR/Case6a/25
141. James Brown	'a man of colour, belonging to the band of the 69th Regiment' who was 'secretly married, he never having obtained permission from his commander to marry' Ann Lovick and was 'shortly after drowned'	1822	Norwich and Ipswich	*Norfolk Chronicle*, Saturday 19 October 1822
142. Unnamed	'a man of colour undertook to run nine miles in fifty-two minutes [...] he ran without shoes and performed his task (with great ease) within the given time. He appeared on the ground the following day to perform twelve miles in one hour and ten minutes, which he was prevented from doing by a fall of rain'	1825	North Walsham	*Norwich Mercury*, Saturday 28 May 1825
143. Joshua Wise	Burial: 'an African'	1826	Holbrook	SRO/FB94/01/7
144. Young Richmond	'a man of colour, calling himself Young Richmond, undertook for a trifling consideration to walk from the Bull Inn, Downham Market, to a measured half mile and back on the Lynn Road and back seven times in an hour; which arduous feat he accomplished in gallant style, by perfectly fair walking, two minutes within the limited time'	1828	Downham Market	*Norwich Mercury*, Saturday 17 May 1828
145. Name unknown 146. Name unknown	Letter: 'Two mulattoes, or blacks'	1830	Cromer	NRO/GTN/9/40

215

147. Name unknown	Newspaper report: 'a man of colour'	1820	Little Walsingham	*Norwich Mercury*, 4 December 1830
148. James Doubleday	Directory listing as 'negro' in 1836 and 'Blackamore' in 1845. Also stated to be 'victualler'; son of James Doubleday (entry 150)	1814–62	Colton	William White, *History*, pp. 770 and 434; NRO/PD/345/3
149. James Doubleday or Ann Doubleday (nee Hammond)[4]	Baptism of James (entry 150); the grandparents of James Doubleday 'negro' (entry 148)	1782	Welborne	NRO/PD/634/2
150. James Doubleday or Martha Doubleday	Parents of James Doubleday 'negro' (entry 148)	1781–1862	Welborne/ Colton	NRO/PD/345/6
151. John Doubleday	Siblings of James Doubleday (entry 150)	1788	Colton	NRO/PD/345/9
152. Eliz. Doubleday		1789	Welborne	NRO/PD/643/3

[4] There is no definitive indication as to which of James' ancestors were African, so his father, his siblings and his grandparents have been included here.

216

153. Martha Doubleday		1810	Colton	NRO/PD/345/2
154. John Doubleday	Siblings of James Doubleday 'negro' and 'Blackamore' (entry 148)	1812	Colton	NRO/PD/345/2
155. Maria Doubleday		1817–77	Colton	NRO/PD/345/6
156. William Doubleday		1808	Colton	NRO/PD/345/2
157. Henry Doubleday		1821	Colton	NRO/PD/345/3
158. Samuel Samuels	Burial: 'a man of colour, a native of Jamaica'	1796–1842	Spixworth	NRO/PD/536/28
159. Unknown	'Miles' black wife of Lessingham'	Date unknown	Lessingham	Rye, 'The Ballad of Arthur of Bradley', in Evelyn-White, *The East Anglian*, pp. 177–80, at p. 179

Appendix B: The Surname 'Blackamore', 1500–1800

The Surname 'Blackamore' (with variants) in Norfolk and Suffolk, 1500–99

Name	Event/Date	Location	Other information	Source
1. Roger Blackamore	1543 at baptisms of his children, entries 2 and 3	Ipswich	–	England Births & Baptisms 1538–1975
2. Robert Blackamore	Baptism: Feb 1544	Ipswich	Father: Roger Blackamore	England Births & Baptisms 1538–1975
3. Anne Blackamore	Baptism: Aug 1546	Ipswich	Father: Roger Blackamore	England Births & Baptisms 1538–1975
4. Margery Blackamore	Marriage: 1547	Thorndon	Spouse: John Grater	England, Boyd's Marriage Indexes, 1538–1850
5. Marable Blackamore	Burial: 10 Jul 1559	Woodbridge	–	National Burial Index for England & Wales
6. Joan Blackmore	Burial: 7 Jan 1562	Ipswich	–	National Burial Index for England & Wales
7. Thomas Blackeamore	Burial: 10 Mar 1565	Ipswich	–	National Burial Index for England & Wales

				National Burial Index for England & Wales
8. Clement Blackmore	Burial: 1 May 1569	Ipswich	-	-
9. Elizabeth Blackmoore	Baptism: 26 Dec 1575	Hadleigh	-	England Births & Baptisms 1538–1975
10. Awdry Blackamore	Baptism: 17 Apr 1578	Layham	Father: Robt. Blackamore	England Births & Baptisms 1538–1975
11. Edward Blackamore	Baptism: 28 Feb 1579	Layham	Father: Robt. Blackamore	England Births & Baptisms 1538–1975
12. Robert Blackmore	Marriage: 8 Jul 1580	Ashill	Spouse: Elizabeth	NRO/PD/548/1
13. Robert Blackamore	Baptism: 17 Apr 1582	Layham	Father: Robt. Blackamore	England Births & Baptisms 1538–1975
14. Robert Blackmore	Marriage: 26 Nov 1584	Ashill	Spouse: Anne	NRO/PD/548/1
15. Anne Blackamore	Burial: 6 Jan 1584	Layham	Father: Robert Blackamore	England Births & Baptisms 1538–1975
16. Margret Blackmore	Marriage: 4 May 1585	Hadleigh	Spouse: Thomas Warren	England Births & Baptisms 1538–1975
17. Alice Blackamore	Baptism: 17 Nov 1590	Layham	Father: Robt. Blackamore	England Births & Baptisms 1538–1975
18. John Blackamore	Baptism: 5 Jan 1594	Layham	Father: Robt. Blackamore	England Births & Baptisms 1538–1975

The Surname 'Blackamore' (with variants) in Norfolk and Suffolk, 1600–99

Name	Event/Date	Location	Other information	Source
1. Judie Blackamore	Marriage: 31 Oct 1602	Nayland	Spouse: John Thorne	SRO/FB64/D1/1
2. Elz Blackamore	Marriage: 1604	Hadleigh	Spouse: John Spels	England, Boyd's Marriage Indexes, 1538–1850
3. William Blackmore	Baptism: 27 Sep 1610	Yarmouth	Son of Thomas and Ann	NRO/PD/28/1
4. William Blackmor	Marriage: 23 May 1611	Norwich: St John Timberhill	Spouse: Mary Farrer	NRO/PD/74/1
5. John Blackmor	Baptism: 2 Feb 1612	Norwich: St John Timberhill	–	NRO/PD/74/1
6. Edward Blackamore	Marriage: 1613	Little Wenham	Spouse: Mary Wolly	SRO/FB183/D/1/1
7. Thomasine Blackamore	Baptism: 19 Jan 1615	Norwich: St Andrew	Father: William	NRO/PD/165/1
8. Alice Blackamore	Marriage: 1616	Hadleigh	Spouse: Will Hall	England, Boyd's Marriage Indexes, 1538–1850
9. William Blackmore	Baptism: 28 Jul 1616	Norwich: St Peter Parmentergate	Father: William	NRO/PD/162/2

10. Anna Blackmor	Baptism: 25 May 1617	Hadleigh	Father: John	England Births & Baptisms 1538–1975
11. John Blackmor	Baptism: 21 Feb 1618	Hadleigh	Father: John	England Births & Baptisms 1538–1975
12. Richard Blackmer	Baptism: 23 Aug 1620	Hadleigh	Father: Edward Blackmer	England Births & Baptisms 1538–1975
13. Thomas Blakemore	Marriage: 6 May 1636	Norwich: St Julian	Spouse: Elizabeth	NRO/PD/31/1
14. Susannah Blakemore	Baptism: 21 Mar 1637	Norwich: St Julian	Parents: Thomas and Elizabeth	NRO/PD/31/1
15. William Blackmore	Marriage: 12 Apr 1637	Norwich: St John Timberhill	Spouse: Katheren Wardly	NRO/PD/74/41
16. Thomas Blackmore	Baptism: 22 Oct 1637	Norwich: St Lawrence	Father: Willyam	NRO/PD/58/1
17. Mary Blackamore	Baptism: 12 May 1642	Norwich: St John de Sepulchre	Father: Wyll 'Black a more'	NRO/PD90/2
18. John Blackamore	Baptism: 3 Aug 1644	Norwich: St John de Sepulchre	Father: 'Wylliam Blackamore'	NRO/PD90/2
19. Jane Blackamore	Marriage: 20 Nov 1645	Higham	Spouse: Isaac Spicer	SRO/FB74/D1/1

20. Edward Blackmore	Baptism: 28 Nov 1652	Norwich: St John Timberhill	Father: William	NRO/PD/71/1
21. William Blackmore	Burial: 27 Mar 1655	Norwich: St John Timberhill	Father: William	NRO/PD/71/1
22. Mary Blakeamor	Baptism: 9 May 1660	Norwich: St Peter Parmentergate	Father: John	NRO/PD/162/4
23. William Blackamoor	Baptism: Oct 1663	Norwich: St Peter Parmentergate	Father: John	NRO/PD/162/4
24. Robert Blackmore	Marriage: 23 Jan 1665	Norwich: St James with Pockthorpe	Spouse: Susan Bryant	NRO/PD/11/1
25. John Blakemoore	Baptism: 6 Aug 1665	Norwich: St Peter Parmentergate	Father: John Blakemoore	NRO/PD/162/4
26. Robert Blackmore	Baptism: 18 Feb 1666	Norwich: St James with Pockthorpe	Parents: Robert and Susan	NRO/PD/11/1
27. John Blackemore	Baptism: 6 Aug 1665	Norwich: St Peter Parmentergate	Father: John	NRO/PD/162/4
28. Edm. Blackemore	Baptism: 2 Feb 1668	Norwich: St Peter Parmentergate	Parents: John and Sissly	NRO/PD/162/4

29. Eliz. Blackemore	Baptism: 13 Sep 1668	Norwich: St James with Pockthorpe	Parents: Robert and Susan	NRO/PD/11/1
30. Christin Blakamour	Baptism: 14 Nov 1670	Norwich: St Peter Parmentergate	Parents: John and Sisly	NRO/PD/162/4
31. Susan Blackamore	Baptism: 12 Mar 1672	Norwich: St James with Pockthorpe	Parents: Robert and Susan	NRO/PD/11/1
32. Robert Blackamore	Baptism: 11 Dec 1673	Norwich: St James with Pockthorpe	Parents: Robert and Susan	NRO/PD/11/1
33. Elizabeth Blackamore	Marriage: 13 Feb 1675	Norwich: St Peter Hungate	Spouse: John Dilney	NRO/PD/61/1
34. Thomas Blackamoore	Baptism: 25 Jun 1676	Norwich: St James with Pockthorpe	Parents: Robert and Susan	NRO/PD/11/1
35. John Blackamoore	Baptism: 29 Feb 1680	Norwich: St James with Pockthorpe	Parents: Robert and Susan	NRO/PD/11/1
36. Elizabeth Blackmore	Burial: 2 Jan 1681	Saxmundham	Daughter of Mark Blackmore & Emm.	Suffolk Early Burials Index

				National Burial Index for England & Wales
37. Richard Blackmoore	Burial: 5 Jun 1681	Hacheston	–	–
38. Mary Blackmore	Baptism: 23 Aug 1682	Norwich: St James with Pockthorpe	Parents: Robert and Susan	NRO/PD/11/1
39. Thomas Blackmore	Marriage: 1 Nov 1677	Norwich: St Stephen's	Spouse: Elizabeth Walwyn	England Marriages 1538–1973
40. John Blackmore	Marriage: 14 Jul 1678	Norwich, St Mary in the Marsh	Spouse: Mary Whitlock	NRO/PD/499/2
41. Mary Blackmore	Baptism: 12 Oct 1678	Norwich: St Stephen's	Father: Thomas	NRO/PD/484/2
42. John Blackmore	Baptism: 15 Dec 1679	Norwich: St Stephen's	Father: Thomas	NRO/PD/484/2
43. Elizabeth Blackmore	Baptism: 13 Feb 1680	Norwich: St Stephen's	Father: Thomas	NRO/PD/484/2
44. William Blackamoore	Marriage: 29 May 1690	Norwich: St Peter Parmentergate	Spouse: Sarah Newton	NRO/PD/162/4
45. Mary Blackamoore	Baptism: 29 Mar 1691	Norwich: St Peter Parmentergate	Father: William Blackamoore	NRO/PD/162/4
46. Mark Blackmore	Burial: 9 Oct 1691	Saxmundham	–	Suffolk Early Burials Index

47. William Blackamore	Burial: 29 Apr 1701	Norwich: St Peter Parmentergate	Father: William Blackamoore	NRO/PD/162/4
48. Mary Blackamoore	Marriage: 27 Mar 1687	Norwich: St Peter Parmentergate	Spouse: Joseph King	NRO/PD/162/4
49. Thomas Blackmore	Burial: 3 Feb 1690	Norwich: St Stephen's	Father: Thomas	NRO/PD 484/2
50. John Blackmoor	Marriage: 3 Oct 1691	Norwich: St Gregory's	Spouse: Hannah Chitrin	NRO/PD/59/1
51. John Blackmoore	Baptism: 18 Jul 1692	Norwich: St Stephen's	Father: Thomas	NRO/PD 484/2
52. Susannah Blakemore	Baptism: 21 Mar 1696	Norwich: St Julian	Parents: Thomas and Elizabeth	NRO/PD/31/1
53. John Blackmoore	Burial: 12 May 1697	Blythburgh	-	National Burial Index for England & Wales
54. Sara Blackmore	Baptism: 27 Mar 1698	Norwich: St Julian	Parents: Thomas and Sara	NRO/PD/31/1
55. Christian Blackamore[1]	Marriage: 24 Apr 1698	Norwich: St Peter Parmentergate	Spouse: William Earl	NRO/PD/162/4

[1] Possibly the same person as entry 30.

The Surname 'Blackamore' (with variants) in Norfolk and Suffolk, 1700–1800

Name	Event/Date	Location	Other Information	Reference
1. Robert Blakemore	Baptism: 21 Apr 1700	Norwich: St Julian	Parents: Robert and Elizabeth	NRO/PD/31/1
2. Jane Blackamore	Burial: 23 Apr 1700	Norwich: St Peter Parmentergate	Parent: William	NRO/PD/162/4
3. Mary Blackmore	Burial: 7 Jan 1701	Norwich: St John the Baptist at Maddermarket	'An ancient widow'	NRO/PD/461/1
4. William Blackamore	Baptism: 29 Apr 1701 Burial: 29 Apr 1701	Norwich: St Peter Parmentergate	Father: William	NRO/PD/162/4
5. Mary Blackmore	Married: 29 Aug 1702	Thurgarton	Spouse: Humphrey Garwood	NRO/PD/221/2
6. Ann Blackmore	Burial: 14 Jan 1704	Norwich: St Peter Parmentergate	Father: Will	NRO/PD/162/4
7. Elizabeth Blackamore	Married: 8 Apr 1705	Norwich: St Stephen	Husband: Richard Dicker	NRO/PD/484/3
8. Eliz. Blackmor	Baptism: 12 Nov 1705	Norwich: St Julian	Parents: Robert and Eliz.	NRO/PD/31/1
9. Sarah Blackmore	Married: 1706	Benhall	Spouse: Edward Reeve	England, Boyd's Marriage Indexes, 1538–1850
10. Richard Blackmore	Married: 1707	Hoxne	Spouse: Mary Self	England, Boyd's Marriage Indexes, 1538–1850

11. Peter Blackamoor	Baptism: 25 Oct 1708	Norwich: St Julian	Parents: Robert and Elizabeth	Norfolk Bishop's Transcripts Baptisms and NRO/PD/31/1
12. Thomas Blackamore	Married: 4 Jul 1708	Norwich: St Stephen	-	Norfolk Bishop's Transcripts Marriages
13. Samuel Blackmore	Married: 4 Jul 1713	Norwich: St Stephen	Spouse: Mary Church	NRO/PD/484/4
14. John Blackmore	Married: 17 Apr 1714	Norwich: St George Colgate	Spouse: Judith Harvey	NRO/PD/7/3
15. Susan Blackmore	Married: 1714	Beccles	Spouse: John Denny	England, Boyd's Marriage Indexes, 1538–1850
16. Mary Blackmoore	Married: 8 Oct 1716	Norwich: St Julian	Married: Francis Moore	NRO/PD/31/1
17. Benjamin Blackamore	Baptism: 5 Jan 1716/7	Norwich: St James with Pockthorpe	Parents: Sam and Mary	NRO/PD/11/3
18. William Blackmore	Burial: 17 Dec 1715	Norwich: St Peter Parmentergate	-	NRO/PD/162/5
19. Ann Blackmore	Burial: 16 Oct 1719	Norwich: St Peter Mancroft	-	NRO/PD/26/16
20. Elizabeth Blackmore	Married: 12 Nov 1719	Norwich: St Julian	Married: Robert Lelly	NRO/PD/31/1
21. Thomas Blackmore	Burial: 19 Apr 1720	Norwich: St Stephen	-	NRO/PD/484/34

22. Mary Blackmore	Baptism: 12 Feb 1721	Norwich: St James with Pockthorpe	'base daughter of Mary Blackmore'	NRO/PD/11/5
23. Sara Blackmoor	Marriage: 1721	Snape	Spouse: John Crisp	England Marriages 1538-1973
24. Christian Blackmore (f)	Baptism: 4 Sep 1725	Norwich: St Stephen	Parents: Samuel and Mary	NRO/PD/484/4
25. Judith Blackmore	Burial: 4 Jun 1727	Norwich: St George Colgate	-	NRO/PD/7/3
26. Elizabeth Blakemore	Burial: 5 Oct 1729	Walberswick	-	National Burial Index for England & Wales
27. Christopher Blackamore	Married: 19 Oct 1731	Norwich: St Peter Parmentergate	Married Susan Dunk	NRO/PD/162/5
28. William Blakemore	Burial: 8 Jun 1732	Halesworth	-	National Burial Index for England & Wales
29. Robert Blackamore	Burials: 2 Aug 1732	Norwich: St Julian	Parents: Christopher and Mary	NRO/PD/31/2
30. Eliz. Blackamoor	Married: 5 Mar 1733	Norwich: St Helen	Married: Thomas Law Both of St Peter Mancroft	NRO/PD/94/2
31. Mary Blakamore	Baptised: 24 Mar 1734 Burial 11 Apr 1734	Norwich: St Peter Parmentergate; Norwich: St Julian	Parents: Christopher and Susan Blackamore	NRO/PD/162/5; NRO/PD31/2

228

Name	Event/Date	Place	Parents/Spouse	Source
32. Elizabeth Blackmore	Baptism: 19 Oct 1735	Norwich: St Peter Parmentergate	Parents: Christopher and Susan	NRO/PD/162/5
33. Witchingham Blackmore	Burial: 4 May 1736	Walberswick	-	National Burial Index for England & Wales
34. Peter Blackmore	Married: 27 Jun 1736	Norwich: St Peter Mancroft	Spouse: Mary Scate	NRO/PD/26/9
35. Mary Blackmore	Baptised: 27 Feb 1737 Burial: 13 Jul 1737	Norwich: St Julian	Parents: Chris and Susan	NRO/PD/162/5; NRO/PD/31/2
36. Benjamin Blackmore	Married: 15 Oct 1737	Norwich: St Peter Southgate	Married: Eliza Watering	NRO/PD/163/2
37. Christopher Blackmore	Baptised: 16 Jul 1738 Buried: 24 Jul 1738	Norwich: St Julian	Parents: Christopher and Susanna	NRO/PD/31/2
38. Christopher Blackmore	Baptised: 30 Sep 1739 Buried: 29 Nov 1739	Norwich: St Peter Parmentergate; Norwich: St Julian	Parents: Christopher and Susan	NRO/PD/162/5; NRO/PD/31/2
39. Alice Blackmore	Burial: 5 Nov 1739	Norwich: St Etheldreda	-	NRO/PD/4/2
40. Susanna Blackmore	Burial: 3 May 1740	Norwich: St Julian	-	NRO/PD/31/2
41. Mary Blackmore	Baptism: 20 Jan 1742	Norwich: St Peter Southgate	Parents: Benjamin and Elizabeth	NRO/PD/163/2

42. Peter Blackmore	Marriage: 20 Aug 1742	Norwich: St Peter Mancroft	Spouse: 'widower' married Sarah Thompson 'widow'	NRO/PD/26/9
43. Robert Blackamore	Baptism: 4 Sep 1743	Norwich: St Peter Mancroft	Parents: Peter and Sarah	NRO/PD/26/27
44. Christian Blackmoor	Baptism: 2 Feb 1744	Norwich: St Peter Southgate	Parents: Benjamin and Elizabeth	NRO/PD/163/2
45. Sarah Blackmore	Baptism: 3 Feb 1745	Norwich: St Peter Mancroft	Parents: Peter and Sarah	NRO/PD/26/27
46. Jonathan Blackmore	Baptism: 1 Jun 1746	Norwich: St Peter Southgate	Parents: Benjamin and Elizabeth	NRO/PD/163/2
47. Anne Blackmoor	Baptised: 3 Aug 1746	Norwich: St Peter Mancroft	Parents: Peter and Sarah	NRO/PD/26/2
48. Robert Blackmore	Burial: 18 Sep 1747	Norwich: St Peter Mancroft	Aged 4	NRO/PD/26/17
49. William Blakemore	Burial: 15 Sep 1748	Norwich: St Peter Southgate	-	NRO/PD/163/2
50. Anne Blackmore	Baptism: 24 Jan 1747 Buried: 6 Sep 1748	Norwich: St Peter Mancroft	Parents: Peter and Sarah	NRO/PD/26/2; NRO/PD/26/17
51. Mary Blackmore	Baptism: 4 Jan 1750 Buried: 17 Jul 1750	Norwich: St Peter Mancroft	Parents: Peter and Sarah	NRO/PD/26/2; NRO/PD/26/17

52. Samuel Blackamoor	Baptism: 3 Apr 1750 Buried: 13 Oct 1817	Norwich: St Peter Southgate; Norwich: St Peter Parmentergate	Parents: Benjamin and Elizabeth	NRO/PD/163/3; NRO/PD/162/19
53. Robert Blackamore	Baptism: 11 Nov 1750	Norwich: St Peter Mancroft	Parents: Peter and Sarah	NRO/PD/26/27
54. Peter Blackamore	Baptised: 22 Oct 1752 Burial: 15 Feb 1754	Norwich: St Peter Mancroft	Parents: Peter and Sarah	NRO/PD/26/2; NRO/PD/26/17
55. Elizabeth Blackmore	Married: 19 May 1752	Norwich: St Julian	Husband: Daniel Spencer	NRO/PD/31/2
56. William Blackemore	Baptism: 17 Jul 1752	Lowestoft: St Margaret	Parents: Henry and Hannah	NRO/PD/589/4
57. Christopher Blackemore	Married: 3 Sep 1754	Norwich: St Julian	Married: Elizabeth Ives	NRO/PD/31/9
58. Christian Blackamoor	Married: 25 Dec 1755	Norwich: St Mary Coslany	Married: Charles Havers	NRO/PD/1/9
59. Elizabeth Blackmore	Baptism: 24 Aug 1755	Norwich: St Peter Southgate	Parents: Benjamin and Elizabeth	NRO/PD/163/3
60. Benjamin Blackmore	Burial: 9 Jan 1759	Norwich: St Peter Southgate	-	NRO/PD/163/3
61. Christopher Blackmore	Burial: 16 Jul 1759	Norwich: St Julian	-	NRO/PD/31/2
62. Elizabeth Blackamore	Married: 12 Feb 1761	Hingham	Married: Thomas Rich	NRO/PD/575/11

63. Minter Blackmore	Married: 18 Oct 1762	Dickleburgh	Samuel Clemence	NRO/PD/704/12
64. Sarah Blackamore	Married: 19 May 1765	Norwich: St Peter Mancroft	Married: Thomas Clarke	NRO/PD/26/9
65. Peter Blackmore	Burial: 30 Jun 1767	Norwich: St Peter Mancroft	'Aged 59'	NRO/PD/26/17
66. Jonathan Blackmore	Banns: 30 Jul 1769	Norwich: St Ethelreda	With: Barbara Lanham	NRO/PD/4/8
67. Jonathan Blackmore	Baptised: 10 Dec 1769	Norwich: St Ethelreda	'Base born son of Barbara Lanham'	NRO/PD/4
68. Christian Blackmore	Buried: 24 Nov 1769	Norwich: St Peter Parmentergate	Aged 25	NRO/PD/162/5
69. Robert Blackmore Clarke	Burial: 20 Aug 1771	Norwich: St John Timberhill	'infant'	NRO/PD/74/43
70. Elizabeth Blackmore	Burial: 6 Apr 1778	Norwich	-	England Deaths & Burials 1538–1991
71. Jonathan Blackmore	Married: 16 Jan 1783	Great Yarmouth	Married: Ann Clarke	NRO/PD/28/67
72. Samuel Blackmore	Married: 5 Dec 1784	Trowse	Married: Susannah Piken	NRO/PD/216/5
73. Alfred Blackamore	Baptism: 30 Jan 1786	Norwich: St Peter Parmentergate	Parents: Samuel and Susanna	NRO/PD/162/6

74. Thomas William Blackamore	Burial: 27 Jan 1790	Norwich: St Peter Parmentergate	'Son of Samuel and Susanna Blackamore'	NRO/PD/162/7
75. Jonathan Blackmore	Burial: 7 Feb 1790	Great Yarmouth	Parents: John and Ann 'aged 6 years'	NRO/PD/28/20
76. Jonathan Blackmore	Baptism: 24 Feb 1791	Great Yarmouth	Parents: John and Ann	NRO/PD/28/20
77. Thomas Clark 'late Blackamore'	Burial of spouse: May 1792	Norwich: St Peter Parmentergate	Burial of Sarah Clark 'widow of Thomas Clark late Blackamore aged 48 years'	NRO/PD/162/7
78. Benjamin Blackmore	Baptism: 8 July 1792	Great Yarmouth	Parents: John and Ann	NRO/PD/28/20
79. Mary Blackmoore (possibly 'a' crossed out)	Married: 1 Oct 1792	Norwich: St Gregory's	Married: William Adcock widower, she was a spinster	NRO/PD/59/9
80. Sarah Blackamore	Burial: 19 Apr 1795	Norwich: St Peter Parmentergate	'widow of Peter Blackamore aged 88 years'	NRO/PD/162/7
81. Edmund Purvey Blackmore	Baptism: 11 Apr 1796	Great Yarmouth	Parents: Jonathan and Anne	NRO/PD/28/20

Appendix C: Plantation Ownership in Norfolk and Suffolk, 1650–1833

Family Name	Location	Plantation Details	Source
1. Arcedeckne	Glevering Hall, Suffolk	Golden Grove and Norbrook estates, Jamaica	SRO/HB26/412; HB26/12012
2. Barclay	Norwich	Unity Valley Pen, Jamaica	NRO/RQG/537/493X1, David Barclay's Letter Book 1788–1809; Barclay, *An account*
3. Beckford	Somerley, Suffolk	Roaring River, Williamsfield, Fort William, Jamaica	NRO/YD/87/9, Youell Diaries, 23 October 1774; Casid, *Sowing*, p. 60; Sheridan, 'Beckford'; Elizabeth A. Bohls, *Slavery and the Politics of Place: Representing the Colonial Caribbean, 1770–1833* (Cambridge University Press, 2014), p. 28
4. Berney	Kirby Bedon, Norfolk	Hanson Plantation, Barbados	NRO/FEL/884/556X4, Journal and ledger of Hanson Plantation, Barbados, of Sir John Berney, 1792
5. Blake	Langham, Suffolk	Montserrat and St Christopher	SRO/HA546/2/23, 30–1, 34–6; HA546/6/1–11
6. Bland	Norwich	Winyou River near George Town in Craven County, South Carolina	NRO/MC/403, 731X9
7. Burton/Fisher	Norwich and Great Yarmouth, Norfolk	Chiswick, Jamaica	St Thomas-in-the-East, Surrey	LBSO, Thomas Burton, https://www.ucl.ac.uk/lbs/person/view/21886; Palmer, *Perlustration*, pp. 393–4
8. Capper-Reid	Ipswich, Suffolk	Friendship, Jamaica	LBSO Biography of Ann Capper (née Reid), https://www.ucl.ac.uk/lbs/person/view/746178682

9. Colhoun	West Wretham Manor, Wretham, also Thorpe Hall, Hasketon, Suffolk, and Great Hockham	Mount Pleasant Plantation, St Croix; 'Colhouns', Nevis	David R. Fisher, 'Colhoun, William MacDowall (fl.1758–1821), of Wretham, nr. Thetford, Norf. and St. Kitts', in R. Thorne (ed.), *The History of Parliament: the House of Commons 1790–1820* (London, 1986) <http://www.historyofparliamentonline.org/volume/1790-1820/member/colhoun-william-macdowall-1758-1821> [accessed 1 October 2020]; Pares, *A West India Fortune*; Nisbet, 'Sugar'.
10. Dalling	Earsham Hall, Norfolk	Donnington Castle, Jamaica	NRO/MEA/6/1/660X8
11. Daniell	Snettisham, Norfolk	Paradise Estate, Dominica	LBSO, Biography of Thomas Daniell, https://www.ucl.ac.uk/lbs/person/view/2146643847
12. Davers	Rougham, Suffolk	Davers, Barbados	Will of Sir Robert Davers of Barbados and Rushbrooke, 1688
13. Frere	Occold, Suffolk; Harleston, Norfolk	Barbados	From Hotten, *The Original*, p. 461
14. Greene	Bury St Edmunds, Suffolk	Nicola Town; Phillips; Turtle(?) Island, all in St Christopher	LBSO, Biography of Benjamin Greene, https://www.ucl.ac.uk/lbs/person/view/25002; Wilson, *Greene King*; Wilson, 'Greene family'
15. Gurley	Needham Market, Suffolk	Peter's Hope, St Vincent	LBSO, Biography of Mary Selby Gurley (née Johnston), https://www.ucl.ac.uk/lbs/person/view/2146644165
16. Hervey/Ellis	Ickworth, Suffolk	Montpelier, Jamaica	Hervey Family Archive, SRO/HA/507
17. Long	Saxmundham, Suffolk	Lucky Valley and St David's, Jamaica	SRO/HA18/GB and GD

18. Longe/Howse	Spixworth, Norfolk	Unnamed estate, St Christopher (possibly Camp Estarte)	LBSO, Biography of Catherine Longe (née Jackson), https://www.ucl.ac.uk/lbs/person/view/2146645403
19. Middleton	Barham, Suffolk	Crowfield Plantation, South Carolina	SRO/HA93/2/3243-4
20. Molineux	Garboldisham, Norfolk and St Christopher	Crisp Estate, St Christopher	NRO/BL/X6/21
21. Peete	Norwich	Ferry Pen, Jamaica	*Norwich Mercury*, 16 April, and 14 June 1783; *Norfolk Chronicle*, 12 January 1788; PROB 11/1378/199, PROB 11/1169/71
22. Penrice	Great Yarmouth, Norfolk	Jamaica	NRO/BER/484/691X5
23. Pocklington	Chelsworth, Suffolk	Hyde Plantation, Jamaica	SRO/HA552/2H/2
24. Scott	Garboldisham, Norfolk	Retreat Estate and Clarendon Park, Jamaica	NRO/PROD 11/1551
25. Thellusson	Rendlesham, Suffolk	Bacolet Estate, Las Cuevas Estate, Grenada	SRO/HB/416/D1/3/1
26. Woodley	Eccles, Norfolk	Greenland Estate, St Christopher	PROB 11/1462/55
27. Worrell	Ipswich, Suffolk	Sturges, Barbados	LBSO, Biography of Jonathan Worrell senior, https://www.ucl.ac.uk/lbs/person/view/-131609571

Bibliography

Primary Sources

Unpublished Correspondence and Manuscript Sources

The National Archives, Public Record Office, Kew, London

ADM/7/83, No. 111 Admiralty Passes
IR1 Series Britain, Country Apprentices 1710–1808
PROB/11/1232/158 Will of Crisp Molineux of Garboldisham, Norfolk, 1792
PROB/11/391/419 Will of Sir Robert Davers, 1688
PROB/11/216/350 Will of Seth Hawley
PROB/11/1319/184 Will of Mary Ann Steele, Spinster of Bloomsbury, Middlesex, 1799
T/64/72 Ships belonging to GB or British Persons entering Jamaica, 1775–85
T/64/276A/273 Record of Ships to the Coast of Africa, 1734–54

The Norfolk Record Office, Norwich

ANF 11 Records of the Archdeaconry of Norfolk, Probate, Probate inventories
AYL 20 The Aylsham Papers, Papers of the Browne family of Poringland, etc., Miscellaneous Browne papers
AYL 49 The Aylsham Papers, Papers of the Doughty family of Hanworth
AYL 201 The Aylsham Papers, Papers of the Doughty family of Hanworth – Doughty wills and family settlements
AYL 304 The Aylsham Papers, Miscellaneous deeds and papers of the Paston family, earls of Yarmouth
AYL 535 The Aylsham Papers, Papers of the Doughty family of Hanworth – Doughty family title deeds
AYL 831 The Aylsham Papers, Papers of the Doughty family of Hanworth, Doughty wills and family settlements
BL AQ 2/13 Bradfer-Lawrence Collection, Antiquarian Papers: King's Lynn: catalogue of mayors and annual occurrences, 1204–1693
BL CS Bradfer-Lawrence Collection, Philip Case Papers 1423–20th century
BL F Bradfer-Lawrence Collection Families, Individuals, Autographs, Typed extracts from letter books of Crisp Molineux
BL MC Bradfer-Lawrence Collection, Miscellanea 1300–20th century
BL Y Bradfer-Lawrence Collection, The Yarmouth Letters, 1660–88

COL 7 The Colman Manuscript Collection, Literary, Pious, Musical and Autobiographical MSS

COL 9 The Colman Manuscript Collection, Society of United Friars [1666]–1926

DCN Records of the Dean and Chapter of Norwich Cathedral

FEL 539 Fellowes of Shotesham Collection, Estate Papers Estate: Non-Fellowes, Berney estate

FEL 884 Fellowes of Shotesham Collection, Household, Business and Personal, Non-Fellowes, Sir John Berney

FX 323 Photocopies of King family correspondence, including letters from James King, alias Warner, at sea and in Jamaica

GUN 82-83 Rolfe Family Papers, Personal Papers, Books and Publications; Norfolk and Norwich Archaeological Society publications

KL C The Records of King's Lynn Unreformed Corporation

KL TS King's Lynn Borough Archives, Trustees for the port of King's Lynn under an Act for the relief of maimed and disabled seamen and widows and children of those killed in the merchant service 1747–1827

LEST Le Strange of Hunstanton Collection, Main Deposit Family Wills, Probates etc.

MC 403 Testamentary and Financial Records of Michael Bland, merchant, and brewer, of Norwich and London, 1736–1832

MC 42 Estate, Manorial and Personal Records of the Wyche family of Hockwold, 1374–1896

MC 50 Folkes of Hillington (Additional), [? 1312]–20th century

MC 265 Stanford Sale Agreement, 1546, and Pengelly Letters, 1665, 1674

MC 757 Collection letters and miscellaneous documents, 1655–1882

MC 1503 Bill of sale by Jacob Preston to William Manning, 29 May 1784

MEA 6 Meade of Earsham, Donnington Castle Estate, Jamaica, 1780–1851

MEA 10 Meade of Earsham, Dalling Family, 1503–1906

NCR 5b-c Leet rolls, 1287–1391 (with gaps)

NCR 12A Norwich Quarter Sessions files, interrogations, and depositions

NCR 16a/26 Norwich Mayor's Court Book

NCR 20a Norwich Quarter Sessions Minute Book

PRA Pratt Family of Ryston Hall, Norfolk Wills, Settlement, and related papers

PD/11/11 Parish Records of St James with Pockthorpe

PD/12/1 Parish Records of St Martin at Palace, Norwich

PD/13/1 Parish Records of Stradsett

PD/26 Parish Records of St Peter Mancroft, Norwich

PD/28/1 Parish Records of Great Yarmouth St Nicholas

PD/28/14 Parish Records of Great Yarmouth St Nicholas

PD/31/1 Parish Records of St Julian, Norwich

PD/39/2 Parish Records of St Margaret with St Nicholas, King's Lynn

PD/39/84 Parish Records of St Margaret with St Nicholas, King's Lynn

PD/58/1 Parish Records of St Lawrence, Norwich

PD/59/1 Parish Records of St Gregory, Norwich

PD/61/1 Parish Records of St Peter Hungate, Norwich
PD/69/1 Parish Records of Drayton
PD/71/1 Parish Records of Fritton (Norfolk)
PD/74/1 Parish Records of St John Timberhill with All Saints and St Michael
 at Thorn, Norwich
PD/74/41 Parish Records of St John Timberhill with All Saints and St Michael
 at Thorn, Norwich All Saints
PD/90/2 Parish Records of St John de Sepulchre, Norwich Baptisms
PD/100/364 Parish Register, Diss
PD/105/1 Parish Records of Kessingland
PD/162/2 Parish Records of St Peter Parmentergate, Norwich
PD/162/4 Parish Records of St Peter Parmentergate
PD/197/2 Parish Records of Garboldisham
PD/221/1 Parish Records of Thurgarton
PD/311/1 Parish Records of Hockwold cum Wilton
PD/422/1 Parish Records of Hainford, Registers
PD/451/98 Parish Records of Gaywood with Bawsey and Mintlyn
PD/484/2 Parish Records of St Stephen, Norwich
PD/519/3 Parish Records of Earsham
PD/548/1 Parish Records of Ashill
PD/573/1 Parish Records of Burnham Westgate
PD/575/1 Parish Records of Hingham
PD/589/1 Parish Records of St Margaret, Lowestoft
PD/608/1 Parish Records of Holkham
PD/696/16 Parish Register, Great Ringstead
PD/698/1 Parish Register, Old Hunstanton (St Mary's)
PD/711/1 Parish Records of North Walsham
RQG/537 Gurney of Bawdeswell Collection, Gurney and Related Families,
 Barclay Family
SF/6 Records of the Society of Friends in Norfolk, Minute Books, Registers and
 Account Books, Records of the Quarterly Meeting, Minutes of the Men's
 Meeting, Norfolk and Norwich Quarterly Meeting, 26 Sep 1781–31 Dec 1794
WKC/7 Family and Estate Papers of the Ketton-Cremer Family of Felbrigg Hall,
 13th–20th century
Y/C Great Yarmouth Borough Archives, Town Clerk's Department pre-1835
Y/D/41 Great Yarmouth Borough Archives, Private Deposits
YD/87/9 Youell Diaries

The Suffolk Record Office, Ipswich and Bury St Edmunds

FL619/4/2 Parish Register of Rougham
FB64/D1/2 Parish Register of Nayland
FB74/D1/4 Parish Register of Higham
FC61/D1/1 Parish Register of Sibton

FL543/4/3 Parish Register of Bury St Edmunds
FB81/D1/3 Parish Register of Hadleigh
FL523/4/1 Parish Register of Barningham
FL622/4/1 Parish Register of Ipswich St Mary
FB94/D1/7 Parish Register of Ipswich St Nicholas
FC105/D1/2 Parish Register of Brandeston
FL622/4/1 Parish Register of Great Saxham
FC73/D1/1 Parish Register of Yoxford
FC129/D1/3 Parish Register of Aldeburgh
FB98/D1/3 Parish Register of Ipswich St Clement
FB123/D1/4 Parish Register of Mellis
FL522/4/3 Parish Register of Bardwell
FL541/4/4 Parish Register of Bury St Edmunds St James
FL125/d1/2 Parish Register of Henstead
FC164/D1/4 Parish Register of Tunstall
FC129/D1/3 Parish Register of Aldeburgh
HA 93 Middleton Family of Shrubland Park
HA 546 Blake Family of Langham; West Indies estates
HB 26 Golden Grove Estate
HB 416 Estate Records of the Thellussons, Barons Rendlesham
HB 26/412 Records of the Golden Grove Estate, Jamaica
HA 507 Hervey Family, Estate Papers
HB 26 Vanneck family, Lords Huntingfield
HA 552 Pocklington Family of Chelsworth

Other Archives

London, British Library, Harley MS 304, ff. 75r–78v, 'Kett's Demands Being in Rebellion'
HA/A/26 Holkham Hall, Holkham household accounts
CB27 York City Archives, Chamberlains' Book
M23 Royal Norfolk Regimental Museum, West, and East Norfolk Militia Scrapbook 1804–1900

Paintings

National Trust Collection NT/1210329, 'A Boy and a Girl and a Blackamoor Page', Anglo-Dutch School, Part of the Bedingfeld collection; presented to the National Trust by Sybil Lyne-Stephens, Lady Paston-Bedingfeld (1883–1985), 1961
AG567 'Cotton', Norwich c.1823 watercolour 32x23, the Docker collection of portraits by John Dempsey in the collection of the Tasmanian Museum and Art Gallery, Hobart

AG574 'Black Charley, bootmaker, Norwich', 1823, watercolour 31.5x22.7, the Docker collection of portraits by John Dempsey in the collection of the Tasmanian Museum and Art Gallery, Hobart
'The Yarmouth Collection', Anglo-Dutch School, c.1665, Norfolk Museums Service

Printed Primary Sources

Contemporary books and articles

A copy of the poll for the Knights of the Shire for the County of S. taken at Ipswich, Aug. 30 1727 R. Goodrich, Esq.; High Sheriff. Candidates, Sir W. Barker, Sir J. Danvers, Baronets, J. Holt, Esquire (Ipswich, 1727)

The Calendar of the Freemen of Lynn, 1292–1836 (Norwich, 1913)

The Gentleman's Magazine (London, 1810 and 1815)

Barclay, David, An account of the emancipation of the slaves of Unity Valley Pen Jamaica (London, 1801)

Burke, John, A genealogical and heraldic history of the landed gentry of Great Britain and Ireland (2 vols, London, 1863), Vol. 2

Chambers, John, A General History of the County of Norfolk: Intended to Convey All the Information of a Norfolk Tour (Norwich, 1829)

Collinges, John, 'Sermon. 50. Man's Destruction of himself', in Several Discourses Concerning the Actual Providence of God: Divided Into Three Parts (London, 1678)

Creed, Henry, Extracts from the Registers of Mellis (Suffolk, 1853)

Cromwell, Thomas Kitson, Excursions in the county of Suffolk (London, 1819)

Crouse, J., The History and Antiquities of the County of Norfolk (Norwich, 1781)

Debrett, John, Debrett's Peerage of England, Scotland, and Ireland (London, 1820)

Gurney, Daniel, Household and Privy Purse Accounts of the Lestranges of Hunstanton, from A.D. 1519 to A.D. 1578: Communicated to the Society of Antiquaries (London, 1834)

Hall, Edward, The union of the two noble and illustrate famelies of Lancastre [and] Yorke (1st edn plus variant) (1 vol., London, 1548)

Harrod, Henry, 'Notes on the Records of the Corporation of Great Yarmouth', Norfolk Archaeology Vol. IV (1851)

Hervey, S.H.A., (ed.), Rushbrook Parish Registers, 1567–1850 with Jermyn and Davers Annals (Woodbridge, 1903)

Lawrence-Archer, J.H., Monumental Inscriptions of the British West Indies from the Earliest Date (London, 1875)

Le Strange, Hamon, Norfolk's Official Lists (Norwich, 1890)

Mackerell, Benjamin, The History and Antiquities of the Flourishing Corporation of King's-Lynn in the County of Norfolk (Norwich, 1738)

Mackie, Charles, Norfolk Annals, Volume I, 1801–1850 (Norwich, 1901)

McMahon, Benjamin, Jamaican Plantership (London, 1839)

Oliver, Vere Langford, (ed.), *Caribbeana: being miscellaneous papers relating to the history, genealogy, topography, and antiquities of the British West Indies* (London, 1914)

Palmer, Charles John, *The Perlustration of Great Yarmouth, with Gorleston and Southtown: III* (Great Yarmouth, 1875)

Parkin, Charles, *The history and antiquities of the city of Norwich* (Lynn, 1783)

Ramsay, James, *An Essay on the Treatment and Conversion of African Slaves in the British Sugar Colonies* (London, 1784)

Report of the Directors of the African Institution (London, 1813)

Report of the Committee of the African Institution (London, 1814)

Renny, Robert, *An History of Jamaica* (London, 1807)

Savage, James, *A genealogical dictionary of the first settlers of New England, Volume 1* (Boston, 1860)

Southey, Robert, *Lives of the British Admirals: With an Introductory View of the Naval History of England, Volume 2* (London, 1833)

Swinden, Henry, *History and antiquities of the ancient burgh of Great Yarmouth* (Norwich, 1772)

The Monthly Magazine, 20 (1805)

Uring, Nathaniel, *The Voyages and Travels of Captain Nathaniel Uring* (Reprinted London, 1928, first published 1726)

——, *A Relation of the Late Intended Settlement of the Islands of St. Lucia and St. Vincent, in America: in Right of the Duke of Montagu, and Under His Grace's Direction and Orders, in the Year 1722* (London, 1725)

White, William, *History, Gazetteer, and Directory of Norfolk* (Norfolk, 1836)

Wright, John, *The American Negotiator: Or, The Various Currencies of the British Colonies in America* (1765)

Official Books and Publications

'Report concerning the Military Labourers stationed at Brimstone Hill and other liberated Negroes residing in that Island, 24 October 1823', pp. 20-1, in *Slave Trade (Three Volumes) (2), Papers relating to Slaves in the Colonies &c: Volume 22* (1827)

Newspapers

Daily Advertiser
Norfolk Chronicle
Norwich Gazette
Norwich Mercury
Public Advertiser
The Ipswich Journal

BIBLIOGRAPHY

Secondary Sources

Acemoglu, Daron, Simon Johnson and James Robinson, 'The rise of Europe: Atlantic trade, institutional change, and economic growth', *American Economic Review* (2005), 546–79

Alexander, J. Neil, 'The Shape of the Classical Book of Common Prayer', in Charles Hefling and Cynthia Shattuck (eds), *The Oxford Guide to The Book of Common Prayer: A Worldwide Survey* (Oxford; New York, 2006)

Allen, Robert C., 'Agriculture during the Industrial Revolution, 1700–1850', in Roderick Floud and Paul Johnson (eds), *The Cambridge Economic History of Modern Britain 1700–1860* (Cambridge, 2004), pp. 96–116

Allen, Theodore, *The Invention of the White Race* (London, 1997)

Amor, Nicholas, *Late Medieval Ipswich: Trade and Industry* (Woodbridge, 2011)

Amussen, Susan Dwyer, *Caribbean Exchanges: Slavery and the Transformation of English Society, 1640–1700* (Chapel Hill, 2007)

Anderson, Richard, 'The Diaspora of Sierra Leone's Liberated Africans: Enlistment, Forced Migration, and "Liberation" at Freetown, 1808–1863', *African Economic History* (2013), 101–38—with Alex Borucki, Daniel Domingues da Silva, David Eltis, Paul Lachance, Philip Misevich and Olatunji Ojo, 'Using African Names to Identify the Origins of Captives in the Transatlantic Slave Trade: Crowd-Sourcing and the Registers of Liberated Africans, 1808–1862', *History in Africa* (2013), pp. 165–91

Andrews, K.R., *Trade, Plunder and Settlement: Maritime Enterprise and the Genesis of the British Empire, 1480–1630* (Cambridge; New York, 1984)

—, *Spanish Caribbean: Trade and Plunder, 1530–1630* (New Haven, 1978)

Andrews, Kenneth R. (ed.), *The Last Voyage of Drake and Hawkins* (London Second Series, 1972)

Angiolini, Franco, 'Slaves and Slavery in the Early Modern Tuscany (1500–1700)', *Italian History & Culture*, 3 (1997), 67–82

Anglo, S., 'The court festivals of Henry VII: a study based upon the account books of John Heron, treasurer of the chamber', *Bulletin of the John Rylands University Library*, 43 (1960–1), 12–45

Appleby, J.C., 'Pirates and Communities: Scenes from Elizabethan England and Wales', in J.C. Appleby and P. Dalton (eds), *Outlaws in Medieval and Early Modern England: Crime, Government and Society, c.1066–c.1600* (Farnham, England; Burlington, VT, 2009), 149–72

Aravamudan, Srinivas, *Tropicopolitans: Colonialism and Agency, 1688–1804* (Durham, NC, 1999)

Arena, Carolyn, 'Indian Slaves from Guiana in Seventeenth-Century Barbados', *Ethnohistory*, 64 (2017), 65–90

Arkell, Tom, 'Poll Tax, Marriage and King', in Kevin Schurer and Tom Arkell (eds), *Surveying the People* (Oxford, 1992)

Armstrong, D.V., 'Capitalism and the Shift to Sugar and Slavery in Mid-Seventeenth Century Barbados', *Historical Archaeology*, 53 (2019), 468–91

Ascott, Diana E., Fiona Lewis, and Michael Power, *Liverpool, 1660–1750: People, Prosperity and Power* (Liverpool, 2006)

Ayres, James, *Art, Artisans and Apprentices: Apprentice Painters and Sculptors in the Early Modern British Tradition* (Oxford; Philadelphia, 2014)

Bardsley, Charles, *English Surnames: Their Sources and Significations* (London, 1815)

Barney, John, 'Shipping in the Port of King's Lynn, 1702–1800', *Journal of Transport History*, 20 (1999), 126–41

Barr, Juliana, 'From Captives to Slaves: Commodifying Indian Women in the Borderlands', *Journal of American History*, 92 (2005), 19–46

Barry, Jonathan, *The Tudor and Stuart Town 1530–1688: A Reader in English Urban History* (London, 1990)

Bartels, Emily, *Speaking of the Moor: From Alcazar to Othello* (Philadelphia, 2008)

Barthelemy, Anthony G., *Black Face, Maligned Race: The Representation of Blacks in English Drama from Shakespeare to Southerne* (Baton Rouge; London, 1987)

Beckles, Hilary, *A History of Barbados: From Amerindian Settlement to Caribbean Single Market* (Cambridge, 2006)

——, 'A "Riotous and Unruly Lot": Irish Indentured Servants and Freemen in the English West Indies, 1644–1713', *William and Mary Quarterly*, 47 (1990), 503–22

——, *Black Rebellion in Barbados: The Struggle Against Slavery, 1627–1838* (Bridgetown, 1984)

——, 'Plantation Production and White "Proto-Slavery": White Indentured Servants and the Colonisation of the English West Indies, 1624–1645', *The Americas*, 41 (1985), 21–45

——, '"The Williams Effect": Eric Williams's Capitalism and Slavery and the Growth of West Indian Political Economy', in B. Solow and S. Engerman (eds), *British Capitalism and Caribbean Slavery: The Legacy of Eric Williams* (Cambridge, 2004), pp. 303–31

Bekale, Marc Mvé, 'Memories and mechanisms of resistance to the Atlantic slave trade: the Ekang Saga in West Central Africa's epic tale the Mvet', *Journal of African Cultural Studies*, 32 (2020), 99–113

Berlin, Ira, *Many Thousands Gone: The First Two Centuries of Slavery in North America* (Cambridge, MA, 1998)

Berry, Daimi Ramey, '"Broad is de road dat leads ter death": Human Capital and Enslaved Mortality', in Sven Beckert and Seth Rockman (eds), *Slavery's Capitalism: A New History of American Economic Development* (Philadelphia, 2016), pp. 146–62

Billings, Warren, 'The Cases of Fernando and Elizabeth Key: A Note on the Status of Blacks in Seventeenth-Century Virginia', *William and Mary Quarterly*, 3rd ser., 30 (1973), 467–74

Blackburn, Robin, *The Making of New World Slavery: From the Baroque to the Modern, 1492–1800* (London, 1997)

244

Blythe, Ronald, James Woodford, and John Beresford (eds), *The Diary of a Country Parson, 1758–1802* (Norwich, 1999)

Bohstedt, J., *The Politics of Provisions Food Riots: Moral Economy and Market Transition in England, c. 1550-1850* (Burlington, VT, 2010)

Bono, Salvatore, 'Slave Histories and Memories in the Mediterranean World', in Maria Fusaro, Colin Heywood, and Mohamed-Salah Omri (eds), *Trade and Cultural Exchange in the Early Modern Mediterranean: Braudel's Maritime Legacy* (London; New York, 2010), 97–116

Boose, Lynda E., '"The getting of a lawful race": racial discourse in early modern England and the unrepresentable black woman', in Margo Hendricks and Patricia A. Parker (eds), *Women, "Race", and Writing in the Early Modern Period* (London, 1994), pp. 35–54

Bowden, P.J., *The Wool Trade in Tudor and Stuart England* (London, 1962)

Breen, T.H., and Stephen Inness, *"Myne Owne Ground": Race and Freedom on Virginia's Eastern Shore, 1640–1676* (New York; Oxford, 1980)

Bremer, Francis J., *John Winthrop: America's Forgotten Founding Father* (Oxford, 2005)

Bridenbaugh, Carl, *Vexed and Troubled Englishmen, 1590–1660* (Oxford, 1968)

Brodt, Barbel, 'East Anglia', in David Michael Palliser (ed.), *The Cambridge Urban History of Britain: Volume 1, 600–1540* (Cambridge, 2000)

Brown, Christopher L., *Moral Capital: Foundations of British Abolitionism* (Chapel Hill, 2006)

Brown, Vincent, *The Reaper's Garden* (Cambridge, MA, 2008)

Browne, William, Percy Reaney, and Richard Wilson (eds), *A Dictionary of English Surnames* (London; New York, 2006)

Brubaker, Rogers, and Frederick Cooper, 'Beyond "Identity"', *Theory and Society*, 29 (2000), 1–47

Burnard, Trevor, *Mastery, Tyranny, and Desire: Thomas Thistlewood and his Slaves in the Anglo-Jamaican World* (Chapel Hill, 2004)

——, and G. Riello, 'Slavery and the new history of capitalism', *Journal of Global History*, 15 (2020), 225–44

——, and Kenneth Morgan, 'The Dynamics of the Slave Market and Slave Purchasing Patterns in Jamaica, 1655–1788', *William and Mary Quarterly*, 58 (2001), 205–28

——, and John Garrigus, *The Plantation Machine: Atlantic Capitalism in French Saint-Domingue and British Jamaica* (Philadelphia, 2016)

——, 'West Indian Identity in the Eighteenth Century', in Christopher Morris and John D. Garrigus (eds), *Assumed Identities: The Meanings of Race in the Atlantic World* (1st edn, Texas, 2010), 71–88

Bush, Jonathan A., 'The First Slave (and why he matters)', *Cardozo Law Review*, 18 (1996), 610–15

Bush, M.L., *The Pilgrimage of Grace: A Study of the Rebel Armies of October 1536* (Manchester, 1996)

Butcher, David, *Lowestoft, 1550–1750: Development and Change in a Suffolk Coastal Town* (Woodbridge, 2008)

—, *Medieval Lowestoft: The Origins and Growth of a Suffolk Coastal Community* (Woodbridge, 2016)

Butler, Kathleen Mary, *The Economics of Emancipation: Jamaica & Barbados, 1823–1843* (Chapel Hill, 1995)

Campbell, P.F., *Some Early Barbadian History* (Letchworth, 1993)

Campling, Arthur, *East Anglian Pedigrees* (Norfolk, 1940)

Canny, Nicholas, 'English Migration into and across the Atlantic during the Seventeenth and Eighteenth Centuries', in Nicholas Canny (ed.), *Europeans on the Move: Studies on European Migration, 1500–1800* (Oxford; New York, 1994), pp. 39–75

Carson, Jane, 'The Will of John Rolfe', *The Virginia Magazine of History and Biography*, 58 (1950), 58–65

Cawsey, Kathy, 'Disorienting Orientalism: Finding Saracens in Strange Places in Late Medieval English Manuscripts', *Exemplaria*, 21 (2009), 380–97

Chadwick, Esther, *Figures of Empire: Slavery and Portraiture in Eighteenth-Century Atlantic Britain* (New Haven, 2014)

—, '"This deepe and perfect glosse of Blacknesse": Colour, Colonialism, and *The Paston Treasure*'s Period Eye', in Andrew Moore, Nathan Flis, and Francesca Vanke (eds), *The Paston Treasure: Microcosm of the Known World* (New Haven; Norwich, 2018)

Charlesworth, A., *Social Protest in a Rural Society: The Spatial Diffusion of the Swing Disturbances 1830–31* (Norwich, 1979)

Chater, Kathleen, *Untold Histories: Black People in England and Wales during the Period of the British Slave Trade, c 1660–1807* (Manchester; New York, 2009)

Checkland, S.G., 'Finance for the West Indies, 1780–1815', *The Economic History Review*, NS, 10 (1958), 461–9

Chitty, C.W., 'Aliens in England in the Seventeenth Century to 1660', *Race & Class*, 11 (1969), 189–201

Christopher, Emma, *Slave Ship Sailors and Their Captive Cargoes, 1730–1807* (New York, 2006)

Coldham, Peter, *Emigrants from England to the American Colonies, 1773–1776* (Baltimore, MD, 1998)

Colley, Linda, *Captives: Britain, Empire and the World, 1600–1850* (London, 2002)

Coombs, John C., 'Others Not Christians in the Service of the English', *The Virginia Magazine of History and Biography*, 127 (2019), 212–38

Corfield, Penelope, 'East Anglia', in Peter Clark and David Michael Palliser (eds), *The Cambridge Urban History of Britain: Volume 2, 1540–1840* (Cambridge, 2000)

Costello, Ray, *Black Salt: Seafarers of African Descent on British Ships* (Liverpool, 2012)

Coster, W., *Baptism and Spiritual Kinship in Early Modern England* (London; New York, 2016)

——, '"From Fire and Water": The Responsibilities of Godparents in Early Modern England', in D. Wood (ed.), *The Church and Childhood, Studies in Church History*, 31 (Woodbridge, 1994), 301–12

Cressy, David, *Birth, Marriage and Death: Ritual, Religion and the Life Cycle in Tudor and Stuart England* (Oxford; New York, 1997)

Cummings, Brian (ed.), *The Book of Common Prayer: The Texts of 1549, 1559, and 1662* (Oxford, 2011)

Cundall, Frank, *Historic Jamaica* (London, 1915)

Curtin, Philip D., *The Rise and Fall of the Plantation Complex: Essays in Atlantic History* (Cambridge; New York, 1990)

Dabydeen, David, John Gilmore and Cecily Jones (eds), *Oxford Companion to Black British History* (Oxford; New York, 2007)

Darity, Jr., William, 'British Industry and the West Indies Plantations', *Social Science History*, 14 (1990) 117–49

Davies, C.S.L., 'Slavery and Protector Somerset: The Vagrancy Act of 1547', *The Economic History Review*, 2nd ser., 20 (1966), 533–49

Davis, David Brion, 'Foreword', in David Eltis and David Richardson, *Atlas of the Atlantic Slave Trade* (New Haven; London, 2010)

——, *Slavery and Human Progress* (New York, 1984)

——, *Inhuman Bondage: The Rise and Fall of Slavery in the New World* (Oxford, 2006)

Davis, Ralph, *The Rise of the Atlantic Economies* (London, 1973)

Davis, Robert C., *Christian Slaves, Muslim Masters: White Slavery in the Mediterranean, the Barbary Coast, and Italy, 1500–1800* (Basingstoke, 2004)

——, 'The Geography of Slaving in the Early Modern Mediterranean', *Journal of Medieval and Early Modern Studies*, 37 (2007), 57–74

de Vries, Jan, *The Industrious Revolution: Consumer Behaviour and the Household Economy, 1650 to the Present* (New York, 2008)

Deneen, Patrick J., *Why Liberalism Failed* (New Haven, 2019)

Dimmock, Matthew, 'Converting and Not Converting "Strangers" in Early Modern London', *Journal of Early Modern History*, 17 (2013), 457–78

Donoghue, John, '"Out of the Land of Bondage": The English Revolution and the Atlantic Origins of Abolition', *American Historical Review*, 115 (2010), 943–74

Drescher, Seymour, *Econocide: British Slavery in the Era of Abolition* (Pittsburgh, 1977)

——, 'Free Labour versus Slave Labour, The British and Caribbean Cases', in Stanley L. Engerman (ed.), *Terms of Labour: Slavery, Serfdom, and Free Labour* (Stanford, CA, 1999)

——, 'White Atlantic? The Choice for African Slave Labour in the Plantation Americas', in David Eltis, Frank D. Lewis, and Kenneth L. Sokoloff (eds), *Slavery in the Development of the Americas* (Cambridge; New York, 2004), 31–69

Dresser, Madge, 'Slavery and West Country Houses', in Madge Dresser and Andrew Hann (eds), *Slavery and the British Country House* (Swindon, 2013), pp. 12–29

—, *Slavery Obscured: The Social History of the Slave Trade in an English Provincial Port* (New York, 2001)

Duffy, E., *The Stripping of the Altars: Traditional Religion in England, 1400–1580* (New Haven, CT; London, 1992)

Dunn, Penelope, 'Trade', in Carole Rawcliffe and Richard Wilson (eds), *Medieval Norwich* (London; New York, 2004), 213–34

Dunn, Richard S., *Sugar and Slaves: The Rise of the Planter Class in the English West Indies, 1624–1713* (Chapel Hill, 1972)

Dyer, Alan D., and David M. Palliser (eds), *The Diocesan Population Returns for 1563 and 1603* (Oxford, 2005)

Ecclestone, A.W., and J.C. Ecclestone, *The Rise of Great Yarmouth* (Norwich, 1959)

Edwards, Paul, 'The Early African Presence in the British Isles,' in Jagdish S. Gundara and Ian Duffield (eds), *Essays on the History of Blacks in Britain: From Roman Times to the Mid-twentieth Century* (Aldershot, 1992), pp. 9–29

Edwards, Paul, and James Walvin, 'Africans in Britain, 1500–1800', in Martin L. Kilson and Robert I. Rotberg (eds), *The African Diaspora: Interpretive Essays* (Cambridge, MA, 1976), pp. 173–204

El Hamel, Chouki, *Black Morocco: A History of Slavery, Race, and Islam* (Cambridge, 2012)

Eltis, David, 'Coerced and Free Migrations from the Old World to the New', in David Eltis (ed.), *Coerced and Free Migration: Global Perspectives* (Stanford, CA, 2002), pp. 33–74

—, 'New Estimates of Exports from Barbados and Jamaica, 1665–1701', *William and Mary Quarterly*, 3rd ser., 52 (1995)

—, *The Rise of African Slavery in the Americas* (Cambridge, 2000)

—, and David Richardson, 'Prices of Slaves Newly Arrived in the Americas, 1673–1865', in David Eltis, Frank D. Lewis, and Kenneth L. Sokoloff (eds), *Slavery in the Development of the Americas* (Cambridge, 2004), pp. 181–218

—, and Stanley L. Engerman, 'The Importance of Slavery and the Slave Trade to Industrializing Britain', *The Journal of Economic History*, 60 (2000), 123–44

Emmer, P.C., *The Dutch Slave Trade, 1500–1850* (trans. Chris Emery) (New York; Oxford, 2006)

Engerman, Stanley L., 'Europe, the Lesser Antilles and Economic Expansion, 1600–1800', in Robert L. Paquette and Stanley L. Engerman (eds), *The Lesser Antilles in the Age of European Expansion* (Gainsville, FL, 1996), 147–65

Ewing, W.C., 'The Norwich Conspiracy of 1570', *Norfolk Archaeology*, 5 (1859)

Fields, Barbara J., 'Ideology and Race in American History', in J. Morgan Kousser and James M. McPherson (eds), *Region, Race and Reconstruction: Essays in Honour of C. Vann Woodward* (New York, 1982), pp. 143–77

Finley, Moses, *Ancient Slavery and Modern Ideology* (New York, 1980)

Fletcher, Anthony, and Diarmaid MacCulloch, *Tudor Rebellions*, 6th edn (London, 2015)

Ford, Charles, 'People as Property', *Oxford Art Journal*, 25 (2002), 3–16

French, Anna, 'Raising Christian children in early modern England: Salvation, education and the family', *Theology*, 116 (2013), 93–102

——, '"Trembling and groaning depart": Disputing the devil in Christian baptism', *Theology*, 118 (2015), 331–7

French, Christopher J., 'Productivity in the Atlantic Shipping Industry: A Quantitative Study', *Journal of Interdisciplinary History*, 17 (1987), 613–38

Fryer, Peter, *Staying Power: Black People in Britain since 1504* (Atlantic Highlands, NJ, 1984)

Fumerton, Patricia, *Unsettled: The Culture of Mobility and the Working Poor in Early Modern England* (Chicago; London, 2006)

Games, Alison, *Migration and the Origins of the English Atlantic World* (Cambridge, MA, 1999)

Gaskill, Malcolm, *Between Two Worlds: How the English Became Americans* (Oxford, 2014)

George, M. Dorothy, *London Life in the Eighteenth Century* (London, 1926)

Gerbner, Katharine, 'The Ultimate Sin: Christianising Slaves in Barbados in the Seventeenth Century', *Slavery and Abolition*, 31 (2010), 57–73

Gerzina, Gretchen, *Black England: Life Before Emancipation* (London, 1995)

Ghirelli, Michael, *A List of Emigrants from England to America, 1682–1692* (Baltimore, 1989), pp. 28–75

Given-Wilson, Chris, 'Service, Serfdom and English Labour Legislation, 1350–1500', in Anne Curry and Elizabeth Matthew (eds), *Concepts and Patterns of Service in the Later Middle Ages* (Woodbridge, 2000), pp. 21–37

Goetz, Rebecca Anne, 'Rethinking the "Unthinking Decision": Old Questions and New Problems in the History of Slavery and Race in the Colonial South', *Journal of Southern History*, 75 (2009), 599–612

——, *The Baptism of Early Virginia: How Christianity Created Race* (Baltimore, 2012)

——, '"The Child Should Be Made a Christian": Baptism, Race, and Identity in the Seventeenth-century Chesapeake', in Morris and Garrigus (eds), *Assumed*, pp. 46–70

Goodman, Jordan, *Tobacco in History: The Cultures of Dependence* (London; New York, 1993)

Grady, Kyle, 'Zora Neale Hurston and Humoral Theory: Comparing Racial Concepts from Early Modern England and Post-Abolition America', *Shakespeare Studies*, 46 (2018), 144–9

Gragg, Larry, *Englishmen Transplanted: The English colonization of Barbados, 1627–1660* (Oxford; New York, 2003)

Grant, Daragh, '"Civilizing" the Colonial Subject: The Co-Evolution of State and Slavery in South Carolina, 1670–1739', *Comparative Studies in Society and History*, 57 (2015), 606–36

Gray, Todd, *Devon and the Slave Trade: Documents on African Enslavement, Abolition and Emancipation from 1562 to 1867* (Exeter, 2007)

Greenfield, Sidney M., 'Madeira and the Beginnings of New World Sugar Cane Cultivation and Plantation Slavery: A Study in Institution Building', in Vera Rubin and Arthur Tuden (eds), *Comparative Perspectives on Slavery in New World Plantation Societies* (New York; Harmondsworth, 1977), pp. 536–52

Griffin, Carl, 'Swing, Swing Redivivus, or Something After Swing? On the Death Throes of a Protest Movement, December 1830–December 1833', *International Review of Social History*, 54 (2009), 459–97

—, '"There Was No Law to Punish That Offence": Re-Assessing "Captain Swing": Rural Luddism and Rebellion in East Kent, 1830–31', *Southern History*, 22 (2000), 131–63

Griffiths, Elizabeth (ed.), *Her Price is Above Pearls: Family and Farming Records of Alice Le Strange, 1617–1656* (Norfolk, 2015)

—, '"A Country Life": Sir Hamon Lestrange of Hunstanton, Norfolk (1583–1654)', in Richard W. Hoyle (ed.), *Custom, Improvement and the Landscape in Early Modern Britain* (Farnham, Surrey; Burlington, VT, 2011)

Guard, Timothy, *Chivalry, Kingship and Crusade: The English Experience in the Fourteenth Century* (Cambridge, 2013)

Guasco, Michael, *Slaves and Englishmen: Human Bondage in the Early Modern Atlantic World* (Philadelphia, PA, 2014)

Habib, Imtiaz, *Black Lives in the English Archives, 1500–1677: Imprints of the Invisible* (Aldershot, 2008)

—, 'Sir Peter Negro, and the blacks of early modern England: Colonial inscription and postcolonial excavation', *Literature Interpretation Theory*, 9 (1998), 15–30

Hacker, J. David, 'From "20. and odd" to 10 million: the growth of the slave population in the United States', *Slavery & Abolition*, 41 (2020), 840–55

Haigh, Christopher, 'Liturgy and Liberty: The Controversy over the Book of Common Prayer, 1660–1663', *Journal of Anglican Studies*, 11 (2013), 32–64.

Hall, Kim, 'Guess Who's Coming to Dinner? Colonization and Miscegenation in "The Merchant of Venice"', *Renaissance Drama*, 23 (1992), 87–111

—, *Things of Darkness: Economies of Race and Gender in Early Modern England* (Ithaca, NY, 1995)

—, 'Reading What Isn't There: "Black" Studies in Early Modern England', *Stanford Humanities Review*, 3 (1993), 22–33

Hamilton, Douglas, *Scotland, the Caribbean and the Atlantic World 1750–1820* (Manchester, 2005)

Hancock, David, *Citizens of the World: London Merchants and the Integration of the British Atlantic Community, 1735–1785* (Cambridge, 1995)

Handler, Jerome S., 'Custom and law: The status of enslaved Africans in seventeenth-century Barbados', *Slavery & Abolition*, 37 (2016), 233–55

—, with M. Conner and K. Jacobi, *Searching for a Slave Cemetery in Barbados, West Indies: A Bioarchaeological and Ethnohistorical Investigation* (Southern Illinois University: Center for Archaeological Investigations, Research Paper No. 59, 1989)

——, and Matthew C. Reilly, 'Contesting "White Slavery" in the Caribbean: Enslaved Africans and European Indentured Servants in Seventeenth-Century Barbados', *New West Indian Guide*, 91 (2017), 30–55

Hanks, Patrick, Richard Coates, and Peter McClure (eds), *The Oxford Dictionary of Family Names in Britain and Ireland* (Oxford, 2016)

Hansen, David, *Dempsey's People: A Folio of British Street Portraits 1824–1844* (Canberra, 2017)

——, '"Remarkable Characters": John Dempsey and the Representation of the Urban Poor in Regency Britain', *The British Art Journal*, 11 (2010), 75–88

Hardman Moore, Susan, *Abandoning America: Life-stories from Early New England* (Woodbridge, 2013)

Harper, Raymond L., *A History of Chesapeake, Virginia* (Charleston, 2008)

Harvey, I.M.W., 'Was there popular politics in fifteenth-century England?', in R.H. Britnell and A.J. Pollard (eds), *The McFarlane Legacy: Studies in Late Medieval Politics and Society* (Stroud; New York, 1995), 155–74

Hatcher, John, 'English Serfdom and Villeinage: Towards a Reassessment', *Past & Present*, 90 (1981), 3–39

Helfman, Tara, 'The Court of Vice Admiralty at Sierra Leone and the Abolition of the West African Slave Trade', *Yale Law Journal*, 115 (2006), 1122–56

Heller-Roazen, Daniel, *The Enemy of All: Piracy and the Law of Nations* (New York, 2009)

Heywood, Linda M., and John K. Thornton, *Central Africans, Atlantic Creoles, and the Foundation of the Americas, 1585–1660* (New York, 2007)

——, 'In Search of the 1619 African Arrivals', *The Virginia Magazine of History and Biography*, 127 (2019), 200–11

Heywood, Stephen, 'The Chapel of St George King Street, Great Yarmouth', *Norfolk Historic Environment Record No. 4336* (2009)

Higginbotham Jr., A. Leon, *In the Matter of Colour: Race and the American Legal Process: The Colonial Period* (New York, 1978)

——, and Barbara Kopytoff, 'Racial Purity and Interracial Sex in the Law of Colonial and Antebellum Virginia', in Werner Sollors (ed.), *Interracialism: Black-White Intermarriage in American History, Literature, and Law* (Oxford; New York, 2000), pp. 81–140

Higman, B.W., *Jamaica Surveyed: Plantation Maps and Plans of the Eighteenth and Nineteenth Centuries* (Kingston, Jamaica, 2001)

——, *Montpelier, Jamaica: A Plantation Community in Slavery and Freedom, 1739–1912* (Barbados, 1998)

——, *Plantation Jamaica, 1750–1850: Capital and Control in a Colonial Economy* (Kingston, Jamaica, 2008)

——, 'The West India Interest in Parliament, 1807–1833', *Historical Studies*, 13 (1967), 1–19

Hill, Christopher, *The World Turned Upside Down: Radical Ideas during the English Revolution* (Harmondsworth, 1975)

——, 'The Norman Yoke', in Christopher Hill (ed.), *Puritanism and Revolution: Studies in Interpretation of the English Revolution of the Seventeenth Century* (London, 1969)

Hilton, R.H., 'Freedom and Villeinage in England', *Past & Present*, 31 (1965), 3–19

Hindle, Steve, *The State and Social Change in Early Modern England, c. 1550–1640* (Basingstoke, 2000)

Hiskey, Christine, *Holkham: The Social, Architectural and Landscape History of a Great English Country House* (Norwich, 2016)

Hobsbawm, E.J., and G. Rudé, *Captain Swing* (London, 1970)

Horn, James, *Adapting to a New World: English Society in the Seventeenth Century Chesapeake* (Chapel Hill; London, 1994)

Hotten, John C. (ed.), *The original lists of persons of quality: emigrants; religious exiles ... and others who went from Great Britain to the American plantations 1600–1700* (New York, 1931)

Howes, David, 'Introduction: Empires of the Senses', in David Howes (ed.), *Empire of the Senses: The Sensual Culture Reader* (Oxford; New York, 2005)

Hudson, Pat, 'Slavery, the slave trade and economic growth: a contribution to the debate', in Catherine Hall, Nicholas Draper, and Keith McClelland (eds), *Emancipation and the Making of the British Imperial World* (Manchester, 2014), pp. 36–59

Hughes, Paul L., and James F. Larkin (eds), *Tudor Royal Proclamations Vol. 3: The Later Tudors, 1588–1603* (New Haven, 1969)

Hyams, Paul, 'The Proof of Villein Status in the Common Law', *English Historical Review*, 89 (1974), 721–49

Inikori, Joseph E., *Africans and the Industrial Revolution in England* (Cambridge, 2002)

——, 'Slavery and the Development of Industrial Capitalism in England', in Barbara Solow and Stanley Engerman (eds), *British Capitalism and Caribbean Slavery* (Cambridge, 1987), pp. 79–101

Ives, Eric, *The Reformation Experience: Living Through the Turbulent 16th Century* (Oxford, 2012)

James, Philip, and M.H. Combe Martin, 'General Notes', *Journal of the Royal Society of Arts*, 117 (1968), 34–45

Jewson, C.B., *The Baptists in Norfolk* (London, 1957)

——, *The Jacobin City* (Glasgow, 1975)

Jones, Eldred D., *The Elizabethan Image of Africa* (Washington, DC, 1971)

Jones, Peter, 'Swing, Speenhamland and Rural Social Relations: the "Moral Economy" of the English Crowd in the Nineteenth Century', *Social History*, 32 (2007), 271–90

Jordan, Don, and Michael Walsh, *White Cargo: The Forgotten History of Britain's White Slaves in America* (New York, 2007)

Jordan, Winthrop D., *White Over Black: American Attitudes Toward the Negro, 1550–1812* (2nd edn) (Chapel Hill, 2012)

Kaplan, Paul H.D., 'Italy, 1490–1700', in David Bindman and Henry Louis Gates Jr. (eds), *From the "Age of Discovery" to the Age of Abolition: Artists of the Renaissance and Baroque*, Vol. 3 (Cambridge, MA; London, 2010), 95–9

Kaufmann, Miranda, *Black Tudors: The Untold Story* (London, 2017)

—, 'Caspar Van Senden, Sir Thomas Sherley and the Blackamoor Project', *Historical Research*, 81 (2008), 366–71

—, '"Making the Beast with Two Backs": Interracial Relationships in Early Modern England', *Literature Compass*, 12 (2015), 22–37

—, 'Sir Pedro Negro: What Colour was His Skin?', *Notes and Queries*, 55 (2008), 142–6

Kennet, David H., 'Caister Castle, Norfolk and the Transport of Brick and other Building Materials in the Middle Ages', in Robert Odell Bork and Andrea Kann (eds), *The Art, Science, and Technology of Medieval Travel* (London, 2008), 55–67

Kerling, N.J.M., 'Aliens in the County of Norfolk, 1436–85', *Norfolk Archaeology*, 33 (1963)

Ketton-Cremer, R.W., *A Norfolk Gallery* (London, 1948), pp. 56–94

—, *Norfolk Assembly* (London, 1957)

Knutson, Rosalyn L., 'A Caliban in St Mildred Poultry', in Tetsuo Kishi, Roger Pringle, and Stanley Wells (eds), *Shakespeare and Cultural Traditions: the Selected Proceedings of the International Shakespeare Association World Congress, Tokyo, 1991* (Newark, NJ, 1994), pp. 110–26

Kolchin, Peter, 'Variations of Slavery in the Atlantic World', *William and Mary Quarterly*, 59 (2002), 551–4

Korhonen, Anu, 'Washing the Ethiopian white: conceptualising black skin in Renaissance England', in T.F. Earle and K.J.P. Lowe (eds), *Black Africans in Renaissance Europe* (Cambridge, 2007), 94–112

Kowaleski, M., 'The Shipmaster as Entrepreneur in Medieval England', in Ben Dodds and Christian Liddy (eds), *Commercial Activity, Markets and Entrepreneurs in the Middle Ages* (Woodbridge, 2011)

Lewis, Mary, 'Work and the Adolescent in Medieval England AD 900–1550: The Osteological Evidence', *Medieval Archaeology*, 60 (2016), 138–71

Lewis, Tamara E., '"Like Devils out of Hell": Reassessing the African Presence in Early Modern England', *Black Theology*, 14 (2016), 107–20

Linebaugh, Peter, and Marcus Rediker, *The Many-Headed Hydra: Sailors, Slaves, Commoners, and the Hidden History of the Revolutionary Atlantic* (2nd edn) (Boston, 2013)

Little, Kenneth, *Negroes in Britain: A Study of Racial Relations in English Society* (London, 1948)

Livesay, Daniel, *Children of Uncertain Fortune: Mixed-Race Jamaicans in Britain and the Atlantic Family, 1733–1833* (Williamsburg, VA; Chapel Hill, 2018)

Loomba, Ania, *Gender, Race, Renaissance Drama* (Manchester, 1989)

—, 'Periodization, Race, and Global Contact', *Journal of Medieval and Early Modern Studies*, 37 (2007), 595–620

Lowe, Kate, 'The Stereotyping of Black Africans in Renaissance Europe', in T.F. Earle and K.J.P. Lowe (eds), *Black Africans in Renaissance Europe* (Cambridge, 2010), pp. 17–47

——, 'Visible Lives: Black Gondoliers and Other Black Africans in Renaissance Venice', *Renaissance Quarterly*, 66 (2013), 412–52

Lugo-Ortiz, Agnes, and Angela Rosenthal, *Slave Portraiture in the Atlantic World* (New York, 2013)

MacCulloch, Diarmuid, 'Bondmen under the Tudors', in Claire Cross, David Loades, and J.J. Scarisbrick (eds), *Law and Government under the Tudors* (Cambridge, 1988)

——, 'Kett's Rebellion in Context', in Paul Slack (ed.), *Rebellion, Popular Protest, and the Social Order in Early Modern England* (New York, 1984), 36–59

Maguire, Richard, 'Presenting the History of Africans in Provincial Britain: Norfolk as a Case Study', *History*, 99 (2014), 819–38

——, 'The Black Middle Class in nineteenth and early twentieth-century Norfolk', *Norfolk Archaeology*, 67 (2017), 511–22

Maitland, F.W., *Domesday Book and Beyond: Three Essays in the Early History of England* (Cambridge, 1897)

Matthews, C.M., *English Surnames* (London, 1966)

McCusker, John J., and Russell R. Menard, *The Economy of British America, 1607–1789* (Chapel Hill, 1985)

McKinley, Richard Alexander, *Norfolk and Suffolk Surnames in the Middle Ages* (Volume 2 of English Surnames Series) (London, 1975)

Menard, Russell R., *Sweet Negotiations: Sugar, Slavery, and Plantation Agriculture in Early Barbados* (Charlottesville; London, 2006)

——, 'Reckoning with Williams: "Capitalism and Slavery" and the Reconstruction of Early American History', *Callaloo*, 20 *Eric Williams and the Postcolonial Caribbean: A Special Issue* (1997), pp. 791–9

Meniketti, M., 'The Bush Hill Sugar Plantation: A West Indies Case Study in Developmental Capitalism', *Historical Archaeology*, 54 (2020), 212–39

Metters, G. Alan, 'Corn, Coal and Commerce: Merchants and Coastal Trading in Early Jacobean King's Lynn', *International Journal of Maritime History*, 23 (2011), 49–178

Michaud, Francine, 'From apprentice to wage-earner: child labour before and after the Black Death', in J Rosenthal (ed.), *Essays on Medieval Childhood: Responses to Recent Debates* (Donnington, 2007), pp. 73–90

Miller, W.E., 'Negroes in Elizabethan London', *Notes and Queries*, 8 (1961), 138

Minns, Chris, and Patrick Wallis, 'Rules and reality: quantifying the practice of apprenticeship in early modern England', *Economic History Review*, 65 (2012), 556–79

Mintz, Sidney, *Sweetness and Power: The Place of Sugar in Modern History* (New York, 1985)

Moens, W.J.C., *The Walloons and their Church at Norwich: 1565–1832* (London, 1888)

Molineaux, Catherine, *Faces of Perfect Ebony: Encountering Atlantic Slavery in Imperial Britain* (Cambridge, MA; London, 2012)

Morgan, Edmund S., *American Slavery, American Freedom: The Ordeal of Colonial Virginia* (New York, 1975)

Morgan, Kenneth, *Bristol and the Atlantic Trade in the Eighteenth Century* (Cambridge, 1993)

—, 'Building British Atlantic Port Cities: Bristol and Liverpool in the eighteenth century', in Daniel Maudlin and Bernard L. Herman (eds), *Building the British Atlantic World: Spaces, Places, and Material Culture, 1600–1850* (Chapel Hill, 2016), pp. 212–28

—, 'Liverpool's Dominance in the British Slave Trade, 1740–1807', in David Richardson, Suzanne Schwarz, and Anthony Tibbles (eds), *Liverpool and Transatlantic Slavery* (Liverpool, 2007), 14–42

—, 'The Economic Development of Bristol, 1700–1850', in Madge Dresser and Philip Ollerenshaw (eds), *The Making of Modern Bristol* (Bristol, 1996), 48–75

Morgan, Philip D., *Slave Counterpoint: Black Culture in the Eighteenth-Century Chesapeake and Lowcountry* (Chapel Hill; London, 1998)

—, 'Black Experiences in Britain's Maritime World', in D. Cannadine (ed.), *Empire, the Sea and Global History* (Basingstoke, 2007), 105–33

—, 'British Encounters with Africans and African Americans, 1600–1780', in Bernard Bailyn and Philip Morgan (eds), *Strangers within the Realm: Cultural Margins of the First British Empire* (Chapel Hill, 1991)

Morris, Thomas D., *Southern Slavery and the Law, 1619–1860* (Chapel Hill, 1996)

Murphy, Martin, 'The Barbary Pirates', *Mediterranean Quarterly*, 24 (2013), 19–42

Myers, Norma, *Reconstructing the Black Past: Blacks in Britain 1780–1830* (London; Portland, OR, 1996)

Nadalo, Stephanie, 'Negotiating Slavery in a Tolerant Frontier: Livorno's Turkish Bagno (1547–1747)', *Mediaevalia*, 32 (2011), 275–324

Neeson, J.M., *Commoners: Common Right, Enclosure and Social Change in England, 1700–1820* (Cambridge, 1993)

Niebrzydowski, Sue, 'The Sultana and Her Sisters: Black Women in the British Isles before 1530', *Women's History Review*, 10 (2001), 187–210

Nisbet, Stuart M., 'Sugar and the Early Mercantile Identity of Glasgow', *Scottish Archives*, 19 (2013), 65–82

O'Brien, Ellen, 'Sites of Servant Memory in the English Country House: Frederick Gorst and the Gladstone Vase', *Life Writing*, 16 (2019), 369–84

Oestmann, Cord, *Lordship and Community: The Lestrange Family and the Village of Hunstanton, Norfolk* (Woodbridge, 1994)

Oldham, James, *English Common Law in the Age of Mansfield* (Chapel Hill, 2004)

Onyeka, *Blackamoores: Africans in Tudor England, Their Presence, Status and Origins* (London, 2013)

O'Shaughnessy, Andrew Jackson, 'The Formation of a Commercial Lobby: The West India Interest, British Colonial Policy and the American Revolution', *The Historical Journal*, 40 (1997), 71–95

——, *An Empire Divided: The American Revolution and the British Caribbean* (Philadelphia, PA, 2000)

Parent, Anthony, *Foul Means: The Formation of a Slave Society in Virginia, 1660–1740* (Chapel Hill, 2003)

Pares, Richard, *A West India Fortune* (London, 1950)

Patten, John, 'Population Distribution in Norfolk and Suffolk during the Sixteenth and Seventeenth Centuries', *Transactions of the Institute of British Geographers*, 65 (1975), 45–65

Paygrave-Moore, Peter (ed.), 'King's Lynn Land Tax Assessment 1693' (Transcribed) (Norfolk, 2000)

Pelling, M., 'Child health as a social value in early modern England', *Social History of Medicine*, 1 (1988), 135–64

Pelteret, David A.E., *Slavery and Early Medieval England from the Reign of Alfred to the Early Twelfth Century* (Woodbridge, 1995)

Pestana, Carla Gardina, *The English Atlantic in an Age of Revolution, 1640–1661* (Cambridge, MA; London, 2004)

Pitt-Rivers, Julian, 'Race, Colour and Class in Central America and the Andes', in John J. Johnson, Peter J. Bakewell, and Meredith D. Dodge (eds), *Readings in Latin American History, Volume II, The Modern Experience* (Durham, 1985), pp. 313–28

Poole, S., '"A Lasting and Salutary Warning": Incendiarism, Rural Order and England's Last Scene of Crime Execution', *Rural History*, 19 (2008), 163–77

Post, Charles, 'Agrarian Class Structure and Economic Development in Colonial British North America: The Place of the American Revolution in the Origins of US Capitalism', *Journal of Agrarian Change*, 9 (2009), 453–83

Postma, Johannes, *The Dutch in the Atlantic Slave Trade, 1600–1815* (Cambridge, 2008)

Pound, John F. (ed.), *The Norwich Census of the Poor 1570* (London, 1967)

——, 'An Elizabethan Census of the Poor: The Treatment of Vagrancy in Norwich, 1570–1580', *University of Birmingham Historical Journal*, 8 (1961–2), 135–51

Quinn, David B., 'Turks, Moors, Blacks and Others in Drake's West Indian Voyage', *Terrae Incognitae*, 14 (1982), 97–104

Rabin, Dana, '"In a Country of Liberty?": Slavery, Villeinage and the Making of Whiteness in the Somerset Case (1772)', *History Workshop Journal*, 72 (2011), 5–29

Rainbird Clarke, R., *East Anglia* (Wakefield, 1975)

Rawley, James A., *London, Metropolis of the Slave Trade* (Columbia, 2003)

——, and Stephen D. Behrendt, *The Transatlantic Slave Trade: A History* (Lincoln, NE; London, 2005)

Ray, Michael, 'A Black Slave on the Run in Thirteenth-Century England', *Nottingham Medieval Studies*, 51 (2007), 111-19

Rediker, Marcus, *Between the Devil and the Deep Blue Sea: Merchant Seamen, Pirates, and the Anglo-American Maritime World, 1700-1750* (Cambridge, 1987)

Reed, M., 'The Peasantry in Nineteenth-Century England: A Neglected Class?', *History Workshop*, 18 (1984), 53-76

——, 'Nineteenth-Century Rural England: A Case for "Peasant Studies"', *Journal of Peasant Studies*, 14 (1986), 78-99

Richards, Paul, 'The Hinterland and Overseas Trade of King's Lynn 1205-1537: An Introduction', in Klaus Friedland and Paul Richards (eds), *Essays in Hanseatic History: The King's Lynn Symposium 1998* (Dereham, 2005), pp. 10-21

Richardson, David, 'Slavery and Bristol's "Golden Age"', *Slavery and Abolition*, 26 (2005), 35-54

Riches, Naomi, *The Agricultural Revolution in Norfolk* (London, 1967)

Roberts, Justin, *Slavery and the Enlightenment in the British Atlantic, 1750-1807* (New York, 2013)

Rodger, N.A.M., 'The Law and Language of Private Naval Warfare', *The Mariner's Mirror*, 100 (2014), 5-16

Rolfe, A. Neville, 'The Ancestral Home of John Rolfe', *William and Mary Quarterly*, 13 (1933), 137

Rollison, David, 'Exploding England: the dialectics of mobility and settlement in early modern England', *Social History*, 24 (1999), 1-16

Rommelse, Gijs, *The Second Anglo-Dutch War (1665-1667)* (Hilversum, 2006)

Rönnbäck, Klas, 'Sweet business: quantifying the value added in the British colonial sugar trade in the 18th century', *Revista de Historia Económica/Journal of Iberian and Latin American Economic History*, 32 (2014), 223-45

——, 'On the economic importance of the slave plantation complex to the British economy during the eighteenth century: a value-added approach', *Journal of Global History*, 13 (2018), pp. 309-27, at p. 319.

Rorabaugh, W.J., *The Craft Apprentice: From Franklin to the Machine Age in America* (New York; Oxford, 1988)

Rose, Susan, *England's Medieval Navy 1066-1509* (Havertown, 2013)

Rosenheim, James A., 'Robert Doughty of Hanworth: A Restoration Magistrate', *Norfolk Archaeology*, 38 (1983), 296-9

Rubin, Alfred P., *The Law of Piracy* (Newport, 1988)

Ruddock, Alwyn A., 'Alien Merchants in Southampton in the Later Middle Ages', *English Historical Review*, 61 (1946), 1-17

Rushforth, Brett, '"A Little Flesh We Offer You": The Origins of Indian Slavery in New France', *William and Mary Quarterly*, 60 (2003), 777-808

Ryden, David Beck, *West Indian Slavery and British Abolition, 1783-1807* (Cambridge; New York, 2009)

Rye, C.G., and J.G. Hurst, 'Medieval Pottery from Great Yarmouth', *Norfolk Archaeology*, 34 (1968), 279-92

Sacks, David Harris, and Michael Lynch, 'Ports 1540–1700', in David Michael Palliser, Peter Clark, and Martin J. Daunton, *The Cambridge Urban History of Britain*, Volume 2 (Cambridge, 2000), pp. 377–424

Samson, Ross, 'The End of Medieval Slavery', in Allen J. Frantzen and Douglas Moffat (eds), *The Work of Work: Servitude, Slavery, and Labour in Medieval England* (Glasgow, 1994), pp. 95–124

Saul, A., 'The Herring Industry at Great Yarmouth, 1280–1400', *Norfolk Archaeology*, 38 (1983), 38–41

——, 'English Towns in the Late Middle Ages: the Case of Great Yarmouth', *Journal of Medieval History*, 8 (1982), 75–88

Savage, M., 'Space, networks and class formation', in N. Kirk (ed.), *Social Class and Marxism: Defences and Challenges* (Abingdon; New York, 1996), pp. 58–86

Schama, Simon, *Rough Crossings* (London, 2005)

Schwartz, Stuart B., *Sugar Plantations in the Formation of Brazilian Society: Bahia, 1550–1835* (Cambridge, 1985)

Schwarz, Suzanne, 'Reconstructing the Life Histories of Liberated Africans: Sierra Leone in the Early Nineteenth Century', *History in Africa*, 39 (2012), 175–207

——, 'Extending the African Names Database: New Evidence from Sierra Leone', *African Economic History*, 38 (2010), 137–63

Seaman, Peter (ed.), *Norfolk Hearth Tax Exemption Certificates 1670–1674: Norwich, Great Yarmouth, King's Lynn and Thetford* (London; Norwich, 2001)

Sheridan, Richard B., *Sugar and Slavery: An Economic History of the British West Indies, 1623–1775* (Kingston, 1994)

——, 'Planter and historian: the career of William Beckford of Jamaica and England, 1744–1799', *The Jamaican Historical Review*, 4 (1964), 36–58

Sherwood, Marika, 'Blacks in Tudor England', *History Today*, 53 (October 2003), 40–2

Sluiter, Engel, 'New Light on the "20. and Odd Negroes" Arriving in Virginia, August 1619', *William and Mary Quarterly*, 54 (1997), 395–8

Smith, S.D., *Slavery, Family, and Gentry Capitalism in the British Atlantic: The World of the Lascelles, 1648–1834* (Cambridge, 2006)

——, 'Gedney Clarke of Salem and Barbados: Transatlantic Super-Merchant', *The New England Quarterly*, 76 (2003), 499–549

Smith, Woodruff D., *Consumption and the Making of Respectability, 1660–1800* (New York; London, 2002)

Snell, K.D.M., 'The apprenticeship system in British history: the fragmentation of a cultural institution', *History of Education*, 25 (1996), 303–21

——, 'The culture of local xenophobia', *Social History*, 28 (2003), 1–30

Sommers, Susan Mitchell, *Parliamentary Politics of a County and Its Town: General Elections in Suffolk and Ipswich in the Eighteenth Century* (Westport, CT; London, 2002)

Spufford, M., *Contrasting Communities in the Sixteenth and Seventeenth Centuries* (Cambridge, 1974)

Spurdle, Frederick G., *Early West Indian Government: Showing the Progress of Government in Barbados, Jamaica and the Leeward Islands, 1660–1783* (Palmerston North, New Zealand, 1962)

Squires, William Henry Tappey, *Through Centuries Three: A Short History of the People of Virginia* (Portsmouth, VA, 1929)

St Clair, William, *The Grand Slave Emporium* (London, 2006)

Starkey, David J., 'Voluntaries and Sea Robbers: A review of the academic literature on privateering, corsairing, buccaneering and piracy', *The Mariner's Mirror*, 97 (2011), 127–47

Stirland, A., *Men of the Mary Rose: Raising the Dead* (Stroud, 2005)

Strong, James, *New Exhaustive Concordance of the Bible* (Nashville, c.1985)

Sykes, Peter (ed.), *Borough of King's Lynn 1524–1835 Part One: An Index of Mayors, Aldermen, Common Councillors, Officials and some others* (Norwich, 2002)

——, 'King's Lynn Borough Records: The Quit Rental of 1697, An Annotated Transcription' (Norfolk, 2004)

——, 'King's Lynn. The Poll Tax and Aid of 1689: Annotated and Indexed' (Norfolk, 2005)

——, 'Notes on Houses in the Riverside Streets of King's Lynn and their known Owners and Tenants up to 1849' (Norfolk, 2003)

Tate, W.E., *The Parish Chest: A Study of the Records of Parochial Administration in England* (Chichester, 1983)

Tattersfield, Nigel, *The Forgotten Trade: comprising the log of the Daniel and Henry of 1700 and accounts of the slave trade from the minor ports of England, 1698–1725* (London, 1991)

Taylor, Charles, *A Secular Age* (Cambridge, MA; London, 2007)

Taylor, Iain, 'One For the (Farm) Workers? Perpetrator Risk and Victim Risk Transfer During the "Sevenoaks Fires" of 1830', *Rural History*, 28 (2017), 137–59

Temperley, Howard, *White Dreams, Black Africa: the Antislavery Expedition to the Niger, 1841–1842* (New Haven, CT; London, 1991)

Thomas, Hugh, *The Slave Trade: the Story of the Atlantic Trade, 1440–1870* (New York, 1999)

Thompson, Alvin O., 'Race and Colour Prejudices and the Origin of the Trans-Atlantic Slave Trade', *Caribbean Studies*, 16 (1976-7), 29–59

Thompson, E.P., *The Making of the English Working Class* (London, 1963)

——, 'The Moral Economy of the English Crowd in the Eighteenth Century', *Past and Present*, 50 (1971), 76–136

Thompson, Roger, *Mobility and Migration: East Anglian Founders of New England, 1629–1640* (Amherst, 1994)

Thorndale, William, 'The Virginia Census of 1619', *Magazine of Virginia Genealogy*, 33 (1995), 155–70

Thornton, John K., *Central Africans, Atlantic Creoles, and the Foundation of the Americas, 1585–1660* (Cambridge; New York, 2007)

—, 'The African Experience of the "20. and Odd Negroes" Arriving in Virginia in 1619', *William and Mary Quarterly*, 55 (1998), 421-34

Tittler, Robert, 'The English Fishing Industry in the Sixteenth Century: The Case of Great Yarmouth', *Albion*, 9 (1977), 40-60

Tolan, John, *Saracens: Islam in the Medieval European Imagination* (New York, 2002)

Tomlins, Christopher, *Freedom Bound: Law, Labour, and Civic Identity in Colonizing English America, 1580–1865* (New York, 2010)

Traub, Valerie, 'Mapping the Global Body', in Peter Erickson and Clark Hulse (eds), *Early Modern Visual Culture: Representation, Race, and Empire in Renaissance England* (Philadelphia, 2000)

Turner, J.M., 'Pablo Fanque "an Artiste of Colour"', *King Pole*, 89 (1990), 5-9

Underdown, David, *A Freeborn People: Politics and the Nation in Seventeenth-Century England* (New York, 1996)

Ungerer, Gustav, *The Mediterranean Apprenticeship of British Slavery* (Madrid, 2008)

—, 'Portia and the Prince of Morocco', *Shakespeare Studies*, 31 (2003), 90-3

—, 'Recovering a Black African's Voice in an English Lawsuit: Jacques Francis and the Salvage Operations of the Mary Rose and the Sancta Maria and Sanctus Edwardus, 1545–1550', *Medieval and Renaissance Drama in England*, 17 (2005), 255-71

—, 'The Presence of Africans in Elizabethan England and the Performance of *Titus Andronicus* at Burley-on-the-Hill, 1595/96', *Medieval and Renaissance Drama in England*, 21 (2008), 19-55

van Cleve, George, '"Somerset's Case" and Its Antecedents in Imperial Perspective', *Law and History Review*, 24 (2006), 601-45

van der Linden, Marcel, 'Reconstructing the origins of modern labour management', *Labour History*, 51 (2010), 509-22

Vasconcellos, Colleen A., *Slavery, Childhood, and Abolition in Jamaica, 1788–1838* (Athens, GA, 2015)

Vaughan, Alden T., 'The Origins Debate: Slavery and Racism in Seventeenth-Century Virginia', in Alden T. Vaughan, *Roots of American Racism* (New York, 1995), 36-174

—, and Virginia Mason Vaughan, 'Before Othello: Elizabethan Representations of Sub-Saharan Africans', *William and Mary Quarterly*, 3rd ser., 54 (1997), 19-44

Vieira, Alberto, 'Sugar Islands: The Sugar Economy of Madeira and the Canaries, 1450–1650', in Stuart B. Schwartz (ed.), *Tropical Babylons: Sugar and the Making of the Atlantic World, 1450–1680* (Chapel Hill, 2004), pp. 42-84

Walker, Christine, 'Pursuing her Profits: Women in Jamaica, Atlantic Slavery and a Globalising Market, 1700-60', *Gender & History*, 26 (2014), 478-501

Wallis, P., 'Apprenticeship and Training in Premodern England', *Journal of Economic History*, 68 (2008), 832-61

Walvin, James, *Black and White: The Negro and English Society 1555–1945* (London, 1973)

—, *Black Ivory: A History of British Slavery* (Oxford, 2001)

—, *From the Fringes to the Centre: The Emergence of British Black Historical Studies* (London, 1982)

—, *The Black Presence: A Documentary History of the Negro in England, 1555–1860* (London, 1971)

—, *The Trader, the Owner, the Slave: Slavery and its Abolition* (London, 2007)

Weissbourd, Emily, "'Those in Their Possession': Race, Slavery, and Queen Elizabeth's 'Edicts of Expulsion'", *Huntington Library Quarterly*, 78 (2015), 1–19

Wells, Calvin, and Helen Cayton, 'The Human Bones (from North Elmham Park)', in *East Anglian Archaeology Report No. 9, Norfolk, North Elmham, Volume II* (Norfolk, 1980), 259–62

Wells, R., 'Crime and Protest in a Country Parish: Burwash 1790–1850', in J. Rule and R. Wells (eds), *Crime, Protest and Popular Politics in Southern England 1740–1850* (London, 1997), 169–236

—, 'The Moral Economy of the English Countryside', in A.J. Randall and A. Charlesworth (eds), *Moral Economy and Popular Protest: Crowds, Conflict and Authority* (Basingstoke, 1999), 209–71

Wenley, Robert, 'Robert Paston and the Yarmouth Collection', *Norfolk Archaeology*, 4 (1991), 113–44

Wheeler, Roxann, *The Complexion of Race: Categories of Difference in Eighteenth-Century British Culture* (Philadelphia, 2000)

Whiteman, Anne, and Mary Clapinson (eds), *The Compton Census of 1676: A Critical Edition*, Records of Social and Economic History: New Series, Vol. 10 (Oxford, 1986)

Whittle, J., 'Lords and Tenants in Kett's Rebellion 1549', *Past & Present*, 207 (2010), 3–52

—, *The Development of Agrarian Capitalism: Land and Labour in Norfolk, 1440–1580* (Oxford, 2000)

Wiecek, William M., 'Somerset: Lord Mansfield and the Legitimacy of Slavery in the Anglo-American World', *University of Chicago Law Review*, 42 (1974), 86–146

Willan, Thomas Stuart, *Studies in Elizabethan Foreign Trade* (Manchester, 1959)

Williams, C.H. (ed.), *English Historical Documents 1485–1558* (New York, 1967)

Williams, Eric, *Capitalism & Slavery* (New York, 1961, orig. 1944)

—, *The Economic Aspect of the Abolition of the West Indian Slave Trade and Slavery* (Lanham, MD, 2014)

Williams, Gomer, *History of the Liverpool Privateers: and Letters of Marque with an Account of the Liverpool Slave Trade, 1744–1812* (Liverpool, 1897)

Williams, N.J., *The Maritime Trade of the East Anglian Ports, 1550–1590* (Oxford, 1988)

Wills, Mary, 'At War with the "Detestable Traffic": The Royal Navy's Anti-Slavery Cause in the Atlantic Ocean', in Christer Petley and John McAleer (eds), *The Royal Navy and the British Atlantic World, c. 1750–1820* (London, 2016), 123–46

——, *Envoys of Abolition: British Naval Officers and the Campaign Against the Slave Trade in West Africa* (Oxford 2019)

Wilmot, Swithin R., 'Not "Full Free": The Ex-Slaves and the Apprenticeship System in Jamaica, 1834–1838', *Jamaica Journal*, 17 (1984), 2–10

Wilson, Charles, *England's Apprenticeship, 1603–1673* (London, 1965)

Wilson, Richard G., *Greene King: A Business and Family History* (London, 1983)

——, 'Introduction', in Carole Rawcliffe, Richard Wilson, and Christine Clark (eds), *Norwich Since 1550* (London; New York, 2004)

——, 'Journal of a Tour through Suffolk, Norfolk, Lincolnshire and Yorkshire in the Summer of 1741', in Christopher Harper-Bill, Carole Rawcliffe, and Richard Wilson (eds), *East Anglia's History: Studies in Honour of Norman Scarfe* (Woodbridge, 2002), pp. 259–88

Wood, Andy, 'Fear, Hatred and the Hidden Injuries of Class in Early Modern England', *Journal of Social History*, 39 (2006), 803–26

——, *Riot, Rebellion and Popular Politics in Early Modern England* (London, 2002)

——, 'Tales from the "Yarmouth Hutch": Civic Identities and Hidden Histories in an Urban Archive', *Past & Present*, 230 (2016), 213–30

——, *The 1549 Rebellions and the Making of Early Modern England* (Cambridge, 2007)

Wood, Betty, 'Freedom and Bondage in English Thought', in Betty Wood, *The Origins of American Slavery: Freedom and Bondage in the English Colonies* (New York, 1998), pp. 9–19

Wood, Ellen Meiksins, 'The Agrarian Origins of Capitalism', *Monthly Review*, 50 (1998)

Wright, Franklin W., 'Introduction: Race and Identity in the New World', in Morris and Garrigus (eds), *Assumed*, pp. 1–17

Wrightson, Keith, *English Society, 1580–1680* (London, 1982)

——, *Ralph Tailor's Summer* (New Haven, 2011)

Wrigley, Tony, *English County Populations in the Later Eighteenth Century* (Cambridge Group for the History of Population and Social Structure, Department of Geography, University of Cambridge. An ESRC Funded Project, Male Occupational Change and Economic Growth 1750–1851)

Wrigley, E.A., 'Rickman Revisited: The Population Growth Rates of English Counties in the Early Modern Period', *The Economic History Review*, 62 (2009), 711–35

Yaxley, David (ed.), *Oxnead 1654–56: Accounts of Oxnead Hall, Home of Sir William Paston* (Dereham, 2014)

Yungblut, Laura Hunt, '"Mayntayninge the indigente and nedie": The institutionalization of social responsibility in the case of the resident alien communities in Elizabethan Norwich and Colchester', in Randolph Vigne and Charles Littleton (eds), *From Strangers to Citizens: The Integration of Immigrant Communities in Britain, Ireland and Colonial America, 1550-1750* (Brighton; London, 2001), pp. 99-105

Zahedieh, Nuala, 'Colonies, copper, and the market for inventive activity in England and Wales, 1680-1730', *Economic History Review*, 66 (2013), 805-25

——, *The Capital and the Colonies: London and the Atlantic Economy, 1660-1700* (Cambridge, 2010)

Zins, Henryk, *England and the Baltic in the Elizabethan Era* (Manchester, 1972)

Unpublished Theses

Barney, John M., 'The merchants and maritime trade of King's Lynn in the eighteenth century' (Unpublished Ph.D. Dissertation, University of East Anglia, 1997)

Metters, G.A., 'The Rulers and Merchants of King's Lynn in the Early Seventeenth Century' (Unpublished Ph.D. Dissertation, University of East Anglia, 1982)

Saul, A., 'Great Yarmouth in the Fourteenth Century: A Study in Trade, Politics and Society' (Unpublished Ph.D. Thesis, University of Oxford, 1975)

Winkelman, Winnifred V., 'Barbadian Cross-currents: Church-State Confrontation with Quaker and Negro, 1660-1689' (Unpublished Ph.D. Dissertation, Loyola University Chicago, 1978)

Web-based Sources

Oxford Dictionary of National Biography

Beckett, J.V., 'Coke, Thomas William, first earl of Leicester of Holkham (1754-1842), politician and agriculturist', ODNB <https://www.oxforddnb.com/view/10.1093/ref:odnb/9780198614128.001.0001/odnb-9780198614128-e-5831> [accessed 6 August 2012]

Gragg, L., 'Steele, Joshua (c. 1700-1796), plantation owner and writer on prosody', ODNB <https://www.oxforddnb.com/view/10.1093/ref:odnb/9780198614128.001.0001/odnb-9780198614128-e-26345> [accessed 30 January 2017]

Kaufmann, Miranda, 'Blanke, John (fl. 1507-1512), royal trumpeter', ODNB <https://www.oxforddnb.com/view/10.1093/ref:odnb/9780198614128.001.0001/odnb-9780198614128-e-107145> [accessed 31 December 2019]

Laughton, J., and A. Lambert, 'Irby, Frederick Paul (1779-1844), naval officer', ODNB<https://www.oxforddnb.com/view/10.1093/ref:odnb/9780198614128.001.0001/odnb-9780198614128-e-14444> [accessed 12 August 2020]

Lemmings, D., 'Pengelly, Sir Thomas (1675-1730), judge', ODNB <https://www.oxforddnb.com/view/10.1093/ref:odnb/9780198614128.001.0001/odnb-9780198614128-e-21837> [accessed 15 November 2019]

```

Lowe, W., 'Keppel, George, third earl of Albemarle (1724–1772), army officer and politician', ODNB <https://www.oxforddnb.com/view/10.1093/ref:odnb/9780198614128.001.0001/odnb-9780198614128-e-15441> [accessed 6 February 2019]

Matthew, H., 'Harbord, Edward, third Baron Suffield (1781–1835), politician', ODNB <https://www.oxforddnb.com/view/10.1093/ref:odnb/9780198614128.001.0001/odnb-9780198614128-e-12232> [accessed 20 March 2020]

McGrath, C.I., 'Wyche, Sir Cyril (c. 1632–1707), government official', ODNB <https://www.oxforddnb.com/view/10.1093/ref:odnb/9780198614128.001.0001/odnb-9780198614128-e-30117> [accessed 7 February 2017]

Orbell, J., 'Greene, Benjamin Buck (1808–1902), merchant', ODNB <https://www.oxforddnb.com/view/10.1093/ref:odnb/9780198614128.001.0001/odnb-9780198614128-e-48874> [accessed 24 January 2020]

Rowe, J., 'Lestrange [Le Strange], Sir Thomas (c. 1490–1545), landowner and administrator', ODNB <https://www.oxforddnb.com/view/10.1093/ref:odnb/9780198614128.001.0001/odnb-9780198614128-e-16515> [accessed 21 July 2017]

Rye, Walter, 'The Ballad of Arthur of Bradley', in Charles Harold Evelyn-White, The East Anglian (Lowestoft, 1800), pp. 177–80 <https://archive.org/details/eastanglianorno04whitgoog/page/n190/mode/2up> [accessed 22 October 2019]

Sheridan, R., 'Beckford, William (1744–1799), sugar planter and historian', ODNB <https://www.oxforddnb.com/view/10.1093/ref:odnb/9780198614128.001.0001/odnb-9780198614128-e-1904> [accessed 27 January 2020]

Spain, J., 'Dalling, Sir John, first baronet (c. 1731–1798), army officer and colonial governor', ODNB <https://www.oxforddnb.com/view/10.1093/ref:odnb/9780198614128.001.0001/odnb-9780198614128-e-53621> [accessed 6 February 2019]

Tilton, R., 'Rolfe, John (1585–1622), colonist and entrepreneur', ODNB <https://www.oxforddnb.com/view/10.1093/ref:odnb/9780198614128.001.0001/odnb-9780198614128-e-24018> [accessed 6 February 2019]

Watt, J., 'Ramsay, James (1733–1789), surgeon and slavery abolitionist', ODNB <https://www.oxforddnb.com/view/10.1093/ref:odnb/9780198614128.001.0001/odnb-9780198614128-e-23086> [accessed 6 February 2019]

Wilson, R., 'Greene family (per. 1801–1920), brewers', ODNB, retrieved 24 January 2020, from https://www.oxforddnb.com/view/10.1093/ref:odnb/9780198614128.001.0001/odnb-9780198614128-e-50414 [accessed 28 August 2016]

Woodward, W., 'Winthrop, John (1606–1676), colonial governor and physician', ODNB <https://www.oxforddnb.com/view/10.1093/ref:odnb/9780198614128.001.0001/odnb-9780198614128-e-29779> [accessed 19 October 2019]
```

The History of Parliament

Cruickshanks, Eveline, 'Coke, John I (1635–71), of Holkham, Norf.', in B.D. Henning, *The History of Parliament: the House of Commons 1660–1690* (London, 1983) <http://www.historyofparliamentonline.org/volume/1660-1690/member/coke-john-i-1635-71>

Drummond, Mary M., 'Windham, William (?1705–89), of Earsham, Norf.', in L. Namier and J. Brooke (eds), *The History of Parliament: the House of Commons 1754–1790* (London, 1964) <http://www.historyofparliamentonline.org/volume/1754-1790/member/windham-william-1705-89>

Fisher, David. R., 'Colhoun, William MacDowall (fl.1758–1821), of Wretham, nr. Thetford, Norf. and St. Kitts', in R. Thorne (ed.), *The History of Parliament: the House of Commons 1790–1820* (London, 1986) <http://www.historyofparliamentonline.org/volume/1790-1820/member/colhoun-william-macdowall-1758-1821> [accessed 1 October 2020]

Harrison, Richard, 'Jermyn Wyche, (c.1670–1720), of Hockwold, Norf.', in D. Hayton, E. Cruickshanks, and S. Handley (eds), *The History of Parliament: the House of Commons 1690–1715* (Cambridge, 2002) <http://www.historyofparliamentonline.org/volume/1690-1715/member/wych-%28wyche%29-jermyn-1670-1720> [accessed 1 June 2018]

Hayes, Brian, 'Molineux, Crisp (1730–92), of Garboldisham, Norfolk', in L. Namier and J. Brooke (eds), *The History of Parliament: The House of Commons 1754–1790* <http://www.historyofparliamentonline.org/volume/1754-1790/member/molineux-crisp-1730-92> [accessed 1 October 2020]

Other Electronic Sources

'Admissions to the Freedom of York: Temp. James II (1685–88)', in Francis Collins (ed.), *Register of the Freemen of the City of York: Vol. 2, 1559–1759* (Durham, 1900), pp. 161–6. British History Online <http://www.british-history.ac.uk/york-freemen/vol2/pp161-166> [accessed 2 February 2020]

Bitterman, Rusty, and Margaret McCallum, *The Pursuit of Gentility in an Age of Revolution: The Family of Jonathan Worrell*, Acadiensis, 43 (2) (November 2014) <https://journals.lib.unb.ca/index.php/Acadiensis/article/view/22685/26326>

Calendar of Close Rolls, Henry III: Volume 10, 1256–1259 (London, 1932), at p. 444, <https://babel.hathitrust.org/cgi/pt?id=mdp.35112103127173&view=1up&seq=5> [accessed 17 May 2018]

Calendar of the Patent Rolls preserved in the Public Record Office: Henry VI, Vol.VI, A.D. 1452–1461 (London, 1910) <https://dcms.lds.org/delivery/DeliveryManagerServlet?dps_pid=IE47017> [accessed 20 July 2019]

Calendar of the Patent Rolls preserved in the Public Record Office: Edward IV, Henry VI, 1467–1477 (1900) <https://dcms.lds.org/delivery/DeliveryManagerServlet?dps_pid=IE100801> [accessed 1 March 2019]

Davy, Henry, *Views of the seats of the noblemen and gentlemen in Suffolk* (1827) <https://landedfamilies.blogspot.com/2015/04/162-arcedeckne-of-glevering-hall.html>

Ekwe-Ekwe, Herbert, *Geopolitics or Blatant Sophistry?*, Latitude: Rethinking Power Relations – for a decolonised and non-racial world, <https://www.goethe.de/prj/lat/en/dis/21909728.html> [accessed 7 October 2020]

Federici, Cesare, *Voyage and trauaile* (trans. Thomas Hickock) (London, 1588). Facsimile edition published online at < http://tei.it.ox.ac.uk/tcp/Texts-HTML/free/A00/A00611.html> (University of Oxford Text Archive)

Hurd, John C., *The Law of Freedom and Bondage in The United States* (1858), p. 179, <https://archive.org/details/lawoffreedombond00hurd/page/180/mode/2up> [accessed 7 September 2017].

Kingsbury, Susan Myra (ed.), *The Records of The Virginia Company of London, III* (Washington, 1933) <https://archive.org/details/recordsofvirgini03virg/page/242/mode/2up?q=rolfe>

Kingsley, Nicholas, Landed Families of Britain and Ireland, '(162) Arcedeckne of Glevering Hall', <https://landedfamilies.blogspot.com/2015/04/162-arcedeckne-of-glevering-hall.html> [accessed 25 March 2019].

Legacies of British Slave Ownership Database, <https://www.ucl.ac.uk/lbs>

Ligon, Richard, *A True & Exact History of the Island of Barbadoes* (1673), <https://archive.org/details/A-true-exact-history-of-the-island-of-Barbadoes-Illustrated-with-a-map-of-the-is-PHAIDRA_o_361036/page/n65/mode/2up>

Lincoln, Solomon, *An Address Delivered Before the Citizens of the Town of Hingham: On the Twenty-eighth of September, 1835, Being the Two Hundredth Anniversary of the Settlement of the Town* (Hingham, MA, 1835) <https://archive.org/details/addressdelivered1835linc> [accessed 3 February 2019]

Reconnecting Diverse Rural Communities: Black presences and the legacies of slavery and colonialism in rural Britain, c.1600–1939 <https://www.nottingham.ac.uk/isos/research/rural-legacies.aspx>

'Sessions Books: 1690', in W.J. Hardy (ed.), *Middlesex County Records: Calendar of Sessions Books 1689–1709* (London, 1905), pp. 1–26. British History Online <http://www.british-history.ac.uk/middx-county-records/session-bks-1689-1709/pp1-26> [accessed 21 October 2020]

Steele, Robert (ed.), *Medieval Lore from Bartholomaeus Anglicus* (trans. from the Latin by John Trevisa) (London, 1893), <https://archive.org/details/b29011152/page/120/mode/2up?q=moors> [accessed 9 February 2019]

'The Ancestors and Descendants of John Rolfe with Notices of Some Connected Families, *The Virginia Magazine of History and Biography*, 21 (1913), pp. 105–6, <http://www.jstor.org/stable/4243251>

'The Ancestors and Descendants of John Rolfe with Notices of Some Connected Families (Continued)', *The Virginia Magazine of History and Biography*, 21 (1913), pp. 208–11, <http://www.jstor.org/stable/4243266>

The Trans-Atlantic and Intra-American slave trade database, <https://www.slave-voyages.org/>

Waters, Henry Fitzgilbert, 'The Gedney and Clarke Families of Salem, Massachusetts', *Essex Institute Historical Collections*, 16 (1879), p. 242, <https://archive.org/details/essexinstitutehiv16esse/page/242/mode/2up?q=gedney>

Winthrop, Henry, 'Letter to John Winthrop, 15 October 1627', Winthrop Papers (W. 1. 27; 5 Collections, VIII. 180–1), Massachusetts Historical Society, Boston, <http://www.masshist.org/publications/winthrop/index.php/view/PWF01d254> [accessed 12 June 2019]

Winthrop, Henry, 'Letter to Emmanuel Downing, 22 August 1627', Winthrop Papers (W. 1. 25; 5 Collections, VIII. 179–80), <http://www.masshist.org/publications/winthrop/index.php/view/PWF01d249> [accessed 17 June 2019]

Woods, R., *Norfolk furies and their foyle* (London, 1615), B2, ProQuest, <https://search-proquest-com.uea.idm.oclc.org/docview/2240885474?accountid=10637> [accessed 2 February 2020]

Index

Abolitionism, generally 3-4, 16 n.47
   East Anglia 149-50, 168-9,
   179-82
   effect on terms used to describe
   Africans 41-2
   See also William Coke, Frederick
   Paul Irby, William Wright
Abolition of the slave trade in British
   ships 3, 168, 179
Abolition of slavery in British Empire 13
Absentee plantation owners 15, 18,
   138-44
   agents 142-3
   American Revolution, effect
   on East Anglian plantation
   ownership 141
   effect of ownership upon
   appearance of Africans in East
   Anglia 38-9
   opinions of abolition 145
   views of enslaved people 143-4,
   150, 166-8, 190-1, 197
   See also amelioration, Barclay
   family, William Beckford, Berney
   family, Sir Patrick Blake, Bland
   family, bookkeepers, Burton family,
   William Colhoun, Dalling family,
   Daniell family, Sir Robert Davers,
   Davers family, Greene family,
   Longe family, Peete family, Penrice
   family, plantations and plantation
   ownership, John Scott, Thelluson
   family, Jonathan Worrell
Acemoglu, Daron 16
African/Africans
   acceptance into the working class
   and region more generally 2,
   9-21, 37-8, 47-53, 57, 59-61,
   65-73, 77-81, 111-15, 122, 124-31,
   162-77, 178-9, 187-8, 190-200
   arrival and migration in
   East Anglia, general process
   of 13-21, 33-9, 43, 81-100,
   108-9, 151

   changing response to Africans
   in East Anglia generally 10-21,
   39-43, 81, 100-7, 108-15, 119,
   131-2, 150-1, 175-7, 193-4
   descriptor in records, used
   as 1-2, 24, 41-2
   descriptions, changing 39-43
   distribution in East
   Anglia 29-31, 33-9, 42-3, 80
   first documented arrival in East
   Anglia of 13, 22
   free or enslaved in East
   Anglia 33-9, 43, 49-52, 54-6,
   59-61, 65-72, 75-7, 79-80,
   103-7, 108-10, 113-15, 115-17,
   120-2, 128-32, 152-70
   gender composition of 31-2, 43
   identification in records 24-31
   initially connected to ports 33, 43
   legal status of in East
   Anglia 13-14, 69-72, 106-7,
   109-10, 114-15
   Mediterranean origins 108-9
   negative views in East Anglia,
   development of 9, 15-21, 40-3,
   81-100, 143-4, 166-8, 190-1
   negative views generally 15,
   41-2, 44-6, 90-100, 102, 106-7,
   110-11, 131-2, 150-1, 195-200
   'non-African' used as antonym in
   this text 57 n.61
   not automatically connected to
   enslavement or negativity 15,
   46-53, 60-1, 65-72, 79-80,
   98-100
   population of in East
   Anglia 22-31
   surnames, used to identify 25-8
   used as general term in this
   text 2
   See also apprentices, baptism,
   'blackamore', 'black', 'Ethiopian',
   Cartwright's case, class,
   commodification of Africans,

268

Frere family (Barbados)   87-8, 141, 157
Froissart, Jean   26
Fumerton, Patricia   12

Garboldisham   153-4, 166-8, 190, 195
    See also Richard Alexander,
    John Davis, Crisp Molineux,
    Charles Molineux, Charles
    Sheard Molineux, 'mulatto',
    Mary Molineux, Samuel
    Molineux, Sophia Molineux,
    Thomas Crisp Molineux
    Montgomerie, Samuel Stanton,
    Robert Taylor
Garrigus, John   149
Gatford, Lionel   101, 103
Gaskill, Malcolm   83
Gedney, John   85
George, Dorothy M.   2
Gerbner, Katherine   110, 111
German, Thomas   156
See also John Brown, Anthrobus Morgan
Gibbs, John   168
Glevering Hall, see Arcedeckne family,
    Henry Norbrook
Goetz, Rebecca   95, 100, 111-12
Golden Grove plantation, see Arcedeckne
    family
Gooding Robert, see Oxford 'an East
    India Black'
Grady, Kyle   10
Grant, Daragh   94-6
Grafton   136
Gravell, John   89
Great Massingham, see William Snoring
Great Saxham, see John Browne, Thomas
    German, Anthrobus Morgan
Great Yarmouth   1, 44, 106, 199
    economics and trade   23-4, 33,
    48-9, 53-4, 85-6, 144-6, 147
    executions   46-7
    merchant links with colonies, 144-6
    migrants from   85, 89, 103
    piracy   49-50
    town records   28
    See also abolitionism, Burton
    family, Eylys, foreigners, John 'the
    niger', Livorno, Penrice family,

William Pigott, pirates, Edward
    Steele, Samuel Ward
Greene family   139 n.35, 141, 142
    See also absentee plantation
    owners, St Christopher
Grey, Benjamin   172, 188
    See also crime
Griffin, Carl   190, 191
Guasco, Michael   14 n.43, 66-7 n.20, 92

Habib, Imtiaz   3, 25-8, 76, 111-12
Hadleigh, see Blackamore family
    (Ipswich), Robert Smith
Hall, Kim   46, 63-4
Halletts plantation, see Joshua Steele
Handler, Jerome   15, 40, 48, 92, 98-9
Hanson family   89, 139 n.14
Hanson plantation, see Berney family
Hanworth, see William Doughty
Harbord, Edward (third Baron
    Suffield)   189-91
Hardyngham, William (master of la
    Margaret)   50
Harper, George   86
Harriett   146
Hartley, Anne   114
Harvey, I.M.W,   192-3
Hawkins, Sir John   51, 70
Hawkins, Henry   89, 102
Hawley, Henry (Governor)   103-4
Hawley, Seth   100, 103-6
    See also Doughty family, Peter
    Lynn, Thoroughgood family
Heacham, see Baptist, Lestrange family
Heathe, Irby Amelia Frederick   183-4
    See also Freeman, Charles
    Fortunatus, Frederick William
    (Captain RN) Irby, Paolo
    Loando, Edward Makenzie,
    Sierra Leone
Hellet, Mary   152-3
Henstead, see Joseph Diana
Hervey family   190
Heywood, Linda M.   51, 93
Hicks, John William   156
    See also John Brown, Anthrobus
    Morgan, Thomas German, Mills
    family

275

See also Peter Lynn, Crisp
Molineux, African 'Swing' rioters,
Robert Taylor and family
Muslim   32, 41, 45–6, 48, 55, 65, 70
conversion of   32, 65, 79
manumission of in Italy   55
See also baptism, Bartholomew
'sometime a Saracen', 'More',
Saracen
Musicians, African   123–4
See also 'Black with a French
horn', employment of Africans,
Robert Smith
Myers, Norma   2

Nacton, *see* William Strap
Narford, *see* John Ong
Native Americans   74, 94, 96, 98
See also Meotaka
'Native of Jamaica' (description)   24,
41–2, 156, 158, 169
See also John Brown, Sigismunda
Beckford, Samuel Samuels
Nayland, *see* Sir Patrick Blake, Stephen
Tucker
'Near slavery' and 'slavish servitude'
definition, as distinct from chattel
slavery   13–15
general   19–20, 31, 32, 51, 70–1,
81, 115, 119, 152–69
not automatic   120–3, 128–31,
162–74, 197–9
See also Baptist, Rosanna Blunt,
'Captain Uring's Black', William
Byrom, Amber and Cuffee
Cross, Joseph Diana, Rachel
Fitshoe, Mary Hellet, Peter
Lynn, Christiana Niger, Thomas
Rundell, Samuel Samuels, slavery,
Robert Taylor, Stephen Tucker,
'ye black boy'
'Negro' (descriptor)
Colonial context   87, 90, 110,
113–14, 114 n.21, 131, 143–4, 147, 149
derivation of   40
general   24–5, 30, 39–40, 64, 87,
135 n.12, 181, 188, 195–7

negative views of   42, 90–7, 125
See also Elizabeth Barnes, Cross
family, Davers family, James
Doubleday, Barlow Fielding, Jerome
Handler, Mary Hellet, Jeremiah
Rowland, Henry Norbrook, 'A
negro, a servant to Mr Machett',
William Strap, William Suza,
Stephen Tucker, 'White Negro
Woman', William 'a negro'
'Negro, a servant to Mr Machett'   163–4
Neville/Woods narrative   68
See also rebellions of 1549
Nevis, *see* Thomas Carter
New England   85–6, 145
Newmarket, *see* 'Pauper, an African'
Nichols, John   173
See also crime
'Niger' (descriptor)
derivation of   54–5
general   39–40
See also Anthonius Niger,
Christiana Niger, John 'the niger',
Mary Niger
Niger, Anthonius (Essex)   54
Niger, Christiana   54, 108–9, 111, 129
Niger, Mary   108
Norbrook, Hannah, 165
Norbrook, Henry   164–5
See also Arcedeckne family, family,
marriage
Norfolk, for economy and geography, *see*
East Anglia
North Carolina   145
Norwich   1, 23, 63, 65–6
See also John Brown, Blackamore
families, Charley (bootmaker),
Cotton (street trader), Joseph
Diana, John Gibbs

Oestmann, Cord   75
Ong, John   172
See also crime
Onyeka   3, 33, 102, 129
Orpheus HMS, *see* Barlow Spence
Osborne, Sarah Hopkins   186
See also Joshua Steele

Slave ships   18, 132, 135-7, 146, 182, 184
  See also Charming Sally, Elizabeth,
  King's Lynn
Sherrad David, *see* 'Little Black Man'
Shrimpson, Martha   89
Sierra Leone   134-5, 181, 182-5
  See also Charles Fortunatus
  Freeman, Frederick William
  Irby (Captain RN), Irby Amelia
  Frederick Heathe, Paolo Loando,
  Edward Makenzie, Sierra Leone,
  'captured negroes'
Skippon, Philip   116
Slatia, Anna   185, 186
  See Edward Steele, Joshua Steele,
  Katherine Steele, mulatto
Slave Trade Abolition Act, 1807 (Britain),
  see apprentices
Slaves
  use of term in Norfolk and
  Suffolk   152-3, 163
  See also Cross family, near slavery,
  plantation owners, slavery, slave
  ships, slave trade, slavish servitude
Slaveholders, *see* absentee plantation
  owners, plantations
Slave ships
  generally   7-8
  from Norfolk and Suffolk   133-7
Slave trade
  English involvement in   51-2, 147
Slavery
  associated with social
  situation   13-21, 66-72, 79, 96,
  102, 109-10, 178-88
  chattel slavery   13-14, 19-20, 52,
  81-105, 131, 169, 171, 183, 185
  connected to capitalism   3-4,
  9, 10-13, 16-21, 64-8, 71-2,
  81-100, 113, 130-2, 133-5,
  150-1, 197
  gradual correlation to physical
  appearance   99-100, 102
  involvement an economic
  decision   146-50
  lack of discussion of legal
  situation in East Anglia   14, 65

  specific local East Anglian ideas
  of   14-15, 18-21, 65-72, 96-7,
  98-9
  problems in using models from
  slavery in Americas in understanding
  early modern England   11
  property rights   13-14, 98-9
  Medieval England   66-7
  metaphor for illegitimate use of
  power   92-3
  not associated with skin
  colour up to mid-1600s in East
  Anglia   13-15, 65-72, 93, 96-7
  not limited to Africans   65,
  69-71, 93
  'slave societies' and 'societies with
  slaves'   20, 99
  See also abolitionism, African/
  Africans, 'bonde' men,
  Bartholomew 'sometime a
  Saracen', Cartwright's Case,
  capitalism, colonial ideas about
  enslavement, 'near slavery',
  rebellions of 1549, serfdom,
  slave trade, slave ships, 'slavish
  servitude', villeinage, unfree
  labour
Slaving ports   3-4, 7, 137
  See also Bristol, King's Lynn,
  Liverpool, London,
'Slavish servitude', *see* 'near slavery'
Smith, Robert   123-4, 129-30, 171
  See also employment of Africans,
  musicians
Snell, Keith   191
Somerley Hall, *see* Sigismunda Beckford,
  William Beckford
Somerleyton, *see* Sigismunda Beckford,
  William Beckford
Somerset Case   13-14, 71 n.16
South Carolina   94-6, 141, 145
  See also Thomas Bland
Snoring, William and family   31, 38,
  124-6, 129, 172
  See also crime
Spain and Spanish   64, 75, 101
  See also Edicts of Expulsion